The Disappearing State?

The Disappearing State?

Retrenchment Realities in an Age of Globalisation

Edited by

Francis G. Castles

Professor of Social and Public Policy,
University of Edinburgh, UK

Edward Elgar

Cheltenham, UK • Northampton, MA, USA

Published by
Edward Elgar Publishing Limited
Glensanda House
Montpellier Parade
Cheltenham
Glos GL50 1UA
UK

Edward Elgar Publishing, Inc.
William Pratt House
9 Dewey Court
Northampton
Massachusetts 01060
USA

A catalogue record for this book
is available from the British Library

Library of Congress Cataloguing in Publication Data

The disappearing state?: retrenchment realities in an age of globalisation/
    edited by Francis G. Castles.
        p.   cm.
    Revisions of papers presented at a workshop held Mar. 2006 in
        Delmenhorst, Germany.
    Includes bibliographical references and index.
    1. Expenditures, Public. 2. OECD countries—Appropriations and
expenditures. 3. Government spending policy. 4. Government spending
policy—OECD countries. I. Castles, Francis Geoffrey.
HJ7461.D57   2007
352.4—dc22
                                                            2007001385

ISBN 978 1 84542 297 4 (cased)

Printed and bound in Great Britain by MPG Books Ltd, Bodmin, Cornwall

Contents

List of contributors   vii
Preface and acknowledgements   ix

1   Introduction   1
    Francis G. Castles

2   Testing the retrenchment hypothesis: an aggregate overview   19
    Francis G. Castles

3   Data on the functions of government: where are we now?   44
    Neil Fraser and Paul Norris

4   The changing cost of government: trends in the state
    overhead budget   75
    Richard Parry

5   Sinking budgets and ballooning prices: recent developments
    connected to military spending   103
    Thomas R. Cusack

6   Expenditure on public order and safety   133
    Paul Norris

7   Testing the retrenchment hypothesis: educational spending,
    1960–2002   159
    Manfred G. Schmidt

8   The real race to the bottom: what happened to economic
    affairs expenditure after 1980?   184
    Herbert Obinger and Reimut Zohlnhöfer

9   A mortgage on the future? Public debt expenditure and its
    determinants, 1980–2001   215
    Uwe Wagschal

10 Moving beyond expenditure accounts: the changing
    contours of the regulatory state, 1980–2003   245
    Nico A. Siegel

Index   273

Contributors

Francis G. Castles is Professor of Social and Public Policy at the University of Edinburgh. He has been a leading international figure in comparative public policy research for nearly three decades and is author or editor of 20 books, many of them with a focus on social expenditure and the welfare state.

Thomas R. Cusack is Senior Research Fellow and Head of the Working Group on Institutions, States and Markets at the Science Centre, Berlin. He has published extensively on public finance and issues relating to defence economics over many years.

Neil Fraser is Senior Lecturer in Social Policy at the University of Edinburgh. His main research interests are in economic and employment policy as well as the economic appraisal of social policies.

Paul Norris is a doctoral candidate in the School of Social and Political Studies, University of Edinburgh. He has a keen interest in comparative public policy research with particular reference to criminal justice issues.

Herbert Obinger is Professor of Social and Public Policy at the University of Bremen and its Research Centre on Transformations of the State (TranState). He has published widely in the fields of comparative welfare state research and comparative political economy.

Richard Parry is Reader in Social Policy at the University of Edinburgh. His research centres on the processes of public resource allocation and of multi-level governance, especially in the United Kingdom.

Manfred G. Schmidt is Professor of Political Science at the University of Heidelberg and is one of Germany's leading social scientists. He has contributed extensively to the comparative analysis of welfare states and is a leading authority on issues relating to democracy and to the German political system.

Nico A. Siegel is Senior Research Manager at TNS Infratest Social Research Munich, having previously been a Lecturer in Public Policy at the University of Kent. He has published widely in the areas of comparative welfare state research and comparative political economy.

Uwe Wagschal is Professor of Comparative Politics at the University of Heidelberg. He publishes mainly on issues such as tax reform, the determinants of public debt, welfare state reform and the effects of direct democracy.

Reimut Zohlnhöfer is Assistant Professor of Political Science at the University of Heidelberg In 2004/05, he was John F. Kennedy Memorial Fellow at the Center for European Studies at Harvard University. His research focuses on comparative public policy.

Preface and acknowledgements

This book contains studies emanating from an international collaborative research project on the political economy of recent public expenditure development that has been in progress since 2003 under the convenership of Francis G. Castles, Professor of Social and Public Policy at the University of Edinburgh. Early in 2003, the majority of the authors of these studies held a two-day meeting at the University of Edinburgh on the topic of *Globalization and the Public Purse: The Missing Dimension*, a meeting made possible by a grant from the Anglo-German Foundation and additional funding from the School of Social and Political Studies of the University of Edinburgh. At that meeting, it was agreed that continued data gathering and analysis across a wide range of functional areas of public spending would be fruitful and might eventually lead to the publication of a book on the determinants of public spending in areas hitherto largely untreated by existing comparative political economy research. It was further agreed that scholars from the Edinburgh Social Policy subject area would take responsibility for data gathering and that each of those who had attended the Edinburgh meeting would undertake the analysis of a particular category of spending with a view to reporting their findings to a project workshop to be held at a later date.

That workshop took place at the Hanse-Wissenschaftskolleg (HWK) in Delmenhorst in Germany over three days in March of 2006, with the proceedings going under the title of *The Disappearing State?* All those who had met in Edinburgh participated in the Delmenhorst meeting, together with three additional scholars recruited to give a broader coverage of spending areas. The papers presented and discussed at the Delmenhorst workshop were rewritten and reworked over the following six months and constitute the chapters of this book. The authors of these chapters collectively wish to acknowledge the generosity of the Hanse-Wissenschaftskolleg in funding the Delmenhorst meeting. The HWK also provided valuable support for the project by making the editor an HWK Fellow for three-month periods in both 2006 and 2007, allowing him to conduct research related to the project as well as to undertake coordinating and editorial tasks associated with the preparation of the volume. Finally, the editor wishes to acknowledge the facilities made available to him by the Political Science Department of the Research School of Social Sciences at the Australian National University in preparing the manuscript for publication while he was an Adjunct Professor in that department.

1. Introduction

Francis G. Castles

1.1 LOOKING FOR RETRENCHMENT IN THE WRONG PLACE

The rationale of this book is to examine a phenomenon, the scholarly account of which is both extremely puzzling and seriously incomplete. The phenomenon in question is an apparent reversal in the trajectory of public expenditure development in the countries of Western capitalism that has been widely interpreted as going from a phase of expansive growth in the immediate post-war decades to one of marked cutbacks and retrenchment over the past quarter-century. The story as it is commonly told is one of the burgeoning of the public expenditure state as a consequence of total war and the rise of socialist collectivism and its more recent decline in the face of the onslaught of a globalising economy and a reassertion of economic liberalism, with the tipping-point between these two phases of post-war development occurring sometime around the early 1980s. No one is arguing that this reversal of trajectory means that the state is about to disappear entirely, or even that it is likely to return to its former 'Night Watchman' role as a mere guarantor of contracts and protector of the 'King's peace'. There are, however, scholars from a variety of disciplines and commentators on both Left and Right, who would argue that the policy reforms of recent decades have set in motion a decisive retreat of the post-war interventionist state, and some quite ready to maintain that, in a greater or lesser number of countries, that process is already well under way (see Jessop, 2002; Schuknecht and Tanzi, 2005).

The main terrain for both scholarly and popular debate on the trajectory of public expenditure development since the early 1980s has been the welfare state. That is for several reasons. The growth of the positive state after World War II has been widely construed as being substantially a consequence of the state's assumption of a much extended role in the fields of income maintenance, health and other caring services, with average social expenditure levels in the 18 countries featuring in the analysis of Chapter 2 of this volume going up from just above 10 per cent of GDP in 1960 to only just below 20 per cent two decades later (see Castles, 2006, Table 2). A not unnatural corollary of this functionally specific expansion of the role of the state has been the assumption that any reversal in the trend of post-war expenditure development would occur in the area of its most recent growth. Thus it is understandable that the state that has been seen as being under attack and at risk of retrenchment in the present era has been the welfare state. It is no less understandable that it has been the ideological and scholarly defenders of the welfare state who have often been most sensitive to the threat of impending social spending cuts.

The assumption of the inherent reversibility of post-war welfare states has been further reinforced by the thrust of theorising about the forces shaping the trajectory of public expenditure growth over recent decades. Because, in earlier decades, public expenditure growth had been essentially welfare state growth, a previous generation of sociologists and political scientists had seen it as appropriate to identify the forces explaining the growth of the post-war state by focusing on the socio-economic and political antecedents of social expenditure growth (see, amongst many others, Wilensky, 1975; Korpi, 1978; Castles, 1982). Now, in the late 1970s and early 1980s, under circumstances widely interpreted as a 'crisis' of excessive public spending (see OECD, 1981), neo-classical economists and their neo-liberal popularisers began to focus on what they saw as the deleterious consequences of high levels of social spending, arguing that big welfare states could not compete in increasingly globalised markets because high levels of 'non-productive' state spending constituted a source of economic inefficiency leading to higher prices, reduced economic growth and runaway levels of both unemployment and inflation (for a summary of some of these arguments, see Gough, 1996).

However articulated, the way out of this dilemma of expenditure-induced economic stagnation was seen by those who diagnosed the problem in this manner as being self-evident. In order to restore Western economies to their full economic potential or, indeed, for politicians to win democratic elections in an era in which voting intentions are primarily shaped by economic outcomes, it was necessary to cut back the government expenditure and concomitant taxation of business inputs that served as a shackle on competitiveness in global markets. Moreover, what was necessary was simultaneously seemingly ineluctable, since nations failing to curtail their spending would by the very logic of the argument suffer catastrophic economic or political consequences and, most probably, both. As Margaret Thatcher, the neo-liberal doctrine's populariser *extraordinaire* was wont to put it: there simply was 'No Alternative'.

But this is where the puzzle comes in, because, despite a huge investment in research, virtually all the scholarly studies, which have investigated such claims by addressing comparative evidence of recent social expenditure development in advanced industrial nations, have come to the conclusion that, despite reductions in the generosity of certain programmes (see Korpi, 2003; Allan and Scruggs, 2004), overall cutbacks in welfare spending have been confined to a very small number of countries. Indeed, evidence from studies of trends right across the OECD make it clear that the overall trend of social expenditure as a percentage of GDP has been modestly upwards since the early 1980s and that global market pressures have played a negligible role compared to domestic factors in shaping cross-national spending differences (see, as representative of a substantial literature, Garrett, 1998; Pierson; 2001, Swank, 2002; Castles, 2004). On the basis of these findings and those of a wide variety of individual country case studies (see, for example, the studies in Kuhnle, 2000; Clasen, 2001; Leibfried, 2001), the consensus of the comparative literature has been that the case for widespread public expenditure retrenchment has been much exaggerated and that, therefore, the arguments for a globalisation-fuelled 'race-to-the-bottom' in public spending must be rejected.

The premise from which this volume starts is that, whilst these conclusions may well be valid, they are certainly premature and that, in turn, is because of the incompleteness of the empirical evidence on which they are based. What economic theorising on the likely consequences of economic globalisation and comparative research on the possible 'dismantling' or disappearance of the state have in common is that both have focused almost exclusively on propositions concerning and trends characterising the postwar development of social spending. However, construing social expenditure in the manner common to the international agencies (the OECD, ILO and Eurostat), which collect, process and disseminate the relevant data, as the sum of spending on income maintenance programmes, health provision and other caring services, this aggregate of spending currently amounts to only around 50 per cent of total public expenditure across the OECD and, for much of the post-war era, considerably less (see Therborn, 1983; Castles, 2006, Table 5). In other words, social expenditure is only a part of public expenditure and, although becoming markedly more salient during the second half of the twentieth century, and certainly now the largest single functional category of public spending, has never been anything like a predominant part. It therefore follows that what has been happening to social expenditure over recent decades is only part of the story of what has been happening to state expenditure as a whole and to the state as a whole.

To come to well grounded conclusions about the trajectory of the development of the state in recent decades, we need to look beyond social expenditure to other areas of expenditure by the modern state, including the costs of public administration, military defence, public order and safety, education, various aspects of economic affairs and public debt interest payments and, indeed, beyond expenditure itself to the expansion or contraction of the state's regulative activities in these areas. Hence the foremost objective of the studies making up this volume has been to move beyond the narrow confines of social expenditure research with the purpose of ascertaining whether, taking developments in other areas of public spending and regulation into account, the same conclusions hold: that there has been no widespread public expenditure contraction over recent decades and that cross-national differences in the reach of the state are largely attributable to domestic rather than global pressures. Or, to contextualise that objective in terms of the emergent social expenditure-focused problematic of the comparative literature from the mid-1970s onwards, the question we seek to answer in this book is whether those who have been seeking to identify globally induced expenditure retrenchment tendencies over recent decades have failed to find them simply because they were looking in the wrong place.

1.2   MAPPING THE MISSING DIMENSION

Comparative political economy's strong tendency to use social expenditure development as its effective measure of the reach of the state undoubtedly owes much to the particular thrust of theorising concerning the causes and consequences of increasing – and, subsequently, decreasing – post-war state intervention. It is arguable, however, that those seeking to describe the trajectory of statist development during these years did not really have a great deal of choice in the matter. This was because, until quite recently, social expenditure has been the only really significant functional category of spending adequately and routinely reported by international agencies and, hence, readily available for comparative analysis; first in the ILO's volumes on *The Cost of Social Security*, reporting expenditure from the early 1950s onwards, and used as a data source by all the early comparative studies of the determinants of public expenditure outcomes, and then in occasional OECD publications culminating in the *OECD Social Expenditure Database* (SOCX), reporting disaggregated data for nine expenditure programmes for all member countries from 1980 onwards and now favoured as the preferred data source for most comparative work in this area of spending.

The only other officially validated and functionally defined cross-national spending series were to be found in the *UNESCO Statistical Yearbook*, reporting expenditures (and personnel levels) in the area of education and in the OECD's *Economic Outlook* database, reporting member states' levels of debt interest repayments, although another series on military spending was published by the Stockholm International Peace Research Institute (SIPRI) from 1970 onwards. The problem was that even adding together all the available expenditure categories did not generate an adequate evidence base for describing trends across non-social budget areas as a whole. Too much of what was important was missing, most conspicuously spending on the administrative functions of government, on public order and safety, community services and economic affairs. Without a fully reported functional breakdown of public expenditure categories, shifts in the trajectory of spending outside of the social expenditure area remained unknown and, effectively, unknowable: a *terra Australis incognita* or missing dimension of political economy research. Mapping this missing dimension is one of the main purposes of the research reported here.

We seek to accomplish this mapping exercise by reference to three kinds of data, which, in combination, allow us to provide a fuller account than any previously of the changes taking place in non-social expenditure in Western developed nations over the past quarter-century. Some of this data comes from established cross-national data series, but much of it is only newly available and some of it is generated by new methods. Even so, the information available to us remains incomplete in many details, with deficiencies both in respect of the time-period covered and the number of countries available for comparison. It is, however, we believe, sufficient to permit conclusions concerning the recent trajectory of public expenditure development more nuanced and more firmly grounded in evidence than those preceding them. Moreover, even in areas where the data available to us do not allow us to establish the recent trajectory of expenditure development over a span of more than just a few years – and this is true in the areas of general public services treated in Chapter 4 and public order treated in Chapter 6 – the mapping and analysis these chapters undertake is useful both in establishing the baseline for future expenditure change and in providing an account of some of the more significant factors shaping expenditure levels at the present time. The object of maps is not just to locate where one has come from, but also the starting-point for the route ahead.

The three kinds of data used to map non-social spending in the studies constituting this volume may be characterised as follows.

1.2.1 Residual Estimates of Aggregate Core Expenditure

An important source of data this volume uses for mapping the missing dimension of non-social public expenditure could, in principle, have been used in the past, but, in practice, depends for its validity on a belief in the reliability of the information from which it derives, which could not readily be assumed before the late 1990s. The technique by which these data are obtained is best described as the estimation of residuals. Its logic rests on the simple accounting identity that the total outlays of general government are definitionally equivalent to the sum of the social plus the non-social expenditures of general government. The availability of cross-national data on total outlays has never been in question, although National Accounts definitions have periodically changed and, as noted above, social expenditure is the one functional category of spending to be available throughout the post-war period. This means that, in principle, it would always have been possible to generate a set of annual estimates of aggregate non-social expenditure by deducting total social expenditure from total outlays for successive years. However, prior to the publication of the first provisional version of the *OECD Social Expenditure Database* (SOCX) (OECD, 1996), changes in the categorisation of social spending and the unreliability of the national attribution of expenditure items to particular programmes would have made it difficult to believe that the resulting series was more than broadly indicative of trends. The first set of estimates using this technique, with non-social expenditure data reported for the years 1984 and 1997 in 19 OECD countries, was published in an article by this author in 2001 (Castles, 2001). Subsequently, with the aim of sketching the development of public expenditure and its main aggregates over the entire post-war era, and with strong cautionary warnings about the potential unreliability of the estimates so derived, I used pre-SOCX social expenditure data to esti-mate aggregate non-social expenditure figures for 18 countries for both 1960 and 1970 and, with much greater confidence, because the estimates were derived from SOCX data, for 1980, 1990 and 2001 (Castles, 2006).

It is these latter estimates for the period from 1980 onwards that I use in Chapter 2 of this volume to provide an aggregate overview of the retrench-ment hypothesis as it applies to both social and non-social spending aggre-gates. In that chapter, and subsequently in the remainder of the volume to refer to its findings, the term 'non-social spending' is replaced by the term 'core spending' (for an alternative usage of the same term to capture a similar, but not identical, residually-derived, expenditure concept, see Hagfors and Saari, 2006). This term is preferred to non-social expenditure, because, although this aggregate is derived as a residual, it is quite inap-propriate to view the functional categories of spending of which it is com-posed as being in some way of lesser significance than spending for social purposes. Core spending is a useful term because it designates the central-ity of the functions much of this spending serves. General public services are the sinews of modern democratic government and the maintenance of external defence and public order are tasks of the state much, much older than the provision of mass welfare. Education, not infrequently construed as a component of the welfare state, is unlikely to become less important in a society ever more reliant on the cultivation of advanced human capital skills. In the immediate post-war decades, government intervention in economic affairs, often involving high levels of public spending, was generally seen as absolutely pivotal to the efficient management of a mixed economy and, although as later chapters in this volume demonstrate in some detail, public expenditure in this area has been declining markedly over recent decades, a state control once underpinned by public spending is now quite frequently secured by regulatory means (see Chapter 10 below).

The use of residually derived core expenditure estimates in Chapter 2 is vital to the architecture of our account of the trajectory of recent public expenditure change in two important ways. First, they make it possible to identify core expenditure developments in a far greater number of countries from an earlier date than could be obtained by any other means, with, as already noted above, some capacity to describe broadly indicative trends in core spending from 1960 onwards and the means of generating reasonably reliable estimates for most OECD countries from 1980 onwards. In contrast, the data on functional categories of spending we go on to describe in the next section are only available for a comparably large number of countries from the mid-1990s onwards. However, most accounts of public expenditure reversal and retrenchment locate the origins of such changes in a period well before such functional data are available for more than a quite limited range of countries, so that, without this residual mapping technique, it would be impossible to say whether these accounts applied in the area of core spending or not.

Second, the availability of estimates of core spending allows us to contrast developments in social and non-social areas of spending after 1980, to ask whether they were moving to the beat of a single drum and to identify factors accounting for changes in the balance between these types of expenditure over time and in different countries. It is not the intention of this introduction to provide a detailed account of findings which emerge more comprehensibly from the detailed analysis of later chapters, but it is worth making clear that the post-1980 trajectories of social and core expenditure were quite different. Chapter 2 confirms the findings of the comparative social expenditure literature, that cuts in welfare spending as a percentage of GDP were few and far between after 1980, but demonstrates no less clearly that a contraction in core spending was the OECD norm. This marked contrast between types of spending aggregate does not necessarily mean that a globalisation-induced 'race-to-the-bottom' missing in the social expenditure arena is present in the arena of core spending, but it does quite definitely mean that comparing and contrasting what was occurring in the areas of social and core spending provides us with a basis for elaborating a different and a fuller account of how the state has been weathering the changes of the past quarter-century than is currently available in a literature which focuses on social expenditure alone. Later chapters in this volume, like that earlier social expenditure research, also concentrate on particular categories of spending, and so are equally constrained in what they can tell us about the forces leading to change in the relative salience of different types of expenditure (although see the analysis of trade-offs against military expenditure in Chapter 5). Chapter 2 is, therefore, the main place in this book to look for a discussion of the factors shaping the dynamic of public expenditure change as a whole.

1.2.2   A Functional Breakdown of Government Expenditure: The COFOG Data

The newly available data used in this volume derive from a data classification originally elaborated in the 1960s as part of a revised system of National Accounts (SNA68), which were only sporadically reported by a quite limited group of nations in the 1970s and 1980s, and for which data for a reasonably large subset of the advanced industrial nations for dates commencing in the early to mid-1990s are only now being reported by Eurostat and the OECD. This data classification is known as the *Classification of the Functions of Government* and is almost universally referred to by its acronym, COFOG. COFOG provides a complete breakdown of general government expenditure into functional spending categories. Prior to the 1990s, there were 14 categories. Now there are ten elaborated as follows: general public services; defence; public order and safety; economic affairs; environmental protection; housing and community amenities; health; recreation, culture and religion; education; and social protection. Health plus social protection spending are together closely equivalent, although not quite identical, to total social expenditure as measured in SOCX. It therefore follows that the sum of the remaining functions together is substantially equivalent to what we here describe as core expenditure.

Chapter 3 of this volume, by Neil Fraser and Paul Norris, discusses the evolution of the COFOG data set, reproduces and discusses data from the only study to bring together available COFOG-based data for the 1970s and 1980s (Oxley and Martin, 1991) and collects and provides a preliminary analysis of the COFOG data now available for the 1990s and the early years of the 2000s. This chapter has several important functions for the research undertaken in this volume and research in the area of comparative political economy in the future. First, it provides a summary of what we currently know about trends in the development of the separate functional categories of spending in the 1980s and 1990s for the countries reporting such data. These trends are summarised in Tables 3.1 and 3.3 and it is worth glancing ahead to these tables to dispel any notion that expenditure change in different spending areas was in any single direction during these decades. Second, the authors of the chapter use these functional spending data to provide an empirical check on the accuracy of the core spending estimates of Chapter 2, a test from which these estimates escape largely, although not wholly, unscathed. This reinforces our confidence in the broad thrust of the findings reported in Chapter 2. Third, the data collected by this chapter on functional spending in 14 countries from 1990, 18 from 1995 and 19 from 2002 onwards (see Appendix 3B of Chapter 3) constitute a solid starting-point for future comparative analysis along the lines of that which has become increasingly common and increasingly sophisticated in the area of social spending over the past three decades. Even if these data by themselves allow us only to discern quite recent trends, combined with data for later years, which international agencies now seem committed to providing on a routine basis, they offer the prospect and possibility of a substantial extension of comparative public expenditure analysis beyond its present largely social expenditure focus.

Finally, Chapter 3 is important because it is the primary source of data for some of the later chapters in this volume. This is particularly true of Chapter 4 by Richard Parry, which uses COFOG data on general public services spending to derive a more refined category of *state overhead* spending, and Chapter 6 by Paul Norris, which uses COFOG public order and safety data (as well as separate sources of data on spending on policing and prisons) as a basis for identifying the factors shaping this sometimes controversial function of the modern state. Chapter 8 on economic affairs spending by Herbert Obinger and Reimut Zohlnhöfer also starts out by using COFOG numbers, but then shifts its attention to an OECD series on subsidies to industry reporting over a much longer time-period. It should be noted, however, that some chapters for which COFOG data are available for the 1990s rely instead on other expenditure series (see below) and that there are COFOG categories – including environmental protection, housing and community affairs and recreation, culture and religious affairs – where average levels of spending are too low (for figures, see Appendix 3B) and the categorisation of spending too disparate to warrant separate chapters. There remain serious problems in the categorisation of the environmental protection series (see discussion in Chapter 3), but one suspects that, in future, this will become a highly significant and much expanded category of spending throughout the industrialised world.

The chapters on the state overhead budget and public order spending represent one extreme of the analytical endeavour in this volume, with a focus, in some ways, as much exploratory as analytical. Because the COFOG-based data sets they largely rely on provide information for a reasonably large number of countries only for a brief span of years from the mid-1990s onwards, these chapters obtain relatively weak leverage on the question of whether the functional areas of spending they discuss have experienced a major reversal in recent decades, although the evidence they provide for the years for which data are available is of a steady-state or, possibly even, a modestly increasing trajectory of spending. Interestingly, too, these are the only areas of spending discussed in this volume where strong convergence effects are not observed, but whether this is because the time-span of the spending observed in these chapters is too short or too recent or because trends in these areas are shaped by a different dynamic from that governing other spending areas is impossible to tell. Data availability problems notwithstanding, however, these chapters are, in some ways, the most pioneering of all the contributions to this volume, since they seek to explore areas of expenditure never before subject to cross-national analysis. Why countries differ in the size of their state overhead expenditure is a question that potentially unlocks a whole series of issues pertaining to levels and trends of the cost of administering particular political systems. Why countries differ in their responses to criminal justice issues is not a new question, but one never before explored using public expenditure data. The answers to these questions given by Chapters 4 and 6 for the period at and around the turn of the millennium, together with a continuing flow of the relevant COFOG data for later years, will most certainly be of assistance to scholars seeking to identify the dynamic of spending in these areas in later comparative research.

1.2.3   Existing Data Series

Apart from Chapters 4 and 6, the remaining chapters in this volume reporting on functional categories of spending, and the further and final chapter discussing regulatory intervention in economic affairs, all rely on existing series reporting data back to the 1980s or even earlier. Chapter 5, by Tom Cusack, uses the long available SIPRI data set as its primary source on military spending. Chapter 7, by Manfred Schmidt, on trends in educational spending, uses the OECD's *Education at a Glance* series as its main source and reports data going back to the mid-1970s. As noted previously, Herbert Obinger and Reimut Zohlnhöfer's Chapter 8 discussion of spending on economic affairs starts out by using COFOG data for the 1990s, but bases its main analysis on an OECD series reporting levels of industrial subsidies in member countries since 1980. Uwe Wagschal's Chapter 9 discussion of the factors determining levels and changes in debt interest repayments bases its findings on figures available for member countries from the OECD *Economic Outlook* database in some cases going back to the 1970s. Finally, Nico Siegel's analysis of economic regulation in Chapter 10 makes use of series on the extent and character of product market regulation and employment protection legislation emanating from OECD research published only quite recently but reporting data over a period of two or more decades.

Earlier we noted that adding all the existing series of non-social functional spending data together could not produce anything like a realistic series on total non-social or 'core' spending because data on so many categories were missing. However, what these data series going back to the 1980s or earlier can tell us is what has happened to particular categories of spending over a substantially longer span of years than is available from the COFOG data. This means that we can not only contrast the growth of aggregate social spending over the past quarter-century with the decline in aggregate core spending over the same period, but also identify in which categories of core spending the most significant cutbacks occurred and whether they occurred in the 1980s or 1990s. While Chapters 4 and 6 offer tentative, but necessarily period-constrained, evidence of a lack of systematic retrenchment in state overhead and public order spending, Chapters 5, 7 and 8 locate quite generalised cutbacks in spending on defence, education and industrial subsidies taking place either over the period as a whole or, in the case of defence, since around 1990. Chapter 10 identifies similar downward trends in market-restricting product market regulation and temporary employment protection legislation, while Chapter 9 reports a rather different pattern of a sharp increase in debt repayment expenditure in the 1980s and early 1990s and a no less rapid decline in the decade thereafter.

Taken together, the three kinds of data examined in this volume provide us with a picture of the past quarter-century's trajectory of public spending which, rather than having a missing dimension, is multidimensional in character. This is a picture with clear implications for the proper assessment of the supposed phenomenon of a generalised public expenditure reversal commencing some time in the 1980s. Some categories of spending (primarily social expenditure comprising the COFOG categories of social protection and health) have expanded, while others (as described above) have declined. COFOG-based evidence for the 1990s demonstrates no clear trend in either state overhead or public order spending and the data overview in Table 3.4 of Chapter 3 of the COFOG categories of spending not separately reported in this volume are suggestive of a similar conclusion. Moreover, the analysis of aggregate spending in Chapter 2 demonstrates that, over the period as a whole, average increases in social expenditure outweighed aggregate cuts in core spending, so that average levels of OECD total outlays were actually somewhat higher in 2001 than they had been in 1980.

This is a body of evidence that makes it extremely difficult to accept the proposition that any widespread reversal in the developmental trend of public spending took place during these years. Using expenditure as a percentage of GDP as our measuring rod, it is clear that no retrenchment occurred in either aggregate social spending or total outlays and that the most that might reasonably be claimed is that recent decades have witnessed a trend towards core expenditure retrenchment. Even then, however, there must be caveats. The notion of retrenchment sits rather uneasily with cutbacks, which, in many countries, in the 1990s at least, were largely constituted by declining debt interest payments rather than a reduced provision of services and by reductions in military spending made possible by the 'peace dividend' resulting from the end of the Cold War. Retrenchment is a term usually employed with negative connotations and these were developments largely welcomed by Western mass publics. Moreover, the shift in the overall balance of public spending from core to social spending that occurred in these years might simply be seen as the continuation of the long-run postwar trend towards an increased salience of welfare state spending, with the only significant difference from the past the fact that it was taking place under circumstances of fiscally constrained total expenditure. On the other hand, there clearly were new departures, conspicuous amongst them the fact that the undoubtedly major cutbacks occurring in economic affairs spending were accompanied by a no lesser transformation in the field of economic regulation. Arguably, then, what was new and systemic in these years was a shift away from state intervention in economic affairs of a kind consonant with the neo-liberal doctrines of the era: a retrenchment not of the core, but of one of its most significant components.

1.3   ACCOUNTING FOR CORE EXPENDITURE DEVELOPMENT

Such conclusions and speculations are as far as we can reasonably go on the basis of a description of trends in expenditure development. To take the discussion further requires us to locate the factors shaping these trends. Clearly the argument for retrenchment of greater or lesser proportions would be much strengthened by the identification of a factor leading to cutbacks in expenditure and regulation across a broad front, with globalisation obviously the front-runner in the scholarly literature. That is not, however, the only reason for moving beyond a description of expenditure trends to a search for their determinants. The very fact of the recognition of the multidimensional character of public spending patterns immediately poses questions concerning the factors shaping patterns of change in different spending domains. In principle, such questions are of precisely the same nature as those addressed by a generation of researchers seeking to establish the determinants of changes in social expenditure over the past three or more decades. The studies constituting this volume seek to extend this kind of analysis to the categories of public expenditure constituting core spending for two reasons. One is that that is necessary to complete our investigation of whether the cutbacks in these areas can legitimately be seen as aspects of a coherent process of core expenditure retrenchment. The other is that we wish to demonstrate the possibility of broadening the focus of comparative political economy research beyond a single dimension to embrace the whole of public expenditure development and, indeed, beyond public expenditure as such to other phenomena, such as economic and other forms of regulation, which define the reach of the modern state. In this final section of the introduction and, once again, without any detailed summary of individual chapter findings, we identify some of the more general conclusions that emerge from our analysis of the determinants of the different core spending categories treated in this volume and note their implications for the idea of a concerted cutback across the entire area of core spending or, at least, across more than just one or two spending areas.

A first important point to note is that the analyses in the chapters that follow neither employ an identical statistical technique nor explore anything like an identical array of hypotheses to account for expenditure and regulatory variation. On the methodological front, what is common to all these studies is the use of some kind of multivariate method, allowing the identification of a variety of influences on expenditure or regulatory development, but the precise technique employed differs. Some chapters contextualise their multivariate modelling through extensive prior bivariate analysis and one of these relies on what is described as an 'easily accessible substitute for a classical regression-based multivariate explanation'. Other chapters report 'best-fit' equations and still others provide a variety of iterations of their models, testing the explanatory power of different combinations of variables. The chapter on military spending, precisely because it rests on the longest and strongest body of data, uses pooled time-series methods, while the remaining chapters bow to the realities of a situation in which the data required are only now becoming available and base much of their analysis on relatively small-n cross-sections of, typically, 18 to 20 countries. This latter technique has many problems of which the authors are well aware. Here, given the inadequacies of the data discussed throughout the volume, the only alternative would be to abandon cross-national analysis altogether.

In respect of hypothesis testing, the authors have not followed any self-imposed party line. All came to their chapters with an awareness of the twin objectives of this study – to assess whether the category of spending they were considering was subject to retrenchment pressures and to open up that category of spending to comparative political economy analysis – but the balance between the objectives was necessarily partly a function of the availability of data, so that, for instance, those utilising COFOG data alone were unable to speak meaningfully to the issue of retrenchment tendencies manifested much before the early to mid-1990s. In any case, the apparently conflicting demands of examining factors supposedly common across all expenditure areas and of locating factors theoretically specific to particular spending areas were always going to be resolved in favour of the latter, since without the fullest possible specification of the cross-national variance through area-specific variables, the impact of common factors could not be properly ascertained. The result is a multiplicity of models constituted of many and diverse variables, with just a few factors (often themselves differently specified in different chapters) common to most chapters in the volume. These common factors include tests for the presence of expenditure convergence, partisanship and trade dependency effects, the latter variable serving, as elsewhere in the literature, as a measure of susceptibility to global economic pressures.

A summary presentation of our findings in respect of these three factors serves as a taster for what is to come and as a set of headline conclusions on which need to be superimposed the complex detail that can only come from addressing the argument and modelling of particular chapters.

- *Outcomes convergence* Much the strongest common finding of this volume is of a convergence of outcomes in most Western industrialised countries. This applies both to the social and core expenditure aggregates and to the majority of functional categories making up core expenditure as well as to the realm of economic regulation. The exceptions – state overhead and public order spending – are exceptions not because of contrary evidence, but because of a lack of data to establish trajectories of spending over more than just a few years. In many cases, the catch-up (or catch-down) coefficients reported in this volume are extraordinarily strong, by themselves accounting for half or more of cross-national variation in the period under review. What this tells us is that, although countries were becoming much more alike in respect of each separate category of spending, change was not occurring in the kind of uniform direction presupposed by a 'race-to-the-bottom' scenario. One obvious source of a compressed distribution of spending applying across many categories of expenditure was the fact that the countries of the New Southern Europe, which in 1980 had only recently emerged as fully-fledged democratic systems, increased their public spending virtually right across the board. At the same time, however, there were conspicuous high spenders in particular areas that, over the course of the 1980s and 1990s, came back to the pack. Dramatic instances include Canada in the area of educational spending, Portugal and Norway in the area of total economy subsidies, the Netherlands in respect of aggregate social expenditure and both Belgium and Ireland in respect of aggregate core spending. No less dramatic cuts in product market regulation took place in Belgium and Japan and in temporary employment protection in Sweden and Italy. It is possible, although not considered in the scholarly literature, that widespread cutbacks of this nature could represent a kind of attenuated retrenchment process, with countries cutting back not so much on total spending, but on classes of expenditure where a previous trajectory of development had left them substantially out of kilter with significant others.

- *Party Control Still Matters* A key argument from a previous generation of social expenditure studies was that the partisan complexion of government was a major factor shaping the growth of spending and a key plank of theorising around the sources of social expenditure retrenchment is that the old partisan divide no longer makes a great deal of difference (Huber and Stephens, 2001; Green-Pedersen, 2002; Kittel and Obinger, 2003). It is a natural extrapolation from the social to the core expenditure area to hypothesise that partisanship may once have influenced other categories of spending as it did social expenditure and that this effect may also have disappeared with the passing of time. The first part of that hypothesis is confirmed in this study more strongly than the second part, with the aggregates of social and core spending strongly and positively shaped by prior Left incumbency at the beginning of the period and still noticeably, if perhaps less strongly so, at the end of the period. Partisanship is also shown to influence nearly all of the separate categories of spending in some way in one time-period or another (military expenditure is the big exception), although change effects are often harder to discern than level effects and the Left is not always a predictor of higher levels of spending. That depends on the policy area in question. Studies in this volume show that expenditure on prisons and the size of the budget deficit were both higher in countries in which Right cabinet incumbency was greatest. Thus cross-national differences in patterns of partisan incumbency remain a significant factor accounting for the absence of any single direction of public expenditure development in the countries of advanced capitalism over the past quarter of a century.

- *The evidence on globalisation*   In the literature on social expenditure, the effects of trade dependency are contested. Early studies (Cameron, 1978; Katzenstein, 1985) suggested that countries faced with external vulnerability tended to spend more to protect their citizens. Globalisation theorists argue that, under present economic circumstances, this logic is reversed and that, the more a country is exposed to the world economy, the more it will be required by market imperatives to cut back on spending and taxing that constitute a burden on export competitiveness (again, see Gough, 1996). In this book on changing patterns of core expenditure, every chapter except that on public order spending seeks to identify the effects of trade dependency as measured by a country's level of imports plus exports as a percentage of GDP, and some chapters further test for globalisation effects by examining the impact of trade flows. The vast majority of these tests yield wholly negligible coefficients. In fact, only one of the chapters on particular categories of core spending reports a negative and significant finding and that is in the rather unlikely area of military spending. The finding ceases to be significant, however, when expenditure convergence is controlled for and, arguably, therefore, may be regarded as spurious. The only other negative trade dependency effect is reported in Chapter 2 and relates to change in aggregate core spending minus net debt repayment expenditure in the 1980s. This is an ostensibly important finding because it suggests that core spending as a whole declined more strongly in countries more exposed to world market forces and that, therefore, globalisation factors may have been implicated in what we earlier identified as the nearest thing to a broad-based retrenchment tendency encountered at any point in this analysis. However, because aggregate core spending at the beginning of the period was actually quite significantly higher in countries with exposed economies and because at the end of the period there is no sign that it was significantly lower, Chapter 2 interprets the finding for the 1980s less as evidence of a systemic globalisation effect than of a one-off fiscal adjustment by countries whose earlier high levels of spending had left them dangerously overexposed in an uncertain economic climate.

So the evidence for globalisation-induced cutbacks in expenditure turns out to be as weak as the evidence for a dramatic reversal of trajectory across most categories of spending. Not only has the state not disappeared, but the main account offered for that phenomenon fails nearly all the tests asked of it. Nevertheless, as this book shows very clearly, there were categories of public spending that were cut during these years and, in some instances, so severely as to amount, in the words of one these chapters, to 'a real race to the bottom'. Rather than looking to sweeping theories accounting for expenditure cuts in general, the very fact that different spending categories manifest quite different patterns of growth and decline suggests a need to analyse each area in its own right. That, of course, is precisely what the substantive chapters of this book attempt to do and in a far more nuanced way than can possibly be captured in a summary introduction. For the present, our mapping of the multidimensional aspects of the modern state suggests that we should be wary of generalised trends and generalised conclusions. It may be, however, that what we learn of the factors shaping these diverse areas of spending will ultimately make it possible to identify more complex patterns of change and causation than identified in the present literature. However, whether that is the case or not, measurement and analysis of a multidimensional universe will certainly tell us far more about what has been happening to the state over the past quarter-century than can possibly be learned by continuing to insist on looking for retrenchment in the wrong place.

REFERENCES

Allan, J. and L. Scruggs (2004), 'Political partisanship and welfare state reform in advanced industrial societies', *American Journal of Political Science*, **48** (3), 496–512.

Cameron, D. (1978), 'The expansion of the public economy: a comparative analysis', *American Political Science Review*, **72** (4), 1243–61.

Castles, F.G. (ed.) (1982), *The Impact of Parties: Politics and Policies in Democratic Capitalist States*, London: Sage Publications.

Castles, F.G. (2001), 'On the political economy of recent public sector development', *Journal of European Social Policy*, **11** (3), 195–211.

Castles, F.G. (2004), *The Future of the Welfare State*, Oxford: Oxford University Press.

Castles, F.G. (2006), *The Growth of the Post-war Public Expenditure State: Long-term Trajectories and Recent Trends*, Bremen: TranState Working Papers, no. 35, 1–69.

Clasen, J. (ed.) (2001), *What Future for Social Security? Debates and Reforms in National and Cross-National Perspective*, The Hague: Kluwer Law International.

Garrett, G. (1998), *Partisan Politics in the Global Economy*, Cambridge: Cambridge University Press.

Gough, I. (1996), 'Social welfare and competitiveness', *New Political Economy*, **1** (2), 209–32.

Green-Pedersen, C. (2002), *The Politics of Justification*, Amsterdam: University of Amsterdam Press.

Hagfors, R. and J. Saari (2006), 'Does the stability and growth pact crowd out social expenditure? Latent crowding out and the Lisbon strategy', *Espanet Conference*, 21–3 September, Bremen.

Huber, E. and J. Stephens (2001), *Development and the Crisis of the Welfare State*, Chicago: University of Chicago Press.

Jessop, B. (2002), *The Future of the Capitalist State*, Cambridge: Polity Press.

Katzenstein, P. (1985), *Small States in World Markets*, Ithaca: Cornell University Press.

Kittel, B. and H. Obinger (2003), 'Political parties, institutions, and the dynamics of social expenditure in times of austerity', *Journal of European Public Policy*, **10** (1), 20–45.

Korpi, W. (1978), *The Working Class in Welfare Capitalism*, London: Routledge and Kegan Paul.

Korpi, W. (2003), 'Welfare-state regress in Western Europe: politics, institutions, globalization and Europeanization, *Annual Review of Sociology*, **29**, 589–609.

Kuhnle, S. (ed.) (2000), *The Survival of the European Welfare State*, London: Routledge.

Leibfried, S. (ed.) (2001), *Welfare State Futures*, Cambridge: Cambridge University Press.

OECD (1981), *The Welfare State in Crisis*, Paris.

OECD (1996), 'Social expenditure statistics of OECD member countries (provisional version), Paris.

Oxley, H. and J.P. Martin (1991), 'Controlling government spending and deficits: trends in the 1980s and prospects for the 1990s', *OECD Economic Studies*, No.17, Paris.

Pierson, P. (ed.) (2001), *The New Politics of the Welfare State*, Oxford: Oxford University Press.

Schuknecht, L. and V. Tanzi (2005), *Reforming Public Expenditure in Industrialised Countries: Are There Trade-offs?*, European Central Bank, Working Paper no. 435, 1–44.

Swank, D. (2002), *Global Capital, Political Institutions, and Policy Change in Developed Welfare States*, Cambridge: Cambridge University Press.

Therborn, G. (1983), 'When, how and why does a welfare state become a welfare state?', paper presented at the ECPR Workshops, March, Freiburg.

Wilensky, H. (1975), *The Welfare State and Equality*, Berkeley: University of California Press.

2. Testing the retrenchment hypothesis: an aggregate overview

Francis G. Castles

2.1 INTRODUCTION

Much of this book is concerned with mapping trends in particular pro-grammes of core expenditure in OECD countries over recent decades. This chapter is different in focusing on the big aggregates of spending: total social and core expenditures, each, on average, currently constituting around 50 per cent of OECD public budgets. We commence our study with these broader aggregates of spending, for several reasons. First, because much of the debate on public sector retrenchment and the retreat of the state has focused on trends in social expenditure, it is important to establish from the very beginning whether expenditure in this area has really been contracting. Second, the very fact that social and core spending are of roughly equal weight in public budgets suggests the obvious, and hitherto largely unexam-ined, possibility that retrenchment trends may have been just as prominent in the programmes making up core spending. Third, while the optimum strategy for investigating trends in core spending might well be to investigate how particular programme changes had contributed to public spending development as a whole, reasonably complete programme data are, in an appreciable number of cases, only available for the period after 1990. In most accounts, retrenchment pressures began at least a decade earlier, so it is vital to find some alternative leverage on what was taking place in this period.

A possible way forward is to use long-standing OECD data series to gen-erate estimates of aggregate core spending from 1980 onwards by the simple technique of deducting total social expenditure as reported in the OECD Social Expenditure Database (SOCX) from total government outlays (for a discussion of this technique of estimating core spending, see Chapter 1, above, and Castles, 2006). These estimates, although calculated as residuals, are not intrinsically less reliable than the series from which they are derived and which have been routinely used in comparative public policy research, although it should be noted that mostly quite minor differences between SOCX and COFOG definitions of social expenditure mean that, even were we to be able to calculate the sum of COFOG core spending categories, the figure obtained would not be identical to the residual estimates arrived at here. In what follows, we seek to establish whether aggregates of social and core spending have manifested similar or divergent patterns of growth over recent decades and the nature of the factors shaping each. Answers to these questions allow us to come to conclusions about the appropriateness of seeing the present era as one of widespread expenditure retrenchment and of the retreat of the state.

2.2 TRENDS

Table 2.1 contains data on levels of social and core spending in 18 OECD countries in 1980 and 2001 and change in social and core spending in these countries for the periods 1980–90, 1990–2001 and 1980–2001. With a view to identifying patterns of similarity and difference between countries sharing cultural and linguistic commonalities, Table 2.1 groups the countries under examination into four families of nations: the English-speaking countries, Scandinavia, continental Western Europe and Southern Europe. Data for Japan is also reported, although that country is not included in any of these families of nations groupings. The 18 countries compared include most long-term OECD members. However, New Zealand and Switzerland are excluded because of missing data and Norway because its reliance on North Sea oil revenue makes it increasingly difficult to compare meaningfully that country's public finances with those of other OECD nations. As a means of assessing the extent of similarity in spending patterns amongst nations, the summary statistics for levels of spending include a measure of the coefficient of variation (CV) of the sample distribution. To assess the extent to which countries are converging over time, the columns reporting change include a measure of *catch-up*, which is simply the correlation between the initial level of expenditure and subsequent expenditure change, with strong negative coefficients indicative of increasing similarity amongst this sample of 18 OECD countries.

An initial glance at the summary statistics section of Table 2.1 suggests three apparently clear-cut findings:

1. That social expenditure continued to grow throughout the 1980s and 1990s, while core expenditure development was static or declining.
2. That the general tendency of the changes taking place over the past quarter-century has been broadly convergent in character.
3. That expenditure growth in the 1980s was appreciably stronger than expenditure growth in the 1990s.

Support for the first of these findings is extremely strong and confirms the suspicion that retrenchment theorists may have been mistaken in their single-minded focus on social expenditure. What these figures tell us is that, in the vast majority of these countries, it was not the welfare state, but the core expenditure state, that was being cut back during these decades. Between 1980 and 2001, average OECD levels of social expenditure increased by 3.9 per cent of GDP or by 21 per cent over their 1980 average levels of 18.8 per cent of GDP. Over the same period, average core spending levels declined by 1.4 per of GDP, equivalent to almost 6 per cent of their 1980 average level of 24.3 per cent of GDP. Moreover, this contrast between still increasing social expenditure levels and declining or static core expenditure levels is not just a matter of averages, but applies to all family of nations' expenditure comparisons and to the vast majority of individual country cases. Some scholars (Mishra, 1990; Clayton and Pontusson, 1998) have attributed welfare expenditure growth in these years to increased spending on unemployment, but SOCX data on unemployment benefit and active labour market spending suggest that such increases contributed only marginally to the social expenditure growth noted in Table 2.1.

The evidence for a general process of expenditure convergence also appears extremely strong, with a substantial decline in the coefficients of variation for both expenditure aggregates and with all six catch up coefficients decidedly negative and all but that for 1980–90 social expenditure statistically significant. A possible objection might be to argue that the undoubtedly greater magnitude of both social and core expenditure growth in Southern Europe between 1980 and 2001 gives an impression of a generalised process of convergence, when, in reality, the phenomenon was restricted to a rather small group of countries, the catch-up trajectory of which was conditioned by their economic and political underdevelopment in the decades before 1980. However, excluding Southern European countries from the sample and recalculating catch-up coefficients still points to a similar conclusion, with all the coefficients remaining negative and all but one greater than –0.40.

The third apparent finding from Table 2.1, that expenditure growth was higher in the 1980s than in the 1990s, remains true in respect of social expenditure even when we adjust for changes in unemployment-related expenditure in these decades. However, in the case of core expenditure, what appears to be a no less decisive contrast between no-change expenditure development in the 1980s and a general trend towards expenditure cutbacks in the 1990s turns out to be far more problematic than it appears on the surface. That is because the core expenditure figures take no account of the quite substantial changes in net debt interest payments that took place during these periods. In the 1980s, such payments were rising steeply partly because

Table 2.1   Levels and changes in total social expenditure and core
             expenditure, 1980–2001

	Social expenditure				
	1980	1980–1990	1990–2001	1980–2001	2001
Australia	11.3	2.9	3.8	6.7	18.0
Canada	14.3	4.3	−0.4	3.9	18.2
Ireland	19.0	−0.4	−4.8	−5.2	13.8
United Kingdom	17.9	1.6	2.3	3.9	21.8
United States	13.3	0.1	1.4	1.5	14.8
Family mean	*15.2*	*1.7*	*0.5*	*2.2*	*17.3*
Denmark	29.1	0.2	−0.1	0.1	29.2
Finland	18.5	6.3	0.0	6.3	24.8
Sweden	28.8	2.0	−1.9	0.1	28.9
Family mean	*25.5*	*2.8*	*−0.7*	*2.2*	*27.6*
Austria	22.9	1.2	1.9	3.1	26.0
Belgium	24.1	2.8	0.3	3.1	27.2
France	22.6	4.2	1.7	5.9	28.5
Germany	23.0	−0.2	4.6	4.4	27.4
Netherlands	26.9	0.7	−5.8	−5.1	21.8
Family mean	*23.9*	*1.7*	*0.5*	*2.3*	*26.2*
Greece	11.5	9.4	3.4	12.8	24.3
Italy	18.4	6.4	1.0	7.4	25.8
Portugal	10.9	3.0	7.2	10.2	21.1
Spain	15.9	3.6	0.1	3.7	19.6
Family mean	*14.2*	*5.6*	*2.9*	*8.5*	*22.7*
Japan	10.6	1.0	5.7	6.7	16.9
Summary statistics					
Overall mean	*18.8*	*2.7*	*1.1*	*3.9*	*22.7*
CV/Catch-up	*33.0*	*−0.35*	*−0.53*	*−0.62*	*21.8*

Sources and notes: Social expenditure as a percentage of GDP as reported in OECD
(2004a). Core expenditure is equivalent to total expenditure of general government (data
from OECD, *Economic Outlook*, various dates) minus total social expenditure. CV
designates the coefficient of variation, which is reported for measures of level of
expenditure. Catch-up is the correlation between the level of spending at the beginning of
each period and change in spending during that period. Means subject to rounding errors.

the general level of public debt was increasing and partly because interest
rates had increased dramatically. Through the 1970s, real interest rates had
been generally rather low and sometimes even negative, but, from the time
of the second oil shock, governments began to take a less accommodative

Core expenditure				
1980	1980–1990	1990–2001	1980–2001	2001
20.1	0.7	−1.6	−0.9	19.2
24.5	2.9	−3.8	−0.9	23.6
30.3	−7.7	−2.9	−10.6	19.7
25.1	−4.7	−1.2	−5.9	19.2
18.1	1.3	0.9	2.2	20.3
23.6	*−1.5*	*−1.7*	*−3.2*	*20.4*
27.1	2.2	−3.2	−1.0	26.1
19.6	0.9	3.8	4.7	24.3
31.3	−3.0	−0.2	−3.2	28.1
26.0	*0.0*	*0.1*	*0.2*	*26.2*
25.2	−0.7	0.4	−0.3	24.9
34.2	−6.1	−6.0	−12.1	22.1
23.5	−0.5	1.0	0.5	24.0
24.9	−2.6	−1.4	−4.0	20.9
28.9	−2.4	−1.6	−4.0	24.9
27.3	*−2.5*	*−1.5*	*−4.0*	*23.4*
18.9	8.5	−1.5	7.0	25.9
23.5	4.9	−5.5	−0.6	22.9
23.5	4.4	−2.7	1.7	25.2
16.3	6.2	−2.5	3.7	20.0
20.6	*6.0*	*−3.1*	*3.0*	*23.5*
21.8	−1.7	0.7	−1.0	20.8
24.3	*0.1*	*−1.5*	*−1.4*	*22.9*
19.8	*−0.72*	*−0.63*	*−0.84*	*11.8*

stance to inflation, raising rates to the 'relatively high average levels' that persisted until the early 1990s, after which they declined continuously and quite markedly (OECD, 1993).

Changes in net debt interest payments (the determinants of which are discussed in Chapter 9 of this volume) are significant for core expenditure change in both substantive and theoretical terms. From 1980 to 1990, the average level of debt interest paid by these 18 countries went up from 1.8 to 4.3 per cent of GDP. From 1990 to 2001, debt interest payments went down from 4.3 to 2.8 per cent of GDP. Unlike unemployment-related social expenditure changes, these are changes of sufficient magnitude to alter the entire perspective of what was happening to core expenditure in these decades. Theoretically, the point is that a higher level of debt interest servicing, just like a higher level of unemployment-related expenditure, is not an unalloyed good in the sense of affording citizens higher levels of service provision, but rather may be seen as a response to problems largely or wholly of a government's own making. Because the notion of retrenchment is often seen as being as much about levels of provision as of expenditure, it is therefore important to assess the extent to which trends in core spending are artefacts of change in debt interest payment levels.

A way of doing this is to deduct changes in net debt interest payments from core spending levels and changes, as shown in Table 2.2. Comparing these figures to those in the core expenditure figures in Table 2.1 shows a world turned entirely on its head. Between 1980 and 1990, average levels of core spending minus debt interest payments went down from 22.5 per cent of GDP to 20.1 per cent, a cutback of almost exactly 10 per cent on 1980 levels. Between 1990 and 2001, however, the sharp decline in net debt interest payments resulting from the interest rate cuts of the period was sufficient to turn around a 1.5 per cent of GDP core expenditure reduction, leaving the average level of core spending minus debt payments unchanged. This reversal of the temporality of cutbacks is just as apparent at the individual country level as it is in terms of averages, with 15 of these 18 countries experiencing reductions in core expenditures minus debt interest payments in the first period, and a far more balanced picture of cuts and increases in the second. In real provision terms, then, a strong case can be made for arguing that the expenditure cuts occurring in these decades were a phenomenon of the 1980s rather than of the 1990s.

Before turning to hypotheses that might explain these trends, it is also worth remarking on some of the family of nations' patterns revealed by Tables 2.1 and 2.2, some highly predictable in terms of the literature and others more surprising. The strong growth profile and catch-up trajectory of the Southern European nations is, of course, precisely what might be expected on the basis of a convergence-based account of recent public expenditure trends. Summing social and core expenditure growth over the period as a whole to obtain total outlays, the only other family of nations to be in positive territory was Scandinavia. That fits nicely with the 'politics matters' hypothesis, although, interestingly, Scandinavian spending superiority is more pronounced in the area of core expenditure than in that of social expenditure, which is the domain in which the claims of the partisan model have been most comprehensively tested.

The really big surprise, however, is the absence of any significant difference between either the social or core expenditure profiles of the

Table 2.2   Levels and changes in core expenditure minus net debt interest payments in 18 OECD countries, 1980–2001

	1980	1980–1990	1990–2001	1980–2001	2001
Australia	19.2	−1.9	0.0	−1.9	17.3
Canada	22.6	−0.4	−1.5	−1.9	20.7
Ireland	26.8	−10.4	3.1	−7.3	19.5
United Kingdom	22.0	−4.3	−0.5	−4.8	17.2
United States	17.0	−1.0	2.0	1.0	18.0
Family mean	*21.5*	*−3.6*	*0.6*	*−3.0*	*18.5*
Denmark	26.6	−1.1	−1.2	−2.3	24.3
Finland	20.6	1.6	1.4	3.0	23.6
Sweden	31.7	−2.3	−2.0	−4.3	27.4
Family mean	*26.3*	*−0.6*	*−0.6*	*−1.2*	*25.1*
Austria	23.5	−1.8	0.4	−1.4	22.1
Belgium	28.8	−11.6	−1.3	−12.9	15.9
France	22.7	−2.1	0.6	−1.5	21.2
Germany	23.6	−3.5	−2.0	−5.5	18.1
Netherlands	26.5	−4.3	0.0	−4.3	22.2
Family mean	*25.0*	*−4.7*	*−0.5*	*−5.1*	*19.9*
Greece	16.9	0.7	1.6	2.3	19.2
Italy	18.8	−0.3	−1.5	−1.8	17.0
Portugal	20.4	−1.1	2.7	1.6	22.0
Spain	16.0	3.4	−2.2	1.2	17.2
Family mean	*18.0*	*0.7*	*0.2*	*0.8*	*18.9*
Japan	20.8	−2.0	0.6	−1.4	19.4
Summary statistics					
Overall mean	*22.5*	*−2.4*	*0.0*	*−2.3*	*20.1*
CV/Catch-up	*19.3*	*−0.65*	*−0.24*	*−0.73*	*15.2*

Sources and notes: Core expenditure figures from Table 2.1. Net debt interest payments also from OECD, *Economic Outlook*, various dates. CV designates the coefficient of variation, which is reported for measures of level of expenditure. Catch-up is the correlation between the level of spending at the beginning of each period and change in spending during that period. Means subject to rounding errors.

English-speaking and continental Western European families of nations, and that, taking account of the effect of debt interest payments on changes in core spending, the average extent of cutbacks in continental Western Europe was actually much greater than in the English-speaking world. The column for overall change in Table 2.2 reveals that, between 1980 and 2001, core spending minus debt interest payments declined by 5.1 per cent of GDP in the former grouping as compared to 3 per cent of GDP in the latter.

All five countries in the continental grouping experienced significant expenditure reductions over these decades, with Germany's cutback of 5.5 per cent of GDP more than matching the Netherlands' 4.3 per cent and more than compensating for the German post-unification increase in social spending of 4.6 per cent shown in Table 2.1.

These findings are clearly anomalous. They do not fit the received view that 'liberal' welfare regimes are inherently more expenditure-averse than 'conservative' ones (Esping-Andersen, 1990). Nor are they seemingly compatible with the fact that the neo-liberal parties that dominated governments across much of the English-speaking world during this period were rhetorically, at least, far more committed to public expenditure retrenchment than the more consensus-oriented parties and governments of continental Western Europe. Conjoined with the findings that social expenditure was rising throughout the period and that, taking into account debt interest payment changes, the core expenditure cutbacks which occurred took place in the 1980s rather than the 1990s, they are departures from the standard account of recent expenditure trends and of the factors shaping them that any successful account of recent expenditure development must seek to explain.

2.3   HYPOTHESES

The remainder of this chapter seeks to locate reasons why recent trends in public expenditure development depart so radically from those expected. To do this, we model the expenditure levels and changes reported in Tables 2.1 and 2.2 using simple regression methods. These cross-sectional models are derived by identifying which of a series of factors, hypothesised to be influential in shaping public expenditure trends over these years, best accounts for the expenditure variation exhibited by the countries under analysis here. In this section, we provide a brief account of the argument underlying each hypothesis and identify the variable or variables used to test that hypothesis in the modelling exercise that follows.

- *Catch-up and convergence*   Essentially, the logic informing the idea that expenditure development follows a catch-up path leading to greater convergence in expenditure policy outcomes is one of inertial forces propelling expenditure growth to inherent limits implicit in programme design (see, for various adumbrations, Aaron, 1967; Flora, 1986; Pierson, 2000). Programmes grow rapidly at first, but tend to stabilise as they become more mature, that is, achieve the extension their architects envisaged. The argument that programme maturation helps to account for expenditure trends rests largely on the fact that different countries adopt programmes at different times. Initially, this implies increasing divergence amongst countries as some experience rapid programme growth and others none at all. However, as more and more countries adopt a given expenditure programme, there will come a time when the early adopters enter the programme maturation phase, whilst the programmes of late adopters continue to grow rapidly. Expenditure levels will then converge as countries with lower levels of spending begin to catch up with those who initiated their programmes earlier. Arguably, a similar logic of intended programme design may also help explain government efforts to cut back spending, where, as a consequence of lower than predicted economic growth (see below), programme expenditure has exceeded original targets. The universally negative and generally significant correlations between initial levels of spending and subsequent spending reported in Tables 2.1 and 2.2 provide strong *prima facie* evidence that catch up has been occurring on a major scale. In our modelling, we test whether the initial expenditure level variable used to detect the presence of catch up in these tables remains a significant predictor of expenditure outcomes when we take account of the effects of variables deriving from other hypotheses.

- *Economic slowdown*   Economic slowdown has featured prominently in the literature on retrenchment as the trigger event precipitating efforts to cut back expenditure levels. The literature is, however, strongly divided about the relationship between economic growth and spending, with an influential view, following the lead of the public finance pioneer, Alfred Wagner (1883), seeing growth as a potent force for greater spending, but with others arguing that, since spending is measured as a percentage of GDP, all other things being equal, higher growth will mean lower expenditure increases (Wildavsky, 1975). Both views could, in fact, be simultaneously correct, with the Wagnerian perspective explaining why new programme adoption slowed so rapidly right across the OECD in the wake of the 1970s oil shocks, and with the counter argument providing a logic explaining why it was countries like Japan and Ireland, with the most rapid rates of economic growth, which have manifested the lowest rates of post-war expenditure growth. Since the analysis here is exclusively cross-national in character, the clear expectation is that it will be the negative relationship that will be most prominent in our findings. In our modelling of expenditure levels, the test variable is a nation's average rate of economic growth in the 20 years preceding the year in which expenditure levels are being measured. In our modelling of expenditure changes, it is the average rate of economic growth for the period in question. Data for constructing these variables come from Armingeon et al. (2004) and are derived from OECD sources.

- *An increasing debt burden*   As noted previously, during the 1970s and 1980s many OECD countries sought to sidestep potential resistance to the higher taxes required to fund new or existing expenditure programmes by increasing levels of public borrowing (the classical analysis of the fiscal limits to expenditure development may be found in Peacock and Wiseman, 1961). In 1970, the average level of gross financial liabilities of general government in the 18 OECD countries analysed here was 34.4 per cent of GDP; in 1980, 40.9 per cent; in 1990, 63.7 per cent; and, in 2001, 70.0 per cent (data from OECD, *Economic Outlook*, various years). However, increasing real interest rates after 1980 meant that higher debt levels automatically translated through to substantially higher net debt interest payments which, by 1980, were, in several countries, a significant component of core spending. In that year, the average level of net debt interest payments of the five most indebted OECD countries was 3.8 per cent of GDP. Ten years later, the equivalent average was a massive 8.2 per cent of GDP. The obvious implication is that high levels of indebtedness lead to higher levels of core spending when interest rates are rising and to declining expenditures at times when interest rates are falling. A major complication, however, is that a higher debt repayment requirement is, in itself, a potent incentive to cut back other expenditure programmes. This means that expenditure outcomes are likely to be subject to contradictory pressures, with escalating debt interest payments pushing core spending levels upwards at just the same time that governments read the same entrails as warning of the need for greater fiscal stringency. In what follows, we seek to disentangle these effects by contrasting the impact of indebtedness levels on core expenditure levels initially including and subsequently excluding the impact of debt interest payments. A negative relationship between public debt and expenditure change once debt interest payments are discounted would be indicative of an effect separate from that of the automatic outcome of interest rate changes.
- *New politics/new risks*   A significant group of scholars, who have confronted the contradiction between predictions of wholesale social expenditure retrenchment and the fact that, over the past quarter-century, the vast majority of countries have actually expanded their spending, have argued that retrenchment pressures have been overwhelmed by the electoral necessity for governments to respond to

demands for increased spending on existing social programmes and to initiate new programmes to cope with what the literature increasingly describes as the 'new social risks' (see Taylor-Gooby, 2004) of life in post-industrial societies. Although these scholars have suggested that such developments represent a 'new politics of the welfare state' (see the contributions to the volume of that name edited by Paul Pierson, 2001), in effect what is being argued is that, under modern conditions, social needs – old and new – trump traditional partisan politics in shaping social expenditure outcomes. Leaving aside for the moment whether that is actually the case, and largely unconsidered by the 'new politics' paradigm itself, is the possibility that strong pressures for the maintenance and extension of the social budget could constitute an important reason why governments might look around for alternative expenditure arenas (that is, those constituting core spending) in which to undertake whatever expenditure retrenchment may be considered necessary. In what follows, we consider four different hypotheses relating to need. Old needs variables include population ageing (percentage of the population aged 65 and over) and unemployment rates. New needs variables include deindustralisation (as operationalised by Iversen, 2001, p. 61) and the extent of female labour force participation. Data for all of these variables come or are derived from figures contained in OECD *Labour Force Statistics* (various years).

• *Politics still matters*   The idea that the partisan preferences of political actors have been superseded by a 'new politics of the welfare state' is a point of serious contention in the literature. 'New politics' findings, such as those of Huber and Stephens (2001, p. 221) of a 'sharp narrowing of political differences in the 1980s', have been challenged by studies demonstrating the continuing impact of partisan incumbency on welfare state entitlements (see, amongst others, Korpi, 2003; Allan and Scruggs, 2004; Hacker, 2004). The concern here, however, is less with points scoring between the protagonists of the old and new politics of the welfare state and more with establishing how far hypotheses developed to account for social expenditure patterns apply in the area of core spending. Research on the role of partisanship in this area is not well developed. However, some at least of the functions served by core spending, including particularly education and economic affairs, resonate strongly with traditional Left partisan aspirations and there is no reason why politics should matter less in these than in any other expenditure contexts. In the modelling that follows, we operationalise Left partisanship in two ways designed to distinguish between immediate and longer-term effects of incumbency. A *Left impact* variable measures the average share of Left cabinet seats in a country over a given period of expenditure change (the 1980s or the 1990s), while a *Left legacy* variable measures the average share of Left cabinet seats from a date early in the post-war period (1950) to the point in time at which the expenditure comparison is made. This latter variable seeks to capture the extent to which Left party aspirations have been built into taken-for-granted policy agendas. Data again come from Armingeon et al. (2004).

- *The threat of globalisation*   Much the most influential explanation for perceived expenditure retrenchment trends in the period since the early 1980s has been the 'crisis threat' of globalisation leading to a 'race to the bottom' in social spending (see Castles, 2004, and, for the most recent and comprehensive study, Brady, Beckfield and Seeleib-Kaiser, 2005). This account involves a complete reversal of earlier theorising on the impact of open economies, which suggested that it was precisely the countries most exposed to outside influences that were most likely to experience state intervention to compensate workers for this additional economic vulnerability (see Cameron, 1978; Katzenstein, 1985; and, more recently, Rieger and Leibfried, 2003). An *a priori* objection to the 'race to bottom' thesis as applied to social spending is the simple fact (see Table 2.1 above) that such expenditure continued to rise throughout the 1980s and 1990s. Clearly, however, that does not apply to core expenditure, where the same table shows average expenditures declining after 1990 and, taking account of net debt interest payments, already falling sharply in the 1980s, with no less than 15 of the 18 countries covered in this analysis experiencing reduced spending as a percentage of GDP during the period. An obvious hypothesis, therefore, is that what globalisation effects there have been are likely to have been concentrated in the area of core spending, with the 'new politics of the welfare state' quite possibly deflecting policy makers from effecting cuts in social expenditure. In the modelling exercise that follows, the extent of globalisation is measured by variables capturing the openness of economies to international trade and to cross-border capital flows. The trade variable is operationalised as is conventional in the literature by a measure of imports and exports as a percentage of GDP, with data coming from OECD *Historical Statistics* (various years). The capital flows variable used is a measure of the average level of foreign direct investment in a given country for each of the expenditure change periods featuring in the analysis, with data calculated from OECD, *Foreign Direct Investment in OECD Countries* (various years) and IMF *Balance of Payments Statistics* (various years).

2.4 FINDINGS

In this final substantive section of the chapter, we present cross-sectional, linear regression models of variation in levels of total public social expenditure and core spending in 18 OECD countries in 1980 and 2001 and of change in these aggregates over the periods 1980–90, 1990–2001 and 1980–2001. The choice of a research design based on successive cross-sections rather than on pooling data for different years is informed by both methodology and strategy of comparison considerations. On the methodological front, it can be argued that, rather than increasing the number of cases observed, all that data pooling really does is to proliferate observations of those cases (see Kittel, 1999). However, even if this were not the case, the problem with pooling is that it produces findings by averaging variation over time, whereas our purpose is to account for variation in levels of spending at different times and in changes in spending patterns over different time periods. Clearly, in order to identify diverse patterns of association at different times requires a strategy of comparison that maintains a clear separation between the instances being compared. By its very nature, pooled time-series analysis breaches that requirement.

The downside of not using pooled time-series techniques is the relatively small number of cases on which conclusions concerning the association of variables rest. However, while this is a difficulty inherent in our chosen research strategy, there are still ways of assessing the coherence and robustness of the findings that emerge from the analysis. The best test of the coherence of the models under consideration here is to regard the separate models of variation in levels and changes in a given expenditure aggregate as constituting components of a single account to be judged by whether it makes sense as a whole. This means that our judgment of the reasonableness of our findings is not simply a function of the strength of the statistical relationships located in individual 18-case comparisons, but depends crucially on whether those findings makes sense in light of the findings provided by other models. One test of the robustness of our models is to jackknife equations by removing each case in turn, thereby establishing whether they are dependent on the inclusion of particular cases. Where jackknifing reveals that the exclusion of one or more cases in a given model leads to t-values of less than 2, a robust variant of the model is also reported, including only those variables that do attain the required significance threshold. In what follows, we interpret findings that meet the robustness test as strongly indicative of particular associations of variables, while we regard non-robust terms as suggestive of possible, but as yet unproven, relationships.

The models reported in Tables 2.3 and 2.4 below are derived by taking all the variables identified in the hypotheses elaborated in the previous section and using them to generate best-fit models including only variables that are themselves statistically significant (for a discussion and justification of this methodology, see Castles, 1998). Where a variable identified in a particular hypothesis does not feature in a model, the proper conclusion is that there is insufficient evidence to support the presence of the hypothesised relationship in respect of the level or change in expenditure being modelled. The tables reporting social and core expenditure models are presented together to facilitate contrasts and comparisons of the influence of particular factors on different expenditure aggregates. Data sources for the variables featuring in the models are to be found in the notes and sources section of each table.

Looking at the models featuring in Tables 2.3 and 2.4, the first thing to strike one is the degree of similarity in the factors shaping levels and changes in these expenditure aggregates. This is immediately apparent looking at the models for expenditure levels at the beginning of the period. In the immediate post-war period, cross-national patterns of social and core spending had differed rather markedly, but, by 1980, had converged quite appreciably (see Castles, 2006). These models make it clear why this had occurred. What they tell us is that, by 1980, these aggregates of spending were substantially shaped by the same two factors: the post-war legacy of Left incumbency and the extent of a country's dependence on international trade. The strong impact of Left incumbency clearly offers support for the view that 'politics matters', but so too, indirectly, does the role of trade dependency, for what the positive coefficient in these models demonstrates is not evidence of higher levels of international trade leading to lower spending, but rather the kind of political mobilisation against trade-induced economic vulnerability suggested in the work of scholars such as David Cameron (1978) and Peter Katzenstein (1985).

Similarities are no less apparent when we come to look at the factors shaping expenditure change, but here the common factors are anything but political. Of the six change models, three for each of the expenditure aggregates, five feature a negative term for initial levels of expenditure. In addition, the social expenditure models all contain a negative term for economic growth, as does the model for core expenditure change in the 1980s. Total outlays are, of course, the sum of social and core spending and it is worth noting that initial expenditure levels and economic growth rates are negative and significant predictors of total outlays change throughout (see Castles, 2006). The cumulative evidence of these findings suggests strongly

Table 2.3   Modelling total social expenditure in 18 OECD countries, 1980–2001

	Coefficient	Standard error	*t*-value
1980 level			
Intercept	−19.95	11.92	−1.67
Left cabinet seats 1950–80	0.18	0.03	5.56
Deindustrialization 1980	0.40	0.15	2.61
Imports + exports (IMEX) 1980	0.06	0.03	2.17
Adj. $R^2 = 0.74$			
(Robust variant: 1980 Level = −20.77 + 0.20 (0.04) Left + 0.45 (0.17)			
Deindustrialisation. Adj. $R^2 = 0.68$)			
1980–1990 change			
Intercept	25.54	2.92	4.35
Initial (1980) expenditure level	−0.28	0.07	−3.93
Average GDP growth 1980–90	−2.82	0.65	−4.37
Δ Deindustrialisation 1980–90	0.75	0.20	3.76
Adj. $R^2 = 0.72$			
1990–2001 change			
Intercept	14.18	2.12	7.00
Initial (1990) expenditure level	−0.53	0.09	−5.71
Average GDP growth 1990–2001	−1.59	0.35	−4.50
Left cabinet seats 1991–2001	0.06	0.03	2.47
Adj. $R^2 = 0.71$			
1980–2001 change			
Intercept	22.87	2.47	9.26
Initial (1980) expenditure level	−0.64	0.07	−8.84
Average GDP growth 1980–2001	−2.77	0.60	−4.62
Left cabinet seats 1981–2001	0.05	0.02	2.82
Δ Female labour force 1980–2001	−0.14	0.06	−2.18
Adj. $R^2 = 0.86$			
(Robust variant: 1980–2001 Change = 25.54 − 0.64 (0.09) Initial			
Level − 3.72 (0.67) GDP growth. Adj. $R^2 = 0.77$)			
2001 level			
Intercept	28.91	2.30	12.58
Left cabinet seats 1950–2001	0.08	0.03	2.81
Average GDP growth 1980–2001	−4.19	0.76	−5.51
Imports + exports (IMEX) 2001	0.03	0.01	2.21
Adj. $R^2 = 0.82$			
(Robust variant: 2001 Level = 28.47 + 0.11 Left (0.03) − 3.41 (0.76) GDP growth. Adj.			
$R^2 = 0.78$)			

Sources and notes: Data on social expenditure from Table 2.1. Data on left cabinet seats, imports plus exports as a percentage of GDP and average annual rates of economic growth calculated from Armingeon et al. (2004). The additional data required to extend the left cabinet seats variable back to 1950 come from Castles (1998). The concept of deindustrialisation is from Iversen (2001: 61) and data for this variable are calculated from OECD (2004b). Robust equations are reported where jackknifing leads to a variable in the model failing to meet the significance threshold of a *t*-value in excess of 2.

The disappearing state?

Table 2.4   Modelling core expenditure in 18 OECD countries,
*   1980–2001*

	Coefficient	Standard error	t-value
1980 level			
Intercept	13.08	1.14	11.53
Left cabinet seats 1950–80	0.07	0.02	3.87
Public debt 1980	0.13	0.03	4.43
Imports + exports (IMEX) 1980	0.07	0.02	3.84

Adj. $R^2 = 0.87$

(Alternative variant: 1980 Level $= 24.45 + 0.23$ (0.05) Left $+ 0.19$ (0.04) Imports $+$ exports. Adj. $R^2 = 0.76$)

	Coefficient	Standard error	t-value
1980–1990 change			
Intercept	15.65	3.86	4.06
Initial (1980) expenditure level	−0.70	0.09	−7.55
Average GDP growth 1980–90	−4.21	0.73	−5.74
Δ Age 65 + 1980–90	1.92	0.44	4.40

Adj. $R^2 = 0.84$

	Coefficient	Standard error	t-value
1990–2001 change			
Intercept	2.46	0.98	2.52
Public debt 1990	−0.06	0.01	−4.45

Adj. $R^2 = 0.53$

	Coefficient	Standard error	t-value
1980–2001 change			
Intercept	15.36	3.02	5.09
Initial (1980) expenditure level	−0.45	0.17	−2.59
Public debt 1980	−0.14	0.05	−3.01

Adj. $R^2 = 0.79$

(Robust variant: 1980–2001 Change $= 8.38 - 0.24$ (0.04) Public debt. Adj. $R^2 = 0.72$)

	Coefficient	Standard error	t-value
2001 level			
Intercept	20.84	0.95	22.00
Left cabinet seats 1950–2001	0.07	0.03	2.65

Adj. $R^2 = 0.26$

(No robust variant can be calculated)

Sources and notes: Data on core expenditure from Table 2.1. Data on left cabinet seats, imports plus exports as a percentage of GDP and average annual rates of economic growth calculated from Armingeon et al. (2004). The additional data required to extend the left cabinet seats variable back to 1950 come from Castles (1998). Public debt as here measured is equivalent to gross financial liabilities of general government as a percentage of GDP and come from OECD, *Economic Outlook,* with missing data supplied by Uwe Wagschal. Robust equations are reported where jackknifing leads to a variable in the model failing to meet the significance threshold of a t-value in excess of 2.

that programme convergence and economic growth differentials are the main keys to understanding cross-national variance in overall public expenditure trends during these decades.

Finally, there are also similarities (although less marked ones) in the factors influencing expenditure levels in 2001. Both Left incumbency over the post-war period as a whole and economic growth over the past 20 years strongly shape present-day distributions of social expenditures and, although the finding is not robust, there is also evidence that core spending levels in 2001 reflect past patterns of Left incumbency. On the other hand, it should also be noted that the earlier similarity of higher spending in countries with greater trade dependence had diminished over time, now showing up only in a non-robust relationship with 2001 social spending.

These latter findings have implications for two of the most influential theories of recent public expenditure development. On the one hand, the persistence of a Left legacy term in the 2001 levels models suggests that, whatever evidence there may be for a 'new politics of the welfare state', it has as yet not had the effect of superseding the 'old politics' of the partisan shaping of public expenditure outcomes. Admittedly, the partisan link with core spending levels has become more tenuous over time, but the significant term for Left impact featuring in the model for social expenditure change in the 1990s suggests that, for this particular sample of countries in this particular time period, partisan influence may actually have been becoming stronger just when the 'new politics' literature suggests it should have been getting weaker.

On the other hand, the declining significance of trade openness might be interpreted by some as evidence of the beginnings of a shift to the kind of 'race-to-the bottom' scenario envisaged by globalisation theory. If so, the shift has so far been restricted entirely to core spending, where the strong positive linkage of 1980 had, by 2001, almost entirely disappeared, although entering the trade dependency term in the 2001 model still produces a very marginally positive coefficient. In the social expenditure arena, the positive relationship, although no longer robust, is still clearly discernible. Differences in spending patterns between open and closed economies may be diminishing, but there is, as yet, no evidence that open economies are on track to become systematically low spenders in the manner predicted by globalisation theory.

With one extremely significant exception to be discussed at length below, dissimilarities in the models are less salient than similarities. Evidence of a Left impact effect on social expenditure growth in the 1990s has already been mentioned and other effects particular to social expenditure development include a positive relationship with deindustrialisation in 1980 and with change in deindustrialisation during the 1980s, as well as a negative relationship with the growth of the female labour force in the period 1980–2001. Table 2.4 also shows a positive link between the share of the population aged 65 years and over and core expenditure development in the 1980s. Of these findings, those relating to the impact of deindustrialisation are easiest to reconcile with the theoretical literature, providing some limited support for the 'new politics' position by demonstrating that, in this period at least, social expenditure was significantly shaped by the emergence of new social risks. The evidence, however, is quite specific to the 1980s, and there is no sign that this factor influenced the trajectory of social expenditure change in the 1990s or was strong enough to have an impact on social spending levels at the turn of the century, arguably because the shift to deindustrialisation is now more or less complete in all the long-term members of the OECD (see Iversen, 2001).

The remaining one-off differences are less easy to reconcile with the standard hypotheses drawn from the literature. Female labour force participation is a test variable for another adumbration of the 'new politics' thesis, that new needs produce new spending, which is obviously contradicted by the non-robust negative relationship featuring in the 1980–2001 social expenditure model. However, this is, almost certainly, a finding which should be discounted, since it results entirely from the experience of two countries – Ireland and the Netherlands – which, during this period, experienced extremely strong growth in female labour force participation from a base markedly lower than that of any other of the 18 countries included in this analysis, while also experiencing high rates of economic growth that contributed to cuts in social spending as a percentage of GDP. Although there are possible scenarios by which these developments might be linked, it seems more likely that the association is spurious. Population ageing is also a measure of need and one whose impact on spending is undoubted. The anomaly here, though, is that this factor is not linked to social expenditure, which is where the literature tells us to expect ageing pressures to have direct knock-on effects, but to core spending, where reasons for a positive association are far less obvious. In the absence of such reasons, we can only note the finding and the fact that, excluding the population ageing term, the terms entering the 1980s core expenditure model are unchanged and no less robust, although, of course, the overall model has a somewhat reduced degree of explained variation (Adj. $R^2=0.64$).

The exception to the rule that differences in the factors shaping the different expenditure aggregates are less salient than similarities is the appearance of a public debt term in three of the core expenditure models but in none of the social expenditure models. It is possible to argue that the inclusion of a debt term in the 1980 core expenditure model in Table 2.4 is inappropriate on the grounds that high spending is likely to be as much a cause as a consequence of debt and, for that reason, the table includes an alternative variant of the model excluding the debt term. There can, however, be no reasonable doubt concerning the models for core expenditure change for the periods 1990–2001 and 1980–2001, in which prior debt levels feature as the only robust predictor of core expenditure change and, of themselves, account for somewhere between 50 and 70 per cent of explained expenditure variation. Thus the headline story of the models featuring in Table 2.4 is that the marked cutbacks occurring in core expenditure in the 1990s right across the OECD would appear to have been driven largely by the extent of these countries' public indebtedness.

However, in discussing the debt burden hypothesis, it was noted that high levels of public indebtedness might influence spending in two possible ways: first, as an automatic consequence of the impact of changing interest rates on net debt interest payments and, second, because increased borrowing costs give governments strong incentives to find matching savings. The first mechanism would suggest a positive relationship between debt and expenditure change in the 1980s, when real interest rates were increasing, and a negative relationship in the 1990s, when they were declining. The findings in Table 2.4 provide strong evidence supporting the latter prediction, but not the former. However, the second mechanism, leading to offsetting expenditure cuts as borrowing costs increased, might supply the reason why increasing real interest rates failed to lead to higher core expenditure levels during the course of the 1980s, with real programme cuts masking the effects of interest rate rises. A strategy for disentangling these effects is to model levels and changes in core expenditure minus net debt interest payments and to compare the results with those for core expenditure in Table 2.4. The models presented in Table 2.5 make such a comparison possible.

The models for 1980 and 2001 levels of core expenditure minus debt interest payments and for change over the period 1980–2001 that appear in Table 2.5 are more or less identical to the corresponding models for core expenditure appearing in Table 2.4. However the Table 2.5 model for change in the 1980s is quite dramatically different from its Table 2.4 counterpart, while, without the inclusion of debt interest payments as part of the dependent variable, it is impossible to identify any variables significantly linked to expenditure change in the 1990s. The key variables in the modified 1980s model are negative terms for public debt and trade dependence, which wholly supersede earlier catch up and economic growth terms. The negative trade dependency term provides the only statistical support in this chapter for something akin to a globalisation effect, although the absence of any such findings in the models for expenditure change in the 1990s and expenditure levels in 2001 suggests that the finding

Table 2.5   *Modelling core expenditure minus net debt interest payments in*
              18 OECD countries, 1980–2001

	Coefficient	Standard error	t-value
1980 level			
Intercept	15.46	1.34	11.58
Left cabinet seats 1950–80	0.09	0.02	3.75
Imports + exports (IMEX) 1980	0.08	0.02	4.02
Adj. $R^2 = 0.70$			
1980–1990 change			
Intercept	5.83	1.18	4.93
Public debt 1980	−0.12	0.03	−3.95
Imports + exports (IMEX) 1980	−0.05	0.02	−2.76
Adj. $R^2 = 0.76$			
1990–2001 change			
No model can be calculated			
1980–2001 change			
Intercept	10.85	2.58	4.21
Initial (1980) expenditure level	−0.35	0.14	−2.58
Public debt 1980	−0.13	0.03	−3.88
Adj. $R^2 = 0.73$			
(Robust variant: 1980–2001 Change = 4.99 − 0.18 (0.03) Public debt.			
Adj. $R^2 = 0.64$)			
2001 level			
Intercept	17.80	1.07	16.72
Left cabinet seats 1950–2001	0.08	0.03	2.68
Adj. $R^2 = 0.27$			
(No robust variant can be calculated)			

Sources and notes: Data on net public interest payments from OECD, *Economic Outlook*,
Paris (various years). Other notes and sources as in Table 2.4.

is probably better interpreted as marking a one-off retreat from previous
high spending policies than as evidence for the advent of a new era of globally induced low spending. However, as we shall see below, this trade
dependency effect does help us understand why the countries of continental Western Europe were in the vanguard of expenditure cuts during the
1980s.

The emergence in Table 2.5 of a strong public debt finding for the 1980s
and its disappearance in the 1990s, read in conjunction with the entirely
contrary findings in Table 2.4 and what we know of real interest rate developments during this period, tells an even more fascinating story. The fact

that the negative impact of public debt is markedly higher when debt interest payments are not included in core spending strongly suggests that, in the 1980s, high debt levels led to spending cuts, not because of any automatic interest rate effect, but rather because the increased cost of borrowing gave governments huge incentives to seek matching expenditure savings. That this effect disappeared after 1990 suggests that such incentives diminished once governments began to reap the automatic expenditure savings resulting from lower real interest rate levels. The real story of change in core spending during these decades is that levels of public debt were the driving force throughout, but that the effects of debt were mediated by different mechanisms at different times, with the trajectory of interest rate changes the obvious factor determining which mechanism was dominant at any given time. When interest rates were rising, highly indebted countries had to make significant cuts in public spending; when interest rates were falling, the public expenditure cuts made themselves.

Earlier we argued that any successful account of recent public expenditure trends needed to explain why core spending was more subject to cutbacks than social spending, why real retrenchment tendencies were restricted to core spending in the 1980s and why the countries of continental Western Europe experienced greater expenditure cutbacks than the countries of the English-speaking family of nations. The analysis here provides most of the answers. In the 1990s, the big headline cutbacks in core spending were automatic consequences of the impact of declining interest rates on net debt interest payments and, hence, endogenous to that area of spending. In the previous decade that was not so and, in principle, governments might have chosen to cut social as much as core spending in their attempts to match the increased cost of borrowing.

However the evidence here suggests that it was precisely during the 1980s that deindustrialisation served to boost and protect existing social expenditure levels, so it is possible to argue that the operation of the 'new politics of the welfare state' prevented cuts in social expenditure, possibly at the cost of making core expenditure cuts greater. The reason that real expenditure cutbacks occurred in the 1980s and not in the 1990s is simply that it was in the 1980s that debt levels, magnified by high and increasing interest rates, became a serious problem to governments across the OECD. Faced by net debt interest payments of as much as 10 per cent of GDP, policy makers had to effect major cuts, enter into new borrowing commitments or find ways of altering current perceptions of what constituted a 'tolerable burden of taxation'. For governments seeking to win democratic elections, a preference for borrowing and, wherever possible, covert (that is, blame avoidance maximising), expenditure cuts is scarcely surprising.

That leaves the question of why the countries of continental Western Europe turned out, despite the virulence of the anti-statist rhetoric of leaders such as Thatcher and Reagan, to be bigger cutters of core expenditure than the countries of the English-speaking world, and the answer is provided in Table 2.5. In 1980, the countries of the English-speaking world and those of continental Western Europe had very similar average public debt levels (46.4 and 44.6 per cent of GDP respectively), which were appreciably higher than those of Scandinavia and Southern Europe (both around 33 per cent of GDP). However, in 1980, the countries of the English-speaking world were far less trade-dependent than those of continental Western Europe, imports plus exports averaging 55.1 per cent of GDP in the former and 81.4 per cent in the latter. Debt levels in 1980 were, therefore, a factor driving the two families of nations to similar cost-cutting exertions, but continental Western Europe's far greater trade dependence, which had earlier been a factor promoting higher levels of spending, provided a further incentive to austerity in the 1980s, which, according to the figures in Tables 2.1 and 2.2, persisted, although on a lesser scale, through into the 1990s.

2.5   CONCLUSION

This chapter has examined aggregate data on changes in social and core spending between 1980 and 2001 with a view to establishing whether a realistic case can be made that this was a period in which there was significant public expenditure retrenchment or that witnessed the emergence of forces with the potential to undermine the public expenditure state over the long term. Conclusions on both counts are largely negative.

The evidence provided in Table 2.1 confirms the findings of the majority of studies of social expenditure during this period: that, although after 1980 the growth trajectory of the welfare state was slowing, cutbacks actually occurred only in a small minority of countries. On the other hand, Tables 2.1 and 2.2 also show that the majority of countries experienced cuts in core spending and, still more, in core spending minus net debt interest payments. In terms of a verdict on overall expenditure retrenchment, what is significant, however, is that social expenditure growth outweighed core expenditure decline over the period as a whole and that there is evidence that the real cutbacks in core programme provision of the 1980s were a one-off phenomenon attributable to a conjuncture of high levels of indebtedness and high real interest rates, which policy makers across the OECD appear committed never to allow to recur.

Rather than pointing to an enduring and deep-seated process of retrenchment reversing the public sector expansion of the early post-war decades, the analysis here suggests that the dominant trend of public spending over recent years has been convergent in character, with much of the upward movement in social expenditure coming from the catch-up of the countries of Southern Europe and much of the downward movement in core spending from the efforts of the countries of continental Western Europe to reduce their fiscal vulnerability under circumstances of increasing debt. These adjustments made, the probable course of future public expenditure growth is likely to be one of 'steady-state' development, with cross-national relativities of both social and core spending modestly influenced by continuing partisan differences and, in the case of social expenditure, perhaps more decisively, by fluctuations in economic performance.

The probability of a continuing steady-state development could only be realistically challenged if we could identify a factor or factors capable of overriding existing commitments to democratic electorates of continuing levels of social and core expenditure provision. That, of course, is why the debate over the public expenditure effects of increased international economic interdependence has been so important, because, in increasing trade and capital flows, globalisation theory purports to have identified factors with just such implications. However, the findings here suggest that, for much of the period under discussion, trade openness was associated with higher levels of both social and total public expenditure, and that its only demonstrable negative impact was a one-off effect on core spending in the 1980s, making it more difficult for countries with open economies to maintain their formerly more generous spending levels. In none of the models elaborated did the extent of foreign direct investment have any significant effect (either positive or negative) on OECD expenditure outcomes.

It is appropriate to conclude with the caveat that these conclusions may apply only at the aggregate level. At the programme level things could well be quite different. The impetus for bringing together a group of scholars to study developments in core spending was a view that the expenditure programmes in this area had received far too little attention in the comparative literature and that, given the evidence of continuing social expenditure growth, might be a more fertile place to discover retrenchment effects. The evidence here does not identify any generalised retrenchment tendency, but certainly does point to a greater proclivity to cut core spending. Within limitations of data that, as the next chapter points out, are, in some cases, all too real, the remainder of this book seeks not only to locate the factors driving expenditure change in different core spending programmes, but also to identify whether some of these programmes have been cut back more consistently and more severely than others.

REFERENCES

Aaron, H. (1967), 'Social security: international comparisons', in O. Eckstein (ed.), *Studies in the Economics of Income Maintenance*, Washington, DC: Brookings Institution.

Allan, J. and L. Scruggs (2004), 'Political partisanship and welfare state reform in advanced industrial societies', *American Journal of Political Science*, **48** (3), 496–512.

Armingeon, K., P. Leimgruber, M. Beyeler and S. Menegale (2004), 'Comparative political data set 1960–2002', Institute of Political Science, University of Berne.

Brady, D., J. Beckfield and M. Seeleib-Kaiser (2005), 'Economic globalization and the welfare state in affluent democracies, 1975–2001', *American Sociological Review*, **70** (6), 921–48.

Cameron, D. (1978), 'The expansion of the public economy: a comparative analysis', *American Political Science Review*, **72** (4), 1243–61.

Castles, F. (1998), *Comparative Public Policy: Patterns of Post-war Transformation*, Cheltenham, UK and Northampton, MA, USA: Edward Elgar.

Castles, F. (2004), *The Future of the Welfare State*, Oxford: Oxford University Press.

Castles, F. (2006), *The Growth of the Post-war Public Expenditure State: Long-term Trajectories and Recent Trends*, TranState Working Papers, no. 35, Bremen.

Clayton, R. and J. Pontusson (1998), 'Welfare state retrenchment revisited', *World Politics*, **51** (1), 67–98.

Esping-Andersen, G. (1990), *The Three Worlds of Welfare Capitalism*, Cambridge: Polity Press.

Flora, P. (ed.) (1986), *Growth to Limits: The Western European Welfare States Since World War II*, vol. 1, Berlin: De Gruyter.

Hacker, J. (2004), 'Privatizing risk without privatizing the welfare state: the hidden politics of social policy retrenchment in the United States', *American Political Science Review*, **98** (2), 243–60.

Huber, E. and J. Stephens (2001), *Development and the Crisis of the Welfare State*, Chicago: University of Chicago Press.

IMF (various years), *Balance of Payments Statistics*, Washington, DC.

Iversen, T. (2001), 'The dynamics of welfare state expansion: trade openness, deindustrialization and partisan politics', in P. Pierson (ed.), *The New Politics of the Welfare State*, Oxford: Oxford University Press, pp. 45–79.

Katzenstein, P. (1985), *Small States in World Markets*, Ithaca: Cornell University Press.

Kittel, B. (1999), 'Sense and sensitivity in the pooled analysis of political data', *European Journal of Political Research*, **35** (2), 225–53.

Korpi, W. (2003), 'Welfare-state regress in Western Europe: politics, institutions, globalization and Europeanization', *Annual Review of Sociology*, **29**, 589–609.

Mishra, R. (1990), *The Welfare State in Capitalist Society*, Toronto: University of Toronto Press.

OECD (1993), 'Are real interest rates high?', *Economic Outlook*, no. 53, 23–30.

OECD (2004a), *Social Expenditure Database* (SOCX) *1980–2001*, Paris.

OECD (2004b), *Labour Force Statistics, 1980–2002*, Paris.

OECD (various years), *Economic Outlook*, Paris.

OECD (various years), *Historical Statistics*, Paris.

OECD (various years), *Foreign Direct Investment in OECD Countries*, Paris.

Peacock, A. and Wiseman, J. (1961), *The Growth of Public Expenditures in the United Kingdom*, Princeton, NJ: Princeton University Press.

Pierson, P. (2000), 'Increasing returns, path dependence, and the study of politics', *American Political Science Review*, **94** (2), 251–68.

Pierson, P. (ed.) (2001), *The New Politics of the Welfare State*, Oxford: Oxford University Press.

Rieger, E. and S. Leibfried (2003), *Limits to Globalization*, Cambridge: Polity Press.

Taylor-Gooby P. (ed.) (2004), *New Risks, New Welfare: The Transformation of the European Welfare State*, Oxford: Oxford University Press.

Wagner, A. (1883), *Finanzwissenschaft*, 2nd edn, Leipzig: C.F. Winter (reprinted and partly translated in R. Musgrave and A. Peacock (eds) (1958), *Classics in the Theory of Public Finance*, London: Macmillan).

Wildavsky, A. (1975), *Budgeting. A Comparative Theory of Budgetary Processes*, Boston: Little, Brown.

3. Data on the functions of government: where are we now?

Neil Fraser and Paul Norris

3.1 INTRODUCTION

This chapter is concerned with assessing the evolution of usable data on spending on the functions of government available comparatively for different countries. These are data known by the UN and other international agencies as COFOG – Classification of Functions of Government.

Some functionally classified public expenditure data, for example for social spending, defence spending and education spending, exist in quite long time-series for a number of countries. It was recognised early in the development of comparable National Accounts that a cross-national breakdown of public expenditure by function would be valuable, for example to compare the welfare effort or the defence effort of different countries. Four international agencies, the IMF, the OECD, the UN and EU, were involved in collecting these data from national statistical offices, but the reporting of these data over all functions of government was only patchy in the 1970s and 1980s. Most effort then was devoted to producing comparable data on public social expenditure.

In the 1990s, a revised COFOG and a greater determination to collect and publish the results made comparative research on both social and non-social expenditure much more feasible. In the early 1990s, the quality of the data available on non-social expenditure was perhaps comparable to that for social expenditure in the mid-1970s, when comparative welfare state research started in earnest. However, the data on the new basis are only being asked from countries back to 1990, making for an awkward break in series at that time-point. As part of the process of assessing these data, we attempt in this chapter to test how well other data used in this book correspond to the emerging COFOG data. We also include in the appendixes data on the old COFOG basis for 11 countries between 1979 and 1989, assembled by Oxley and Martin 1991, and data on the new COFOG basis for 19 countries between 1990 and 2002, which we have assembled from Eurostat (2006) and OECD (2006) sources.

3.2 PUBLIC EXPENDITURE AS A MEASURE OF GOVERNMENT ACTIVITY

Public expenditure as used here is expenditure by 'general government', the primarily tax-financed part of the public sector. It does not include public corporations selling output at market prices.

Expenditure is not a measure of output, of what government achieves. Rather, it is the most universally recognised measure we have of inputs into or the extent of government activity and, hence, is a way of measuring the relative importance of one area compared with others (for example, of welfare effort versus defence effort). As Hofferbert and Budge put it: 'Money is certainly not all there is to policy . . . But most policy implementation will languish without it. . . . Expenditures are clearly a major as well as the most visible and accessible measure of government activities' (Hofferbert and Budge, 1996).

However, although expenditure inputs are a way of assessing the extent of government activity in a given policy area, the measure is very far from perfect. One very important reason that this is the case is that governments seek to achieve their goals by regulation rather than through expenditure programmes. A common instance is where governments mandate other (frequently business) actors to provide expenditures equivalent to cash programmes. Examples include second-tier pensions and sickness benefits in many countries (Castles, 1994). In many countries also, regulation is used as an important instrument of environmental protection and economic regulation is used in place of economic subsidies.

An example of the difference that counting regulative interventions can make to comparisons normally made in expenditure terms was the inclusion, in the late 1980s, of state-regulated expenditure by German business enterprises on industrial apprenticeships in German public education spending totals on the ground that such expenditure could properly be considered as part of public educational effort (Heidenheimer, 1996), a classificatory move that transformed Germany overnight from an educational expenditure laggard to an expenditure leader. An early quantitative study of public sector activity, which discusses regulation (and tax expenditures) as part of 'public sector off-budget activity', is to be found in Saunders and Klau (1985). In the final chapter of this book, Nico Siegel examines the extent to which regulation is replacing public expenditure as an instrument of public intervention in economic affairs.

The trend to separating finance and provision in government, as in 'public–private partnerships', might be seen as a further weakening of public expenditure as an indicator of the extent of government activity. These partnerships typically involve state financing with the private sector providing costly infrastructure. But if the finance continues to be public, then public expenditure still captures the scale of government commitment. Full privatisation would be a different matter, but that is less common in the area of 'general government' than in the wider public sector. Mechanisms such as the 'private finance initiative' in the UK do, however, alter the timing of public expenditure by substituting an annual charge over the life of the project for the conventional lump-sum public investment (accounting on an 'accruals' basis, which is coming into public sector accounting, will also spread investment costs).

The separation of finance and provision means that expenditure and employment are very different indicators. An example is provided by the reorganisation of the British National Health Service in 1989. By this reform, hospital employees became employees of Trusts and no longer counted as public employees in spite of the fact that Trusts remained financed by government. In expenditure terms, much less had changed than in apparent employment terms.

Expenditure, in this chapter and generally throughout this study, will be expressed as a percentage of GDP. In relation to any one function of government, this ratio identifies the quantum of available resources the country puts into that function and, hence, a yardstick of national commitment to particular policy goals. GDP measures productive capacity and tax capacity. Comparing expenditures without dividing by GDP involves complications of converting to a common currency and allowing for inflation over time. However, use of PE/GDP ratios does mean that change in the ratio can be due to change in either public expenditure or GDP, as our analysis will note at times. Countries with rapid economic growth, such as Ireland with 10 per cent GDP growth in the 1990s, may have a declining PE/GDP ratio despite quite appreciable increases in real public expenditure.

Public expenditure by function has been used not only for comparing the extent of national commitment to particular policy objectives, but also as a testbed for theories of the growth of the state, such as economistic theories (including 'public choice' theories), sociological theories premised on the impact of socio-economic factors, and political science theories emphasising the key role of parties and institutions. Modern social science techniques of comparison imply some level of quantification and, expenditure apart, there are only limited alternative measures (employment is one, but it cannot deal with transfers or – as noted above – the separation of finance and provision). Social expenditure, with the most developed comparative data set and apparently self-evident implications of partisan difference in likely spending patterns, has been the primary focus of such research. The greater availability of COFOG data pertaining to a wide range of functional categories and range of diverse activities of government should make it possible to extend such research.

Public expenditure is classified, not only by function, but also by economic category; that is, distinguishing public consumption expenditure, transfers and investment. Research seeking to explain cross-national differences in these categories includes work by Castles (1982) (public consumption expenditure, transfers and subsidies), Lane and Ersson (1990) (public consumption expenditure, social security expenditure), Castles (1998) (civilian public consumption expenditure) and Sturm (1998) (government capital spending). Arguably, however, these categories of spending are of lesser policy relevance than functional breakdowns for policy research because they do not tell us unambiguously where government is directing its efforts (for instance, health interventions may be made through transfers or through public consumption expenditure). As a consequence, research on the determinants of economic categories of spending has been rather eclipsed by research on the factors shaping welfare state inputs and outcomes. As we shall see later, it may be possible to combine functional data with data organised by economic category to provide more nuanced accounts of public policy development.

3.3 THE IDEA OF A FUNCTIONAL EXPENDITURE BREAKDOWN

A functional expenditure breakdown is an important development compared with conventional government accounts, which reflect the organisational structure of governments. Departmental responsibilities change over time and differ between countries. Some countries will organise medical education under health services, others under education. The internationally agreed COFOG assigns it to education. Research and development may be organised in a central agency, but in the COFOG classification it is classified according to the particular function it serves. A functional breakdown is meant to be given and applicable to all countries and years. The data from such a breakdown facilitate cross-national analysis of governmental inputs to the degree that the allocation of transactions to functions for each country is undertaken in the manner stipulated by the functional classification.

3.3.1 Early Efforts

Social expenditure was the first functional category of public expenditure to be collected comparatively. ILO's *The Cost of Social Security* dates from the late 1940s (ILO, 1952, and subsequently) and the OECD began collecting and reporting social expenditure data in the 1970s (for example, OECD, 1976). OECD published a full data set, with analysis, of member states' social expenditure in 1985, with figures from 1960 onwards (OECD, 1985). This data set has been continued and further elaborated to the present day and is now routinely provided on a biannual basis in CD-Rom form (known as the OECD Social Expenditure Database, or SOCX for short). The reason for the initial focus on social expenditure in the OECD is summed up in the title of their report on a conference on social policies in the 1980s, *The Welfare State in Crisis* (OECD, 1981). Anxiety about the future viability of the welfare state stemmed from the conjunction of the huge expansion in social spending of the 1960s and 1970s and the slowdown in economic growth that took place following the oil shocks of 1973–4 and 1979–80.

The data analysed in subsequent chapters of this book include some time-series which are separate from, and older than, the general functional breakdown we are discussing here. Such is the case with military expenditure (see Chapter 5), education expenditure (Chapter 7), subsidies to industry (Chapter 8) and public interest payments (Chapter 9). In the case of military and education expenditure, we test below for the levels of association between these series and the military and education figures in the general functional (COFOG) breakdowns. High levels of association suggest that both series can be used for comparative purposes with some level of confidence.

As part of the move to international standardisation of national accounting, a 'classification of the functions of government' (COFOG) was devised and incorporated into the System of National Accounts agreed at the United Nations in 1968 (known as SNA68). A further publication in 1980 (UN, 1980) details how the 14 major groups of public expenditure can be subdivided into 61 groups and 127 subgroups. It is reported there that 100 member states of the UN were then regularly supplying public finance statistics to the UN, many of them including some kind of functional breakdown of government expenditures. Once SNA68 was agreed, the UN, OECD, IMF and EU asked their member states to report data on that basis annually. However, how carefully that was done was mainly up to individual country statistical offices. The functions identified for international comparability would inevitably cut across departmental boundaries in each country. A particular source of inconsistency in old COFOG (as we shall call the pre-1999 classification system) was in the different ways countries classified debt interest payments. Florio (2001) shows that Germany and Denmark included their interest payments (and only their interest payments) in the 'Expenditure not classified by major group' category, but that the United Kingdom, Italy and Australia did not.

The publication of these data by these international agencies was very patchy up to the 1990s. The following European Union countries regularly reported a COFOG breakdown of general government expenditure: Denmark, Germany, France, Ireland, Italy, Portugal, Spain, UK (Eurostat, 1997). The OECD regularly reported only the same countries plus Norway, Iceland, Australia and (from 1989) New Zealand (OECD, 1994). An early attempt to summarise the OECD data (based on data for just nine countries) can be found in Saunders and Klau (1985); see Table 8 for 1970 and Table 9 for 1981. Oxley and Martin (1991) were able to assemble OECD data for 11 countries for 1979 and 1989 (see Appendix 3A to this chapter). Some other countries provided a COFOG breakdown only for the final consumption expenditure of general government.

The IMF reports probably the fullest range of old COFOG data in terms of both number of countries and years in their *Government Finance Statistics Yearbooks* (IMF, annual). These data are used in some empirical work, especially by economists (for example Kneller et al., 1999). However, a problem in using these data to assess differential national expenditure effort is that they are, generally, not consolidated by level of government, but presented separately for central, regional and local governments. As functions are performed at different levels of government in different countries, cross-national comparisons using unconsolidated data are likely to be highly misleading.

For the most part, the *UN National Accounts* present a COFOG breakdown only of final consumption expenditure of general government. The UN uses OECD and Eurostat sources for data for their member states and only corresponds directly with statistical offices in the remaining countries (personal communication, UN). The World Bank takes UN data and presents them in ratio-to-GDP form.

Certain functions of government – for example defence, education, health and income transfer programmes, along with different types of expenditure, for instance interest on public debt, and public investment – are presented in series form for OECD countries going back to dates before World War II and up to 1995 by Tanzi and Schuknecht (2000). This research on public expenditure development uses individual country data plus specialized international sources like SIPRI (Stockholm International Peace Research Institute) for defence and UNESCO (United Nations Educational Social and Cultural Organisation) for education. Apart from these specialised international sources, there is a potential reliability problem where internationally standardised categories of spending are not used.

An ambitious effort to assemble COFOG data for 1970 to 1997 for 26 OECD countries is that by economists, Sanz and Velázquez, who use it to analyse convergence in government expenditure composition (Sanz and Velázquez, 2004). Their basic source is *OECD National Accounts*, supplemented by data from national agencies, Eurostat, IMF and World Bank. Given the gaps in the OECD data, theirs' must have been a heroic effort, for example, in consolidating IMF data to arrive at accurate figures for general government expenditure categories. This data set does not yet appear to be available for research by other scholars.

3.3.2   The New COFOG Classification

A new System of National Accounts, SNA1993 (EU Commission, IMF, OECD, UN, World Bank, 1993), was agreed by all the international agencies in 1993 and introduced into their questionnaires to member states over the succeeding years. The European Union developed its own version of this accounting system known as ESA95 (ESA = European System of Accounts) needed for the creation of monetary union. SNA93/ESA95 in turn led to a new COFOG with 10 categories of expenditure in 1999 (UN, 2000).

The new COFOG is being published for years going back to 1990 by the OECD, Eurostat and the IMF and replaces the old COFOG, which identified 14 functional expenditure categories. The IMF has published an account of how the new and the old categories compare (IMF, 2001b). Many functions remain the same, but the changes there have been still make it difficult to translate old into new throughout. We will be using data for 1990–2002 on the new COFOG basis and figures constructed by Oxley and Martin for the 1980s using OECD data on the old COFOG basis.

The categories (pre-1990) are General Public Services, Defence, Public Order and Safety, Education, Health, Social Security and Welfare, Housing and Community Amenities, Recreational, Cultural and Religious affairs, Economic Services (five sub-divisions) and Expenditure not classified by major group, while the categories (post-1990) are General Public Services, Defence, Public Order and Safety, Economic Affairs, Environmental Protection, Housing and Community Amenities, Health, Recreation, Culture and Religion, Education and Social Protection. The following changes should be noted.

1.   The category of 'Expenditure not classified by major group' has disappeared. It largely consisted of public debt transactions (although not invariably: see Florio, 2001), which are now included in the General Public Services category (but we have made them a separate category, because we are interested both in the factors determining the extent of debt repayments (see Chapter 9) and in the role debt repayment has

played in shaping the dynamic of overall public expenditure development (see Chapter 2 above)).
2. A new category of 'Environmental Protection' has been created. This
    is an example of COFOG changing in response to the changing
    salience of governmental activities. This expenditure was, earlier,
    largely included in 'Housing and Community Amenities'. However,
    some countries continue not to separate the categories.
3. Economic services are no longer subdivided (hence, the total number
    of functions comes down from 14 to 10).
4. Research and development is now to be allocated to whichever func-
    tion is the main subject of the research and development.
5. Employer social contributions are now to be explicitly recorded along-
    side wages and salaries.

Other changes are at sub-category level and do not affect what is reported
for the categories as a whole (the level being used in current reporting).

Changes from the old to the new COFOG classification can be expected
to have repercussions in national statistical offices. Statistical offices
develop traditions of accounting which may need to be modified for the
new approach. Changes in the USA are outlined in an article by Galbraith
(2000). The US National Income and Product accounts now present government by function tables with the new COFOG categories (apart from
Environmental Protection). Similarly, the UK *National Accounts Blue
Book* (ONS, 2005) now has a COFOG table.

However the major change is that far more countries have been per-
suaded to report these data to OECD and Eurostat, and to do this on a
regular basis. In the case of the European Union, reporting is now compulsory. This means that comparative analysis of data post-1990 is now
much more practical and, given the greater number of countries reporting, far more promising. Since 2002, the IMF also presents COFOG
figures for general government as well as central and local governments
separately.

A natural question which arises from all this change in data definition is
how close COFOG data for defence and education expenditure are to
longer running comparative data sets for those particular items (from
SIPRI and OECD *Education at a Glance* respectively). In the later chapters
in this volume by Cusack and Schmidt, it is these long-running sources that
are used as the basis for the analysis and the question is whether the use
of COFOG data would make a difference. We tested the Pearson's correlation between 15 EU countries' COFOG figures for defence and education
expenditure and data from the sources used by Cusack and Schmidt
and found, quite coincidentally, correlations of 0.91 for both (defence

expenditure based on 2003 figures, education expenditure based on 2002 figures). This provides strong and welcome reassurance that these different sources are broadly consistent.

3.3.3 Conceptual Problems and Analytical Prospects

The international data-collecting agencies rely on the statistical offices of member governments to arrange their government accounts and national accounts to fit the COFOG categories. In principle, every transaction should be identified as belonging to a COFOG category. In practice, the agencies recognise that, at best, departmental accounts will be subdivided and rearranged to get as close as possible to COFOG categories.

The international agencies can only validate the data sent to them by national statistical offices to a limited extent (personal communication, IMF and Eurostat). They all report that they look for unexpected changes in data from year to year which might indicate mistakes. They give detailed guidance to the national offices about how their questionnaires are to be completed, but they have to rely on the good faith of the national statisticians for their completion, even though the translation of departmental accounts into COFOG categories may be quite difficult.

An important principle in relation to these data is the following:

> All outlays for a particular function are collected in one category of COFOG regardless of how the outlays are implemented. That is, cash transfer payments designed to be used for a particular function, the purchase of goods and services from a market producer that are transferred to households for the same function, the production of goods and services by a general government unit, or the acquisition of an asset for that same function are all in the same category. (IMF, 2001a, 75)

OECD and Eurostat now both report their COFOG data by economic category (for example, final consumption, transfers, investment expenditure). The ratio of transfers to total expenditure can be quite different in different countries. This especially affects social expenditure. These data give scope for analysis of how the expenditure on particular functions varies in different countries, for example how far cutbacks are made in investment, public consumption or transfers. There is evidence, for instance, that different political constellations have preferences for different expenditure types, that is, Christian Democracy for transfers, Social Democracy for services and investment (Castles, 1982, 1998). This suggests that the analysis of functional spending data by economic category might well be a fruitful starting point for embarking on a more nuanced political economy of public investment than has hitherto been possible.

COFOG categories attempt to stipulate how ambiguous elements are to be treated, as with the case of medical education already referred to and the problem of the different aims of subsidies (IMF, 2001a, p. 77). One problem apparently remaining concerns the functional attribution of civil service pension spending. The UK Office of National Statistics report that the COFOG classification is somewhat different from their National Accounts version of general government expenditure, with civil service pensions included twice in COFOG, both as an accruing cost in final consumption (by function) and as a social benefit (ONS, 2005) (see also Parry's more detailed discussion of UK general public services expenditure in Chapter 4).

Governments are increasingly being urged to record expenditure on an accruals basis (at the time economic value is created or exchanged). The IMF in particular is endeavouring to put its *Government Finance Statistics* on that basis. Nevertheless, governments have been accustomed to recording cash flows and that is the basis for COFOG returns here. Eurostat and OECD interpret COFOG data in National Accounts (SNA) terms, whereas the IMF works with accounts for government (*Government Finance Statistics*). This distinction is developed in the IMF *Government Finance Statistics Manual* (2001a), but it is not clear that it has much salience in relation to COFOG data.

It is important to understand the 'general government' concept as used in relation to these data. The general government sector consists of all government units and all non-market, non-profit institutions that are controlled and mainly financed by government (IMF, 2001a). It does not include the expenditures of public corporations or quasi-corporations, these being units which sell all or almost all their output at market prices. This involves an exercise of judgment to distinguish pricing at market levels from pricing at non-market levels.

The term 'general government' is also used when the accounts for the different levels of government (central, regional, local) are consolidated. 'The basic measure of the size of government within the SNA framework is the total consolidated spending of all general government agencies after netting-out transfers between the different levels of government' (Saunders, 1993). As already noted here, the data analysed throughout this book are largely on a 'general government' basis. OECD and Eurostat have used such consolidated figures throughout the period under analysis here, unlike (as noted) the IMF. There are real questions about the consistency of the consolidation undertaken by individual government statistical offices (personal communication, IMF), because these transactions necessarily involve many separate consolidations and a great deal of complexity.

As noted above, COFOG data are currently collected into ten categories, but defining these categories involves identifying a finer breakdown. There is agreement now about two-digit and three-digit categories (UN, 2000), which might be used some day and which might, at least, in principle, permit even more nuanced comparative analysis of the activities of government in particular policy areas.

3.4   DATA FOR THE 1980S

COFOG data for the 1980s, as assembled by Oxley and Martin (1991), are reproduced in Appendix 3A and discussed here. Oxley and Martin's work illustrates the problems there used to be in breakdowns of expenditure by function. Their efforts are widely recognised; for example, see their use by Saunders (1993). They use a regrouping of COFOG into the following economic categories: public goods, merit goods, income transfers and economic services. Under the label of public goods they include the categories of (1) defence and (2) general public services. Under merit goods they include categories (3) education, (4) health and (5) housing and other. Income transfers consist of category (6) income maintenance. Under the label of economic services they include the categories of (7) economic services, (8) public debt and (9) balancing item.

Their regrouping of table SNA5 (old COFOG) with our amendments is as follows:

2.   General public services include 'public order and safety' (and what they call 'other functions of public goods', a category in Oxley and Martin which is zero except for the Nordic countries). There is not the data in OECD or Eurostat in the 1980s to separate 'public order and safety'.

5.   Housing and other=housing and community amenities + recreation, cultural and religious affairs.

6.   Income maintenance=social security and welfare in COFOG (we have removed the sub-divisions in Oxley and Martin).

7.   Economic services=economic services in COFOG (we have removed the sub-divisions).

8.   Public debt interest=property income in table SNA 6 (debt interest was not separately itemised in old COFOG, but generally designated as 'expenditure not classified').

9.   Balancing item='a range of factors including rounding and in some cases, definitional differences, discrepancies and apparent incoherence in the data between SNA tables 5 (COFOG) and 6'.

Oxley and Martin derived their figures from OECD table SNA5 (old COFOG) figures (plus table SNA 6 for debt interest) in the case of Japan, Germany, the United Kingdom, Australia and Austria. Only final consumption expenditure was analysed in COFOG terms for the OECD by the United States, Denmark and Finland (with Norway and Sweden also incomplete), so that further work had to be done by Oxley and Martin to create their data. Most work was done by them in the case of the Netherlands, much of which they constructed from national data.

Table 3.1, which is derived from Appendix 3A, summarises the changes by function. To begin with the total general government expenditure column, this is shown as a rising ratio of GDP between 1979 and 1989 for most of the countries analysed by Oxley and Martin, exceptions being the Netherlands, Germany, UK and Sweden. Using *OECD Economic Outlook* figures one can examine a wider range of countries. This confirms a general picture of rising expenditure relative to GDP. Out of 19 countries, the only reducing ratios are Belgium, Germany, Ireland and UK (Sweden reverses direction compared with the Oxley and Martin figures).

The items increasing as a percentage of GDP in most countries in the 1980s are debt interest (up in all countries except the UK), income transfers (up in all countries except Germany, Australia, and the Netherlands) and health (up in all countries, except for a cut in Sweden and remaining level in Denmark, USA and Austria). One category decreasing in most of the countries is economic services (it rises only in the Netherlands and remains level in Denmark and the United States). Education also declines in most countries (except USA, Austria, Finland and Norway). Defence spending stays level in most countries, declines in UK and Sweden, and rises in the USA and Norway. The figures for US health spending are hard to understand. For the OECD, SOCX shows a rise in US public health spending from 3.7 per cent of GDP in 1980 to 4.5 per cent of GDP in 1989, but it seems that the bulk of public expenditure on health is recorded in income transfers (Oxley and Martin, 1991, annex 1).

Paralleling the earlier aggregate expenditure analysis in Chapter 2 above, but here using Oxley and Martin's data, Table 3.2 focuses on core expenditure and core expenditure minus debt interest. Core expenditure is defined as total expenditure minus income transfers and minus health. Table 3.2 shows core spending was more or less static in the 1980s (except for increases in USA and Denmark and decreases in UK and Sweden) and that core spending minus debt interest was declining markedly in all these countries, except the USA and Norway. This supports Castles' aggregate analysis for the 1980s suggesting that, as interest rates and debt increased, and as neo-liberal views progressively identified the problem as one of undue state intervention, countries generally began to cut back and move towards

Table 3.1 An overview of expenditure changes by function, 1979–89

Country	Defence	General services	Education	Economic services	Health	Housing	Income transfers	Debt interest	Total
Australia	=	=	−	−	+	=	=	+	+
Austria	=	=	=	−	=	=	+	+	+
Denmark	=	+	−	=	=	−	+	+	+
Finland	=	=	=	−	+	=	+	+	+
Germany	=	=	−	−	+	=	−	+	−
Japan	=	=	−	−	+	+	+	+	+
Netherlands	=	−	−	+	+	+	−	+	=
Norway	+	+	+	−	+	−	+	+	+
Sweden	−	−	−	−	−	−	+	+	−
UK	−	=	−	−	+	−	+	−	−
United States	+	+	=	=	=	=	+	+	+
Most common	=	=	−	−	+	=	+	+	+

Note: − indicates expenditure falling by at least 0.4 per cent of GDP; = indicates expenditure which is within 0.3 per cent of GDP of original level; + indicates expenditure rising by at least 0.4 per cent of GDP.

Table 3.2   Core expenditure and core expenditure minus debt interest payments in 11 countries, 1979 and 1989 (percentage of GDP)

Country	Core expenditure		Core expenditure excluding debt interest	
	1979	1989	1979	1989
Australia	21.7	22.1[1]	19.6	17.7[1]
Austria	21.1[3]	21.1[1]	18.3[3]	17.2[1]
Denmark	27.8	31.6[1]	24.3	23.7[1]
Finland	19.8	19.5	18.9	18.1
Germany	22.5	21.8[1]	20.8	19.1
Japan	20.3	19.5	17.7	15.5
Netherlands	28.6	29.5	24.4	22.8
Norway	28[2]	28.7	24.6[2]	24.7
Sweden	29.9[2]	27.0[1]	25.8[2]	21.3[1]
UK	26.3	23.3	21.9	19.7
USA	20.4	23.7	17.6	18.7

Notes:
1. 1988.
2. 1980.
3. 1981.

Source: Oxley and Martin (1991); see Appendix 3A.

Table 3.3   Correlation coefficients between Oxley and Martin's data and Chapter 2 estimates for the ten countries in both data sets

Measures	Pearson correlation
Core expenditure in 1979, 1980 or 1981	0.886*
Core expenditure in 1989 or 1988	0.817*

Note: * significant at the 0.01 level.

regulation in the core expenditure area. This is a hypothesis to be investigated in the later economic policy chapters.

Table 3.3 presents correlation coefficients between the Oxley and Martin data and the Chapter 2 data for core expenditure. The figures are generally reassuring. The discrepancies in start and finish dates (Chapter 2 reports figures for 1980 and 1990; Oxley and Martin for the years indicated in the table) and the interpolations of data from different sources by Oxley and Martin probably explain why the correlations are not stronger.

3.5   DATA FOR THE 1990S AND BEYOND

Expenditure data based on the SNA68 edition of COFOG are available for several countries as late as the mid-1990s (see UN, 1995). However the collection of these data has ended as national statistical offices and international organisations have switched to SNA93. Unfortunately, as outlined earlier in this chapter, the differences in the classification of expenditure between the two systems mean that data from the two systems cannot be combined in a straightforward manner to create continuous time-series. Given that the SNA68 classification has largely been replaced by SNA93, the remainder of this chapter will consider data collected under the most recent system of national accounts.

Cross-national figures based on the SNA93 edition of COFOG (dating back to 1990 for many countries) are available from OECD and Eurostat, while recent editions of the IMF's *Government Finance Statistics Yearbook* also provide data for the period since 2000. Given that data published by the IMF are only available for a handful of years, the remainder of this chapter will concentrate on the data available from OECD and Eurostat, but reference to the IMF data will be made where appropriate.

Appendix 3B provides a snapshot of the data provided by the OECD and Eurostat for the period 1990–2002. The general picture presented by the data in Appendix 3B is optimistic, with data appearing to be available for a majority of those countries commonly considered by studies in comparative political economy for most COFOG expenditure categories and for a range of years since 1990. Comparing the data in Appendix 3A with that in Appendix 3B also suggests that, for the most part, data collected throughout the 1990s might be more disaggregated than those for the 1980s. For instance most countries now provide separate data for Public Order and Safety, where, previously, this was often grouped with General Public Services. Similarly, and, as previously noted, separate data relating to Environmental Protection (a growing area of interest in public policy and research) are now often provided when these were previously grouped with data on Housing and Community Affairs.

Unfortunately, several problems can be identified with the data presented in Appendix 3B, suggesting that the utility of data collected under the new COFOG classification for investigating cross-national variation in government expenditure may be limited, and that, where used, great care should be exercised to ensure the suitability of the data for the analysis being undertaken. While the reporting of COFOG data by SNA93 has been generally good across the OECD, there remain several countries that do not appear to provide data in accordance with the new COFOG classification, including Australia, Canada, New Zealand and Switzerland (Canada has begun to provide data to the IMF but this only covers the period 2000–2003 and no data are available from the OECD). Given the small sample size that is often used in comparative public policy work, these data deficiencies could be expected to have a substantial impact on any analysis either by reducing the overall sample size or by biasing the analysis, because so many of the missing countries are to be found in the English-speaking family of nations identified by Castles (1998, and the present volume).

Of those countries included in Appendix 3B, several do not provide data for the full time-span from 1990–2002. The provision of data improves as latter years are considered and continues to improve over time. For instance, in 2005, Ireland published data back as far as 1990, when they had previously only been available from 1995; and in recent years the USA has started to provide data for all years. Despite these improvements, data for Austria, France, Netherlands and Sweden are generally only available at present from 1995 onwards, while data for Spain are only available from 1999 onwards. Combined with the missing countries identified above, this means that any sample based just on OECD and Eurostat published data starting in 1990 is likely to be too small for all but the most basic of cross-sectional analysis. At points, this has limited the analysis that could be undertaken in this volume, but, given the increasing number of countries now providing data, the prospects seem set fair for increasingly comprehensive comparative analyses in future.

Finally, while the new COFOG breakdown has much to recommend it (for instance, the separation of Environmental Protection spending and the apparent increase in the reporting of separate expenditure for Public Order and Safety), some problems remain concerning the categories used. First, several countries (namely Iceland, Ireland and the United States) do not provide data for the Environmental Protection category. These data are commonly listed as not available, implying that spending under this heading is not simply zero. It would appear that these countries have yet to manage to separate out environmental protection expenditure, but it is not clear if they are following the SNA68 convention of including it with Housing and Community Affairs (most likely) or whether they have mainstreamed environmental policy, meaning it is spread across the full range of functions. Secondly, the new COFOG classification now includes debt transactions as part of General Government Services rather than the old COFOG approach where it was generally put in 'expenditure not classified by major group'. The data published by the IMF are an exception, as under General Public Services they give details of debt transactions as a separate sub-function. Data on debt transactions are available separately from the OECD, suggesting that it should be possible to identify spending under these different heads, but, as discussed below, this appears to provide some inconsistent results.

Table 3.4 follows the logic of Table 3.1, but is derived from Appendix 3B to show the general pattern of expenditure change between 1990 and 2002. While the data used to create this table are not directly comparable to those in Table 3.1 (owing not only to the different accounting systems, but also to the different countries available for comparison in each time period), comparing the two does provide a crude indicator of the similarities and differences in changes in expenditure over the two periods. A major similarity between the two periods can be seen in the way expenditure on welfare issues (in the early period identified as Health and Income Transfers and in the latter period as Health and Social Protection) has generally risen across the OECD. A similarly consistent pattern can be seen with reference to Economic Affairs, which has fallen across nearly all countries in both time periods.

The Housing category in Table 3.1 represents the SNA68 COFOG categories of Housing and Community Affairs as well as Recreation, Cultural and Religious Affairs. These categories are presented separately in Table 3.4 and need to be considered in conjunction with spending on Environmental Protection as this used to be included under Housing and Community Affairs prior to SNA93. The general pattern relating to these functions is one of consistency over both periods (although this may to some extent be a function of the cut-off points used in the construction of Tables 3.1 and 3.4, which are likely to understate the importance of changes in expenditure for categories where the level of expenditure is low).

Possibly the major difference between the two periods can be seen in defence expenditure, which has fallen in nearly all the countries in Table 3.4, in contrast to Table 3.1, where it appears generally stable (and indeed increases in Norway and the United States). This is investigated further in Chapter 5 of this volume, but given the cut-off point for the two tables, and the high number of European countries considered, this change is almost certainly largely attributable to the end of the Cold War and its associated 'peace dividend'.

The trend of Education expenditure also appears to differ between the two time periods. In the 1980s, Education appears to have experienced cuts in expenditure, while the picture for the 1990s appears more varied. Comparing countries that appear in both tables gives the impression of a policy area in which expenditure may be quite volatile. For instance, expenditure in Denmark and the UK fell in the 1980s, but rose in the 1990s, while the opposite occurred in Norway. Additionally, expenditure in Germany and Japan appears to have become stable in the 1990s after falling in the 1980s, while, in the USA, expenditure has begun to increase in the 1990s after appearing quite stable in the 1980s.

The remaining categories in Table 3.4 cannot be directly compared to those in Table 3.1, but Table 3.4 suggests that expenditure on Public Order

Table 3.4 An overview of expenditure changes by function, 1990–2002

Country	General public services (inc. debt repayments)	Defence	Public order and safety	Economic affairs	Environ-mental protection	Housing and community affairs	Health	Recreation, culture and religion	Education	Social protection	Total
Belgium	–	–	+	–	=	=	+	+	=	–	–
Denmark	–	–	=	–	=	=	+	=	+	+	–
Finland	+	=	=	–	=	=	+	=	=	+	+
Germany	–	–	=	+	–	=	+	=	=	+	+
Greece	–	–	n/a	–	+	=	+	=	=	+	–
Iceland	n/a	n/a	=	–	n/a	n/a	+	+	+	+	+
Ireland	–	–	=	–	n/a	n/a	+	=	–	–	–
Italy	–	=	=	–	=	–	=	=	–	+	–
Japan	=	=	=	=	=	=	+	=	=	+	+
Luxembourg	–	–	=	–	–	=	=	+	=	+	+
Norway	–	–	=	–	–	=	+	–	–	–	–
Portugal	–	–	=	–	=	=	+	+	+	+	+
United Kingdom	–	–	=	–	–	–	+	=	+	+	+
United States	–	–	+	=	n/a	n/a	+	=	+	+	–
Most common	–	–	=	–	=	=	+	=	=	+	+/–

Note: – indicates expenditure falling by at least 0.4 per cent of GDP; = indicates expenditure which is within 0.3 per cent of GDP of original level; + indicates expenditure rising by at least 0.4 per cent of GDP.

61

Table 3.5   Estimates of debt interest transactions, 1990–2002 (percentage of GDP)

Country	1990	1996	2002
Austria		4.1	3.4
Belgium	11.9	8.9	6.0
Denmark	7.3	6.4	3.7
Finland	1.4	4.2	2.2
France	2.9	3.9	3.0
Germany	2.8	3.6	3.1
Greece	10.0	12.0	6.4
Iceland	3.8	4.1	3.3
Ireland	7.9	4.6	1.3
Italy	10.5	11.5	5.9
Japan	3.7	3.5	3.1
Luxembourg	0.5	0.5	0.3
Netherlands	5.9	5.6	3.1
Norway	3.5	2.5	1.8
Portugal	8.6	5.7	3.1
Spain		5.2	2.7
Sweden		6.6	3.2
United Kingdom	3.8	3.7	2.0
United States	4.9	4.6	2.9

Note: All countries based on data provided by OECD, March 2005, except for Japan, the data for which is from the OECD, July 2006.

and Safety has remained relatively constant over the 1990s (again this may be a function of the way Table 3.4 is created and the low percentage of GDP commonly spent in this area). Expenditure recorded under General Public Services appears to have fallen across most the countries considered in the 1990s. However, as this category includes expenditure on debt transactions, it is not clear from these data whether this represents a genuine fall in the cost of government or a change in debt repayment obligations (on this see the next chapter).

Table 3.5 presents estimates of expenditure on debt interest repayments for 1990–2002, based on the figures provided in the OECD table 'Summary of General Government Aggregates and Balances' (personal communication from OECD March 2005, also available in OECD, 2006) for the same countries and years as General Public Services data are available in Appendix 3B. This table presents a striking contrast to the change in debt repayments between 1979 and 1989 shown in Table 3.1. As already underlined in the aggregate analysis of Chapter 2, in the 1980s, debt repayment costs were going up in almost all the countries analysed, whereas, in the 1990s, the predominant direction for debt repayment costs is down.

In general, the figures presented in Table 3.5 appear plausible and, for most countries, they are less than the totals given for General Public Services in Appendix 3B. However, this is not the case for Iceland, which appears to have higher levels of expenditure on debt transactions than expenditures on General Public Services, even though the former is meant to be recorded as part of the latter. It is not immediately clear why this is the case, although comparing the data from the OECD with those from the IMF (2005), where debt transactions are explicitly recorded as a sub-function of General Public Services, suggests that the debt interest figures used for Table 3.5 are consistent across different data sources. In contrast, expenditure on General Public Services appears consistent across sources with the exception of the figures for Iceland. A similar pattern can be seen in respect of published data for Japan in OECD (2006). However the OECD was able to provide revised data for Japan, where this issue no longer arose and suggested that the inconsistency was caused by these countries not recording debt transactions as part of General Public Services. No revised data were available for Iceland (personal communication with the OECD, July 2006). Whatever the reason for these apparent inconsistencies, they do provide a good illustration of how cross-checking these relatively new data can assist in highlighting potential sources of error.

Following on from Table 3.2, Table 3.6 presents estimates for the Chapter 2 aggregate category of core expenditure for the period 1990–2002. In this case, core expenditure is defined as total expenditure minus spending on health and social protection. Core expenditure minus debt repayments is calculated by subtracting the figures for debt expenditures given in Table 3.5 (Iceland is excluded because of the apparent inconsistency of the data, as noted above).

Only a handful of countries provide data for 1989/90 in both Tables 3.2 and 3.6, but these estimates (particularly before debt transactions are accounted for) do appear broadly consistent, especially when accounting differences between SNA68 and SNA93 are considered. Table 3.7 provides correlation coefficients between the figures presented in Table 3.6 and the estimates arrived at in Chapter 2 using the residuals method. As with the data from the 1980s (Table 3.3), these correlations appear to suggest that relatively consistent estimates of core expenditure are arrived at even when they are based on different underlying data sources. The one exception is the correlation relating to 1990 spending once debt expenditure is removed. Although part of this discrepancy is likely to be attributable to the fact that the Table 3.6 data for 1990 do not include Sweden, the most extreme case in the corresponding Chapter 2 distribution, the relative weakness of the

Table 3.6   Estimates of core expenditure, 1990, 1996, 2002 (percentage of GDP)

Country	Core expenditure			Core expenditure excluding debt interest		
	1990	1996	2002	1990	1996	2002
Austria		26.2	23.0		22.1	19.6
Belgium	30.2	27.7	25.8	18.3	18.8	19.8
Denmark	28.2	28.1	25.7	20.9	21.7	22.0
Finland	23.5	28.0	22.4	22.1	23.8	20.2
France		25.7	23.2		21.8	20.2
Germany	22.3	20.9	19.6	19.5	17.3	16.5
Greece	32.0	27.1	25.7	22.0	15.1	19.3
Ireland	25.6	22.4	19.4	17.7	17.8	18.1
Italy	31.3	29.1	23.8	20.8	17.6	17.9
Japan	18.4	20.7	18.9	14.7	17.2	15.8
Luxembourg	21.4	21.7	20.5	20.9	21.2	20.2
Netherlands		25.9	24.9		20.3	21.8
Norway	29.1	24.7	21.8	25.6	22.2	20.0
Portugal	28.2	25.6	24.0	19.6	19.9	20.9
Spain			20.5			17.8
Sweden		32.3	27.2		25.7	24.0
United Kingdom	23.1	20.4	19.5	19.3	16.7	17.5
United States	25.0	22.7	21.9	20.1	18.1	19.0

Note: Core expenditure = total expenditure – (health + social protection), all taken from Appendix 3B.
Core expenditure minus debt repayments = total expenditure – (health + social protection + debt interest repayments), total expenditure, health and social protection from Appendix 3B, debt repayments as in Table 3.5.

association may be seen as further calling into question the reliability of attempting to combine debt figures from a separate table with expenditure data presented in the COFOG based table.

3.6   CONCLUSION

International data on public expenditure by function have been evolving since the 1970s, in ways which make them an increasingly valuable resource for comparative research on government activities. The major development has been the elaboration of the international Classification of Functions of Government (COFOG) data standardised by function, which gets around

Table 3.7   Correlations between COFOG data and estimates of
core expenditure for the 1990s and 2000s (from Chapter 2)

Measures	Pearson correlation
COFOG-based core expenditure 1990 with Chapter 2 core expenditure 1990 excluding Japan (n=11)	0.843**
COFOG-based core expenditure 2002 with Chapter 2 core expenditure 2001 (n=16)	0.782**
COFOG-based core expenditure minus debt 1990 with Chapter 2 core expenditure minus debt 1990 (n=11)	0.568*
COFOG-based core expenditure minus debt 2002 with Chapter 2 core expenditure minus debt 2001 (n=16)	0.852**

Note: * significant at the 0.1 level, ** significant at the 0.01 level.

the problem of national data being influenced by different departmental boundaries in different countries. Social expenditure led the way in the publication of data, because of the need to monitor welfare state growth, especially at times of economic slowdown. Non-social expenditure (here called 'core expenditure') has been much more patchily recorded, apart from series for individual categories such as military and education spending. Availability of these data has, however, improved markedly following the revision of the COFOG classification in the 1990s. The data are now being published by international agencies back to 1990 (with a series break occurring in that year). There are still problems with the new data, but there seems to be a resolve to surmount these.

In this chapter we have looked at data for the 1980s derived from OECD sources and assembled by Oxley and Martin (1991). We compared these data with Castles' earlier analysis of core expenditure for the same period. Both are consistent with cutbacks in the core expenditure area in response to rising interest rates, rising debt and the rise of neoliberalism. We have also included a section analysing data for the period 1990 to 2002. Social expenditure takes up a rising share of GDP in most countries during both periods, arguably putting severe pressure on core spending. This pressure was, however, eased by falling debt interest costs in the second period. Pressures on spending were also eased in a number of countries by reductions in defence expenditure with the end of the Cold War. Our analysis here suggests that the continuing rise in social expenditure was made possible by falling shares of GDP for economic affairs, defence and debt repayments, with near level-pegging by other categories of core expenditure. The question that remains is how long these tendencies in core expenditure will persist.

This chapter reveals that data for a new research field are emerging, allowing us to compare government activity across all the functions of government and not restricted to the sphere of social expenditure. Time-series analysis of these new data is, however, limited by the 1990 start date for the New COFOG series. Cross-sectional analysis is limited by the number of countries reporting, but with all EU countries obliged to report (subject to 'derogation' in some cases), OECD countries being actively encouraged, and the IMF having changed to reporting COFOG data on a general government basis, more and more countries are becoming source material. Although much of this book is based on data from other sources, we believe it will soon be possible to undertake comparable and, in some instances, more sophisticated analyses using COFOG data.

ACKNOWLEDGEMENTS

We wish to thank the Carnegie Trust for the Universities of Scotland for the financial support required for Neil Fraser to visit Eurostat in Luxembourg, the IMF in Washington and the UN in New York. We also thank the University of Edinburgh's School of Social and Political Studies for the funding that enabled Paul Norris to assemble the COFOG data that appear in Appendix 3B.

REFERENCES

Castles, F.G. (1982), *The Impact of Parties: Politics and Policies in Democratic Capitalist States*, London: Sage.

Castles, F.G. (1994), 'Is expenditure enough? On the nature of the dependent variable in comparative public policy analysis', *Journal of Commonwealth and Comparative Politics*, **32** (3), 349–63.

Castles, F.G. (1998), *Comparative Public Policy*, Cheltenham, UK and Northampton, MA, USA: Edward Elgar.

EU Commission, IMF, OECD, UN, World Bank (1993), *System of National Accounts 1993*.

Eurostat (1997), *General Government Accounts and Statistics 1985–1996*, Luxembourg.

Eurostat (2006), *Government Finance Statistics*, Luxembourg (http://epp.eurostat. ec.europa.eu/portal/page?_pageid=1996,45323734&_dad=portal&_schema=P ORTAL&screen=welcomeref&open=/gov/publ_exp&language=en&product= EU_MASTER_government&root=EU_MASTER_government&scrollto=0) (last accessed 17/06/2006).

Florio, M. (2001), 'On cross-country comparability of government statistics: public expenditure trends in OECD National Accounts', *International Review of Applied Economics*, **15** (2), 181–98.

Galbraith, J.K. (2000), 'Government spending by function: a new presentation', *Survey of Current Business*, June, 18–23.

Heidenheimer, A.J. (1996), 'Throwing money and heaving bodies: heuristic callisthenics for comparative policy buffs', in L.M. Imbeau and R.D. McKinlay (eds), *Comparing Government Activity*, London: Macmillan, pp. 13–25.

Hofferbert, R.I. and I. Budge (1996), 'Patterns of post-war expenditure priorities in ten democracies', in L.M. Imbeau and R.D. McKinley (eds), *Comparing Government Activity*, London: Macmillan.

ILO (1952, and subsequent), *The Cost of Social Security*, Geneva.

IMF (annual), *Government Finance Statistics Yearbook*, Washington.

IMF (2001a), *Government Finance Statistics Manual 2001*, Washington.

IMF (2001b), *Government Finance Statistics Manual Companion Material 2001*, Washington.

IMF (2005), *Government Finance Statistics Yearbook, 2005*, Washington.

Kneller, R., M.F. Bleaney and N. Gemmell (1999), 'Fiscal policy and growth: evidence from OECD countries', *Journal of Public Economics*, **74**, 171–90.

Lane, J-E and S. Ersson (1990), *Comparative Political Economy*, London: Pinter.

OECD (1976), *Public expenditure on Income maintenance Programmes*, Paris.

OECD (1981), *The Welfare State in Crisis*, Paris.

OECD (1985), *Social Expenditure, 1960–1990*, Paris.

OECD (1994), *National Accounts 1982–94, Detailed Tables*, Paris.

OECD (2006), *National Accounts 1993–2004, Volume IV, General Government Accounts*, Paris.

OECD (bi-annual), *Economic Outlook*, Paris.

ONS (2005), *UK National Accounts Blue Book 2005*, London.

Oxley, H. and J.P. Martin (1991), 'Controlling government spending and deficits: trends in the 1980s and prospects for the 1990s', *OECD Economic Studies*, no.17, Paris.

Sanz, I. and F.J. Velázquez (2004), 'The evolution and convergence of the government expenditure composition in the OECD countries', *Public Choice*, **119**, 61–7.

Saunders, P. (1993), 'Recent trends in the size and growth of government in OECD countries', in N. Gemmell (ed.), *The Growth of the Public Sector*, Cheltenham, UK and Northampton, MA, USA: Edward Elgar.

Saunders, P. and F. Klau (1985), 'The role of the public sector', *OECD Economic Studies*, no.4, Paris.

Sturm, J-E (1998), *Public Capital Expenditure in OECD Countries*, Cheltenham, UK and Northampton, MA, USA: Edward Elgar.

Tanzi, V. and L. Schuknecht (2000), *Public Spending in the 20th Century: A Global Perspective*, Cambridge: Cambridge University Press.

UN (1980), *Classification of the Functions of Government*, Department of International Economic and Social Affairs Statistical Office, statistical papers series M, no. 70, New York.

UN (1995), *National Accounts Statistics: Main Aggregates and Detailed Tables 1995*, New York.

UN (2000), *Classifications of Expenditure according to Purpose*, Department of International Economic and Social Affairs Statistical Office, statistical papers series M, no. 84, New York.

UN (annual), *National Accounts*, New York.

Appendix 3A   Functional breakdown of expenditure as given by Oxley and Martin for 1979 and 1989

	Australia		Austria		Denmark		Finland		Germany		Japan	
	1979	1988	1981	1998	1979	1988	1979	1988	1979	1988	1979	1989
Defence	2.2	2.1	1.1	1.1	2.2	2.1	1.3	1.4	2.8	2.6	0.8	0.9
General services	4.3	4.2	4.2	4.0	5.8	6.5	3.0	3.0	5.5	5.6	3.1	2.8
Education	5.8	5.1	4.3	4.4	7.3	6.9	4.9	5.0	5.0	4.3	4.6	3.5
Health	4.5	5.1	5.2	5.2	5.6	5.3	3.8	4.4	6.1	6.5	4.5	4.9
Housing	1.5	1.6	0.9	0.9	3.0	2.4	1.2	1.3	2.2	1.9	2.2	2.5
Income transfers	7.5	7.4	22.1	23	20.4	22.5	12.9	14.3	19.4	18.5	6.3	7.2
Economic services	5.8	4.7	7.5	6.7	6.0	5.8	8.4	7.3	5.4	4.6	6.6	5.5
Debt interest	2.1	4.4	2.8	3.9	3.5	7.9	0.9	1.4	1.7	2.8	2.6	4.0
Balancing item	0	0	0.3	0	0	0	0.1	0.1	-0.1	0	0.4	0.3
Total expenditure	33.7	34.6	48.4	49.2	53.8	59.4	36.5	38.2	48	46.8	31.1	31.6

	Netherlands		Norway		Sweden		United Kingdom		United States	
	1979	1989	1980	1989	1980	1988	1979	1989	1979	1989
Defence	3.1	2.9	2.9	3.3	3.4	2.4	4.5	4.1	4.9	5.9
General services	8.0	7.1	3.3	4.3	5.1	4.1	3.9	4.2	2.8	3.2
Education	7.4	5.4	6.4	6.9	6.5	5.5	5.2	4.8	4.5	4.6
Health	5.5	5.9	6.5	7.1	7.9	6.9	4.6	5.0	0.9	0.9
Housing	0.5	1.0	2.8	2.2	2.9	2.1	3.8	3.0	0.8	0.6
Income transfers	22.1	21.1	13.8	18.8	24.1	25.8	11.9	12.9	10.8	11.7
Economic services	5.7	6.3	9.9	8.4	7.6	6.9	3.7	3.0	4.5	4.5
Debt interest	4.2	6.7	3.4	4.0	4.1	5.7	4.4	3.6	2.8	5.0
Balancing item	-0.3	0.1	-0.7	-0.4	0.3	0.3	0.8	0.6	0.1	-0.1
Total expenditure	56.2	56.5	48.3	54.6	61.9	59.7	42.8	41.2	32.1	36.3

Note: All data from Oxley and Martin (1991), Table 3, pp. 163–4.

69

Appendix 3B General government expenditure by COFOG function (1993 SNA) as a percentage of GDP (collected from Eurostat 2006 and OECD 2006)[a]

	Austria			Belgium			Denmark			Finland		
	1990	1996	2002	1990	1996	2002	1990	1996	2002	1990	1996	2002
General public services		9.4	7.7	13.3	11.9	9.9	11.2	10.5	8.2	5.3	7.8	6.5
Defence		1.0	0.9	2.0	1.4	1.2	2.0	1.8	1.6	1.6	2.1	1.5
Public order and safety		1.5	1.4	1.2	1.5	1.7	1.1	1.0	1.0	1.3	1.5	1.4
Economic affairs		4.7	5.0	6.0	4.7	4.6	4.6	4.5	3.6	6.5	7.0	4.9
Environmental protection		1.4	0.3	0.5	0.7	0.8	0.3	0.6	0.6	0.2	0.3	0.3
Housing and community affairs		1.1	0.7	0.3	0.4	0.3	0.5	0.6	0.7	0.7	1.0	0.5
Health		7.5	6.6	5.4	6.4	6.5	6.6	6.9	7.0	5.9	6.4	6.3
Recreation, culture and religion		1.1	1.0	0.8	0.9	1.3	1.5	1.7	1.6	1.5	1.4	1.2
Education		6.0	5.8	6.1	6.3	6.1	7.0	7.5	8.2	6.4	6.8	6.1
Social protection		21.7	21.1	18.1	18.1	17.5	21.1	24.1	22.2	19.4	25.6	21.2
Total		55.4	50.7	53.7	52.2	49.8	55.9	59.1	54.9	48.8	60.0	49.9

	France			Germany			Greece			Iceland		
	1990	1996	2002	1991[b]	1996	2002	1990	1996	2002	1990	1996	2002[c]
General public services		8.4	7.4	6.6	6.7	6.2	18.5	15.1	9.8	2.0[d]	1.9[d]	2.4[d]
Defence		2.9	2.3	1.8	1.3	1.2	4.9	2.7	4.4	n/a	n/a	n/a
Public order and safety		1.0	1.0	1.5	1.7	1.7	n/a	0.7	1.3	1.3	1.4	1.6
Economic affairs		3.6	3.2	5.3	4.4	4.0	4.7	4.1	5.5	8.6	6.7	6.2
Environmental protection		0.6	0.7	1.0	0.9	0.5	0.1	0.6	0.6	n/a	n/a	n/a
Housing and community affairs		1.5	1.8	1.0	0.8	1.1	0.1	0.4	0.4	0.8	0.9	1.0
Health		6.7	7.0	5.8	6.4	6.4	1.1	3.5	4.9	6.9	6.9	8.6
Recreation, culture and religion		1.1	1.3	0.9	0.8	0.7	0.1	0.3	0.4	2.2	2.3	2.7
Education		6.5	6.4	4.1	4.4	4.3	3.5	3.2	3.2	4.9	5.4	6.8
Social protection		22.1	22.4	18.2	22.0	22.1	17.1	18.6	19.1	7.8	8.8	9.2
Total		54.5	52.6	46.3	49.3	48.1	50.2	49.2	49.7	41.2	41.3	44.8

Appendix 3B (continued)

	Ireland			Italy			Japan[e]			Luxembourg		
	1990	1996	2002	1990	1996	2002	1990	1996	2002	1990	1996	2002
General public services	9.8	6.6	3.5	13.2	13.7	9.3	6.0	5.7	5.6	5.2	4.4	5.0
Defence	1.4	0.9	0.6	1.5	1.1	1.2	0.9	0.9	1.0	0.9	0.6	0.3
Public order and safety	1.7	1.7	1.4	2.1	2.1	2.0	1.2	1.4	1.4	0.9	0.9	1.1
Economic affairs	5.7	5.8	5.2	6.1	4.7	4.3	4.4	5.3	4.5	5.9	6.3	5.1
Environmental protection	n/a	n/a	n/a	0.7	0.7	0.9	1.3	1.7	1.6	1.3	1.5	1.2
Housing and community affairs	1.7	1.9	2.5	1.3	0.9	0.1	0.7	1.0	0.8	1.0	1.0	1.0
Health	5.7	5.8	6.7	6.4	5.5	6.5	4.5	5.2	6.7	4.8	5.8	4.9
Recreation, culture and religion	0.4	0.5	0.6	0.8	0.9	0.9	0.2	0.2	0.2	1.3	1.8	1.9
Education	4.8	4.9	4.2	5.6	4.9	5.0	3.9	4.0	4.1	4.9	5.1	5.0
Social protection	12.0	10.9	8.8	16.6	17.5	18.2	7.6	9.7	11.7	17.0	19.2	18.2
Total	43.3	39.1	33.4	54.3	52.1	48.5	30.5	34.9	37.5	43.2	46.7	43.6

	Netherlands			Norway			Portugal			Spain		
	1990	1996	2002	1990	1996	2002	1990	1996	2002	1990	1996	2002
General public services		9.5	8.1	7.2	5.7	5.0	11.0	7.9	6.0			5.3
Defence		1.8	1.5	3.3	2.4	2.0	2.0	1.7	1.4			1.1
Public order and safety		1.4	1.7	1.1	1.0	1.2	2.2	1.7	1.9			1.9
Economic affairs		5.0	5.1	8.7	6.4	5.1	5.8	5.8	4.8			4.5
Environmental protection		0.8	0.8	1.1	0.9	0.6	0.4	0.5	0.7			0.9
Housing and community affairs		1.5	1.1	0.5	0.7	0.4	0.8	0.8	0.9			1.1
Health		3.5	4.2	6.8	6.9	7.9	4.0	5.8	6.7			5.2
Recreation, culture and religion		0.9	1.5	1.2	1.2	1.2	0.8	0.9	1.2			1.4
Education		5.0	5.0	6.1	6.2	6.2	5.2	6.2	7.3			4.3
Social protection		20.2	17.1	18.1	17.4	17.8	9.9	12.3	13.6			13.0
Total	54.8	49.6	46.2	54.0	49.0	47.5	42.1	43.7	44.3			38.7

Appendix 3B (continued)

	Sweden			United Kingdom			United States[f]		
	1990	1996	2002	1990	1996	2002	1990	1996	2002
General public services		11.7	9.1	5.1	5.7	4.4	7.2	6.5	5.0
Defence		2.5	2.1	4.1	2.9	2.6	5.7	3.8	3.7
Public order and safety		1.4	1.4	2.1	2.1	2.4	1.7	1.9	2.1
Economic affairs		4.9	4.8	4.2	2.9	2.7	3.7	3.5	3.7
Environmental protection		0.2	0.3	0.5	0.4	0.7	n/a	n/a	n/a
Housing and community affairs		2.6	0.9	1.5	0.9	0.6	0.8	0.8	0.7
Health		6.6	7.0	5.1	5.7	6.3	5.2	6.6	7.1
Recreation, culture and religion		1.9	1.1	0.8	0.7	0.6	0.3	0.3	0.3
Education		7.0	7.4	4.7	4.6	5.5	5.7	5.8	6.3
Social protection		25.9	23.7	14.0	17.0	15.8	6.9	7.2	7.3
Total		64.8	57.9	42.2	43.1	41.6	37.1	36.5	36.3

Notes:

a No data available in either source for Australia, Canada, New Zealand or Switzerland.

b Figures refer to 1991 rather than 1990 owing to reunification.

c Figures from OECD (2006), other years from Eurostat (2006).

d Figures are consistent between OECD (2006) and Eurostat (2006), but appear substantially lower than in IMF (2005). The total for GPS appears less than that for debt transactions, suggesting these data may exclude debt transactions. However, this does not appear to be documented in OECD (2006) or Eurostat (2006) and hence the reliability of these figures should be investigated further before use.

e 1996 and 2002 figures from OECD (2006); 1990 figures from personal communication with OECD (March 2005). Figures for General Public Services appear inconsistent, with Japan claiming to spend less on general public services than on debt interest. Figures for general public services and total expenditure are therefore based on revised data from the OECD (July 2006).

4. The changing cost of government: trends in the state overhead budget

Richard Parry

4.1 INTRODUCTION

In debate on public expenditure trends there remains a fascination with the cost of the state itself – of the overhead in government that is the prerequisite for spending on functional services. We know the tax collector and presidential aide, the clerk at the Parliament, the diplomat and the spy; they are at the heart of the state, shielded from the test of the market and the scrutiny of service users. We may suspect that there are too many of them and that their positions are too secure, but we lack a conceptual structure for evaluating them and setting them in a comparative context. Some public administration categories have high political salience and significance, but the real expenditure drivers lie elsewhere. A legislative building like Norman Foster's new Reichstag in Berlin and Enric Miralles's Scottish Parliament in Edinburgh may be symbolic and expensive and attract inordinate public attention compared to the cost of building and maintaining other government offices. The staffs of ministers and elected representatives stand out more prominently than the routine bureaucracy of functional departments. A Treasury or central budget agency will typically employ a tiny proportion of those involved in tax collection but attract no less attention.

Expenditure analysis in this area is conceptually and methodologically difficult. That is because the COFOG data for the functional category of General Public Services (GPS), which covers these public administration categories of spending, combine two areas of consumption of public resources. The first is *substantive:* the overhead costs of the state that cannot be attributed to programme expenditure, including support for the central administration and legislature, the costs of tax collection, general research and consultancy (including the maintenance of research infrastructure) and consolidated funding streams such as general grants to public and non-public agencies that are not finally spent in functional areas. Such activity measures the efficiency of state organisation and potentially the extent of bureaucratic self-interest. Within the substantive category, we may distinguish the indisputably central legislative and executive functions, or the 'cost of democracy': categories such as parliamentary members and staff, head of government staff, and electoral officers' organisations; the central budget and financial agencies (Treasury/Office of Management and Budget equivalents, national statistics offices, personnel management of the higher civil service); and other non-functional expenditure such as central property and computer facilities.

The second area is *residual:* services that cannot be classified elsewhere; this includes expenditure genuinely 'not elsewhere classifiable' but also expenditure that could have been attributed to a programme given better data. Thus, in order to determine the true costs of government, it is necessary to remove the residual elements, which, as already shown in Chapter 3, is extremely difficult to do on an entirely consistent cross-national basis. This necessarily makes the comparative analysis of this chapter somewhat more tentative and preliminary than others in this volume.

The UN's COFOG classification seeks the maximum level of functional attribution and the lowest statistical residual. In its methodology, administrative expenditure related to programme delivery should in principle be classified as being part of the programme concerned, which would account for the great majority of salaried public officials; and the pension costs of former public employees, a matter of interest and salience given the typically generous schemes for public employees, are now classified as part of social protection. What is left is included in COFOG's 'general public services' category. Such expenditure will vary between countries and over time, and movement of expenditure data to an accrual accounting basis can also have a particular impact on this category.

For all its limitations, we can have increasing confidence in the OECD general public services category. It is intended to be a residual one, with anything that can be allocated to a specific function going into expenditure on that function (this includes ministerial offices, personnel administration and services, planning and statistical services, applied research and experimental development, and intergovernmental transfers, a small exception being the compilation of statistics on functional areas by a central statistical agency). At worst, the data offer the basis for analysing what is here described as the 'state overhead'. At best, we may gain an insight into the level and trends of the cost of administering particular political systems and throw light on important questions such as the following:

- the size of government in Western political and economic systems (noting that most public officials will be counted under programme categories and that the search for a core of central administrative

officials, the imagery of the bloated state important in right-wing ideology, may be elusive or impossible);

- whether the cost of public administration becomes a greater or lesser
  share of the declining aggregate share of non-social expenditure in
  GDP – the disappearance or otherwise of the 'core of the core';
- the costs of multi-level government: whether such systems and the distinct legislatures and executives they maintain impose a burden on
  public administration expenditure not found in unitary systems. There
  are major variations in the number of units of local government in
  European countries and also of patterns of constitutional federalism,
  captured in analyses of federalism such as Lijphart's (1999);
- the effect of party competition on the bureaucratic overhead of the
  state: whether large overheads are left-wing phenomena, reflecting a
  tolerance of large public organisations run on good employer lines and
  protected by state-encouraged trade unions, or common to a range of
  parties on the model of continental European welfare states; and
  whether the typical opposition pitch of 'cutting bureaucracy' as a
  rhetorical route to the simultaneous advocacy of both well-resourced
  public services and tax cuts has any basis in cross-national evidence;
- the distinction between 'front-office' and 'back-office' functions,
  between staff who are serving or interacting with service users (such
  as teachers, doctors and police officers) and those who are providing
  administrative resources to enable this to happen (finance, personnel
  management, purchasing, legal compliance). The presumption is
  that a high ratio of front to back office staff is desirable, and that
  back-office functions tend to expand over time and are either not necessary or should be outsourced. In the United Kingdom, this distinction, set out in a report by Peter Gershon in 2004, was the
  foundation of a programme of cuts in administrative costs of government departments initiated in 2004 (Gershon, 2004). Back-office
  functions in, for example, health, education and social security, will
  be attributed to the functional category from which they derive and
  not to general public services, but the general front-office/back-office
  distinction is important within government as a whole;
- the effects of a greater use of principal–agent organisational forms,
  with external or internal contracts (Lane, 2000, part III). Delivery
  systems dependent on the buying in of services are tending to grow,
  with effects that might include transparency of costings and more
  precise information on administration costs. Equally, contracted-out
  delivery may conceal the true size of the public sector. Contracting
  out is less likely to occur in core political functions (typified by resistance to privatised tax collection);

- our understanding of 'bureaucracy' in the Weberian sense of an introspective apparatus for the organisation of state authority, which would need to be supplemented by public employment numbers, a more accurate and accessible measure of the weight of public sector activity and its distribution between occupational groups, breaking down the monolith of the state and distinguishing the roles of officials at middle and lower levels (Page and Jenkins, 2005).

Because of its partly residual status, expenditure data cannot stand alone as evidence of the true costs of government. That structures our presentation in this chapter. In the first half of the chapter, we offer an analysis of COFOG data adjusted to obtain the best measure of 'state overhead' spending. This analysis, which adopts the same strategy of quantitative cross-national research as the other chapters in this volume, yields suggestive findings accounting for the observed variance in spending in terms of independent variables plausibly hypothesised as relevant explanatory factors. However, in the second part of the chapter, we move on to examine various other characteristics of government – the size of the core government wage bill, the extent of public employment in this area, the multiplicity of governmental units and the efficiency of tax collection – as important dimensions of the state overhead. We also examine some national data (for the United Kingdom, Australia and Canada) in order to illustrate some of the issues arising in the construction of these data. The cumulative message of these different analyses is that, while comparative analysis in this area of expenditure may not be able to achieve the same rigour as in some others, it does provide us with strong evidence that the core of the state – or what, in the terminology of the introduction to this volume, one might call the core of 'core' spending – is a very long way from disappearing.

4.2   EXPENDITURE CONFIGURATIONS

The source of the expenditure data used in this chapter is the 'general public services' category of the COFOG classification. COFOG's current flaws, the unsuitability of some of its categories for analytical purposes, and its reliance on national statistical interpretations of the correct attribution of expenditure, are especially pronounced in seeking to establish a reasonably accurate picture of the costs of government. Nevertheless, the general public services (GPS) categorisation offers us one of the few routinely provided cross-national metrics of the size of government available to us at the present time.

Table 4.1   The components of COFOG general public services

1. 'Public administration' components

011 Executive and legislative organs, financial and fiscal affairs, external
    affairs

0111 executive and legislative organs

including office of the chief executive at all levels of government – office of the
    monarch, governor general, president, prime minister, governor, mayor;
    legislative bodies at all levels of government; advisory, administrative and
    political staffs, libraries and other reference services and physical amenities
    attached to chief executive officers and legislatures

0112 financial and fiscal affairs

including administration of fiscal affairs and services, the inland revenue agency
    and the customs authorities; operation of the treasury or ministry of finance,
    the budget office, the accounting and auditing services

0113 External affairs

013 General services (including personnel, planning and statistical)

0131 General personnel services

0132 Overall planning and statistical services

0133 Other general services

including administration and operation of government-owned or occupied
    buildings, centralised supply, purchasing, computer, data processing and
    printing services; central motor vehicle pools

015 R&D general public services

016 General public services n.e.c.

including voter registration and holding of elections and referendums

2. Non-public administration components

012 Foreign economic aid

0121 Economic aid to developing countries and countries in transition

0122 Economic aid routed through international organisations

014 Basic research

017 Public debt transactions

018 Transfers of a general character between different levels of government

Source: International Monetary Fund, *Government Finance Statistics Manual 2001*,
Washington: International Monetary Fund, pp. 79–82.

The subheads of general public services expenditure are set out in Table
4.1, under the reference numbers of the classification originally set in 1993
and revised in 1999. Selected rubrics from the coding book indicate the kind
of expenditure we are talking about. Four of the GPS subheads are clearly
'public administration' and are listed first in Table 4.1, but four are not. As

the rubrics show, the detailed categories include a mixture of functions of varying cost and symbolism.

The general public services aggregate for 2002 ranges from a low of 3.0 of GDP in Ireland to a high of 10.0 per cent of GDP in the case of Belgium. Analytically, however, the category is of little use as it stands. For our purposes here, we have constructed a more restrictive definition of general public services which we call *state overhead spending*. To arrive at this category, we exclude 'public debt transactions' by subtracting debt interest, for which consistent international data are reported by the OECD. This is a highly variable indicator, ranging from highs of 6.4 per cent of GDP in Greece and 5.9 per cent in Belgium down to 1.3 per cent in Ireland and 0.3 per cent in Luxembourg. This spending on debt repayments reflects a legacy of past borrowing in order to fund spending, and is politically traded off against the whole range of functions and not just GPS. Debt interest is the topic of the penultimate chapter of this book. We also exclude foreign economic aid, which is a proxy for official development assistance as documented on a consistent long-term basis by the OECD's Development Assistance Committee to facilitate monitoring of the United Nations goal to raise overseas aid to 0.7 per cent of GDP. The only nations to have achieved this level are Norway, Denmark, Sweden, the Netherlands and Luxembourg, Denmark alone reaching the level of 1.0 per cent of GDP. Imbeau (1988) has analysed the determinants of such spending and demonstrated the strong influence of partisanship on foreign aid expenditure outcomes.

Greater problems arise with the other two non-public administration categories and the data are not available to separate them. Basic research evidently has little to do with public administration and is usually of an educational or industrial nature. Consolidated, unspecific intergovernmental transfers might end up being applied to the policy responsibilities of the lower level rather than being genuinely non-attributable to functional programmes, although we should not exaggerate the problem as most grants are directly or indirectly linked to a specific service and are netted out when reported in the appropriate functional category.

We must remember that the COFOG coding is an aid to allocation of spending and not a presumption that data will be broken down to the lowest classification. The categories are guides to attribution, not budget lines. In fact, even national statistics rarely provide us with this information. It is tantalising to think that, at the level of actual local spending, they do exist as accounted-for magnitudes and that this information is lost as the aggregates are reported upwards.

The total effect of these adjustments documented in Table 4.2 is that an average of 51 per cent of apparent GPS expenditure is removed, ranging

Table 4.2 *Reconciliation of OECD general public services data with 'state overhead' analytical definition, 2002*

Country	General public services (OECD) as percentage of GDP	Debt interest as percentage of GDP	Official aid as percentage of GDP	State overhead as percentage of GDP	State overhead as percentage of public expenditure
Sweden	9.2	3.3	0.8	5.1	8.7
Netherlands	8.2	2.9	0.8	4.5	9.4
Austria	7.7	3.3	0.3	4.1	8.2
Belgium	10.0	5.9	0.4	4.0	9.1
Luxembourg	4.9	0.3	0.7	3.9	9.0
France	7.1	2.9	0.4	3.8	7.2
Denmark	8.5	3.8	1.0	3.8	6.8
Finland	6.0	2.1	0.3	3.6	7.2
Italy	9.3	5.9	0.2	3.2	6.7
Greece	9.6	6.4	0.2	3.1	6.3
Germany	6.2	2.9	0.3	3.0	6.3
Portugal	6.3	3.1	0.3	2.9	6.4
Norway	5.0	1.8	0.9	2.3	4.9
UK	4.6	2.1	0.3	2.2	5.4
Spain	5.1	2.7	0.3	2.1	5.6
USA	5.0	2.9	0.1	2.0	5.4
Ireland	3.6	1.3	0.3	1.9	5.8

Source: OECD, *National Accounts of OECD countries: Vol. IV General Government Accounts 1992–2003* (Paris: OECD 2004) country tables I (debt interest) and IV; aid data from DAC database (www.oecd.org/dac).

from a high of 68 per cent for Greece to a low of 21 per cent for Luxembourg. 'State overhead' spending on our definition ranges from about 2 per cent to about 5 per cent of GDP, with Sweden and the Netherlands distinct outliers at the top end of the distribution. When expressed as a percentage of public expenditure, the Netherlands and Belgium manifest the highest levels of spending, with over 9 per cent. These aggregates undoubtedly include some non-public administration elements and statistical residuals. Nevertheless, they begin to approximate to a category of analytical value to set alongside the others discussed in this volume.

However, no secure long time-series is available. Oxley and Martin's pioneering efforts in the 1980s showed that 'general services' increased in the 1980s for five of the 11 countries they studied (US, Germany, the United Kingdom, Denmark and Norway) and decreased for five (Japan,

Table 4.3   *State overhead (general public services minus debt repayments and official development assistance) as a percentage of GDP, 1990–2002, by country rank 2002, Europe and USA*

Country	1990	1996	2002	Change 1996–2002
Sweden	n/a	4.5	5.1	0.6
Netherlands	n/a	3.5	4.5	1.0
Austria	n/a	5.0	4.1	−0.9
Belgium	0.7	3.1	4.0	0.9
Luxembourg	4.4	3.1	3.9	0.8
France	3.8	2.7	3.8	1.1
Denmark	3.1	3.3	3.8	0.5
Finland	3.0	3.0	3.6	0.6
Italy	2.4	2.3	3.2	0.9
Greece	n/a	2.9	3.1	0.2
Germany	3.5	2.9	3.0	0.1
Portugal	2.3	2.7	2.9	0.2
Norway	2.6	2.4	2.3	−0.1
UK	1.2	1.8	2.2	0.4
Spain	4.2	n/a	2.1	n/a
USA	2.0	1.8	2.0	0.2
Ireland	4.0	1.9	1.9	0
Mean		3.0	3.3	+0.3
Standard deviation		0.92	1.0	
Coefficient of variation		30.6	30.3	

Source: Calculated from OECD, *General Government Accounts 2004* country tables I (debt interest, GDP) and IV.4 (general public services, total public expenditure); 1990 information supplied by OECD; (Germany 1990 based on 1991 data); aid data from DAC database (www.oecd.org/dac).

Australia, Austria, Netherlands and Sweden, Finland remaining static) against a background of a decline in core spending (see Chapter 3 above, Appendix 3A). For the analysis in this chapter we go back to 1990, the initial year for which OECD has attempted a classification on present-day definitions.

Table 4.3 provides data using this analytical definition for 1990, 1996 and 2002, the latest generally available year. These data in a consistent form are available only for European countries and the United States. These are based on the 1993 COFOG general public services classification. The 1996 and 1990 data are progressively less reliable as they are based upon a reworking of the 1968 COFOG, but they are presented by OECD as a consistent classification. Several EU nations are not available for 1990, and Australia, Canada, Japan and New Zealand are not available on this consistent classification.

The average can be calculated meaningfully for 1996 and 2002. It shows an increase from 3.0 per cent to 3.3 per cent of GDP, a significant finding at time when greater precision was being introduced into the UN categories and should have resulted in the fuller attribution of expenditure into functional categories and out of this general residual one. This 10 per cent average increase in spending over just six years is scarcely indicative of the kind of retrenchment trajectory implied by the prevailing rhetoric of the need for countering the bloated and self-serving state. The stability of the coefficient of variation in Table 4.3 suggests that, unlike other categories of expenditure treated in this volume, there is little convergence in state overhead spending. Of the 17 countries featuring in the table, only two manifest expenditure decline between 1996 and 2002 and only Austria shows a cutback of any magnitude. In consequence, this is one area of spending in which a catch-up trajectory is not apparent. Reported GPS aggregates for 1990 for both Belgium and the United Kingdom are so heavily dominated by debt interest as to suggest that the apparently low state overhead figures are depressed by incomplete attribution of data.

If we arrange the data by families of nations (Scandinavian, continental European, Southern European, English-speaking) as in Table 4.4, we find a similar ranking for Scandinavian and continental European groups (noting the lack of data in some years and the exclusion throughout of Canada and Australia, discussed in greater detail below). Continental European countries figuring at the top of the distribution are closely followed by those of Scandinavia. Southern European countries (with reservations about data adequacy) average below the general mean and the English-speaking countries markedly below.

Table 4.4   State overhead, by families of nations

Family of nations	1990	1996	2002
Continental European	3.1*	3.4	3.9
Scandinavian	2.9*	3.3	3.7
Southern European	3.0*	2.6*	2.8*
English-speaking	2.4	1.8	2.0
Mean (as Table 4.3)		3.0	3.3

Note: * data missing for some countries.

Source: Table 4.3 arranged by families (as defined in Chapter 2).

4.3   ACCOUNTING FOR EXPENDITURE VARIATION

In what follows we explore five hypotheses that might account for this pattern of cross-national variation:

1. that state overhead expenditure is high as a share of GDP where total public expenditure is high, that countries with 'big government' also spend more on general services as an aspect of their extensive welfare state and public sector activities, with career structures for employees, proper personnel procedures, extensive support for elected officials, and a full capability to bring in the revenues required to sustain their public households;

2. that state overhead expenditure is a static overhead of government, required to maintain the executive, fiscal and parliamentary capacity of the state and so is relatively unrelated to the level of other expenditure categories and takes up a larger share of the expenditures of the small spenders;

3. that state overhead expenditure is related to the structure of government, with federal or devolved constitutions and the creation of some combination of multiple levels of government and small size of units all, arguably, positively linked to spending. In the standard account of the public expenditure literature the argument is that decentralization frustrates attempts to increase the size of government as a whole either as a consequence of jurisdictional competition between states and local authorities (Brennan and Buchanan, 1980) or a proliferation of veto points (Tsebelis, 2002). Within the present narrower focus, however, a plausible counter-hypothesis is that, in federal nations and those with a multiplicity of administrative units, the proliferation of jurisdictions leads directly to higher administrative costs;

4. that state overhead expenditure is related to the party composition of government, with leftist parties favouring bigger government and rightist parties opposed to spending that enhances the reach of government and state bureaucracies.

5. that state overhead expenditure is related to economic openness, as measured by trade and capital flows, either positively through a proliferation of state interventions designed to dampen the domestic effects of external vulnerability (Cameron, 1978; Katzenstein, 1985) or negatively through a 'race-to-the-bottom' in which the managerially most efficient nations win in international competition.

A simple preliminary test of these hypotheses is by means of bivariate analysis. Table 4.5 reports correlations between state overhead spending

Table 4.5   Bivariate tests of hypotheses accounting for levels and change in state overhead, 1996 to 2002

	1996	2002	Change: 1996–2002
Total outlays minus state overhead	0.63***	0.68***	0.23
Federalism index	0.29	0.04	−0.29
Imports plus exports	0.14	0.32	0.22
Left legacy	0.63***	0.47*	−0.22
1996 state overhead (Catch Up)			−0.24

Notes and sources: Correlations are Pearson's r. Significance levels: * = ≤0.1; ** = ≤0.05; *** = ≤0.01. Total outlays minus state overhead calculated from OECD, *Economic Outlook* database and Table 4.3 above. For levels, outlays figures are for the same year as the expenditure measure; for change, the outlays figure is for 1996. The Lijphart federalism index is invariant and is from Lijphart (1999: 313). Figures for imports plus exports as percentage of GDP are from Armingeon et al. (2004). For levels, figures are for the same year; for change, the beginning year. Left legacy the measure of long-term Social Democratic cabinet strength used in Castles' earlier chapter in this volume, with figures calculated from Armingeon et al. (2004) plus data for the 1950s from Castles (1998) and, for Luxembourg, from Woldendorp et al. (2000). Figures for 1996 state overhead from Table 4.3 above.

and non-GPS public expenditure, party composition of government (data on long-term Social Democratic cabinet strength), federalism as measured by Lijphart's index and imports plus exports as a proportion of GDP used here as elsewhere in this study as an indicator of the openness of the economy.

The bivariate findings reported in Table 4.5 demonstrate that two of these variables are strongly associated with observed outcomes: the general level of government expenditure other than state overhead spending and long-term Social Democratic incumbency. The weakness of the reported relationships with change in spending is not surprising given the rounding of the small magnitudes involved, although it is at least worth noting that the 1996 to 2002 trend is in the negative and convergent direction that might be expected on the basis of Chapter 2's earlier aggregate analysis of core spending.

Table 4.5 demonstrates the influence of both total outlays and Left partisan incumbency, but these are hardly independent factors given the historical association of big government in the wider sense with Left government. To disentangle this relationship and to control for the effects of the other hypothesised variables, we need to employ multivariate analysis. Table 4.6 below shows that total outlays is substantially the best predictor in both 1996 and 2002 (both significant at the 0.01 threshold), with federalism significant at the 0.05 level in 1996 and at the 0.1 level in 2002.

Table 4.6   *Regression model of state overhead expenditure as a percentage*
              of GDP, 1996 and 2000

	1996	2002
Intercept	−2.05*	−4.36***
Total outlays minus state overhead	0.09***	0.14***
Lijphart's federalism index	0.27**	0.18***
Imports plus exports as per cent GDP	0.01*	0.01*
Adj. R²	0.52	0.72

Notes and sources: As for Table 4.5. Figures are unstandardised regression coefficients.

A positive international trade effect achieving the 0.1 level of significance in 1996 becomes stronger in 2002 with significance at the 0.05 level. The partisan variable, despite its significance in bivariate tests, ceases to be significant in models controlling for the impact of prior outlays.

The way that trade openness might lead to a higher level of state overhead needs amplification, given that the linkages between external vulnerability and the costs of government are far from transparent. In the analysis here, the cases driving the positive relationship are Belgium, the Netherlands and, to a lesser extent, Austria. These countries are not just standardised political entities but have complex and distinctive histories: the Netherlands' pillarised structure of multiple delivery mechanisms, Belgium's strong regions taking on a greater weight than the federal government (with state overhead spending rising from 3.1 per cent of GDP in 1996 to 4.0 per cent in 2002) and Austria's explicit federalism, with numerous regions in a small population. It may be because of their economic openness, and resultant wealth, that these countries can assert their political identity in a full texture of state structures. If so, this suggests that, in respect of this category of spending at least, the trade openness variable may serve as a proxy for a more fundamental underlying factor, perhaps most plausibly described as exposure to external pressure on political autonomy.

The other findings of our multivariate analysis provide evidence against two main lines of argument in the literature. The first is that that federalism is invariably a constraint on public spending as a result either of jurisdictional competition or of veto group restraints. Obinger, Leibfried and Castles (2005) have questioned this conclusion in respect of social expenditure development on the grounds that federalism may be contextually influenced by the stage of welfare state development already achieved. Our finding suggests that different categories of expenditure may respond quite differently to federal decentralisation and that in the case of state overhead spending the influence may even be significantly positive.

This is highly plausible. The regional or intermediate level developed in the mid-twentieth century in response to the demands of political management (evident in, for example, Germany, France, Italy, Spain and the United Kingdom). Some nations (the United States, Australia, Canada and Germany) have explicitly federal constitutions in which the federal components have full rights to order their own public management, and commonalities of practice emerge through policy learning and interchange, not central rules. The right to construct a public service is a basic part of the political development of a devolved territory, especially potent where there is some combination of a territory in political opposition to the national-level government (often the case in Canada, Australia and Germany); where language issues are involved (Québec, Flanders, Catalonia, Wales); and where a region is economically underdeveloped and relies on public sector job opportunities to assist its labour market (the eastern German Länder, Northern Ireland) (McEwen and Moreno, 2005).

Jurisdictions may compete with each other for staff, be vulnerable to pressure from organised labour or clientelistic local interests, and fail to learn best practice from one another. They may duplicate services and lack economies of scale. The difficulty for public debate is to distinguish the unavoidable costs of running a multijurisdictional system from the sub-optimalities of small scale. Voluntary mergers of jurisdictions (for example in major urban areas in the United States) are difficult to achieve; the possibility of incorporation of urban areas into new cities distinct from the major 'downtown', a common phenomenon in the United States, is no less strong a political force than the impetus to consolidate urban agglomerations for planning and transport reasons. Mergers of intermediate units are controversial even when they might make sense for public management: in Germany, Brandenburg and Berlin voted against merger and the city-states of Hamburg and Bremen persist.

The second argument is that 'globalisation', the growing economic interdependence of modern states brought about by increased trade and capital flows, is placing strong downward pressure on public expenditure (for a summary of this argument, see Castles, 2004). It seems reasonable to suppose that these pressures will have their greatest impact in the areas of social and economic policy most directly related to labour costs. Nevertheless, the logic of the argument suggests a strong probability that, if such pressures exist, they are likely to have an impact on politically visible spending in all areas and especially where there are connotations of waste. State overhead spending meets both of these criteria. However, the evidence in Table 4.6 is quite decisive that spending is not negatively affected by economic openness. On the contrary, it would appear that it is the positive assertion of state structures that dominates over any attempts to weaken them in the name of competitiveness.

4.4 ALTERNATIVE INDICATORS

The analysis so far suggests that high state overhead expenditure is primarily an aspect of high public expenditure, with political decentralisation and economic openness also significant variables. Given the residual nature of the data we are working with, this is probably as far as we can go using strictly quantitative analysis. It is, however, worth briefly examining some alternative indicators of the state overhead whose characteristics may contribute to our understanding of why the 'core' of the core is bigger in some countries than others. A clue to the persistence and even the enhancement of high levels of state overhead spending may lie in this area's relative immunity to the challenges of privatisation and marketisation that have applied to public employees in social and economic functions over recent decades. Literature on public management reform stresses difficulties and resistances within national political contexts as much as substantive changes (Peters and Savoie, 1998; Pollitt and Bouckaert, 2000; Butcher and Massey, 2003). Here, we argue that factors such as a concentration of the government wage bill on state overhead employees, high levels of employment in state overhead services, large numbers of administrative units and inefficient tax mechanisms are evidence of such resistances and hence contribute, directly or indirectly, to the levels of state overhead spending we have observed.

4.4.1 The State Overhead Wage Bill

A first approach may come from isolating public expenditure paid as compensation of employees and assessing the share of general public services within that (available for 1996 and 2002, but generally not for 1990). As the difference between the OECD definition of GPS and our state overhead category is represented mainly by transfers and interest payments, not by consumption expenditure, this provides a measure of government expenditure on its own employees that cannot be allocated to functional programmes. The indicator (Table 4.7) requires caution because of varying patterns of service delivery through direct employment, but it does show an upward trend between 1996 and 2002, the average rising from 12.7 per cent to 13.8 per cent. The Nordic countries are in the bottom half of the table, behind the United Kingdom. The Continental European family is decisively at the top of the rankings, showing that its directly compensated

Table 4.7   General public services spending on compensation of employees as a percentage of total general government expenditure on compensation of employees, 1996 and 2002

Country	1996	2002
France	21.5	22.8
Luxembourg	19.0	22.2
Austria	16.9	19.3
Netherlands	17.8	17.4
Greece	19.2	17.1
Belgium	17.8	17.0
Germany	16.6	16.4
UK	10.5	11.8
Italy	10.9	11.7
Sweden	10.4	10.7
Finland	8.4	9.7
Spain	n/a	9.4
Norway	6.9	9.1
Denmark	7.4	7.3
Ireland	7.5	6.9
Average of EU 15 + Norway	12.7	13.8

Source: OECD as Table 4.3, country tables IV.

government employees are concentrated in general, non-functional groups. Put another way, over a fifth of the money paid to government employees in France cannot be attributed to a service delivery category, but only a tenth in Sweden.

4.4.2   State Overhead Employment

A further source of data concerning the size and presence of the public sector comes from public employment data. These are in a worse state comparatively than are public expenditure data because of uncertainties about the status of the many employees who are wholly dependent on the public sector but may titularly have a status as employees of the private or voluntary sectors, or as self-employed. There is still no comprehensive international source. Rose (1985), with a limited range of countries and time-points, is still useful as a source on magnitudes and trends. Hogwood and Peters have been conducting a major survey funded by the United Kingdom Economic and Social Research Council, covering the United States, the United Kingdom, Canada, Australia, New Zealand, Germany,

France, Spain, Denmark and Sweden, the final results of which are still awaited (Hogwood, 2005).

International employment data collected by the OECD and reported in Labour Force Statistics do not include any comprehensive breakdown by sector. The category of 'public administration and defence', including employees of compulsory social security schemes, is of little use for assessing public employment as a whole, but for the purpose of the present discussion it is a useful approximation of the central state (Table 4.8). It might be thought that civilian defence employment, on a long-term downward track, would severely distort these figures, but they now represent too small a share of the total category (in the case of the United Kingdom less than

Table 4.8   *Employment in public administration, defence and compulsory social security as a percentage of the civilian labour force, 1990–2002*

Country	1990	1996	2002
EU 15 + Norway			
France	8.74	9.58	8.56
Italy	n/a	10.55	7.62
Greece	n/a	13.05	7.37
Germany	8.15[1]	9.12	7.33
Netherlands	n/a	7.49	6.52
Belgium	n/a	8.09	6.50[2]
UK	6.61	6.47	6.32
Portugal	8.88	8.67	5.93
Spain	6.85	8.07	5.72
Sweden	n/a	5.85	5.68
Austria	n/a	6.82	5.67
Norway	n/a	6.09	5.64
Luxembourg	n/a	5.82	5.03
Denmark	n/a	5.67	4.88
Ireland	n/a	6.32	4.70
Finland	5.70	5.95	4.57
Average		7.73	6.13
Other English-speaking:			
Australia	5.51	6.43	6.84
Canada	5.16	6.72	7.08
New Zealand	4.45	6.73	7.64

Notes and source: [1] Figure refers to 1991; [2] Figure refers to 1999; OECD, *Labour Force Statistics, 2004*, country table 5.

5 per cent) to do so. Indeed. SIPRI data show that between 1996 and 2002 expenditure on defence personnel by NATO European members held constant in real terms (SIPRI, 2003, appendix 10B).

Data for 2002 show that France is again a considerable outlier, with Italy, Greece and Germany also in a group ahead of the rest. The high-spending Nordic countries cluster at the lower end of the table, suggesting that their large public sectors are oriented towards service delivery, not general public administration. The time-series data show a fall in the percentage in every country between 1996 and 2002 (1990 data are fragmentary, but suggest this is not a long-term trend). The reason for this appears to be a slow rate of growth in public administration numbers at a time of rapid expansion of employment in the economy as a whole. Given that the movement in state overhead expenditure is in the opposite direction, we can suggest that the cost drivers do not take the form of an expansion of numbers of bureaucrats as a share of the workforce (Table 4.8) but may represent increasing relative rewards to those employees (Table 4.7).

4.4.3 Multiple Administrative Units

We can see from the data on compensation and employment that France is at the top for both. Table 4.9 provides a clue to the reasons for this: France

Table 4.9 Western European countries by size and number of local units

Country	Average population of lowest tier	Number of authorities, all tiers
France	1 491	36 880
Greece	1 803	5 878
Portugal	2 352	4 526
Netherlands	2 723	584
Spain	4 997	8 149
Italy	7 182	8 215
Germany	7 900	16 514
Norway	9 000	458
Belgium	11 000	601
Finland	11 206	455
Denmark	18 000	289
Sweden	33 000	333
Ireland	36 100	114
UK	137 000	472

Source: Council of Europe data quoted by Peter John, *Local Governance in Western Europe* (Sage, 2001), Table 2.1.

stands out for its large number of units of government and their small average size, and, as with the pattern of government compensation, the continental European countries (densely populated Belgium apart) are ahead of the Nordic countries, with the United Kingdom and Ireland at the bottom of the distribution. The model of the French commune in which even the smallest town has its *mairie*, its physically rooted local public jurisdiction, is the most characteristic example of a phenomenon possible even when the structure of government itself is neither federal nor fragmented. In France's case, it is one aspect of a general resistance to new public management reforms that stands out in a comparative context (Rhodes and Weller, 2003, p. 30).

4.4.4 Efficiency in Tax Collection

If there is one area which is unambiguously large and unequivocally within the state overhead area of spending, it is tax collection. It is small in relation to the tax take (for instance, United Kingdom government data show that the cost of collection of Inland Revenue taxes in 2004–05 was 0.97 per cent of receipts (HM Revenue and Customs, 2005, annex F, table 1)), but the staff presence is large: the United Kingdom data reported later show that HM Revenue and Customs represent nearly 90 per cent of the central government staff that appear to fall in the state overhead category, and many local staff will also be involved in revenue collection.

The ability to tax is a key principle of the modern state and a key indicator of the efficiency of the state apparatus. The trend of fiscal policy over time is a move from reliance on a range of specific duties (customs levies, stamp duties, taxes on alcohol and tobacco, specific taxes on luxuries) to general taxes on income and expenditure (income tax and value added tax). The impact of these taxes is generalized throughout the population and the economy, and collection becomes semi-automatic through payrolls and turnover. International variations in expenditure on tax collection can be accounted for by variables such as the relative complexity of tax codes, arrangements for central and local collection, separation of income taxes and social security contributions, the degree of review of individual cases and the presence or tolerance of a 'black economy' of undeclared activity. High expenditure on tax collection might in principle pay for itself through the efficiency of revenue collection, but might equally represent an inefficient process. OECD data show that expenditure on information technology as a share of total administration costs for taxation is under 10 per cent in Luxembourg, Portugal, Greece, Belgium, France and Austria and over 15 per cent in Australia, Denmark, the Netherlands, Norway, Spain, the United Kingdom and the United States (OECD, 2005, Table 31). The total administration costs implicit in these data, shown in Table 4.10 below,

Table 4.10   Administration costs of tax collection (latest year) as a percentage of GDP, 2002

Country	Tax administration	State overhead total
Belgium	0.59	4.0
Netherlands	0.55	4.5
Portugal	0.43	2.9
Sweden	0.32	5.1
France	0.28	3.8
Ireland	0.27	1.9
Austria	0.25	4.1
Denmark	0.24	3.8
Finland	0.22	3.6
Italy	0.18	3.2
United States	0.06	2.0
Spain	0.05	2.1

Source: Calculated from OECD, *Survey of Trends in Taxpayer Service Delivery Using New Technology* (Forum on Tax Administration report, February 2005), Table 31. United Kingdom and Greece not available. State overhead total as Table 4.2.

suggest wide international variation – and very probably incomplete data reporting – and expenditure on this component of nearly 15 per cent of the GPS total in the Belgian and Irish cases.

The data are fragmentary because we lack consistent cross-national information on the cost of the tax collection. But it seems clear that the administration of taxation is the single most important component of an analytically defined state overhead category and that new structures of tax policy and tax collection offer many countries the possibility of performing this function more efficiently. In the long run, that might eventually imply a trend towards reduced state overhead spending.

4.5   PERSPECTIVES FROM NATIONAL DATA

It would be possible to pursue the data from national statistics in the case of any of the countries included in the analysis of this chapter and this may be the next stage of research on this topic. This section presents information on the United Kingdom, Canada and Australia as English-speaking countries with comparable systems of government. The United Kingdom is of particular interest as a large country with comprehensive public expenditure data covering all levels of government that is used for planning as well as for statistical purposes. Canada and Australia have the value of not being included in the OECD data set because they do not supply data in the COFOG structure required. Data concerning their spending, therefore, provides information additional to that in our earlier analysis.

4.5.1 Comprehensive State Overhead Data: The United Kingdom

The United Kingdom Treasury's definition of 'total managed expenditure' includes spending by devolved administrations and local government and is set for three years ahead in annual Spending Reviews. It also provides data on administrative expenditure, which, since 2004, has attempted to exclude front-line activities. The Treasury has published a reconciliation of its own categories with COFOG (HM Treasury, 2005a) that shows that it includes EU transactions in the data it supplies internationally. Table 4.11, comparing international data for 2002 and United Kingdom data for the (April–March) financial year 2002–03 shows that about half of the apparent expenditure on general public services disappears into international services and EU funding (receipts from the EU budget to fund EU programmes in the United Kingdom, and the United Kingdom's contribution to the EU, here counted as two expenditure streams not offset against each other).

Approaching the United Kingdom data from the perspective of departments and agencies, data from 2003–04 in Table 4.12 show that the central departments amount to about one-third of the total administration budget,

Table 4.11   United Kingdom general public services data from international and national statistics (£m)

Item	Expenditure
From OECD data, 2002	
COFOG General public services	43 513
debt interest	21 457
State overhead plus aid	22 056
From United Kingdom national data, 2002–03	
Public and common services	11 167
International services	4 721
EU contribution net of abatement and collection	2 276
EU receipts	3 424
Total	21 588

Source: OECD as Table 4.2; HM Treasury, *Public Expenditure Statistical Analyses 2005* (London: The Stationery Office, Cm 6521), Table 3.6.

Table 4.12   *Administration costs of United Kingdom departments, 2003–04*

Department	Expenditure (£m)	Staff ('000s)
Within general public services		
Chancellor of the Exchequer's Departments	4396	108.7
Security and Intelligence Agencies	544	4.5
Other Cabinet Office	112	2.1
Foreign and Commonwealth Office	716	6.0
International Development	197	1.8
Total	5965	123.1
Outside general public services		
Administration costs of other agencies	9182	309.1
Defence civilian staff	2461	91.4

Source: HM Treasury, *Public Expenditure Statistical Analyses 2005*, Table 5.1; Cabinet Office database of Civil Service Staffing, April 2004 (full-time equivalents).

about half of which is pay-related costs. They also employ about 20 per cent of civil servants.

When it comes to cuts in administration budgets, the centre tends to spare itself. Proposals announced in July 2004 to run through to 2008 embodied increases in budgets for the diplomatic and security and stability for central departments, but included cuts in most other departments (by 4.5 per cent in money terms). The Treasury's core staff numbers rose from 1020 in 2001 to 1220 in 2003, but are set to fall to 1050 by 2008 (HM Treasury, 2005b, annex B, table 6). This is trivial when set against the Chancellor's other main department, HM Revenue and Customs, which employed a total of 100 000 in 2004 and set to lose a net 13 000 posts by 2008 (HM Treasury, 2004, Table 2.2). This is a microcosm of the whole issue: government's desire for expansion of its central capacity, the intermittent desire to appear frugal, the importance of tax collection within state overhead spending, and the small scale of the bureaucracy within government as a whole.

4.5.2   Missing Cases: Canada and Australia

We noted earlier that some countries are missing from the OECD data set, notably Japan, Australia and Canada. As pointed out in the previous chapter, Japan's data run into difficulties over the attribution of debt interest. The latter two countries have good national statistics that compare

Table 4.13   *Canada general government services as a percentage of total*
              expenditure

Level of government	1999–00	2000–01	2001–02	2002–03	2003–04
Total	3.4	3.8	3.6	3.6	3.4
Federal	3.3	4.7	3.9	4.1	3.7
Provincial	1.7	1.6	1.7	1.7	1.6

Source: Statistics Canada, *Public Sector Statistics*, Table 2.3; the combined definitions of
the three functions of the Financial Management System, i.e. 11.01 Executive and
Legislative + 11.02 General Administration + 11.99 Other General Government Services
would be similar to the combined definitions of the four COFOG sub-functions: 70111
executive + legislative organs + 70112 financial and fiscal affairs + 7013 general services
+ 7016 general public services n.e.c. The main exception to this would be the building
maintenance and central computer services expenditures which in the FMS are distributed
across other functions' (information from Terry Moore, Statistics Canada).

favourably with the highest international standards, and the reasons for not
supplying data lie in these countries' scrupulousness concerning the treat-
ment of the general and overhead categories. But we can examine data from
national sources. The Canadian government's Financial Management
System is not aligned precisely with COFOG and, hence, Canadian data
are not reported in Table 4.2 above. The omissions are foreign economic aid
and intergovernmental transfers. The aggregate Canadian general government services figure (Table 4.13) is a long way short of any of the other
countries. If we add in foreign affairs and international assistance and
research establishments, the figure for this 'general public services equivalent' comes to 4.3 per cent of general government expenditure in 2002–03,
again lower than that of any other country.

    Australia is another country that does not report its data in a COFOG-
compatible form; it includes superannuation benefits, which should go
under COFOG's social protection heading as public sector occupational
pensions, and most data are supplied to national statisticians under the
heading 'general public services not elsewhere classified' (information from
Robert Bourke, Australian Bureau of Statistics).

    The overall picture (Table 4.14) is of a low share of general public services
in government outlays, comparable to the lowest five countries reported
above (Norway, the United Kingdom, Spain, the United States and
Ireland). As the Australian general public services category includes general
research and foreign economic aid (according to OECD data, about 0.25 per
cent of GDP) as well as the usual central services, Australia may have the
lowest level of spending of all on our definition of GPS. The one comparable piece of data we have is the GPS compensation from the source used in

Table 4.14   *Australia general public services as per cent of total expenditure*

Level of government	2001–02	2002–03	2003–04
Total	6.2	6.0	6.1
Commonwealth	5.0	5.4	4.9
State and local	6.4	5.3	6.4
Total as per cent of GDP	2.2	2.1	2.4

Source: *General Financial Statistics Australia 2003–04* (Canberra: Australian Bureau of Statistics), expenses by selected programmes; information from Robert Bourke, Australian Bureau of Statistics.

Table 4.7 above. Australia's figure of 11.2 per cent for 2002 is again at the lower end of the scale, though it exceeds a number of European, and especially Nordic, countries.

Summarising these single-country data, we find Canada and Australia, the most prominent omissions from the OECD data, are, on the evidence of national statistics, likely to confirm the pattern of low state overhead spending in English-speaking countries. This has implications for our earlier analysis, since Canada and Australia, as notable instances of federal government, challenge the positive relationship between federalism and state overhead spending located in our multivariate analysis. We also find in the United Kingdom data suggestions that the analytical core of state overhead spending, in the sense of the costs of government not functionally attributable, may be much smaller than the COFOG-derived figure.

4.6   CONCLUSION

The conceptual construct that we are seeking to identify is clear: expenditure on general public services that cannot be allocated to any functional category and is the overhead of government and the cost of democratic institutions and the core executive of the state. Getting to these data in a meaningful way that would allow us to do statistical manipulations of them with confidence is more difficult, but we can refine the international classification of general public services to produce a usable analytical definition of state overhead spending. When analysed, the size of the rest of public spending and lesser contributions from federalism and economic openness offer a moderately successful and coherent account of variation amongst countries.

The disappearing state?

Table 4.15   Rankings for EU15 and Norway on various indicators

Country	State overhead (% GDP)[1]	State overhead (% public expenditure)[1]	GPS share of government compensation[2]	Public administration employment[3]	Small units[4]
Sweden	1	4	11	10	12
Netherlands	2	1	4	5	4
Austria	3	5	3	11	n/a
Belgium	4	2	6	6	9
Luxembourg	5	3	2	13	n/a
France	6	6	1	1	1
Denmark	7	8	15	14	13
Finland	8	7	6	6	9
Italy	9	9	10	2	6
Greece	10	12	5	3	2
Germany	11	11	7	4	7
Portugal	12	10	8	8	3
Norway	13	16	14	12	8
UK	14	15	9	7	14
Spain	15	14	13	9	5
Ireland	16	13	16	15	13

Sources: [1] Table 4.2, [2] Table 4.7, [3] Table 4.8, [4] Table 4.9.

Summing up the various data presented here, we can set out rank orders on various indicators (Table 4.15). State overhead spending within GDP is the basic scale on which Sweden ranks ahead of several continental European countries. State overhead spending measured as a percentage of public expenditure pulls down some of the rich, high-spending European countries and places Norway at the bottom of the scale, the only country to contain such spending to under 5 per cent of public expenditure. GPS compensation of employees within total compensation is a useful variable that pushes continental European countries up the ranking, a pattern rein-forced by the data on employment in public administration. The small size of units may provide an explanation of variation under this heading. The United Kingdom and Ireland rank as low spenders and seem to run their central states cheaply and with a small number of government units.

We can tentatively suggest three lines of interpretation of these varia-tions. The most important is the *high public expenditure effect*. Where coun-tries are high spenders generally, their general public services are also high as a consequence of an expensive and institutionalized public sector. Correlation and regression analysis identified this as the main driver of expenditure. This is in some ways a surprising finding, as it seems to diminish the effect of economies of scale on both the expenditure and the revenue side as public sectors expand.

We may also observe an *exposed country effect*. As we saw, globalised trade may be one source of such exposure, and the response it elicits tends to lead to high rather than low state overhead spending. Such effects are unlikely to be massive. All systems require a local presence, and a small country with an integrated system can contain the costs of government. The symbols of statehood – the head of state apparatus and the diplomatic presence – are never going to be large enough to have much impact on aggregate statistics dominated by administrative staff and tax collectors.

A counterbalancing variable is *fragmented government*. Where there are large numbers of units, economies of scale are not possible. This is not just a matter of the number of levels of government, but of the consolidation of local units into larger ones. A large national state may find it necessary for political reasons to perpetuate a multiplicity of intermediate and local jurisdictions. France is the paradoxical example of the European country with the greatest tradition of centralization, but also the greatest proliferation of local units. France is also in the lead in the concentration of government employee compensation falling within the general public services category.

These interpretations must be viewed against a background of continuing caution about the data we currently deploy in this area of analysis. As the examination of three individual countries has shown, it is surprisingly difficult to disaggregate the figures that national statistical administrations supply to OECD as the data are statistical artefacts and not planning totals of expenditure. The United Kingdom is better than most because it plans its public expenditure comprehensively, but its own data show a core of public and common services only half of the GPS figure it reports internationally. There is a general difficulty in drawing the boundary between expenditure that is, or is not, functionally attributable. The COFOG classification adds a further difficulty of requiring research and intergovernmental transfers to be allocated according to their generality. It can also provide a 'data drop' for categories that national statistical classification wish to retain as separate budgetary headings (like the EU contribution in the United Kingdom). When the problem of including data from all parts of general government is also taken into account, the task becomes a serious challenge to the skill and professionalism of national statistical agencies.

This said, it is clear that state overhead expenditure is a category of great theoretical interest in which the availability of data is increasing and its comparability improving. These data allow us to address questions that are often different from those raised within functional service categories. Government is both a provider of services and a source of a distinctive kind of economic activity, the general, non-functional political management of a territory. The privatisation, contracting out and globalisation of these services is partly an expression of the state's wish to pluralise provision of the essential functions for which it has hitherto been seen as responsible. With state overhead spending, the stakes are different. The activities may not be visible to the public and may be protected by legal tenure rights or by public service-wide trade unions able to deploy the industrial power of their more visible members. We do not have a general pattern of explanation of why high or low state overhead spending will be politically resisted or tolerated.

The politics of state overhead are not expenditure-driven. There is no clear category that is both expensive and the subject of regular political debate; salient matters like the cost of an official residence or aircraft are not the expensive ones. In general, central and general staff may represent good value to public policy. Good statistics and financial information are at the heart of good governance. The 'challenge' function of central ministries to functional bureaucratic interests requires a structure to shadow functional activities; typically, budget agencies and heads of government offices will have small teams responsible for each function whose capability would benefit from reinforcement (Wanna, Jensen and de Vries, 2003). Allowing agencies to run their own personnel and property management functions may fit in with rhetoric of decentralisation and reduce numbers at the centre, but it can lead to wasteful duplication and competition. An efficient tax collection agency can pay for itself through the revenues it brings in and the reduction it can effect in the size of the black economy. Even set against drives to 'cut bureaucracy', there is enough positive dynamics behind state overhead expenditure to explain its recent trajectory.

In the admittedly short period of time for which COFOG data are available, we have found no general tendency for state overhead expenditure to decline. In its general, non-functional operations, there is no evidence that the state is disappearing. The continuing refinement of the COFOG system should lead to the fuller attribution of expenditure to functional categories and to a fall in general public services as the residual. In this context, the rise in the state overhead budget between 1996 and 2002 is noteworthy and may be a sign of higher, politically mandated spending at the heart of government, as problems such as territorial management and improved service delivery are addressed by an input of resources. Challenges to public sector costs and efficiency will hit this sector last of all, for they are the institutionalized challengers of the rest of the government operation. The continental European and Scandinavian families of nations remain bigger spenders than the countries of Southern Europe, and the English-speaking countries are the lowest spenders of all. Within state overhead spending, we are likely to find the large presence of tax collection worthy of further comparative investigation. Current trends to multi-level government and a global economy have not, as far as we can tell, caused any decline in the share of state overhead expenditure in the economy. At its heart, the state looks after itself.

ACKNOWLEDGEMENTS

Frank Castles was most helpful in his editorial advice and his assistance with the multivariate analysis. Paul Norris's contribution to the refinement of COFOG data and his advice on statistical methods were also of major benefit to the chapter.

REFERENCES

Armingeon, K., P. Leimgruber, M. Beyeler and S. Menegale (2004), 'Comparative political data set 1960–2002', Institute of Political Science, University of Berne.

Brennan, G. and J.M. Buchanan (1980), *The Power to Tax: Analytical Foundations of a Fiscal Constitution*, Cambridge: Cambridge University Press.

Butcher, T. and A. Massey (eds) (2003), *Modernising Civil Services*, Cheltenham, UK and Northampton, MA, USA: Edward Elgar.

Cameron, D. (1978), 'The expansion of political economy: a comparative analysis', *American Political Science Review*, **72** (4), 1243–61.

Castles, F. (1998), *Comparative Public Policy: Patterns of Post-war Transformation*, Cheltenham, UK and Northampton, MA, USA: Edward Elgar.

Castles, F.G. (2004), *The Future of the Welfare State*, Oxford: Oxford University Press.

Gershon, P. (2004), *Releasing Resources to the Front Line: Independent Review of Public Sector Efficiency*, London: HM Treasury.

HM Revenue and Customs (2005), *Annual Report 2004-05*, London: The Stationery Office, Cm 6691.

HM Treasury (2004), *2004 Spending Review: New Public Spending Plans 2005–08*, London: The Stationery Office, Cm 6237.

HM Treasury (2005a), *Guide to HM Treasury Functional Analyses* (http://www.hm-treasury.gov.uk/economic_data_and_tools/finance_spending_statistics/pes_function/function.cfm).

HM Treasury (2005b), *HM Treasury Departmental Report*, London: The Stationery Office. Cm 6540.

Hogwood, B.W. (2005), *Public Employment as a Lens on Cross-National Learning* (ESRC Full Report of Research Findings and Activities) (www.esrc.ac.uk).

Imbeau, L.M. (1988), 'Aid and ideology', *European Journal of Political Research*, **16** (1), 3–28.

Katzenstein, P. (1985), *Small States in World Markets*, Ithaca: Cornell University Press.

Lane, J.E. (2000), *New Public Management*, London: Sage.

Lijphart, A. (1999), *Patterns of Democracy; Government Forms and Performance in Thirty-Six Countries*, New Haven: Yale University Press.

McEwen, N. and L. Moreno (eds) (2005), *The Territorial Politics of Welfare*, London: Routledge.

Obinger, H., S. Leibfried and F.G. Castles (eds) (2005), *Federalism and the Welfare State*, Cambridge: Cambridge University Press.

OECD (2005), 'Survey of trends in taxpayer service delivery using new technology' (Forum on Tax Administration report), February.

Page, E.C. and B. Jenkins (2005), *Policy Bureaucracy: Government with a Cast of Thousands*, Oxford: Oxford University Press.

Peters, B.G. and D.J. Savoie (eds) (1998), *Taking Stock: Assessing Public Sector Reforms*, Montreal: McGill-Queen's University Press.

Pollitt, C. and G. Bouckaert (2000), *Public Management Reform: A Comparative Analysis*, Oxford: Oxford University Press.

Rhodes, R.A.W. and P. Weller (2003), 'Localism and exceptionalism: comparing public sector reforms in European and Westminster systems', in T. Butcher and A. Massey (eds), *Modernising Civil Services*, Cheltenham, UK and Northampton, MA, USA: Edward Elgar.

Rose, R. (1985), *Public Employment in Western Nations*, Cambridge: Cambridge University Press.

SIPRI (2003), *SIPRI Yearbook 2003*, Oxford: Oxford University Press.

Tsebelis, G. (2002), *Veto Players: How Political Institutions Work*, Princeton: Princeton University Press.

Wanna, J., L. Jensen and J. de Vries (eds) (2003), *Controlling Public Expenditure*, Cheltenham, UK and Northampton, MA, USA: Edward Elgar.

Woldendorp, J., H. Keman and I. Budge (2004), *Party Government in 48 Democracies (1945–1998)*, Dordrecht: Kluwer Academic Publishers.

5. Sinking budgets and ballooning prices: recent developments connected to military spending

Thomas R. Cusack

5.1 INTRODUCTION

Traditionally, the military was one of the major financial commitments of the state. Such relative priority has diminished with the passage of time and, while the Cold War that occupied so much of the last half of the twentieth century drew large amounts of monies into military budgets as states responded to perceived external threats, its passage has generally brought about a widespread retreat. In many Western countries, fewer and fewer resources are devoted to the national defence function. The twentieth century and particularly its latter half also increasingly came to be marked by an extensive rise in the relative prices of military capital. With declining levels of financial commitment and rising costs in weapons systems, the military forces in many of the Western countries have become increasingly hollow.

5.2 THE EVOLUTION OF MILITARY EXPENDITURE

Unlike many other functions of government, the availability of data on military spending generally can be characterised as being unproblematic. This is not to say that there are no difficulties or disputes; rather, it is to say that at least in terms of the Western nations there is fairly widespread acceptance of at least one source, namely the Stockholm International Peace Research Institute's publication (*SIPRI Yearbook: Armaments, Disarmament and International Security*). SIPRI has made publicly available a fairly comprehensive database for the post-World War II era. The SIPRI volume has been published annually since 1970 and provides comparable and continuous annual military expenditure series (in local currency, US constant price dollars, and as a share of GDP) for most countries, going back as far as 1950. Serious problems and disputes were common during the Cold War with regard to the military outlays of the centrally planned economies (see Cusack and Ward, 1981) and the issue of military spending levels in the People's Republic of China remains contentious.

Included within SIPRI's measure of military spending are four major categories of current and capital outlays, for (1) the armed forces along with peacekeeping forces; (2) the defence bureaucracy (and other agencies engaged in military activities); (3) paramilitary forces; and (4) military space activities. SIPRI's definition is based on the NATO approach. It does exclude three things that some would argue should be included; these are outlays on civil defence, payment to military veterans, and servicing of war debt. All in all, SIPRI probably is still the most respected source on military spending for purposes of cross-national comparisons.[1]

Governments' control over national economic resources sharply expanded throughout the West over the last century or so. Whereas total government spending accounted on average for less than 10 per cent of GDP in 1880, this figure rose to about 25 per cent by 1940.[2] Dramatic growth occurred after World War II in both the private and public sectors. However the pace of the latter far outstripped the former. Among the OECD countries, in the typical state, close to 46 per cent of all national product was going to government spending by the end of the twentieth century.

While military spending (and the associated debt repayment outlays arising out of war involvement) once constituted an overwhelming share of the total government household, it has receded in relative importance during modern times. At the end of the nineteenth century, the average military burden on the economy was somewhere around 2 to 3 per cent of GDP; with direct military spending constituting about a quarter of total government outlays. The World Wars of the twentieth century were clearly major drains on national economies. Take World War II, for example. By 1943, military outlays constituted huge burdens on both the Axis and Allied Powers' economies. Within the Axis, 70 per cent of German GDP, 21 per cent of Italian GDP and 43 per cent of Japanese GDP went into the war effort. Among the Allies, Britain's outlays accounted for 55 per cent of its net national expenditure and America's stood at 42 per cent of its GNP (figures from Harrison, 1998, p. 21).

The Cold War was witness to inordinately high defence burdens. These relative shares, however, steadily declined over time and with the passage of the East–West conflict the average burden reached levels not seen since the inter-World War period or the end of the nineteenth century. The twentieth century will not be remembered as a peaceful one. Still, as Ferguson points out: 'after many centuries during which the cost of warfare was the biggest influence on state budgets, that role was usurped in the second half of the 20th century by the cost of welfare' (Ferguson, 2001, p. 27).

Table 5.1   *The development of general government spending over the last century (10 country averages of spending expressed as percentage shares of GDP)*

	Total	Military	Social transfers
1880	9.0	2.1	0.4
1890	10.4	2.5	0.4
1900	12.1	3.2	0.5
1910	14.3	2.9	0.5
1920	18.9	5.0	0.5
1930	21.6	2.1	1.5
1938	24.6	4.1	—*
1950	24.7	3.5	7.1
1960	29.2	4.1	8.9
1970	35.5	3.4	11.9
1980	45.9	3.0	15.2
1990	47.7	2.8	17.2
2000	45.7	1.9	18.5

Note: * not available.

Sources: Cusack and Fuchs (2003), European Commission (2003), Lindert (2004), and various volumes of the OECD's *Economic Outlook* and *Yearbook of National Accounts*.

So, despite the massive violence and mayhem, the century also brought about a marked change in the relative priorities of Western governments in terms of resource allocation. In 1900, military budgets accounted for about a quarter of all government spending (see Table 5.1). By 2000, this share stood at about 4 per cent. Military spending was more than six times the amount spent on social transfers in 1900. This disparity was radically reversed by the end of the twentieth century, with social transfers amounting to nearly ten times the amount spent on the military.

The century-long revision of priorities has been dramatic. Even more impressive is to compare these figures with those of one example from the period 1700 to 1799. This is the British case. Across the entire eighteenth century, spending for the army, navy and ordnance combined alone constituted more than half, that is, 52 per cent, of total public spending.[3] Debt management outlays came to an extremely high 37 per cent and the entire civilian function was funded by the derisible residual of 12 per cent of total state outlays. When one looks at the military budget and compares it with the total public outlays net of debt charges (nearly all of which were incurred to support the military effort in the many years of war involvement during the period), on average it came to 80 per cent of all spending. Why so great a burden? According to Levy (1983), in 52 years of the eighteenth century, Britain was engaged in war against one or more major power. During some of these years, it was involved in two separate major power wars. This count excludes from consideration war involvements against non-major powers or non-state actors. So, whereas the state was once little more than a war-fighting machine with attendant apparatus to garner and administer the revenues to conduct these wars, the military function for most of the Western states has receded to the unspectacular role of being barely more than a minor financial footnote at the beginning of the twenty-first century.

I now focus briefly on the evolution of military spending in the last half of the twentieth century through to the first few years of the twenty-first. In Figure 5.1, three curves are plotted. One shows the trajectory of military spending in the Soviet Union and Russia, its successor state. The source for the Soviet/Russian military spending data is the Correlates of War Project's National Material Capabilities Data Set (<http://www.correlatesofwar. org/>). Note that the values in this graph are presented in terms of US dollars expressed in real or constant prices with the base year being 2000. The price series derives from Johnston and Williamson (2004).

Using SIPRI data, comparable values are plotted separately for the US and the group of the 19 other OECD countries in the list of 20 noted above.

Figure 5.1   Military spending: Soviet Union/Russia, the US and the rest of the West, 1950–2003

Particularly up to the beginning of the 1990s, the three series provide some visual affirmation of the standard explanation of the dynamics of East–West military budgets: a competitive accumulation of arms sustained by rising financial outlays. In addition, the US series is marked by a set of cycles, the first two of which are connected to the mobilisation and demobilisation processes associated with major wars (Korean and Vietnamese). The third American cycle is connected initially with the Reagan build-up (here there is something to be said for the primacy of domestic considerations behind this rise) and the decline connected to the tapering off of the Cold War. On the far right side of the graph one sees the dramatic decline in Soviet/Russian outlays with the demise of the former and collapse of the latter's economy. American outlays declined and stabilised through the 1990s and then took off with the onset of the Bush II administration and its 'war on terror'. While the large residual group of other OECD countries as a whole closely paralleled the Soviet trajectory, these outlays tended to decline after the Cold War. This was followed by a long period of stability.

Altering the measure of military effort to one that reflects the burden on the economy (Figure 5.2), one sees that the average burden to the economy within the 20 OECD economies followed a general downward trend. So,

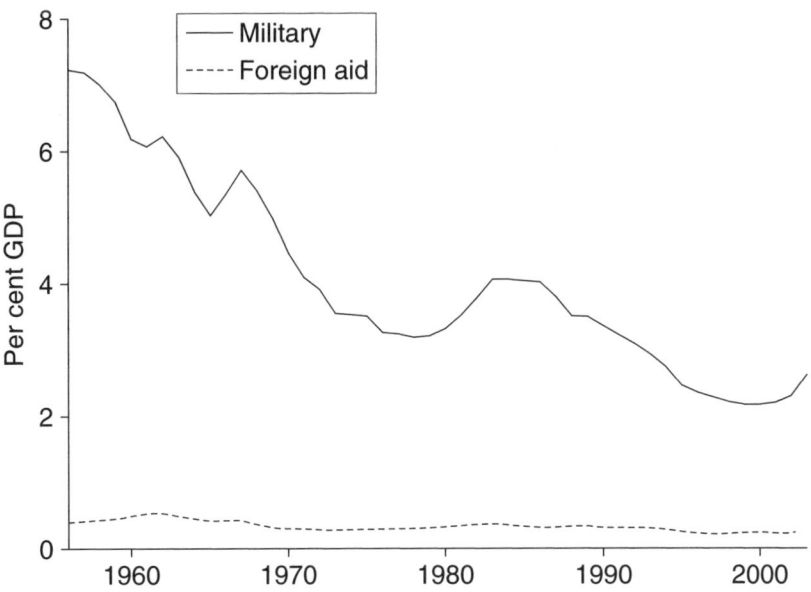

Figure 5.2   Military and foreign aid burdens across 20 OECD countries, 1956–2003 (military and foreign aid expenditures as percentages of GDP)

even if in real terms, per above, the dollar value of military outlays generally rose throughout the last half of the twentieth century, the relative burden tended to decline over time, going from over 7 per cent of GDP in the mid-1950s to close to 2 per cent by the end of the century.

It is notable that, even with the post-Cold War decline in the defence burden, there was no pick-up in share of national economic resources coming from this group of wealthy countries to the Third World in the form of foreign aid (official development assistance, ODA). Although the UN ODA target, adopted in the early 1970s, is 0.7 per cent of GNP, few potential donor countries have ever met the goal. Even the liberation of national economic resources from defence needs brought about by the end of the Cold War was a major disappointment for the group as a whole. This opportunity to employ some of the freed resources for this other important international function was taken by only five of the 20 countries. Indeed, nearly all of the rest cut the amount of relative resources going both to defence and to foreign aid.

Table 5.2 provides a perspective on how the military burdens of individual Western countries developed over the last half-century or so. Starting

Table 5.2 Military spending as a percentage share of GDP

	1960–69	1970–79	1980–89	1990–99	2000–2003
Australia	3.1	2.6	2.6	2.2	1.7
Austria	1.2	1.1	1.2	0.9	0.8
Belgium	3.3	3.1	3.1	1.8	1.3
Canada	3.4	2.0	2.0	1.6	1.2
Denmark	2.8	2.3	2.3	1.8	1.6
Finland	1.7	1.4	1.9	1.7	1.2
FR Germany	4.3	3.4	3.2	1.9	1.5
France	5.5	3.9	4.0	3.2	2.6
Greece	4.1	5.6	6.5	4.9	4.5
Ireland	1.4	1.6	1.7	1.0	0.7
Italy	3.0	2.5	2.3	2.0	2.0
Japan	0.9	0.9	1.0	1.0	1.0
Netherlands	3.9	3.2	3.1	2.2	1.6
Norway	3.5	3.2	3.1	2.6	1.9
Portugal	6.4	5.5	3.3	2.5	2.1
Spain	1.9	1.7	2.3	1.6	1.2
Sweden	4.0	3.4	2.8	2.2	1.9
Switzerland	2.6	2.1	1.9	1.4	1.1
United Kingdom	5.9	4.8	4.8	3.3	2.4
United States	8.8	6.0	6.4	4.2	3.4
Average	3.6	3.0	3.0	2.2	1.8
Std. dev.	1.9	1.5	1.5	1.0	0.9

in the 1960s, one can see a very broad range in share of GDP going to the military, extending from 0.9 per cent in Japan to 8.8 per cent in the United States. Slightly lower levels of defence burdens ensued over the following decades for most countries through the 1980s. With the passage of the Cold War, appreciable drops in this burden came about in the 1990s, and this generally continued through the first few years of the twenty-first century; nevertheless, the relative diversity in burdens sustained continued over the entire period.

5.3   FORCES SHAPING MILITARY SPENDING

I now turn briefly to the mainstream interpretation of the development in Western military budgets in the post-World War II era. It is often difficult to disentangle the external and internal forces that shape the evolution of a nation's military spending (see Stoll, 1982). And while there is a lot to be said for the powerful impact of domestic factors in determining military spending levels (cf. Nincic and Cusack, 1979; Cusack and Ward, 1981), here, instead, it is assumed that external threats play a critical role.

Let us take a simple arms race formulation. In this formulation, the contention is that a nation's military spending (here in constant price US dollars) is a function of an external threat measure (the scale of Soviet/Russian military spending) that acts as a positive force in pushing up military outlays. In addition, an economic term, Y, standing for real GDP in US dollars, is introduced, to capture the effects of income as both an enhancing and constraining force. Natural logs of all the variables in the equation are used, and the model has been estimated on a pooled cross-section of Western countries using six separate and consecutive period averages for all of the variables.[4]

This formulation, whether the US is included in the sample or not, appears to work very well (see Table 5.3). Western nations seem to have responded to variation in Soviet/Russian military outlays in the action/reaction style associated with the classic arms race formulation (see Cusack, 1985b). Income played the expected role with higher real GDP leading to greater military outlays.

An alternative explanation of the forces shaping military outlays, one that conforms to the general line of argument used throughout this volume, is a model that stresses forces that act to restrain and reduce resources going to this function. Certainly the long-term dynamics of the military burden (that is, military spending as a percentage of GDP) would, on the face of it, appear to be subject to downward pressures. Indeed, relative to the aggregate of non-military outlays, it would appear that the military has

Table 5.3   Panel estimates of model capturing the long-term dynamics of military spending

	I Including US	II Excluding US
$\ln(S/R\,MLX)$	0.156*	0.153*
	(3.29)	(3.38)
$\ln(Y)$	0.813*	0.819*
	(31.55)	(32.77)
$\bar{R}^2$	0.989	0.985
Number of cases	120	114
	Country fixed-effects/ panel corrected standard errors	Country fixed-effects/ panel corrected standard errors

Notes: z-statistics in parentheses; * = statistically significant at 0.05 level.

been more prone to the loss of societal resources than have non-military functions. In Figure 5.3, the ratios of the averages of military and non-military spending as shares of GDP in the first few years of the twenty-first century have been plotted against those ratios in the last decade of the Cold War (1980–89).

Ten of the 19 countries for which I have data on the non-military outlay aggregate actually experienced growth over these two decades. Another six experienced modest relative declines (from 3 to 7 per cent), and only three experienced a relative decline of more than ten percentage points. On the other hand, all but one (Japan, which maintained basically the same level of military burden throughout) of the 20 for which I have military burden data experienced declines and most of these declines were extremely large. The average relative decline, indeed, was 36 per cent, with Ireland and Belgium leading the way (both with nearly a 60 per cent relative decline between the decade of the 1980s and the period 2000–2003).

The question suggests itself, then, as to whether pressures, such as those arising from the level of public debt and exposure to international economic forces, have also been at work in driving down the share of economic resources being allocated to the military. Table 5.4 examines this question in some detail by first regressing the levels of defence burdens in three different periods against a set of three variables, including income per capita, trade openness, and the prevailing level of public debt.[5] Income per capita is based on GDP and is measured in thousands of constant price US dollars. Trade openness is the sum of exports plus imports expressed as a percentage of GDP. Finally, debt burden is the public debt expressed also

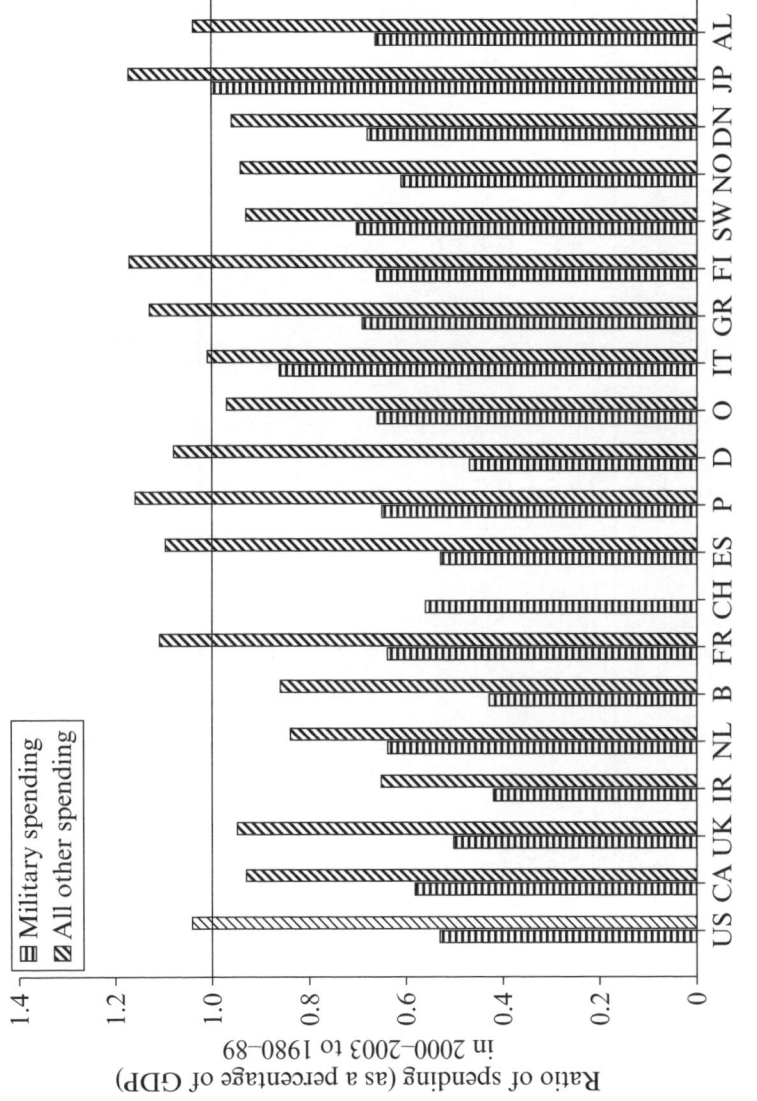

Figure 5.3   Change in spending on military and non-military functions

Table 5.4   The forces of retrenchment and military spending in the post-1980 era

	I Average defence burden for period 1980–89	II Average defence burden for period 1990–99	III Average defence burden for period 2000–2003	IV Change in average defence burden for entire period 1980s–2000s	V Change in average defence burden across each period 1980s–2000s
Income per capita	−0.668 (−1.44)	−0.743 (−1.56)	−0.962 (−1.68)	2.48 (1.94)	−3.08* (−2.70)
Trade openness	−0.019 (−1.36)	−0.012 (−1.50)	−0.012* (−2.40)	−0.005 (−1.67)	−0.003 (−0.50)
Debt burden	0.009 (0.43)	0.002 (0.22)	0.000 (0.01)	−0.002 (−0.50)	−0.003 (−1.50)
Lagged military burden	—	—	—	−0.496* (−9.73)	−0.661* (−3.22)
Soviet/Russian military spending	—	—	—	—	0.494* (22.45)
Constant	10.05* (2.28)	10.13* (1.84)	12.28* (2.08)	−1.96 (−1.47)	—
$\bar{R}^2$	0.04	0.04	0.20	0.83	0.75
Number of cases	20	20	20	20	60
	OLS, cross-section	OLS, cross-section	OLS, cross-section	OLS, cross-section	OLS with country fixed-effects/panel corrected standard errors

Notes:
1. Income per capita is period average for estimates in I–III and V; in IV it is growth rate over the whole period.
2. Trade openness is period average in I–III and V; in IV it is period average of first decade (1980–89).
3. Debt burden is period average in I–III and V; in IV it is period average in first decade (1980–89).
4. Lagged military burden is average defence burden in period immediately preceding.
5. Soviet/Russian military spending is in natural logs for each period.
6. Cols I–IV: t-statistics in parentheses; col. 5: z-statistics; * = statistically significant at 0.05 level.

as a percentage of GDP. Column IV goes beyond this by also looking at the change in the defence burden over the period from the 1980s to the first few years of 2000 and also includes the 'convergence' or 'catch-up effect' (Schmidt, 2006) that might be captured by the previous level of the defence burden. Finally, column V looks at the changes in the defence burden from a pooled perspective, including the first differences for the last three periods under consideration. It also brings into the model the competitive effect of Soviet/Russian military spending.

Columns I to III of Table 5.4 present results on the cross-sectional estimates of the determinants of the levels of defence burdens across three different periods, the 1980s, the 1990s, and the first few years of the new century. The results provide little support for the contention that the restraining effects of the economic variables frequently alluded to in accounting for lower levels of other public spending were also at work in shaping the relative size of the military budget. In only one decade is one of the estimated effects statistically significant; this is the coefficient on the trade openness measure, and it takes on a negative sign. When the convergence effect is also included in a formulation meant to account for the change from the 1980s to the new century (column IV), it turns out to be the only statistically significant factor in shaping these dynamics. None of the putative restraining or dampening effects is detectable. Finally, in column V, it is clear that the arms race effect is the dominant influence on the defence burden. The convergence effect is also at work, and it would appear that the change in the level of affluence, captured by the inter-period first difference in income per capita, acts to lower the overall level of the military burden.

In sum, although the internationalisation of the economy as well as the levels of accumulated public debt may well be important forces in acting as dampening factors in other non-welfare spending functions, their impact hardly registers on the budgetary military burdens countries bear. Instead, it would seem that the rise and decline of a major international military threat to these countries has been a central influence.

5.4 LABOUR, CAPITAL AND THE HOLLOWING OF THE MILITARY

5.4.1 Military Personnel

In the West, to a great extent, the rise and decline in military spending is reflected in the trend in the personnel employed within the military (see Figure 5.4). As the Korean War broke out, total military personnel in this

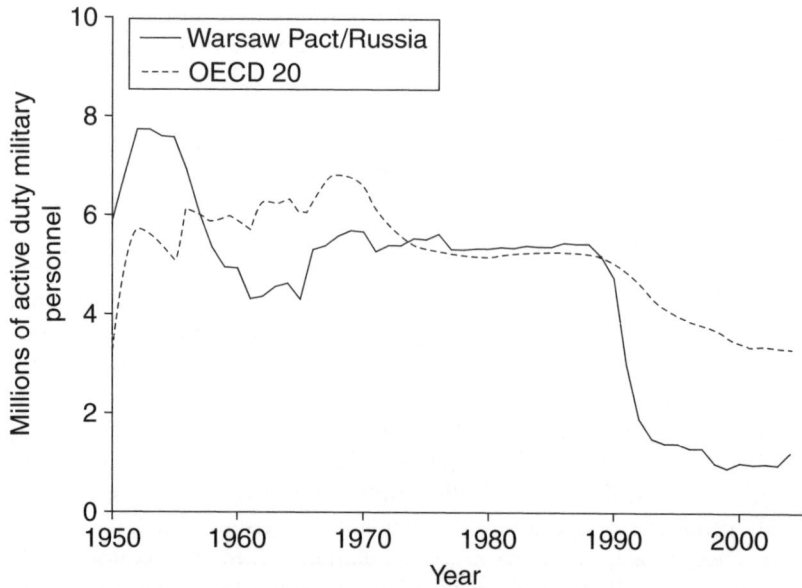

Figure 5.4   East–West military personnel balance

group of 20 OECD countries quickly moved from the level of three to six million soldiers. The total reached its height at the end of the 1960s during the Vietnam War, coming close to seven million and then retreated to around five million by the end of the Cold War. As the East–West conflict terminated, personnel needs lessened and, once again, force levels declined to close to three million active duty soldiers. For the most part, the staffing levels in the West paralleled those within the Warsaw Pact. The latter's dissolution at the beginning of the 1990s provided much of the impetus for the sharp reduction in personnel levels in Western nations.

Conscription was in fairly widespread use throughout much of the West as the Cold War set in. Seventeen of the 20 Western countries for which I have collected data used conscription to meet personnel requirements in the mid-1950s. By the end of the Cold War, fourteen out of the 20 still retained conscription. The Anglo-Saxon countries, here the United Kingdom (in the early 1960s) and Australia and the US (both in the early 1970s), ended reliance on conscription during the Cold War. As of 2006, with Italy scheduled to end conscription, only nine of these 20 states will still be using this means of staffing the military.

This form of coercive labour demand played an important role in maintaining the high levels of military manpower, particularly during the Cold

*Table 5.5   The importance of conscription in supplying military personnel
(conscripts as a percentage of armed forces)*

	1970–79	1980–89	1990–99	2000–2004
Netherlands*	47	47	25	0
Belgium*	33	32	35	0
France*	54	52	44	20
Switzerland	74	84	68	52
Spain*	66	66	62	17
Portugal	73	53	36	18
FR Germany	47	46	43	36
Austria	61	58	43	46
Italy+	65	67	55	26
Greece	74	70	75	64
Finland	79	72	75	61
Sweden	71	72	74	64
Norway	68	65	61	57
Denmark	34	30	29	25

Notes:
Period averages calculated using available annual data drawn from the IISS (various years) Military Balance;
* = conscription ended in Netherlands (1996), Belgium (1994), France (2002), Spain (2002);
+ = conscription will end in Italy in 2006.

War. Data on the importance of conscription in supplying personnel needs are available for 14 of the OECD countries (see Table 5.5). One sees a broad range across these countries and over time. In the 1970s and 1980s, conscription helped supply anywhere from an average of 30 to nearly 84 per cent. This reliance decreased during the 1990s, with two countries ending conscription (Netherlands and Belgium) and quite a number of others lowering their dependence. In the first five years of the present decade, France and Spain ceased using conscription, and most other countries generally lowered their intake.

A variety of reasons have been put forward to justify the use of military conscription. Mulligan and Shleifer (2004), for example, emphasise the regulatory costs and ease with which such a regime of personnel recruitment can be implemented and maintained. However, the principal grounds offered are usually economic. The legal requirement to serve in the military for a significant period of time at low wages is seen as a means of meeting inexpensively what could otherwise be very large personnel requirements and attendant high financial costs. However, leaving aside the costs and risks this imposes on the individuals subject to such forced labour, a number of analysts have pointed out that very few savings actually accrue to governments that use this instrument. Cost savings estimates vary, but generally range between only 5 and 10 per cent of the military budget (van Ypersele de Strihou, 1967; Oneal, 1992).

5.4.2 Military Capital

It has been possible to collect a significant quantity of data on major military capital items for a large number of countries, both East and West. These data have been collected and coded from the International Institute for Strategic Studies' annual publication, *The Military Balance*. The data collection effort has been described in greater detail elsewhere (Cusack, 1985a). The weapons data reflect a country's stock of in-use military capital items as of 1 July of the year for which the data are reported. Note that here the West is defined as the 16 OECD countries described in note 2. Until 1991, with the dissolution of the Warsaw Treaty Organization, the East is defined as being constituted by the following seven countries: East Germany, Poland, Hungary, Czechoslovakia, Bulgaria, Romania and the Soviet Union. Thereafter, it includes only the Russian Federation.

The three data series consider only important military equipment that can be used for conventional combat and exclude items entirely devoted to strategic nuclear purposes. It should be noted that some analysts (see, for example, Lieber and Press, 2006) have concluded that the United States has not only pursued but effectively achieved predominance in the strategic nuclear area. This entails that it has gone beyond the constraints implied by the situation of 'mutually assured destruction' that prevailed during much of the Cold War period and has acquired effective nuclear primacy or hegemony with the ability to launch successfully a nuclear first strike with minimal risk of effective retaliation.

The first series deals with naval forces. It is an annual count of the number of major surface combat vessels (MSCVs); this category includes frigates, destroyer escorts, destroyers, cruisers, battleships and aircraft carriers. The second series is connected to land forces and is a simple annual count of the category of armour conventionally described as main battle tanks (MBTs). The third series deals with the air force's principal offensive weapons platform: fixed-wing combat aircraft (FWCAs), including both fighters and bombers. These three weapons systems data do not extend as far back as the personnel series, but they do cover a significant span of time, namely from the 1960s or early 1970s to the beginning of the twenty-first century.

In the naval area during both the Cold War and beyond, the West held an appreciable lead over the Warsaw Pact in the sheer number of MSCVs.

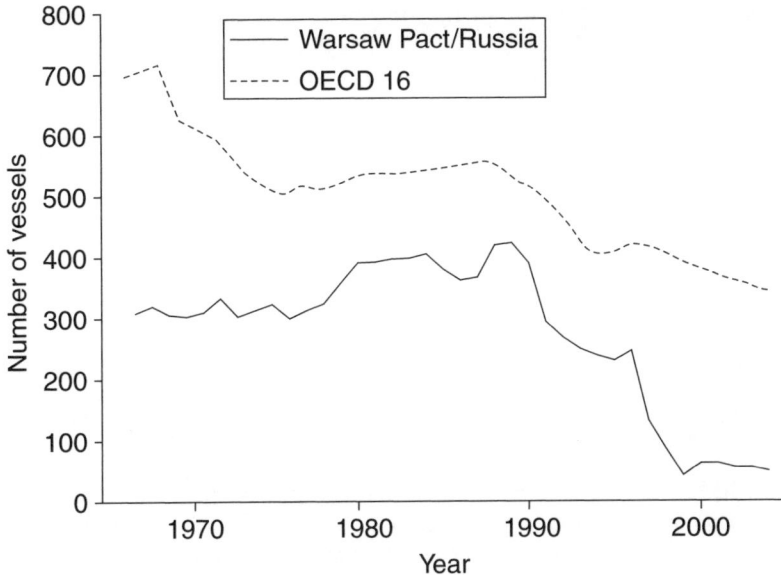

Figure 5.5   East–West naval balance: principal combat surface vessels

One sees that the end of the 1960s marked the beginning of a significant decline in the West's stock of important combat vessels (see Figure 5.5). The decline was principally driven by large cutbacks in American weapons stocks as US involvement in the Vietnam War drew down. This decline was reversed somewhat in the 1980s, partially in response to the Warsaw Pact (mainly Soviet) build-up. Again, with the end of the Cold War, the former potential enemy's stock of capital in this area declined dramatically. A gentler decline was set in train throughout the West.

In terms of land-based military capital items, one can observe a dramatic gap to the apparent advantage of its Eastern competitors (see Figure 5.6). Throughout the Cold War period, the East enjoyed more than a two-to-one advantage. However, it should be pointed out that, inside the Socialist centrally planned economies, counts of the number of capital items, particularly main battle tanks, almost certainly exaggerate the actual number of functioning weapons platforms. Within centrally planned economic systems, there was little or no incentive to produce spare parts. Often, then, a significant portion of existing weapons stocks was cannibalised in order to replace worn-out parts. Nevertheless, on both sides of the East–West conflict, there was a substantial rise in the stock of such weapons through the 1970s and 1980s. And, again, with the end of the Cold War, there were dramatic cutbacks on both sides.

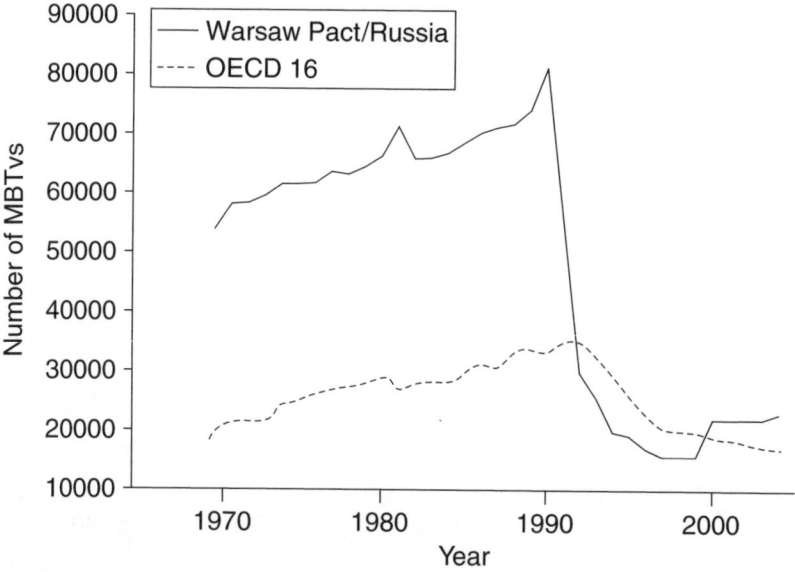

Figure 5.6   East–West land armour balance: main battle tanks

Finally, along the third dimension, the air, one can see that the decline in the Western stock of fixed-wing combat aircraft with the winding down of the Vietnam War was eventually followed by a build-up during the Reagan administrations (see Figure 5.7). With the end of the Cold War, the stock of such weapons systems once again went into decline. Over the entire period, there was an almost consistent downward trend in the stock of these weapons held by the Warsaw Pact countries. Russian stocks plummeted through the 1990s and into the first few years of the new century.

On a country-by-country basis, the picture is generally uniform. Table 5.6 provides information on the country holdings of the three major conventional military capital items for the years 1970, 1980, 1989 and 2004. For most countries, the stocks of these weapons have generally declined, and in quite a number of cases significantly. For example, France, Germany, the United Kingdom and even the United States have greatly cut back on their air, land and naval forces' major weapons stocks, and this despite significant efforts to maintain or actually increase stocks during the last decade of the Cold War. For many of the smaller countries the scope of these cutbacks has sometimes been as large if not greater.

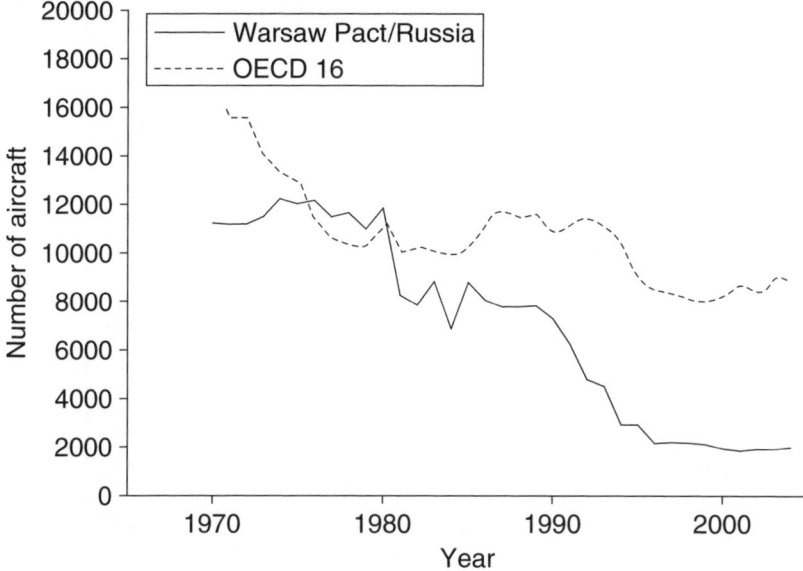

Figure 5.7   East–West aviation balance: fixed-wing combat aircraft

5.4.3   The Dramatic Rise in Prices

In an era of declining capacity or willingness to finance the military and, in particular, to pay the costs of new capital acquisition, in many countries the seemingly ineluctable rise in the relative costs of military capital items has and will continue to hollow out the military might of these nations. Some analysts have remarked upon this feature (see Kirkpatrick and Pugh, 1983; Pugh, 1993; Kirkpatrick, 1995; Augustine, 1997). Note that Kirkpatrick and Pugh (1983), using a variety of sources, report growth rates for a variety of American military weapons systems. The values provided are as follows: infantry anti-tank weapon, 13 per cent; tank, 11 per cent; destroyer, 9 per cent; aircraft, 8 per cent, and aircraft carrier, 6 per cent. They also report an estimate of 8.3 per cent for British combat aircraft in the post-WWII era. Their estimate of aircraft carrier construction cost inflation is exactly the same as that derived here. Their figure on aircraft is slightly lower than the value estimated below for the data I have been able to assemble on fighter aircraft in the US over the period 1916–2005. Other, but similar estimates are also provided by Pugh (1993) for both UK and US weapons procurement.

Indeed, Augustine (1997, p. 107) has suggested that the tendency for the

Table 5.6 Conventional weapons stocks, 1970–2004

	Fixed-wing combat aircraft				Major surface combat vessels				Main battle tanks			
	1970	1980	1989	2004	1970	1980	1989	2004	1970	1980	1989	2004
Australia	224	135	116	152	14	11	12	10	140	90	103	71
Belgium	208	142	126	90	0	4	4	3	640	529	467	143
Canada	280	247	151	140	20	23	19	16	330	114	114	114
Denmark	112	108	89	60	6	10	3	3	298	368	262	231
FR Germany	1080	707	507	384	19	23	14	13	3300	3826	5005	2398
France	740	605	598	478	52	48	43	34	2030	2225	1570	614
Greece	200	264	330	389	12	16	21	14	1100	1510	2219	1723
Italy	425	310	390	220	47	29	33	17	1000	1595	1720	1093
Japan	590	504	362	280	28	48	63	54	685	810	1200	980
Norway	114	123	83	61	7	8	7	3	201	186	187	165
Netherlands	135	161	189	137	32	22	15	15	720	938	913	283
Spain	202	177	217	177	38	28	19	16	600	935	874	552
Sweden	650	430	417	207	16	8	0	0	300	800	985	280
Switzerland	315	377	272	111	0	0	0	0	650	800	820	355
United Kingdom	816	732	570	426	67	70	49	34	900	1171	1561	543
United States	11260	6073	7412	5541	254	191	229	118	11596	12875	15992	7620
Average	1084	693	739	553	38	34	33	22	1531	1798	2125	1073
USSR/Russia	8025	8833	5388	2002	225	310	328	49	41140	50200	54550	22950
PRC	3300	6000	5000	1900	13	29	56	63	8500	11000	9750	8580

Note: Values given for major surface combat vessels in 1970 are from 1971 in the cases of Italy and the United Kingdom, from 1972 in the case of Denmark, from 1974 in the cases of Canada and France, and from 1975 in the case of the PRC. The main battle tanks value in the 1970 column for Norway is actually from 1973.

relative costs of military capital items to rise has achieved a law-like quality. This is summarised facetiously in the quotation below:

> In the year 2054, the entire defence budget will purchase just one aircraft. This aircraft will have to be shared by the Air Force and Navy 3½ days each per week except for leap year, when it will be made available to the Marines for the extra day.

Construction costs of the first two US-built aircraft carriers (the *Saratoga* and the *Lexington*, both entering service in 1927) were 234.5 and 245.7 millions of dollars in constant prices (base year 2000).[6] About 50 years later, the cost of constructing the first of the *Nimitz* class carriers, put into service in 1975, was 4.3 billions of dollars in real 2000 terms; that is, about 20 times the price in real terms of the first two purpose-built carriers. The implied average annual growth rate (above and beyond economy-wide price increases) is close to 6 per cent. Such a growth rate entails a doubling of construction costs over and above economy-wide inflation every 12 years. While this pace of growth is not as great as that seen in the costs of fixed-wing combat aircraft (see below), it is still extremely high and poses grave challenges to governments attempting to keep costs under control while at the same time not diminishing the means employed in the pursuit of state aims. It is fascinating to realise that the problem of Baumol's (1967) disease, first characterized in the 1960s in reference to services as a whole and later often used to explain the growing costs of government because of its heavy reliance on labour in the delivery of services (for example, Beck, 1981), is actually reversed in the case of the military.

Of course, acquisition is not the only cost confronted in fielding a major weapons system. There are additional costs that cannot be avoided. Given the long service life that governments attempt to achieve for these expensive weapons systems, one also needs to take into account the modernisation costs that are periodically required over a long life span as well as the operating and support costs incurred if these systems are to be employed for the purposes for which they were constructed. Finally the deactivation and disposal costs also need to be taken into account. Return to the *Nimitz* class carrier example. To the initial investment of 4.3 billions of dollars, one has to add the mid-life modernisation costs of 2.5 billions, the operating and support costs of 15.6 billions and the deactivation and disposal costs of 0.9 billion. In sum, each of the 12 US aircraft carriers in the US fleet in 2003 entailed a commitment of at least 23.3 billions of dollars. Totalling the costs of the entire fleet of 12 carriers, one comes to the sum of 280 billion dollars (and all of this is without the costs of the expensive aircraft (see below) stationed on these carriers being taken into account) over their anticipated service lives.

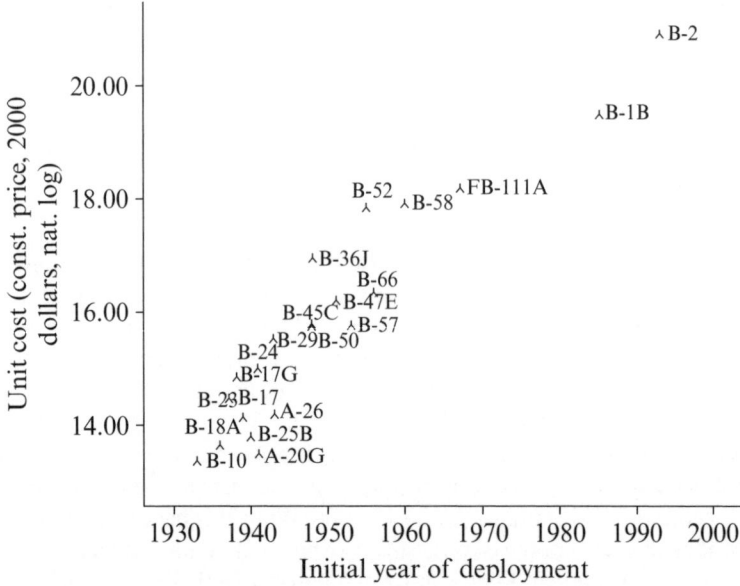

Figure 5.8   Escalating unit costs of US bomber aircraft

Even more dramatic have been the rising relative costs in fixed-wing combat aircraft.[7] Take, for example, bomber aircraft. Figure 5.8 plots the escalating costs of US bomber aircraft over the period from 1933 (when the first US-made bomber, the B-10, went into service) until 1993 (the year the most recent bomber type, the B-2, was initially brought into operation). In real terms, the first bomber cost about 630 thousand dollars. The B-17, one of the workhorse bombers employed during World War II, was introduced at the end of the 1930s, just prior to the war. The B-17G, the more commonly produced of this type, came into service in 1938 and cost 2.8 million dollars in 2000 prices: in other words, four and one half times the real cost of the bomber introduced only five years earlier. Brought into operation only five years later, the B-29 came in at double the price of the B-17G. The B-52, initiated into service 12 years further on, and the mainstay of both the conventional and strategic bomber forces of the American military during the Cold War and beyond, came into operation at a cost ten times as great as the B-29. The most recent bomber type introduced into the American military, the B-2, entered active service in 1993, shortly after the Gulf War. The purchase cost of a single unit was close to 1.2 billion dollars in real terms. This represented an increase of over 2000 per cent in the real dollar cost of a bomber to the American taxpayer.

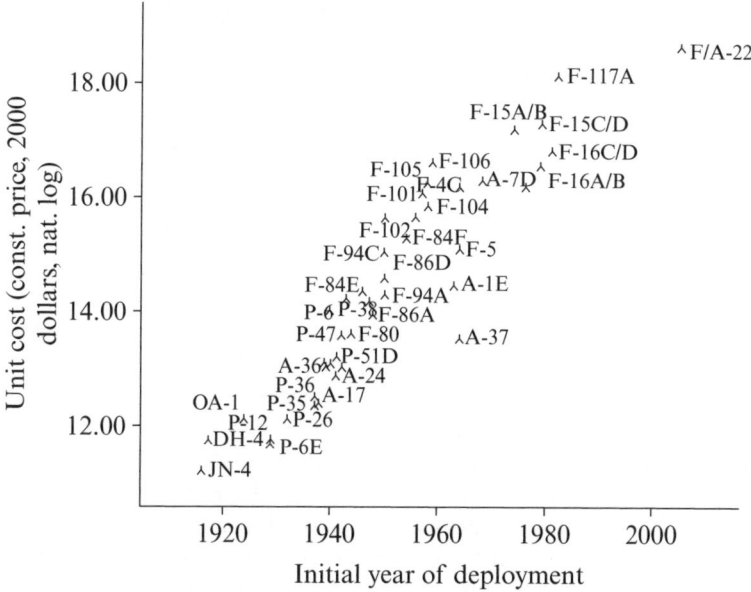

Figure 5.9   Escalating unit costs of US fighter aircraft

Nearly as dramatic has been the rise in real terms of the unit costs of fighter aircraft, of which there has been a far broader and diverse set of acquisitions (see Figure 5.9). The first type for which I have been able to assemble data on both initial year of service and purchase cost is the JN-4, the first mass-produced American aircraft. This two-seat biplane was acquired and put into active service in 1916. In terms of 2000 US dollars, the acquisition cost of this plane was about 70 thousand dollars. The P-39, introduced about 20 years later, shortly before America's entry into World War II, viz., 1939, was acquired at a cost of 470 thousand dollars – nearly seven times the unit costs of the JN-4. The F-84E, one of the main early jet propelled fighters of the American military, was introduced eight years later, after the war. It came in at the cost of 1.37 millions (constant price 2000 dollars), about three times the unit acquisition costs of the P-39. The F4C, introduced at the beginning of direct and intensive American involvement in the Vietnam War, entered active service at a cost of 10.2 million (constant price 2000 dollars), more than seven times the unit acquisition costs of the F-84E. Inflation in real terms over and above what was going on throughout the American economy continued apace. One of the most recent systems-type acquisitions is the stealth fighter, the F-117A, which would first come into operational service during 1982 at a cost of 72 million, to be followed by the 2005 acquisition of the F/A-22 at a unit price of 120 million.

Based on these data, the estimated average annual rates of growth in real unit costs of US bombers and fighter planes were 13.3 and 9.9 per cent, respectively. These estimates are based on the historical data dealing with the unit prices and dates of deployment for 21 individual bombers and 43 fighter aircraft. Note, again, that these inflation rates are over and above those occurring within the economy as a whole. Thus, if the GDP rose by an average annual rate of 1.7 per cent, a modest rate of overall inflation, the implied inflation rate in the cost of a bomber aircraft would be 15 per cent; in other words, a doubling time of less than five years and a quadrupling in unit cost within less than a decade.

Extrapolating, using these rates and the prices of the last acquisitions in these inventories, this would mean that, by the year 2062, were a new fighter aircraft to be developed and acquired, its cost would be 29 billion dollars in 2000 prices. This is 6.7 billion greater than the entire 50-year life span cost of a *Nimitz* carrier. Furthermore, should a new bomber aircraft be developed and added to the inventory in 2062, it would cost 9.17 trillion dollars, a sum close to the size of the entire US economy in the year 2000 as measured in constant price GDP terms (9.92 trillion dollars).

It is interesting to compare these rising real costs with those associated with another major component of military strength, labour. US Department of Defense (DOD) personnel costs have risen at an annual rate over and above economy-wide inflation by 1.8 percent.[8] This estimate is based on annual data on DOD spending on military personnel and taken from the Budget of the United States Government: Historical Tables Fiscal Year 2005, produced by the US Government Printing Office. Personnel data come from the Correlates of War Project. Price data are from Johnston and Williamson (2004).

Contrast this change with the rise in the real costs of the typical civilian employee in the same period. Note that using data on compensation of employees and civilian employment taken from the Council of Economic Advisors' *Economic Report of the President for 2006* and the price data from Johnston and Williamson (2004), the real cost of civilian labour rose at a rate of 1.2 per cent per annum over and above economy-wide inflation. Thus, while inflation in military personnel costs are clearly greater than those found in the civilian labour market, they pale in comparison with the huge inflationary pressures connected to major military capital items.

So, just as in the logic of Baumol's disease (the tendency for productivity in services to lag behind that in manufacturing), the cost of one of two major items in the production function is growing disproportionately (and at a relatively rapid rate). One effect of this is to squeeze the capacity of the governments to maintain existing force levels. In this regard, the end of the

Table 5.7 *The evolution in the number of types of new fixed-wing combat aircraft introduced into the US air fleet*

Period	Total	Of which: Fighters	Bombers
1910–19	2	2	0
1920–29	3	3	0
1930–39	10	5	5
1940–49	19	11	8
1950–59	14	10	4
1960–69	7	5	2
1970–79	4	4	0
1980–89	3	2	1
1990–99	1	0	1
2000–2005	1	1	0

Cold War came at an opportune and fortuitous moment. Demands for newer and even more expensive weapons systems subsided just as already stretched resources were being dramatically reduced.

One of the implications of the rapid relative rise in the unit cost of weapons systems is the decreasing frequency with which new systems are introduced into the military inventory (Lorell, 2003). A very good example of this is to be found in the case of fixed-wing combat aircraft within the US military over the last century or so. Some of the long-run consequences only exaggerate the problem. One begins to see a decline in the frequency with which new systems can be introduced (see Table 5.7 for the American experience in terms of FWCAs). Another consequence, one that generally further heightens acquisition cost pressures, is the ever diminishing size (in terms of the number of firms competing) of the defence capital weapons-building industry (Lorell and Levaux, 1998). This only further heightens cost pressures as industry becomes more oligopolistic, indeed monopolistic, with the consequent price-inflating pressures.

The maintenance of existing force structures has come to pose significant difficulties for most Western nations. With declining overall allocations to the military, this has constrained choices in terms of how the ever more restricted budgets are used. Outside two of the larger powers, such as the US and the UK, most countries for which I have data (see Table 5.8) seem to have forgone the acquisition of new equipment in order to cover personnel and general operating costs – and this in an era when many countries have significantly cut back on personnel. As the level of resources going to the military has stagnated or declined, in most cases smaller shares of these reduced resources have been allocated to the purchase of new

Table 5.8   Changing composition of military budgets

		% share of military budget for personnel	% share of military budget for other purposes	% share of military budget for equipment	Military spending as % share of GDP
US	1986–88	36.4	37.9	25.7	6.4
	2001–03	33.7	41.5	24.8	3.5
Canada	1986–88	46.1	33.4	20.6	2.1
	2001–03	42.8	43.8	13.4	1.2
UK	1986–88	39.6	35.3	25.1	4.6
	2001–03	39.5	36.6	23.9	2.4
Netherlands	1986–88	41.2	39.3	19.5	3.0
	2001–03	48.9	34.2	16.9	1.6
Belgium	1986–88	62.3	25.0	12.7	2.8
	2001–03	70.5	22.7	6.8	1.3
Spain	1986–88	52.1	25.2	22.7	2.2
	2001–03	63.5	23.8	12.7	1.2
Portugal	1986–88	66.1	24.9	9.0	3.2
	2001–03	79.7	14.3	6.0	2.1
F.R. Germany	1986–88	49.1	30.9	19.9	3.0
	2001–03	60.3	26.3	13.4	1.5
Italy	1986–88	58.2	22.0	19.8	2.3
	2001–03	72.6	15.3	12.1	1.9
Greece	1986–88	60.6	20.7	18.8	6.3
	2001–03	66.4	19.6	14.0	4.3
Norway	1986–88	44.8	35.4	19.8	3.2
	2001–03	38.1	39.6	22.2	1.9
Denmark	1986–88	56.4	29.1	14.4	2.1
	2001–03	51.3	31.3	17.4	1.6

equipment. In other words, there appears to be a real trade-off in terms of the level of overall spending and the ability to allocate some of those resources to the purchase of new military capital. As military budgets decline, so too does the purchase of new hardware, and increasingly most of the military budget goes to personnel and operations.

5.5   WIDER TRADE-OFFS

Not only within the military budget, but from the perspective of the broader budget, the question of trade-offs often surfaces. Does military spending come at a direct cost to other government priorities, the classic 'guns/butter' trade-off? If there is a systematic pattern, let us assume that it is symmetric. This means that, if some other major component of government spending suffers as military spending increases, that component gains when military spending decreases. Using this widespread and traditional, but admittedly restrictive, assumption, it is possible to evaluate the question of broader budgetary trade-offs for a number of major items, including social transfers, education spending, health outlays and foreign aid.

Again, using a pooled data set for 20 OECD countries, four trade-off equations have been estimated.[9] These include spending on social transfers, education, health and foreign aid. In each of the formulations, the level of expenditures on a particular category relative to the size of the overall economy serves as the dependent variable. To ascertain whether these relative allocations lose or gain in the budgetary process relative to the military, the military burden term is included. Also included are measures of societal affluence and the partisan character of the government. Note that the last variable in this formulation, DPOP, standing for dependent population as a percentage of total population, is used only in the equations for social transfers and health expenditures. All expenditure variables, $EXP(j)$ and MB, are expressed as percentages of GDP. The societal affluence term, income per capita variable, $YCAP$, is measured in terms of thousands of constant price US dollars. The centre of political gravity (CPG) measure is on a scale, ranging from -100 to $+100$, with very low values indicating a government political orientation on the far left and very high values capturing a government political orientation on the far right (see Cusack and Engelhardt, 2002). Note that it is anticipated that the estimated effect of the income variable is positive, that of the political term to be negative, and that of the dependent population to be positive. Whether the parameter estimate is positive or negative on the military burden term would depend on whether the other spending variable (on the left-hand side of the equation) is complementary or competing. A statistically insignificant parameter would signal that decisions regarding spending on the two items are independent of one another.[10]

OLS with panel-corrected standard errors and country fixed effects was the statistical technique used to estimate the model. The estimation results are presented in Table 5.9. In three of the four equations the parameter on the military burden term is negative. However, one of these parameter estimates – the one for social transfers – is not statistically significant. This finding of a lack of a trade-off between defence and welfare spending is consistent with earlier research (see, for example, Domke et al., 1983). Interestingly, the military burden parameter estimate in the foreign aid equation takes on a positive (and statistically significant) value, suggesting that, rather than being competitive budgetary items, military spending and foreign aid have been complements to one another, rising and declining

Table 5.9   Panel estimates of model capturing the long-term dynamics of military spending

	Social transfers	Education	Health	Foreign aid
Military	−0.136	−0.197*	−0.479*	0.105*
burden	(0.71)	(−2.10)	(−5.15)	(4.57)
Income per	0.326*	0.094*	0.055*	0.023*
capita	(9.31)	(5.88)	(2.04)	(5.75)
CPG	−0.014	−0.019*	−0.016*	0.001
	(−1.00)	(−6.00)	(−3.20)	(1.00)
Dependent	0.582*	—	0.219*	—
population	(13.23)		(4.98)	
$\bar{R}^2$	0.91	0.72	0.84	0.69
Number of	98	84	82	99
cases	Country fixed-effects/panel corrected standard errors	Country fixed-effects/panel corrected standard errors	Country fixed-effects/panel corrected standard errors	Country fixed-effects/panel corrected standard errors

Note: z-statistics in parentheses.

jointly. This relationship is quite the opposite of what one would expect of the idealistic interpretation some analysts give the motives of aid provision (cf. Lumsdaine, 1993). Finally, there seems to have been a competitive relationship between military spending and both health and education outlays. This interpretation, of course, relies on the assumption that trade-offs are a symmetric phenomenon: a change in spending on one component implies a change in the opposite direction for the other component. In terms of the four major civilian spending categories that have been examined, this trade-off relationship appears to occur only between the military budget on the one side, and health and education spending on the other.

5.6   CONCLUSION

Throughout the West, the drain that the military has placed on both government and societal resources generally has diminished since the heydays of the Cold War. This decline was hastened with the culmination of that conflict and the receding international threat. Given the economic pressures that many states confronted from both international and domestic sources, the West can be said to have experienced a fortuitous conjunction of lessening security demands with stable if not rising pressures to allocate more resources to social areas. At least in the areas of health and education, it would seem that governments have been able to move some resources away from the military function to these social purposes.

But in most countries there is little left both in financial terms and with respect to the military capability that financial resources can buy. A good part of the present reduced stocks of military capital in these countries is growing old (therefore potentially obsolete) and wearing out. Should other countries adopt and pay for the materials associated with the so-called 'Revolution in Military Affairs', these Western nations may be confronting external threats that they can no longer meet. Even in the absence of high-tech external threats, the demographic surges outside the West are likely to pose many international security challenges.

The excessive rise in relative prices associated with major military capital items, a rise only partially associated with an increase in real effectiveness, poses a test for many of these states if they are to retain their capacity to provide in some meaningful way for their own military defence. The money available for military purposes is declining or, at best, stagnating. The price per unit of military capital is rising exponentially. For many of the OECD countries, the laws of mathematics assure that something similar to the far-cical outcome described by Augustine will come to the fore sooner rather than later.

At the same time, the ageing problem in the OECD countries will make it more difficult to attract sufficient personnel to the military (Goure, 2000). With shrinking younger age cohorts, the size of the recruitment pool will grow smaller and the costs of attracting people into the military will increase. All of this takes place against a backdrop of popular anti-military sentiment that only makes recruitment more difficult.

Soldiers alone do not make an army. Without modern equipment, the military of many of these countries might better be employed for some internal or international policing purposes or other socially useful activi-ties. The provision of security from external threats would then best be out-sourced and resources found to pay for it. Obviously, one of the more preferable means to do this is through international cooperation. However, cooperation in the security area is one of the most difficult tasks national leaders can undertake.

NOTES

1. See Brozka (1995) for a detailed discussion of alternative sources and the problems endemic to developing reliable and valid measures of military spending.

2. Unless otherwise noted, the figures on government spending in this and the following paragraphs refer to the ten OECD countries listed here: Austria, Canada, Denmark, France, Germany, Italy, Japan, Norway, United Kingdom and United States. Data on these countries are used in Table 5.1. In the data and analysis presented in the rest of the chapter, two larger groups of OECD countries are used. One contains 16 countries (the ten above, less Austria, plus Australia, Belgium, Greece, Netherlands, Spain, Sweden and Switzerland) and the other contains 20 (the 16 above plus Austria, Finland, Ireland and Portugal).
3. These values have been calculated using data drawn from Mitchell (1962, pp. 387–9).
4. The model estimated takes the following form:

$$\ln(MLX_{i,t}) = a_i + \beta_1 \ln(THREAT_t) + \beta_2 \ln(Y_{i,t}) + e_{i,t}.$$

OLS with panel corrected standard errors was used to estimate the model. This was done using country fixed effects and panel corrected standard errors. The time span for the estimates is from 1950 to 2003. Each decade in the last half of the twentieth century is treated as one time unit observation. The four years from 2000 to 2003 constitute the last time unit observation. The cross-sectional units are the 20 OECD countries enumerated earlier. Note that the model is also estimated with 19 countries, dropping the US from the list to test the robustness of the model in the absence of this country.
5. The cross-sectional equation estimated is:

$$MB_i = b_1 + b_2 YCAP_i + b_3 EXIMY_i + b_4 PDB_i + e_i.$$

The necessary modifications were made to estimate the two first-difference models reported in columns 4 and 5.
6. Data related to early US aircraft carrier construction costs derive from MacDonald (1964) and the Federation of American Scientists (2005). Price data are drawn from Johnston and Williamson (2004).
7. Current price data on all US military aircraft are from USAF Public Affairs Division (2005).
8. Annual data on DOD spending on military personnel are taken from the Budget of the United States Government: Historical Tables Fiscal Year 2005, produced by the US Government Printing Office. Personnel data come from the Correlates of War Project. Price data are from Johnston and Williamson (2004).
9. The general form of the equations is as follows:

$$EXP(j)_{i,t} = b_1 + b_2 MB_{i,t} + b_3 YCAP_{i,t} + b_4 CPG_{i,t} + b_5 DPOP_{i,t} + e_{i,t}.$$

10. For a more plausible assumption regarding competition between components of government and competition for scarce resources, see Cusack (1985b).

REFERENCES

Augustine, N.R. (1997), *Augustine's Laws*, Reston: American Institute of Aeronautics and Astronautics.
Baumol, W. (1967), 'Macroeconomics of unbalanced growth: the anatomy of urban crisis', *American Economic Review*, **57**(3), 415–26.
Beck, M. (1981), *Government Spending: Trends and Issues*, New York: Praeger.

Brozka, M. (1995), 'World military expenditures', in Keith Hartley and Todd Sandler (eds), *Handbook of Defense Economics*, vol. I, Amsterdam: Elsevier Science.

Council of Economic Advisors (2005), *Economic Report of the President 2006*, Washington, DC: US Government Printing Office.

Cusack, T.R. (1985a), 'The evolution of power, threat and security: past and potential developments', *International Interactions*, **12**(4), 151–98.

Cusack, T.R. (1985b), 'Contention and compromise: a comparative analysis of budgetary politics', *Journal of Public Policy*, **5**(3), 497–519.

Cusack, T.R. and L. Engelhardt (2002), 'The PGL: file collection: file structures and procedures' (<http://www.wz-berlin.de/mp/ism/people/misc/cusack/d_sets.en.htm#data>).

Cusack, T.R. and S. Fuchs (2003), 'Parteien, Institutionen und Staatsausgaben in den OECD-Ländern', in H. Obinger, U. Wagschal and B. Kittel (eds), *Politische Ökonomie*, Opladen: Leske + Budrich.

Cusack, T.R. and M.D. Ward (1981), 'Military spending in the United States, Soviet Union and People's Republic of China', *Journal of Conflict Resolution*, **25**(3), 429–69.

Domke, W.K., R.C. Eichenberg and C.M. Kelleher (1983), 'The illusion of choice: defense and welfare in advanced industrial democracies, 1948–1978', *American Political Science Review*, **77**(1), 19–35.

European Commission (2003), *Public Finances in EMU 2003*, Brussels: Commission of the European Union.

Federation of American Scientists (2005), Military Analysis Network (<http://www.fas.org/man/>).

Ferguson, N. (2001), *The Cash Nexus: Money and Power in the Modern World, 1700–2000*, London: Penguin.

Goure, D. (2000), 'International security and the aging crisis', Center for Strategic Studies white paper, Washington.

Harrison, M. (1998), 'The economics of World War II: an overview', in M. Harrison (ed.), *The Economics of World War II*, Cambridge: Cambridge University Press.

IISS (various years), *The Military Balance*, Oxford: Oxford University Press.

Johnston, L. and S.H. Williamson (2004), 'The annual real and nominal GDP for the United States, 1789–present', Economic History Services (<http://www.eh.net/hmit/gdp/>).

Kirkpatrick, D.L.I. (1995), 'The rising unit cost of defence equipment – the reasons and the results', *Defence and Peace Economics*, **6**, 263–88.

Kirkpatrick, D.L.I. and P.G. Pugh (1983), 'Towards the Starship Enterprise – are the current trends in defence unit cost inexorable?', *Aerospace*, **10**(5), 16–23.

Levy, J. (1983), *War in the Modern Great Power System, 1495–1975*, Lexington: University Press of Kentucky.

Lieber, K.A. and D.G. Press (2006), 'The rise of US nuclear primacy', *Foreign Affairs*, March/April, pp. 42–54.

Lindert, P.H. (2004), *Growing Public: Social Spending and Economic Growth Since the 18th Century*, vol. 2, Cambridge: Cambridge University Press.

Lorell, M.A. (2003), *The U.S. Combat Aircraft Industry, 1909–2000: Structure, Competition, Innovation*, Santa Monica: Rand Corp.

Lorell, M.A. and Hugh P. Levaux (1998), *The Cutting Edge: A Half-Century of U.S. Fighter Aircraft R&D*, Santa Monica: Rand Corp.

Lumsdaine, D.H. (1993), *Moral Vision in International Politics: The Foreign Aid Regime, 1949–1989*, Princeton: Princeton University Press.

MacDonald, S. (1964), *Evolution of Aircraft Carriers*, Washington: US Government Printing Office.

Mitchell, B.R. (1962), *Abstract of British Historical Statistics*, Cambridge: Cambridge University Press.

Mulligan, C. and A. Shleifer (2004), 'Conscription as Regulation', NBER working paper No. 10558.

Nincic, M. and T.R. Cusack (1979), 'The political economy of U.S. military spending', *Journal of Peace Research*, **16**(2), 101–15.

OECD (various years), *Economic Outlook*, Paris: OECD.

OECD (various years), *Yearbook of National Accounts*, vol. 2, Paris: OECD.

Oneal, J.R. (1992), 'Budgetary savings from conscription and burden sharing in NATO', *Defence Economics*, **3**, 113–25.

Pugh, P.G. (1993), 'The procurement nexus', *Defence Economics*, **4**, 179–94.

Schmidt, M.G. (2006), 'Testing the retrenchment hypothesis: the case of public and private expenditure on education in 21 OECD countries (1960–2002)', paper presented at the workshop on 'The Disappearing State?', Hänse-Wissenschaftskolleg (HWK) Delmenhorst.

SIPRI (various years), *SIPRI Yearbook: Armaments, Disarmament and International Security*, Oxford: Oxford University Press.

Stoll, Richard J. (1982), 'Let the researcher beware: the use of the Richardson equations to estimate the parameters of a dyadic acquisition process', *American Journal of Political Science*, **26**(1), 77–89.

US Department of Commerce (2005), *Budget of the United States Government: Historical Tables Fiscal Year 2005*, Washington, DC: US Government Printing Office.

USAF Public Affairs Division (2005), National Museum of the United States Air Force (<http://www.wpafb.af.mil/museum/air_power/ap.htm>).

Van Ypersele de Strihou, J. (1967), 'Sharing the defence burden among the Western allies', *Review of Economics and Statistics*, **49**, 527–36.

6. Expenditure on public order and safety

Paul Norris

6.1 INTRODUCTION

The protection of citizens and the enforcement of law would appear a key function of government and also clearly qualifies as a 'core' function in more than a purely formal sense. As Heywood (1994, pp. 43–4) writes,

> The central function of a 'minimal' or 'night-watchman' state is the maintenance of domestic order, in effect, the protecting of individual citizens from one another. All states thus possess some kind of machinery for upholding law and order.

Given the apparent importance of maintaining law and order, it might be expected that it would be an area widely addressed in the comparative public policy literature. However, while there is work in criminology considering cross-national variation in individual aspects of criminal justice (for instance Bayley, 1985, with regard to policing levels and Sutton, 2000, with reference to incarceration rates) almost no attention has been paid to variation in overall criminal justice expenditure or effort and its determinants.

Moreover, the comparative research there has been has focused on physical outcomes, such as the number of police officers per 1000 people, rather than expenditure levels. However, as the provision of criminal justice becomes more complex, for instance through the use of private prisons in several countries, it is possible that expenditure data, including the cost to government of using private provision, might provide a better indication of overall resourcing than employment data, generally including only those directly employed by government (see Chapter 3 above for the rationale of this argument).

Comparative work on criminal justice outcomes has also been limited by the lack of comparable data. In contrast to many other policy areas, there are few, if any, truly comparable data sets relating to criminal justice matters. This is largely due to the fact that the roles and responsibilities of those within the criminal justice system can vary substantially from one

Table 6.1   *Number of countries providing data on the resourcing of the*
            criminal justice system to the UNCJS, 1990–2002

		4th survey 1986–90	5th survey 1990–94	6th survey 1995–97	7th survey 1998–2000	8th survey 2000–02
Police	Expenditure	12	17	12	9	10
	Personnel	16	14	19	15	18
Courts	Expenditure	7	7	10	15	11
	Personnel	14	9	15	18	15
Prisons	Expenditure	14	12	9	14	13
	Personnel	14	14	12	14	15

Note: Based on the 19 countries listed in Table 6.2, plus Australia, Canada, New Zealand and Switzerland.

country to another. Two notable exceptions are the *European Sourcebook on Crime and Criminal Justice* (ESCCJ) and the periodic *United Nations Survey of Crime and Justice* (UNCJS), both of which have attempted to get countries to provide data based on common definitions of the different roles within the criminal justice system, for instance policing. However, many countries still provide data without adjustment to match these definitions or with annotations explaining how their definitions differ from those required. As a consequence, comparative work based on these sources needs to be conducted with extreme care and may require substantial primary research to try and ensure the reliability of data.

Assuming that data provided to the UNCJS are comparable between countries and over time, the figures in Table 6.1 suggest that it would be extremely difficult to create a large enough sample of expenditure data to allow for regression-based cross-national analysis. The higher prevalence of data on personnel suggests why this measure has proved a more popular dependent variable in existing research.

6.2   OVERVIEW OF THE DATA

The increased requirement for developed countries to provide a classified breakdown of government expenditure to international organisations such as the OECD might provide an alternative way to tackle the dependent variable issue in comparative work on criminal justice resourcing. Within the COFOG classification of expenditure is a category entitled 'Public Order and Safety'. This category is meant to include all expenditure on policing, the law courts, prisons, the fire service, research and development related to

Table 6.2   Expenditure recorded in COFOG public order and safety category, 1990–2002

Country	Expenditure as a percentage of GDP			Change in expenditure 1990–2002		
	1990	1996	2002	1990–96	1996–2002	1990–2002
Austria	N/A	1.5	1.4	N/A	−0.1	N/A
Belgium	1.2	1.5	1.7	0.3	0.2	0.5
Denmark	1.1	1	1	−0.1	0	−0.1
Finland	1.3	1.5	1.4	0.2	−0.1	0.1
France	N/A	1	1	N/A	0	N/A
Germany	1.5	1.7	1.7	0.2	0	0.2
Greece	N/A	0.7	1	N/A	0.3	N/A
Iceland	1.3	1.4	1.6	0.1	0.2	0.3
Ireland	1.7	1.7	1.4	0	−0.3	−0.3
Italy	2.1	2.1	2	0	−0.1	−0.1
Japan	1.2	1.4	1.4	0.2	0	0.2
Luxembourg	0.9	0.9	1.1	0	0.2	0.2
Netherlands	N/A	1.4	1.7	N/A	0.3	N/A
Norway	1.1	1	1.2	−0.1	0.2	0.1
Portugal	2.2	1.7	1.9	−0.5	0.2	−0.3
Spain	N/A	N/A	1.9	N/A	N/A	N/A
Sweden	N/A	1.4	1.4	N/A	0	N/A
UK	2.1	2.1	2.4	0	0.3	0.3
USA	1.7	1.9	2.1	0.2	0.2	0.4
Mean (all)	1.5	1.5	1.5	0.04	0.08	0.11
Mean (13 countries)	1.5	1.5	1.6	0.04	0.02	0.11
Total N	13	18	19	13	18	13

Notes: No data available for Australia, Canada, New Zealand or Switzerland at any time point; figures subject to rounding errors; data sources as Appendix 3B.

public order and any additional costs relating to the administration of such services (IMF, 2001, p. 83–5). While this constitutes a somewhat imperfect definition of the resources devoted to the realm of criminal justice (for instance, because of the inclusion of the fire service), these data are generally collected by government economic services to match the COFOG classification, and so might avoid some of the jurisdiction-based anomalies associated with data collected through the criminal justice system.

For the countries for which data are available, Table 6.2 shows levels and changes of public order and safety expenditure in the OECD region over the period 1990–2002.

Although the provision of data improves over time, the number of countries for which data are available remains relatively low compared to many of the other policy areas covered in this volume. Under previous COFOG classifications (prior to 1995), while public order and safety appeared as a separate category, some countries lumped together expenditure in this category with that of General Public Services (for discussion of the residual character of this category of spending, see Chapter 4). This situation is improving, with countries slowly going back and providing data for earlier years. However, at the time of writing in the summer of 2006, there are insufficient data to permit regression analysis of expenditure change for the period 1990–2002, much less for the period 1980–2002, as would be required in order to establish whether criminal justice spending had contributed to core expenditure cutbacks after 1980.

Substantively, the figures in Table 6.2 show no general trend over the period. Indeed, the overriding picture is of virtually no change in patterns of spending with a Spearman correlation between expenditure in 1990 and 2002 of 0.831 (p <0.001) and between 1996 and 2002 of 0.872 (p <0.001). In the majority of countries in Table 6.2, spending goes up or down by only 0.1 or 0.2 percentage points of GDP. Changes of this magnitude might well be attributable to data measurement problems rather than representing genuine changes in the size of the public order effort. Data rounding, differences in data recording practices as between countries and, more substantively, the fact that the measure is also influenced by the quite substantial changes in the GDP denominator, all contribute to making analysis on the basis of such small differences more than somewhat perilous. Putting these issues to one side, there is no real evidence of any substantial catch-up trend of the kind that features in other areas of public spending during this period (see the introduction to this volume and many of the chapters on specific policy areas). The Pearson's r correlation between expenditure change 1990–2002 and the 1990 level of public order expenditure is −0.361 and between 1996–2002 change and the 1996 level of spending −0.203. Neither of these relationships even begins to verge on the threshold of statistical significance.

The small number of cases, the absence of any apparent trend and doubts about the reliability of analysing expenditures changes of this magnitude all suggest that a longitudinal analysis, assessing which factors best explain change between 1990 and 2002, is not really feasible. Instead, this chapter will use expenditure data for the year 2000 to suggest some factors that may be worth considering in longitudinal modelling as more data become available. By concentrating on one year it has been possible to gather data from a range of sources, while maintaining comparability with the definitions given in the COFOG literature (full sources for the data are provided under the figures below). It has also proved possible to collect expenditure data on

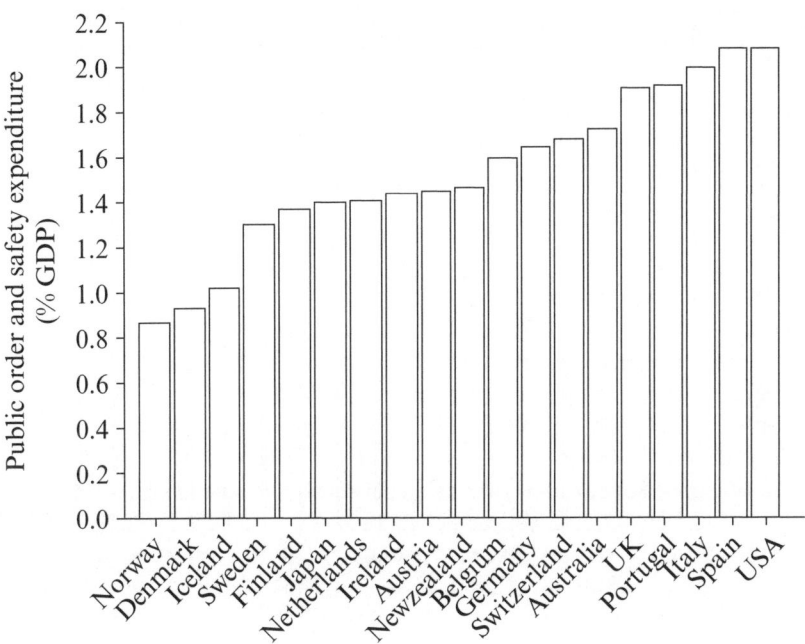

Notes: All data from Eurostat (2006) except Australia, New Zealand and Switzerland – personal contact with National Statistics Office, Japan – OECD (2006), and USA – Bureau of Economic Affairs (2005).

Figure 6.1   *Public order and safety expenditure as a percentage of GDP, 2000*

the specific functions of policing and prisons (which, while identified in the COFOG documentation, are not commonly collected by international bodies). These data are examined to see to what extent studying the overall public order and safety category may conceal differences between cross-national spending patterns in different areas of the criminal justice system.

Figures 6.1, 6.2 and 6.3 report comparative spending levels on aggregate public order and safety, on policing and on prisons respectively. Figure 6.1 shows that the United States ranks first in public order spending, but the figures there do not suggest that the country manifests anything like an outlier status. It is, however, often argued that the USA is an atypical case, especially with regard to its levels of incarceration and apparently resource-intensive policies such as 'three-strikes and you are out' and the 'War on Drugs' (see Thorny, 2006). Figure 6.3 suggests that Spain may be a genuine outlier with respect to its expenditure on prisons, a point supported by the fact that its ratio of (Prison Expenditure/GDP)/(Prisoners/Population) of 5.6

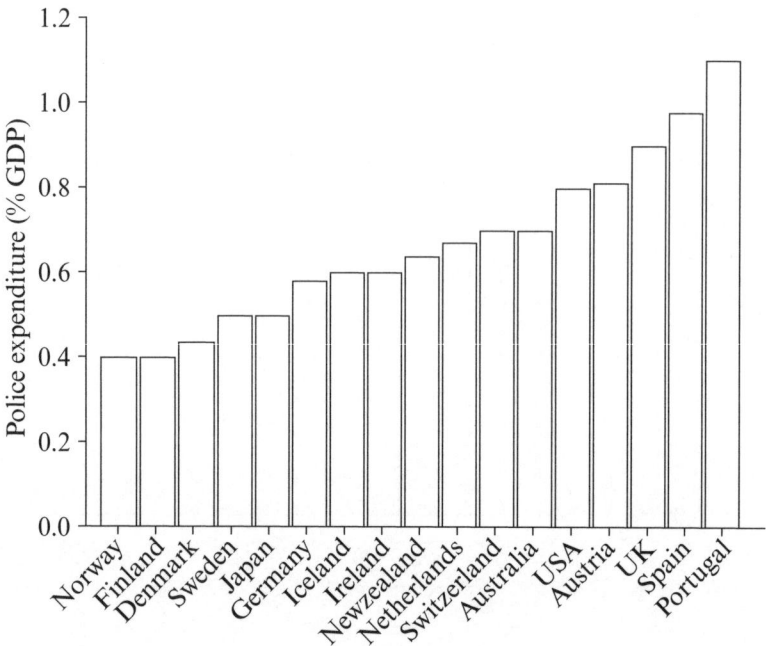

Notes: All data from national statistics offices and based on COFOG subcategory of 'Police', except Australia, Denmark, Ireland – 7th UNCJS and communication with national statistical office and Germany, Netherlands and Portugal: van Dijk and Waard (2000) and own calculations.

Figure 6.2   Police expenditure as a percentage of GDP (I)

contrasts with an average of 2.1 for all other countries (data taken from *World Prison Brief*, 2003). In view of these concerns, subsequent hypothesis testing will be conducted both including and excluding the USA in all instances and including and excluding Spain for analysis concerning prison expenditure.

Table 6.3 shows the Spearman correlations between the three types of expenditure shown above. The relative strength of the correlations suggest that, while countries which spend highly on one part of the criminal justice system are likely to spend highly on other areas, this relationship may hide some subtle differences worthy of further investigation. The order of countries in Figures 6.1–6.3 suggests that expenditure is generally higher in the countries of Southern Europe and in English-speaking countries and generally lower in Scandinavia. These groupings broadly resemble the families of nations identified by Castles (1998, and Chapter 2 above) and suggest that variation in criminal justice expenditure may be related to a range of underlying cultural and historical factors.

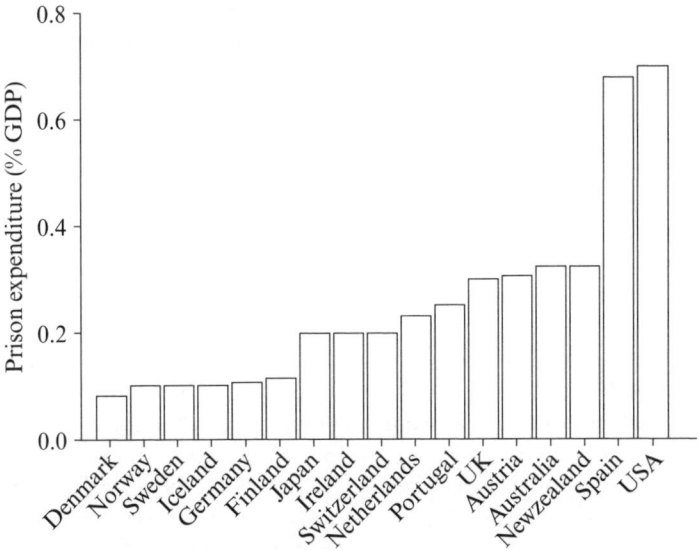

Note: Data sources as for Figure 6.2, except COFOG-based figures now for the subcategory 'Prisons'.

Figure 6.3   Prison expenditure as a percentage of GDP (II)

Table 6.3   Spearman's rho correlations between the different measures of criminal justice expenditure

	Police expenditure	Prison expenditure
Public order and safety	0.84***	0.75***
	(17)	(17)
Police expenditure		0.75***
		(17)

Notes: The numbers in brackets refer to the number of cases considered in each correlation. Data as for Figures 6.1–6.3; *** indicates significance at below the 0.01 level; excluding the USA and Spain makes no difference to the general conclusions.

6.3   POSSIBLE EXPLANATIONS FOR CRIMINAL JUSTICE EXPENDITURE OUTCOMES

6.3.1   Criminal Justice Factors

Expressed simply, the aim of a criminal justice system is to prevent or to deal with crime. As such, it might be expected that spending on criminal justice would be higher where the need for criminal justice services was greatest. What cross-national research there has been has therefore considered the relationship between criminal justice resourcing and the level of crime. This research generally shows a positive linkage between resourcing and recorded crime levels (for example, see Bayley 1985, p. 83, with reference to policing levels). However, these relationships often prove to be statistically insignificant, suggesting that the degree of association is relatively weak.

Beyond a simple relationship between overall crime levels and public order expenditure, it is also possible that the profile of crime may be important in explaining criminal justice resourcing. For instance, violent crimes are generally considered more serious offences and this increase in perceived seriousness may lead to an increase in public and political awareness of the issue (and an increased desire for action). Therefore changes in the level of violent crime would seem likely to lead to changes in policy. Some evidence in support of this proposition can be found in existing research considering personnel levels. Kangaspunta et al. (1998, pp. 66–8) show that the level of violent crime is positively related to the level of prison staffing (at a 0.05 significance level) based on a sample of 30 countries from Europe and North America. Similarly, Bayley (1985, p. 84) finds that the level of policing is positively related to the number of homicides. Using the level of incarceration, Greenberg and West (2001, p. 617) show that the level of violent crime provides a more significant explanation of inter-country variation than does the overall level of crime.

These studies all rely on recorded crime levels as a basis for their data. However, as already noted, official crime figures should only be used in international comparisons with extreme caution. In effect, apparent differences between countries may be as much a result of differences in definitions and administrative practice as they are of levels of crime (see Newman and Howard, 1999a).

Victim surveys (which ask individuals about their experience of crime) are often considered a more reliable instrument for comparing crime levels across countries. Unfortunately, taking data from both the 1996 and 2000 sweeps of the *International Crime Victim Survey* (ICVS) still only provides information on 13 of the countries used in this study. In general, however, recorded crime figures appear to provide a reasonable indication of the relative position of countries when compared with ICVS data. For example, with regard to the level of assault, there is a Spearman's correlation of just under 0.8 (p-value <0.01) for the countries analysed in this chapter, suggesting that, until victim survey data are available for more countries, recorded crime statistics can provide an alternative indicator.

Another reason for using recorded crime figures is that this may well be the information used in framing criminal justice policy in the first place. To

Table 6.4 *Correlations between patterns of crime and public order*
expenditure

Explanatory factor	Public order and safety expenditure	Police expenditure	Prisons expenditure
Recorded crimes per 100 000 people	−0.360 (19)	−0.449* (17)	−0.284 (17)
Recorded crimes per 100 000 people (excluding drugs offences)	−0.362 (19)	−0.451* (17)	−0.299 (17)
Homicides per 100 000 people	0.138 (19)	0.059 (17)	0.090 (17)
Violent crimes per 100 000 people	0.381* (19)	0.259 (17)	0.328 (17)
Violent crimes as a percentage of total crimes	0.693*** (19)	0.690*** (17)	0.623*** (17)

Notes: Expenditure data from Figures 6.1–6.3. All crime data from Interpol International Crime Statistics (2002). Data refer to 1998 except for New Zealand (1997) and United States. The figure for the UK is based on a weighted average of England and Wales (1998), Scotland (1998) and Northern Ireland (1996 and 2000). Estimates of Drugs offences for the following countries were used from national statistical offices: Australia and the USA.
* indicates significance at the 0.1 level; ** indicates significance at the 0.05 level; *** indicates significance at the 0.01 level. Excluding Spain from the analysis has no effect on the results. Excluding the USA causes the relationship between violent crimes per 100 000 people and prison expenditure to become significant at the 0.1 level.

the extent that this is so, previous concerns may be, to some extent, negated, since what drives policy is as much the perception as the reality of the extent of criminal behaviour.

Table 6.4 reports Pearson's r correlations between public order expenditure as a percentage of GDP and levels and types of crime. All the correlations between total crime per 100 000 of the population and spending are inverse, apparently contradicting the expectation that countries in which crime is more prevalent will have the highest expenditure. However, most of these relationships are statistically insignificant, suggesting that no real conclusions can be drawn. In contrast, the correlations for violent offences have the expected positive sign, but again, for the most part, lack statistical robustness except for relationships with violent crime as a percentage of all criminal activity. This exception suggests strongly that it is the profile of crimes within a country, rather than the nominal level of offences, that drives expenditure.

A possible explanation for the apparent contradiction between the correlations concerning violent crime and those concerning crime in general could be that violent crime (the extent of which is often overestimated by the public, leading to greater public pressure to increase criminal justice spending) is indeed associated with higher levels of public order spending. However, greater resourcing of the criminal justice system could be expected to increase the belief amongst criminals that they will be caught. This makes committing minor offences (which make up the majority of total crime) less appealing, leading to a fall in the general level of crime. If true, this would suggest a reversal in the expected causal ordering of the relationship, with higher expenditures contributing to a fall in the overall incidence of criminal behaviour.

6.3.2 Socio-economic Factors

Table 6.5 shows correlations between the three measures of expenditure and various socio-economic factors that are widely believed to influence criminal justice policy. In their study based on the 5th UNCJS, Newman and Howard (1999b, p. 140) demonstrate that levels of police expenditure

Table 6.5   Correlations between socio-economic factors and public order expenditure

Explanatory factor	Public order and safety expenditure	Police expenditure	Prisons expenditure
GDP per capita (PPP$)	−0.292 (19)	−0.443* (17)	−0.174 (17)
Percentage of households on less than 50% median income	0.654*** (18)	0.737*** (16)	0.477** (16)
Average unemployment during 1990s (%)	0.413** (19)	0.204 (17)	0.539** (17)
Percentage of 25–64-year-olds with completed secondary education	−0.453** (19)	−0.676*** (17)	−0.271 (17)
Percentage of population belonging to majority ethno-linguistic group	−0.455** (19)	−0.357 (17)	−0.664*** (17)

Notes: Expenditure data are from Figures 6.1–6.3. The numbers in brackets represent the number of countries involved in each test. Iceland is excluded from the correlations concerning inequality owing to a lack of suitable data. Significance levels as Table 6.4. Excluding Spain from the prison correlations has no effect on the results. GDP per capita: World Bank (2002); households with less than 50% median income: OECD, 2005 or appropriate National Statistics Office; unemployment (% population average 1990–2000) and percentage of 25–64-year-olds with completed secondary education: both OECD, 2005.

and prison expenditure (both measured in nominal US dollars per capita terms) are positively related to a country's level of GDP (again measured in US dollars per capita). However, these findings may simply be due to the fact that richer countries have more resources to devote to criminal justice matters, an issue that can only be settled by measuring expenditure itself as a proportion of GDP. Comparisons relating physical measures of criminal justice policy to a country's level of development suggest that, as countries become more developed, they devote a lower proportion of available resources to criminal justice issues. For instance, Bayley (1985, p. 77) finds that the number of police per capita is inversely related to a variety of measures of economic development including GNP per capita. Kangaspunta et al. (1998, p. 61) reach similar conclusions based on their sample of countries from Europe and North America, with significance at a 0.05 level. The results in Table 6.5 appear to mirror this pattern, particularly when the USA is excluded from the sample, causing all three correlations to be significant at the 0.05 level.

Inequality is another factor potentially linked to the demand for criminal justice intervention. It is possible that higher inequality will cause greater demand for criminal justice services, for two related reasons. First, as inequality increases, so do the potential gains to be made through criminal activity. Hence increased inequality may cause higher crime and a greater need for a criminal justice system. Second, as inequality increases, the threat of criminality experienced by better-off sections of society may be expected to increase. This is likely to produce an increase in demands for policing and for harsher punishment of offenders. Policies addressing such demands could be expected to increase criminal justice expenditure. This linkage is supported by the literature on incarceration, with Petrovec (2000, pp. 379–81), and Krus and Hoehl (1994, pp. 1493–4) finding strong statistical links between inequality and prison use. The correlations reported in Table 6.5, based on the percentage of households receiving less than 50 per cent of median income, support such findings and show that inequality is positively related to spending and one of the best indicators of expenditure outcomes. The level of unemployment is often regarded as a proxy for inequality and has been found to be positively related to incarceration rates (Sutton, 2000, p. 359). While the link between unemployment and prison expenditure is insignificant, positive correlations with total expenditure and expenditure on prisons tend to support the presumption of linkages between unemployment, inequality and criminal justice outcomes.

Levels of education – also strongly related to, or a proxy for, degrees of social inequality – are also commonly believed to influence the level of crime and therefore the demand for criminal justice services. An inverse relationship seems probable, as the effects of educational achievement could be expected to be the reverse of economic inequality (notably due to the relationship between education and employment opportunities). A lack of educational attainment may also be associated with an increase in feelings of marginalisation and resentment within society, reducing the social inhibitions that discourage crime. Policy responses are likely to include increased spending. Statistically significant relationships fitting this expectation are found by Bayley (1985, p. 77) with regard to policing levels and for the level of incarceration by Sutton (2000, p. 359). Again the correlations in Table 6.5 appear to confirm these findings (especially as the relationship with prison expenditure becomes significant at the 0.1 level when the USA is excluded from the sample).

A country's level of ethno-linguistic fragmentation may also affect criminal justice spending as it has commonly been shown to be associated with the prevalence of crime and, in particular, with violent incidents (Fajnzylber et al., 2002). It seems plausible that this perceived threat will increase as the size of the minority grows. Therefore the size of the criminal justice effort could be expected to be smaller the more dominant is the major ethno-linguistic grouping. The correlations in Table 6.5 again fit theoretical expectations, but the effect of ethnic homogeneity appears greater with regard to prisons than to policing. The relationship with overall public order spending ceases to be significant when the USA is removed from the sample.

Overall, the correlations presented in Table 6.5 appear largely supportive of previous research findings on the relationship between socio-economic factors and the size of the criminal justice effort. At the same time, the fact that removing the USA from the sample has a marked influence on the significance levels of a number of these relationships does suggest that this country may, in at least some respects, prove to be an aberrant case.

Much previous research has suggested there is a strong relationship between the prevalence of violent crime, considered in Table 6.4, and the level of inequality, considered in Table 6.5 (see van Dijk, 1999, p. 32). Both factors may be seen as increasing the demand for criminal justice services because they increase the threat that individuals believe they face from crime. Because these factors are strongly related, it is rarely possible to measure them separately in the kind of small-n multivariate modelling employed throughout this book. Thus, in order to test the threat hypothesis, in Table 6.6 we combine these variables in what is here referred to as the 'Threat Index', which is calculated using the following formula:

$$\text{Threat Index} = (\text{Z-score (inequality)} + \text{Z-score (violent crime as a percentage of total crime)})/2$$

Table 6.6   Correlations with the threat index

Factor	Pearson correlation with threat index
Violent crimes as a percentage of total crimes	0.905** (18)
Percentage of households on less than 50% median income	0.904** (18)
Total public order and safety expenditure as a percentage of GDP	0.737** (18)
Police expenditure as a percentage of GDP	0.771** (16)
Prisons expenditure as a percentage of GDP	0.598* (16)

Notes: Numbers in brackets show the number of countries involved in each correlation.
Iceland is excluded from all models including the Threat Index due to a lack of inequality
data. Expenditure data from Figures 6.1–6.3. Significance as in Table 6.4.

This index is extremely strongly related to both of the original measures from
which it is constituted, suggesting they can properly be considered as aspects
of the same overarching factor. The generally strong correlations between
the Threat Index and the different measures of expenditure examined in this
chapter suggest that, as with the original variables, this factor goes a long way
in explaining cross-national differences in public order spending.

6.3.3   Political Factors

While all politicians insist that crime is wrong and steps should be taken to
reduce it, the political Right has generally viewed the maintenance of public
order as one of its strongest policy areas, often seeing demands for harsher
punishments as a trump card in tight electoral contests (Jacobs and Helms,
2001, pp. 174–6). In contrast, the Left often appears more concerned with
reducing the causes of crime, for instance through increased welfare provision
(Sutton, 2000, pp. 361–3). These differences in attitude could well be reflected
in criminal justice expenditure. Given their apparently tougher stance
towards criminality, it would seem plausible that governments of the Right
will direct more resources towards the criminal justice system. In the area of
the relationship between politics and criminal justice, more than either of the
spheres previously discussed, the existing literature would appear to be dominated by work on the level of incarceration. However, given that incarceration is both expensive and also the result of a country's ability to apprehend
criminals and its willingness to punish them, it might be expected that these
relationships will show up in public order expenditure as a whole.

Anecdotal evidence on the relevance of the Right–Left divide to law and order policy is provided by the observation of Morgan (2000, p. 65) on the coming to power of the Conservative Party in the United Kingdom in 1979: 'The Conservatives (the major Right-wing party in British politics) promised the electorate that, if elected, they would cut public expenditure virtually across the board but increase spending on "law and order" services.'

The first four correlations in Table 6.7 report the association between partisan incumbency and public order spending. The direction of the Left

Table 6.7   Correlations between political factors and public order expenditure

Explanatory factor	Public order and safety expenditure	Police expenditure	Prisons expenditure
Percentage of cabinet seats held by left-wing parties, 1950–98	−0.627*** (18)	−0.341 (16)	−0.414 (16)
Percentage of cabinet seats held by left-wing parties, 1990–98	−0.322 (18)	−0.149 (16)	−0.225 (16)
Percentage of cabinet seats held by right-wing parties, 1950–98	0.595*** (18)	0.543** (16)	0.416* (16)
Percentage of cabinet seats held by right-wing parties, 1990–98	−0.091 (18)	−0.091 (16)	−0.216 (16)
Schmidt index, 1960–98	−0.489** (19)	−0.345 (17)	−0.375 (17)
Schmidt index, 1990–98	−0.321 (19)	−0.122 (17)	−0.218 (17)
Social expenditure, 1990–2000 (% GDP)	−0.403* (19)	−0.433* (17)	−0.417* (17)
Consensus government, 1960–96	−0.495** (17)	−0.718*** (15)	−0.716*** (15)
Consensus government, 1990–96	−0.509** (17)	−0.743*** (15)	−0.671*** (15)

Notes: Expenditure data from Figures 6.1–6.3. All data relating to politics variables are from Armingeon et al. (2005). The numbers in brackets represent the number of countries involved in each test. Iceland is excluded from the correlations concerning cabinet seats held owing to a lack of suitable data. Portugal and Spain are considered to be 100% right-wing governments during their respective dictatorships. * indicates significance at the 0.1 level; ** indicates significance at the 0.05 level; *** indicates significance at the 0.01 level.

cabinet coefficients suggests that increased Left-wing influence does indeed result in lower public order expenditure. Paradoxically, Right incumbency in the 1990s is also negatively associated with spending, but not significantly so. However, measures of cabinet influence over the entire period since 1950 suggest that an enduring legacy of Right-wing politics is associated with higher criminal justice expenditure, and that these relationships are statistically significant. As in Chapter 2, incumbency over the long term appears a more potent factor shaping policy outcomes than partisan balance in the short term.

Most measures of partisan incumbency implicitly import national assumptions of Left and Right positioning in the political spectrum; for instance, locating the American Democrats as being, if not a Left party, certainly not a Right-wing one, when, in international comparison, that may well be what it is (see Jacobs and Helms, 2001, p. 182 with regard to the Clinton administrations). A partisan measure, which seeks to take such international comparisons seriously, is Schmidt's indicator of the political complexion of governments, for which findings are also reported in Table 6.7. These, while less significant than for long-term Right incumbency, are generally consistent with the party incumbency hypothesis.

Beyond the partisan aspects of politics, institutional structures can also influence the shape of government policy. Lijphart (1999, p. 297) argues that a country's incarceration rate is inversely related to the number of parties in government, his argument being that consensual politics, of the kind that results from a proportional representation electoral system, tends to mitigate harsh policy outcomes. Arguably, then, where consensus politics is more common, countries will spend less on their criminal justice systems. The correlations presented in Table 6.7 support this supposition, with the number of parties involved in government, over both the long- and the short-term, strongly inversely related to levels of criminal justice expenditure, although the correlation concerning overall spending and the long-term level of consensual politics does appear dependent on the USA.

As well as its direct influence on criminal justice spending, it is also possible that the nature of a country's politics will have an indirect influence on the need for criminal justice services and hence the resources provided to them. It is well established in the public policy literature that both Left-wing incumbency (Castles, 1998, p. 90) and consensual politics (Lijphart, 1999, p. 95) are associated with more generous welfare systems. Accepting that a more generous welfare system will reduce economic inequality, and that lower inequality will reduce crime, a larger welfare system could be expect to reduce the level of resources required for criminal justice matters. This argument is again supported by the literature on incarceration. Sutton (2000,

p. 361) finds an inverse and significant relationship between a country's level of incarceration and its total welfare payments (as a percentage of GDP), while Jacobs and Helms (2001, pp. 176–7) see such 'latent political cleavages' as a key issue in the relationship between politics and imprisonment. In line with this argument, Table 6.7 suggests that all three measures of expenditure are inversely related to a country's level of welfare expenditure. However, once again, this is a finding the significance of which is dependent on inclusion of the American case, adding yet more weight to the possibility that it may be an atypical case.

In contrast to the correlations in the previous two tables, it does appear that removing Spain from the sample has an affect on the results concerning prison expenditure. This is probably because, as well as its apparent outlier status with regard to prison expenditure (discussed earlier), Spain would appear to be a unique case in terms of partisan politics, having had no Right-wing involvement in government between its return to democracy (in the mid-1970s) and the late 1990s. Removing Spain from the sample does not affect the overall pattern of relationships shown in Table 6.5; however, it does make the partisan incumbency variables more significant, with, for instance, the relationship between the long-tem Schmidt Index and prison expenditure now significant at the 0.05 level.

6.4   MULTIVARIATE ANALYSIS

The bivariate results discussed so far suggest that public order expenditure is affected by many of those factors previous research has found to be related to criminal justice personnel levels. In reality, however, that judgement has to wait on multivariate modelling controlling for the potential impact of all these factors simultaneously. In what follows, regression models are presented showing which combinations of factors best explain cross-national variation in total spending as well as specific spending on both police and prisons.

Given the exploratory nature of these models, a significance level at or below the 0.1 threshold is seen as worthy of comment and as possibly suggestive of insights as to areas for future work. However, models satisfying the standard 0.05 criterion are also presented as indicative of the most satisfactory accounts available on current evidence. Given the concerns over the USA's possible outlier status with regard to criminal justice policy, models excluding this case are also presented. In the case of prison expenditure, for reasons already explained, a model excluding the Spanish case is also elaborated.

6.4.1 Overall Public Order and Safety Expenditure

Table 6.8 presents models with the total level of public order and safety expenditure as the dependent variable. All four models offer support for hypotheses suggesting that the extent of such expenditure is a function of both the threat of crime and the partisan composition of government. Model 1 considers all countries for which data are available with the criterion of variable inclusion significance at the 0.05 level. This model explains slightly more than 50 per cent of the cross-national variance and suggests that, for every additional percentage point in the proportion of violent offences, public order spending will be just under 0.05 of 1 per cent of GDP higher. This model also indicates that those countries with a stronger post-war record of Right incumbency have higher levels of public order expenditure.

Table 6.8   Regression models with public order and safety expenditure as a percentage of GDP as a dependent variable

	Model 1	Model 2	Model 3	Model 4
Constant	1.126***	2.949***	1.134***	1.949***
	(9.94)	(5.85)	(9.72)	(9.07)
Violent crimes as a percentage of total crimes	0.046** (2.87)		0.042** (2.27)	
Threat index		0.144* (1.97)		0.294*** (4.08)
Percentage of population belonging to the main ethno-linguistic group		−0.008* (−1.77)		
Percentage of 25–64-year-olds who have completed secondary education		−0.008** (−2.28)		
Percentage of cabinet seats held by the political right, 1950–1998	0.005** (2.25)		0.005** (2.24)	
Percentage of cabinet seats held by the political left, 1990–98		−0.006** (−2.30)		
Schmidt index of government, 1990–98				−0.149* (−1.87)
Adj R^2	0.543***	0.664***	0.482***	0.518***

Notes: Expenditure data as for Figure 6.1; explanatory variables from Tables 6.4–6.7; significance levels as Table 6.7. Figures in parentheses are t-statistics for coefficients.

Model 2 considers the same countries as Model 1; however, the criterion of inclusion here is significance at the weaker 0.1 threshold. The findings of this model provide support for the general conclusions of the previous model, but with some differences regarding the exact variables that appear important. The inclusion of the Threat Index, with a positive coefficient, and both educational attainment and the size of the ethno-linguistic index with negative coefficients, supports the thesis that conditions conducive to a higher perceived demand for criminal justice services are associated with higher levels of public order expenditure. The inclusion of a more differentiated range of socio-economic factors, as compared to Model 1, also has an apparent impact on how partisan politics enters the explanation. Model 2 suggests that, instead of a significant positive Right incumbency effect, higher Left incumbency is associated with lower levels of public order spending. Given the collinearity of Left and Right partisan variables, this reversal is not particularly surprising and should not be over-interpreted. The same, almost certainly, goes for the fact that the long-term incumbency impact highlighted in Model 1 is replaced in Model 2 by a much shorter-term incumbency effect.

Models 3 and 4 once again consider the total level of public order expenditure, but with the United States now excluded from the sample. The adjusted R^2 values for these models are lower than for Models 1 and 2. However, the overall conclusions are very similar, with nearly identical coefficients. Again the use of the 0.1 criterion sees the Threat Index replace the prevalence of violent crime and, arguably, because this provides a partial control for the extent of economic inequality, the incumbency effect again switches from long-term to short-term. However, in this model, it is the Schmidt Index of Government, 1990–98, rather than cabinet incumbency as such which features most strongly in the explanation. The negative coefficient does, however, support the earlier finding that increased Right incumbency is associated with higher public order spending. Once the United States is excluded from the sample, educational attainment and ethno-linguistic fragmentation cease to be significant, suggesting, perhaps, that herein may lie some of the sources of American criminal justice exceptionalism.

6.4.2 Police Expenditure

Table 6.9 reports multivariate models with the level of police expenditure as the dependent variable. The high R^2 values of these models suggest that they provide a strong indication of the factors accounting for cross-national variance. As with the models concerning public order and safety, the models reported in Table 6.9 all suggest that police expenditure is positively related

Table 6.9   Regression models with police expenditure as a percentage of GDP as a dependent variable

	Model 1	Model 2	Model 3	Model 4
Constant	0.980***	1.541***	0.844***	1.517***
	(7.28)	(2.29)	(3.58)	(4.49)
Percentage of households on less than 50% median income			0.023**	
			(2.18)	
Threat index	0.120***	0.088**		0.101*
	(3.20)	(2.29)		(1.80)
Percentage of population belonging to the main ethno-linguistic group		−0.005**		−0.005*
		(−1.93)		(−1.92)
Percentage of 25–64-year-olds who have completed secondary education	−0.005**	−0.006***	−0.006**	−0.005*
	(−2.35)	(3.10)	(2.53)	(1.88)
Adj R²	0.671***	0.728***	0.673***	0.717***

Notes: Expenditure data as for Figure 6.2; explanatory variables from Tables 6.4–6.7; significance levels as Table 6.7. Figures in parentheses are t-statistics for coefficients.

to some measure of the perceived need for policing services, whether the Threat Index or the level of inequality. However, in contrast to the models for overall public order expenditure, there is no sign in these models that police resourcing is, in any way, a function of partisan difference.

Model 1 in Table 6.9 is based on the full sample of countries for which police expenditure figures are available and includes only variables significant at the 0.05 level. This model, which explains around 67 per cent of the cross-national variance, suggests that a country's police expenditure is strongly associated with its standing on the Threat Index. The only other significant variable to feature in the model is educational completion, with its coefficient indicating that, for every 1 per cent of the population aged 24–65 completing secondary education, police expenditure is lower by around 0.005 per cent of GDP.

Model 2 shows how Model 1 changes once significance at the 0.1 level is the accepted criterion of inclusion. In general, the new model appears highly consistent with the previous findings: for instance, the positive impact of the Threat Index and the negative coefficient associated with education. However, in addition to these factors, the extent of ethno-linguistic fragmentation also enters the model. Once again, this factor appears to be inversely related to the level of expenditure, a finding consistent with the Table 6.8 models and with the hypothesis that countries where the dominant group feels under less threat will spend less on maintaining public order.

Excluding the USA from the sample still provides conclusions broadly similar to those discussed above. This is especially the case in the model using a 0.1 significance threshold, which identifies precisely the same factors irrespective of whether or not the USA is part of the sample. The results are slightly less consistent when we consider the models using a 0.05 significance criterion. When the USA is excluded, it is the level of economic inequality, rather than the Threat Index, which appears to have the greatest impact. However, given the strong empirical and theoretical links between the Threat Index, the prevalence of violent crime and the level of inequality, this change should not be seen as undermining previous conclusions, especially given the similarity of the impact of education on police expenditure, irrespective of which other explanatory variable it is paired with.

The absence of any partisan effect in multivariate modelling suggests that the level of police expenditure is determined largely by factors directly influencing perceived demand, as opposed to party political objectives. This finding also suggests that the apparent political influence on overall public order and safety expenditure is likely to be due to its impact on the use of imprisonment. However, while politics appears to have little direct influence on the level of police expenditure, it is possible that, given the importance of the Threat Index and the level of inequality in Tables 6.5 and 6.6, long-term partisan incumbency could have an indirect influence on police expenditure via its impact on policies towards the welfare state. Such a conclusion fits well with the positive relationship between Right-wing cabinet seats (1950–1998) and police expenditure identified in the bivariate analysis (Table 6.7).

6.4.3   Prison Expenditure

Looking at the entire sample of countries and requiring significance at the 0.05 level produces only one-variable models for cross-national variance in prison expenditure levels. Similarly, no multivariate models can be created if the United States is removed from the sample. However, accepting significance at the 0.1 level and including all available countries in the sample does make it possible to identify a two-variable model (Model 1 in Table 6.10). While this model explains less than half the variation, its findings appear consistent with both theoretical expectations and models relating to other aspects of spending. The Threat Index once again is positively related to expenditure, while Left incumbency over recent years is associated with lower expenditure.

Table 6.10   *Regression models with prison expenditure as a percentage of GDP as a dependent variable*

	Model 1	Model 2	Model 3
Constant	0.341***	0.320***	0.680***
	(5.30)	(6.69)	(3.61)
Threat index	0.097**	0.070**	0.063**
	(2.83)	(2.68)	(2.65)
Percentage of population belonging to the main ethno-linguistic group			−0.004*
			(−1.97)
Percentage of cabinet seats held by the political left, 1990–98	−0.003*	−0.003**	−0.002*
	(1.78)	(2.31)	(1.79)
Adj R^2	0.447***	0.521***	0.613***

Notes: Expenditure data as for Figure 6.3; explanatory variables from Tables 6.4–6.7; significance levels as Table 6.7. Figures in parentheses are t-statistics for coefficients.

The previous bivariate analysis suggested that Spain might be an outlier with regard to prison expenditure, and removing this case from the sample does indeed produce stronger multivariate models. Both Model 1 variables are now significant at the 0.05 level (Model 2) and the R^2 value is somewhat improved. Excluding Spain and accepting significance at the 0.1 level sees the measure of ethno-linguistic fragmentation once again enter the model (Model 3). As previously, with regard to both police resourcing and overall public order spending, this variable is inversely related to expenditure.

6.4.4   Comparative Conclusions

In general, the factors associated with cross-national variation in the different forms of expenditure discussed in this chapter would appear to be relatively consistent. However, there are some differences in the factors associated with expenditure on policing and on prisons. All forms of criminal justice expenditure appear positively related to levels of perceived threat, measured either through the percentage of offences accounted for by violent crime, the level of inequality or the Threat Index. Beyond the level of inequality, the models here suggest that socio-economic factors relating to educational level and ethno-linguistic fragmentation may also have a role to play in explaining the level of criminal justice expenditure. However, the importance of these factors as elements of a general explanation is unclear as they mostly feature in models either including the USA or based on a 0.1 significance threshold, with the one important exception being the relationship between educational achievement levels and police spending. In the earlier bivariate analysis, unemployment was moderately strongly associated with spending outcomes. Unemployment does not, however, feature in any of our multivariate models, arguably because the inequality stemming from this source is at least partially controlled for by other variables which do appear in the models.

As with the incidence of crime and socio-economic factors discussed above, it is possible to reach some basic conclusions about the impact of politics on public order expenditure. Right incumbency, it would appear, has a positive effect, generally, in respect of overall spending and, more specifically, with regard to prisons spending. Although Right incumbency has a significant bivariate effect on police resourcing levels, the impact is not evident in the multivariate analysis. Similarly, while the bivariate analysis of politics on the other measures of expenditure generally tends to pick up long-term partisan effects, it is short-term measures which tend to feature as significant in the multivariate models. This gives support to the idea that politics not only has a direct influence on criminal justice spending, but also, because of its impact on welfare provision, may also have an indirect affect by altering the demand for criminal justice services.

6.5 A NEW SOURCE OF THREAT?

The analysis presented in the previous section has been based on expenditure data for the year 2000. However, the advent of the 'War on Terror' and the perception of an increased threat posed by international terrorist groups occurring since the attacks of 9/11 could be seen as providing a possible new driving force for increased public spending in the area of public safety. The last four years have seen a range of terrorist attacks on the interests of Western countries (for instance, in Madrid, in 2004, and in London, in 2005) and most governments have introduced new stringent security policies to meet this threat. All other things being equal, it seems reasonable to suppose that those countries that have had reason to believe they are facing the greatest terror threat will have been most active in introducing measures to address this concern (and will therefore have experienced the greatest increases in expenditure on public order and safety). Table 6.11 shows the average level of expenditure for the three years either side of 2001 for the 17 countries for which data are available. While the extent of expenditure movement is quite similar to that of the earlier period (predominantly between –0.2 per cent and 0.2 per cent of GDP), and while, as in the case of the data in Table 6.2, doubts concerning the measurement reliability of such relatively small changes must remain, the increase in sample size

Table 6.11   Public order expenditure either side of 2001

Country	1998–2000	2002–2004	Post-9/11 difference
Austria	1.5	1.4	−0.1
Belgium	1.5	1.8	0.3
Denmark	1.0	1.0	0.0
Finland	1.4	1.4	0.0
France	0.9	1.1	0.2
Germany	1.7	1.6	0.0
Greece	0.8	1.1	0.3
Ireland	1.5	1.4	−0.1
Italy	2.0	1.9	−0.1
Japan	1.4	1.5	0.1
Luxembourg	0.9	1.1	0.2
Netherlands	1.4	1.7	0.3
Norway	1.1	1.2	0.1
Portugal	1.7	1.9	0.2
Spain	1.8	1.8	0.0
Sweden	1.4	1.4	0.0
UK	2.1	2.5	0.4
USA	2.0	2.2	0.2
Mean	1.4	1.6	0.2

Notes: Data from OECD (2006) and Eurostat (2006).

does provide the opportunity for an examination of whether there is a *prima facie* case for a link between increased post-9/11 spending and the perceived threat of terrorism.

Much existing cross-national research, which has considered the extent of the terrorist threat, has relied on measures of the number of terrorist events or casualties to make comparisons between countries. However, as argued by Frey, Luechinger and Stutzer (2004), this approach provides a far from ideal measure; in particular, because it only accounts for 'successful' terrorist incidents and does not address any latent terrorist threat that may exist. Recent articles by Abadie and Gardeazabal (2005) and Goldstein (2005) have used the terrorist risk assessments provided in the World Markets Research Centre's (WMRC) 'Global Terrorism Index 2003/4' as an alternative measure of the extent of threat posed by such activities. This is the measure we use here.

Correlating the WMRC's estimate of the level of motivation terrorists may feel towards attacking a particular country with the difference in public order expenditure post-11 September (in Table 6.11 excluding Luxembourg) gives a Pearson's r of 0.409 (p=0.103). While this analysis does not include other factors (such as those considered above with regard to expenditure in 2000) and the relationship is only significant at around the 10 per cent level, it does provide some indication that recent changes in public order expenditure could be related to the perceived threat of terrorist attack and that this factor will need to be considered when enough data become available to allow a more complete longitudinal analysis of expenditure patterns.

6.6   CONCLUSIONS

An absence of adequate data for the period prior to the mid-1990s has meant that this study could not focus centrally on factors driving public expenditure change in the era of retrenchment. The somewhat fragmentary data reported in Table 6.2 suggest no obvious trends in spending, either up or down, although the preceding analysis does suggest the possibility that an enhanced terrorist threat might ultimately produce an upward expenditure gradient.

Despite the limitations of the currently available data, it can be argued that the use of COFOG data to study changes in the shape and size of criminal justice policy could be a useful supplement to current cross-national work based on personnel levels. That is because such data are generally collected independently of the criminal justice system using cross-nationally standardised methods and definitions. Moreover, because public expenditure on private personnel counts as part of the public order budget, spending measures get around a problem of comparability in personnel measurement the salience of which is increasing with the onward march of public order privatisation.

Although the use of public expenditure data may provide a better indicator of the overall public criminal justice effort, this chapter has made no reference to the growth of the private security industry, such as in-house security guards in shopping malls, across industrialised countries. The growth of this industry and its impact on the public criminal justice system has being a long-running area of interest in criminology (see, for instance, Shearing and Stenning, 1983, while an overview of the state of the industry across industrialised countries in the late 1990s can be found in De Waard, 1999). Unfortunately, as De Waard (1999, p. 146) notes, comparable data on this industry are not readily available, although, as with data on public expenditure on public order this situation is beginning to improve (see the Confederation of European Security Industries for data relating to EU member states). The wider availability of such statistics could potentially allow us to investigate the question of whether private expenditure on security is driven by the same factors as public expenditure and, of more interest with respect to issues concerning public expenditure retrenchment investigated in this volume, whether or not increased private security expenditure is a concomitant of reduced public expenditure effort in the criminal justice arena.

Lacking adequate change data and, in any case, judging the extent of change in the 1990s to be quite modest, we have devoted this chapter to an exploratory study of the determinants of public order expenditure at a particular point in time. Our findings suggest that the most important factors accounting for cross-national expenditure variance are similar to those identified in earlier research focussing on personnel levels and incarceration rates, although, importantly, with significant differences in the balance of factors impinging on different aspects of the public order budget. Essentially, this coincidence of findings as between different kinds of data is good news. It suggests strongly that, as better and more comprehensive data on spending in this area become available, such data will increasingly become a more and more valuable tool for public policy and criminological research alike.

REFERENCES

Abadie, A. and J. Gardeazabal (2005), 'Terrorism and the world economy' (http://ksghome.harvard.edu/~aabadie/twe.pdf).

Armingeon, K., P. Leimgrober, M. Beyeter and S. Menegale (2005), 'Comparative political data Set 1960–2003' Institute of Political Science, University of Berne.

Bayley, D. (1985), *Patterns of Policing*, New Brunswick: Rutgers University Press.

Castles, F. (1998), *Comparative Public Policy*, Cheltenham, UK and Lyme, USA: Edward Elgar.

Council of Europe (2000), *European Sourcebook of Crime and Criminal Justice* (http://www.europeansourcebook.org/esb).

De Waard, J. (1999), 'The private security industry in international perspective', *European Journal of Criminal Policy and Research*, **7**, 143–74.

EuroStat (2006), 'Expenditure Dataset' (http://epp.eurostat.cec.eu.int/portal/page?_pageid=1996,45323734&_dad=portal&_schema=PORTAL&screen=welcomeref&open=/gov/publ_exp&language=en&product=EU_MASTER_government&root =EU_MASTER_government&scrollto =0).

Fajnzylber, P., D. Lederman and N. Loayza (2002), 'Inequality and violent crime', *Journal of Law and Economics*, **XLV**, 1–40.

Frey, B., S. Luechinger and A. Stutzer (2004), 'Valuing public goods: the life satisfaction approach', Institute for Empirical Research in Economics, working paper, no. 184, University of Zurich.

Goldstein, K. (2005), 'Unemployment, inequality and terrorism: another look at the relationship between economics and terrorism', Illinois Wesleyan University (http://titan.iwu.edu/~econ/uer/articles/kevin_goldstein.pdf).

Greenberg, D. and V. West (2001), 'State prison populations and their growth, 1971–1991', *Criminology*, **39** (3), 615–53.

Heywood, A. (1994), *Political Ideas and Concepts*, Basingstoke: Macmillan Press.
IMF (2001), *IMF Government Finance Statistics Manual 2001*, downloaded (http://www.imf.org/external/pubs/ft/gfs/manual/pdf/all.pdf).
International Centre for Prison Studies (2003), *World Prison Brief*, Kings College London (http://www.kcl.ac.uk/depsta/rel/icps/worldbrief/world_brief.html).
Jacobs, D. and R. Helms (2001), 'Toward a political sociology of punishment: politics and changes in the incarcerated population', *Social Science Research*, **30** (2), 171–94.
Kangaspunta, K., M. Joutsen and N. Ollus (1998), *Crime and Criminal Justice in Europe and North America 1990–1994*, Helsinki: HEUNI.
Krus, D. and L. Hoehl (1994), 'Issues associated with international incarceration rates', *Psychological Reports*, **75**, 1491–5.
Lijphart, A. (1999), *Patterns of Democracy*, New Haven: Yale University Press.
Morgan, R. (2000), 'The politics of criminology research', in R. King and E. Wincup (eds), *Doing Research on Crime and Justice*, Oxford: Oxford University Press.
Newman, G. and B. Howard (1999a), 'Introduction: data sources and their use', in G. Newman (ed.), *Global Report on Crime and Justice*, New York: Oxford University Press, pp. 1–23.
Newman, G. and B. Howard (1999b), 'Resources in criminal justice', in G. Newman (ed.), *Global Report on Crime and Justice*, New York: Oxford University Press, pp. 121–50.
OECD (2005), *Statistical Database* (www.sourceoecd.org).
OECD (2006), *National Accounts 1993–2004. Volume IV General Government Accounts*, Paris.
Petrovec, D. (2000), 'Poverty and reaction to crime – freedom without responsibility', *European Journal of Crime, Criminal Law and Criminal Justice*, **8** (4), 377–89.
Shearing, C. and P. Stenning (1983), 'Private security: implications for social control', *Social Problems*, **30** (5), 493–506.
Sutton, J.R. (2000), 'Imprisonment and social classification in five common-law democracies, 1955–1985', *American Journal of Sociology*, **106** (2), 350–86.
Thorny, M. (2006), *Thinking About Crime*, New York: Oxford University Press.
UN (2006), *UNCJS website* (http://www.unodc.org/unodc/en/crime_cicp_surveys.html).
Van Dijk, F. and J. Waard (2000), *Legal Infrastructure of the Netherlands in International Perspective*, Ministry of Justice, The Netherlands.
Van Dijk, J. (1999), 'The experience of crime and justice' in G. Newman (ed.), *Global Report on Crime and Justice*, New York: Oxford University Press, pp. 25–64.
World Bank (2002), *World Development Indicators CD-Rom*, New York: World Bank.
World Market Research Centre (2003), *Global Terrorism Index 2003/4*.

7. Testing the retrenchment hypothesis: educational spending, 1960–2002

Manfred G. Schmidt

7.1 INTRODUCTION

Has public spending on education been part of the effort to retrench public expenditure in OECD countries? Is the state possibly withdrawing from funding education? The answer to these questions is partly 'yes' and partly 'no'. It is partly 'yes' because a turnaround in public spending on education did take place in a substantial group of OECD countries from around the mid-1970s. While the period from the early 1960s to the mid-1970s was marked by unprecedented growth in public expenditure on education, public spending on education and training (measured as a percentage of GDP) has declined in many OECD member states since the mid-1970s (see Tables 7.1 and 7.2 below).

However, retrenchment has been only one part of the whole story of financing education before and after 1974. First, the data on the level of public expenditure continue to be indicative of massive public investment in education. In the early twenty-first century, the 21 OECD member countries examined in this chapter invest on average 5.2 per cent of their Gross Domestic Product (GDP) on education (OECD, 2005: 184). This represents a larger proportion than in the early 1960s (see Table 7.1), although public spending on education has increased over the last four or five decades significantly less than public expenditure on health, labour market policy or old age pensions (see, for example, Castles, 1998).

Second, in each of the OECD countries, by far the largest part of total expenditure on education comes from the public purse. For example, 97 per cent of the total education budget in Sweden in the early twenty-first century is funded from public sources. And, even in countries with a larger role of private spending on primary, secondary and, above all, tertiary education, such as the United States of America or Japan, the government's share comprises broadly three-quarters of the total expenditure on education (calculated from OECD, 2005: 184).

Table 7.1 Public expenditure on education in 21 OECD countries, 1960–2002 (percentage GDP)

	Estimates from OECD (1985)			Estimates from OECD (1992)			Estimates from OECD (2005)	
	1960	1975	1980	1975	1980	1987	1991	2002
Australia	3.23	5.37	5.10	6.2	5.6	5.1	4.7	4.4
Austria	2.69	2.99	3.12	6.1	5.6	5.8	5.4	5.4
Belgium	4.57	6.89	6.57	5.9	5.7	5.3	5.4	6.1
Canada	3.70	5.84	5.15	8.5	7.7	6.9	6.7	5.2
Denmark		7.34	7.10				6.1	6.8
Finland	7.85	6.26	5.75	6.5	5.8	5.8	6.1	5.9
France		5.17	4.78	5.6	5.1	5.6	5.4	5.7
Germany	2.85	4.66	4.29	5.2	4.6	4.0	4.0	4.4
Greece	1.95	1.86	2.14	3.4	3.2	3.8	3.4	3.9
Ireland	3.52	5.46	5.43	6.5	6.4	6.2	5.5	4.1
Italy	4.76	4.74	4.67	4.8	4.5	5.0	5.0	4.6
Japan	5.55	3.72	3.60	5.3	5.9	4.5	3.7	3.5
Netherlands	6.72	6.50	6.12	7.4	7.1	6.9	5.6	4.6
New Zealand	3.32	4.15	3.62	6.5	6.7	5.9	5.9	5.6
Norway	4.22	6.10	5.91	6.4	5.8	5.6	6.8	6.7
Portugal				3.3	3.7	4.1	5.5	5.7
Spain							4.4	4.3
Sweden	5.64	5.19	5.49	7.1	8.5	6.9	6.5	6.7
Switzerland	3.33	5.06	5.00	5.3	5.2	5.2	5.4	5.7

UK	4.17	5.93	4.92	6.8	5.7	4.8	5.3	5.0
USA	4.12	6.04	5.31	5.7	4.9	4.8	5.5	5.3
Country mean	4.25	5.22	4.89	5.92	5.67	5.38	5.35	5.22

Notes: Column 1: country; Column 2: OECD (1985), Appendix (at 1970 prices); Column 3: OECD (1985), Appendix (at 1970 prices); data for Denmark and Switzerland: 1979; Column 4: OECD (1985), Appendix (at 1970 prices); Column 5: OECD (1992: 84); Finland 1978. Data on Denmark: OECD (1985:89) and on Spain (1974): Castles (1998: 177); Column 6: OECD (1992: 84); Italy 1986; Column 8: OECD, *Education at a Glance* (various editions); data were taken from the database of Busemeyer (2006); Column 9: OECD (2005: 184); data for Canada: 2000 (OECD, 2003: 243); 1991 was chosen as the first time-point in the 1990s, because the data for 1990, at least in some of the OECD countries, appear overestimated compared to the data for the late 1980s (OECD, 1992: 84) and the post-1991 period.

Third, expenditure cuts on a major scale have not occurred in all OECD member states, but only in a particular group of countries. These are the countries of education retrenchment proper. This group includes the members of the English-speaking family of nations, Finland, Germany, Japan, Norway and the Netherlands. Other OECD countries followed a different trajectory in the post-1974 period in maintaining or expanding the proportion of national resources in education.

These findings show that the state's role in financing education and train-ing is not disappearing. Moreover, the observation that retrenchment has been only one part of the post-1974 experience in expenditure on education raises further questions including the following. How far did retrenchment in public educational expenditure really go? How big is the difference between retrenchment and non-retrenchment? And how are the differences between these groups of countries to be accounted for? These questions guide the analysis presented in this chapter.

Apart from Iceland and Luxembourg (omitted as is standard practice in such comparative work), the analysis in this chapter focuses attention on those OECD member countries with an uninterrupted record of democracy from the mid-1970s onwards (see Table 7.1 below for details). Following the practice of *Education at a Glance*, studies published by the OECD (see, for example, OECD, 2005), public expenditure on education is defined as com-prising total public spending on educational institutions such as schools, uni-versities, educational administration and student welfare services. Expenditure on education covers three dimensions: educational core services, research and development in educational institutions, and educational ser-vices other than instruction (for example, spending on ancillary services, such as meals, transport to schools or housing on the campus). Excluded from the data analysed here is expenditure on education outside educational institu-tions, such as private purchases of educational goods and services.

Data on education spending are taken from OECD (2005) and previous issues of *Education at a Glance* and, for the pre-1990 period, from OECD (1992) and the appendix in OECD (1985). The highest level of compara-bility has been achieved in the estimates of educational spending in the *Education at a Glance* volumes, above all in the data for the post-1994 period. Less comprehensive and less comparable are the data for the pre-1990 period. The two most relevant data sets for this period are OECD (1985) and OECD (1992). OECD (1992: 84) presents data on 19 democra-cies mainly from 1971 until 1987/88. OECD (1985) is the earliest larger comparative data set on educational spending. It covers the period from 1960 to 1981 for 19 countries. However, compared to OECD (1992), the data in OECD (1985) tend to underestimate the magnitude of public spending on education in most countries.

The limited comparability of data on education expenditure suggests a need for caution. Despite considerable improvement in the comparability of the relevant data, the remaining statistical discrepancies in the data on public spending (and still more on the data on private spending) render cross-time comparison risky. For this reason, it is proper to regard the data presented here and the conclusions derived from their analysis as preliminary, although validity tests, such as the construction of trichotomised and dichotomised indicators of the dependent variable (see Table 7.2, columns 7 and 8), lend further support to the lessons drawn from the analysis.

7.2   RETRENCHMENT AND EXPANSION IN PUBLIC EDUCATIONAL EXPENDITURE IN OECD COUNTRIES

The rise of 'big government' in Western democracies in the second half of the twentieth century initially went hand in hand with massive financial investment in primary, secondary and tertiary education. Particularly noteworthy was the increase in spending up to the mid-1970s. From the early 1960s until 1975, for example, the increase in public educational expenditure exceeded the growth in national income in almost all OECD nations for which data are available (see Table 7.1). According to the OECD study *Social Expenditure 1960–1990*, for example, the proportion of GDP allocated to public expenditure on education increased from 1960 to 1975 by 0.86 of 1 per cent of GDP on average – a hitherto unprecedented growth in public expenditure on education (OECD, 1985). However, after 1975, the share of public spending on education as a percentage of GDP declined in a larger group of OECD member countries, measured by the long-term percentage point differences between 1975 and 2002, that is, the year for which the latest data were available (see Table 7.2).

Of course, an average increase of 0.86 percentage points over a period of 16 years was not spectacular compared to growth in other areas of public expenditure during this period. Moreover, retrenchment patterns after 1975 were also, for the most part, moderate in nature. A glance at the summary statistics relating to the columns of Table 7.2 reveals cutbacks of the order of −0.29 percentage points in the period from 1975 to 1980, −0.29 in the 1980s and −0.13 in the 1990s. Finally, the estimate of the extent of change between 1975 and 2002 suggests that the share of education budgets as a percentage of GDP decreased by −0.57 percentage points on average over the period as a whole (see Table 7.2).[1] This is broadly equivalent to one-tenth of the size of education budgets (as a percentage of GDP) in 1975.

Table 7.2   *Change in public expenditure on education (as a percentage of GDP) in 21 OECD countries, 1960–2002 (percentage point differences)*

	1960–1975	1975–1980	1980–1987	1991–2002	1975–2002 (interval-scale retrenchment measure)	1975–2002 (trichotomized retrenchment indicator)	1975–2002 (dichotomized retrenchment indicator)
Australia	2.14	−0.27	−0.5	−0.3	−1.8	−1	−1
Austria	0.30	0.13	0.2	0.0	−0.7	1	0
Belgium	2.32	−0.32	−0.4	0.7	0.2	0	0
Canada	2.14	−0.69	−0.8	−1.5	−3.3	−1	−1
Denmark		−0.23		0.7	−0.5	0	0
Finland	−1.59	−0.52	0.0	−0.2	−0.6	−1	−1
France		−0.39	0.5	0.3	0.1	0	0
Germany	1.81	−0.37	−0.6	0.4	−0.8	0	0
Greece	−0.10	0.28	0.6	0.5	0.5	1	0
Ireland	1.95	−0.03	−0.2	−1.4	−2.4	−1	−1
Italy	−0.01	−0.07	0.5	−0.4	−0.2	0	0
Japan	−1.84	−0.12	−1.4	−0.2	−1.8	−1	−1
Netherlands	−0.22	−0.38	−0.2	−1.0	−2.8	−1	−1
New Zealand	0.83	−0.53	−0.8	−0.3	−0.9	−1	−1
Norway	1.88	−0.19	−0.2	−0.1	0.3	−1	−1
Portugal			0.4	0.2	2.4	1	0
Spain				−0.1	2.6	0	0
Sweden	−0.45	0.30	−1.6	0.2	−0.4	0	0
Switzerland	1.73	−0.06	0.0	0.3	0.4	0	0
UK	1.75	−1.00	−0.9	−0.3	−1.8	−1	−1
USA	1.92	−0.73	−0.1	−0.2	−0.4	−1	−1
Country mean	0.86	−0.29	−0.29	−0.13	−0.57		

Notes: Column 2: calculated from OECD (1985), Appendix; see Table 7.1; Column 3: calculated from OECD (1985), Appendix; see Table 7.1; Column 4: calculated from OECD (1992: 84); see Table 7.1. Data for Italy: 1986. OECD (1992) covers expenditure trends only until 1987 and in some countries until 1988; Column 5: calculated from OECD, *Education at a Glance* (various issues); see Table 7.1; Greece: 1993, Italy and New Zealand: 1992; Column 6: 2002: OECD (2005: 184); data for 1975 was taken from OECD (1992: 84), except for Canada (OECD, 1985, appendix) and Spain (source: Castles, 1998: 177); Columns 7 and 8: in order to check for a potential measurement bias, trichotomized and dichotomous retrenchment indicators were developed. The trichotomized indicator classifies the OECD countries according to the trend in education expenditure in the various sub-periods (1975–80, 1980–87, 1991–2002) in Table 7.1 as follows: −1 = retrenchment (i.e. decreasing expenditure–GDP ratios in each sub-period), +1 = expansion (increase in each sub-period), otherwise = 0. The dichotomous measure in column 8 differentiates between retrenchment (−1) and non-retrenchment (0). Both indicators correlate significantly with the interval-scaled retrenchment variable in column 6 ($r = 0.64$, $s = 0.002$, $N = 21$ and $r = 0.65$), and both are just as significant predictors in the correlations with the various predictors discussed further below as the interval-scale retrenchment indicator.

165

The post-1975 trend of public spending on education in the OECD world comprises two types of retrenchment patterns: 'type I' and 'type II retrenchment'. 'Type I retrenchment' is largely an unintended by-product of a massive change outside education policy, such as a long period of high economic growth which tends to decrease expenditure–GDP ratios over time. In contrast to this, 'type II retrenchment' is marked by intended decreases in education expenditure of small or moderate magnitude, while 'type III retrenchment' would reflect an intended fundamental reduction in spending. But 'type III retrenchment' of public education spending has so far been absent in OECD member countries.

Despite the moderate retrenchment patterns displayed in Table 7.1 and Table 7.2, the patterns of variation in these data call for explanation. Why does public spending on education (as a percentage of national resources) decrease in some countries and why does it continue to grow in others? How is the puzzle to be solved that retrenchment in education expenditure occurred mainly in the English-speaking family of nations, in Japan, the Netherlands and Germany? And why has the share of national resources allocated to public spending on education been growing in another group of countries, above all in the three new democracies of the 1970s – Greece, Portugal and Spain – but also, albeit moderately, in Switzerland and in France (see Table 7.2)?

7.3   WHAT ACCOUNTS FOR RETRENCHMENT AND EXPANSION IN PUBLIC EXPENDITURE ON EDUCATION?

What accounts for differences in public expenditure development since 1975? Why has there been retrenchment in one group of countries and why did education budgets expand in other OECD members? Explaining long-term change in education expenditure is a relatively neglected research area. Exceptions, such as Castles (1998: 174–85) as well as various sections in OECD (1992) and the volumes of the *Education at a Glance* series, such as OECD (2005), prove the rule. In addition to the hypotheses that can be derived from these studies, the empirical exploration in the present chapter has been based on key variables from major theories in comparative welfare state research. Broadly speaking, six schools of thought have dominated this research domain.

1.   One school of thought centres attention on socio-economic variables. Examples include socio-economic theories of social policy, such as that of Wilensky (1975) and, more recently, the hypothesis suggesting

that international markets have grown too powerful for any national government to oppose them successfully (for example, theories of globalisation).

2. A second family of theories explains public policy differences mainly in terms of the power resources of social classes, such as the market power and the political power of labour relative to that of capital and the middle classes. A representative example is Esping-Andersen's (1990) study of *Three Worlds of Welfare Capitalism*.

3. A third theory is the 'partisan theory of public policy'. Policy choices and outputs are, in this view, largely driven by incumbent political parties and the preferences of their social constituencies (see Hibbs, 1977; Castles, 1982, and, for an institution-augmented view, Schmidt, 1996, 2005).

4. According to a fourth school of thought, policy differences are mainly attributable to differences in political and economic institutions as well as to differences in the strategies employed by interdependent collective actors (see, for example, Scharpf, 1987).

5. Policy legacies, path dependence and policy inheritance are emphasized by a fifth school of thought, with examples including the work of Rose and Davies (1994) and policy-oriented studies written by social historians.

6. Finally, the international hypothesis relates differences in policy outputs and outcomes in nation-states to structures and processes at the international level (see, for example, Leibfried, 2005).

The findings on education expenditure changes reported so far and the results obtained from the data analysis for this chapter lend support to important conclusions. The first is that long-term change in the national resources devoted to education from the mid-1970s until 2002 has been influenced by a wide variety of interrelated factors of supply and demand. These include the demographic structure of the population, contraction and expansion in educational enrolment rates and the effects of unemployment on the demand for post-secondary education (OECD, 1992: 12–17),[2] as well as key indicators of the level of economic modernisation, such as economic strength (measured by GDP per capita indicators)[3] and levels of deindustrialisation at the beginning of the retrenchment period.[4]

The second conclusion that emerges from our analysis is that change in expenditure–GDP ratios is not only shaped by social and political 'sources', but also by deep-seated social and political 'causes' (in the sense of Mancur Olson's distinction between two major classes of determinants of policy outputs and outcomes; see Olson, 1982: 4). It is on these 'causes'

that attention is mainly centred in this study. As the data analysis reported
below suggests, the following factors deserve priority in any explanation
of long-term changes in education expenditure–GDP ratios (see Table
7.3).

1. a strong convergence trend;
2. for the countries of Southern Europe intensified by a dual dynamic
    resting on both the transition to democracy and the impact of the level
    of economic modernisation;
3. asymmetric 'family of nations' effects;
4. short-term impacts of incumbent political parties and long-term lega-
    cies of incumbent political parties – above all Social Democratic
    parties on the one hand and parties of secular conservative complex-
    ion on the other;
5. the impact of state-centred or market-oriented routines of problem
    solving outside education on public spending on education;
6. the degree of fiscal decentralisation;
7. fiscal competition of educational spending with, and crowding out by,
    the size of the social budget at the beginning of the retrenchment
    period; and
8. the role of private spending on education, which may partly or totally
    compensate for cutbacks in the public sphere.

7.3.1 Catch-up Processes

The data on education budgets in the post-1975 period indicate massive
convergence based on two different trajectories. The first is a classical catch-
up path, the second a catch-down process of cutting back by the big
spenders prior to or at the beginning of the retrenchment period (see Table
7.1 and Table 7.3). The extent to which a country prioritised education in
relation to its overall allocation of national resources at the beginning of
the retrenchment period, that is, in the mid-1970s, made a difference for
spending in the subsequent periods. In countries which were big spenders
on education in the mid-1970s, such as most of the English-speaking
nations and the Netherlands, the share of the education budgets as a percentage of GDP declined markedly after 1975. Part of that process has
been the larger leeway for action in these nations due to their relatively
larger budgets: big spenders had a greater potential for decreasing their relative share of spending on education. Quite the opposite trend characterised the spending laggards: education budgets began to grow rapidly in
the majority of OECD member countries with low investment in education
and training prior to the mid-1970s.

Table 7.3 *Correlates of change in public expenditure on education as a percentage of GDP (percentage change from 1975 to 2002)*

Theoretical concept/empirical indicator	Pearson's correlation coefficient r	Level of significance	Number of cases
Catch-up/public spending on education in 1975 (% GDP)	r = −0.80	s = 0.000	21
Catch-up continued: impact of the level of economic modernisation/ service sector employment (% total employment) in 1975	r = −0.72	s = 0.000	21
Catch-up continued: impact of new democracies/age of democracy	r = −0.64	s = 0.002	21
Family of nations effects/English family of nations – dummy	r = −0.53	s = 0.014	21
Impact of incumbent political parties/differences between Social Democratic and secular conservative cabinet seat share, 1975–2002	r = 0.48	s = 0.028	21
Long-term legacy of incumbent political parties/cabinet seat share of secular conservative parties in 1950–1975	r = −0.41	s = 0.065	21
Impact of state-centred or market-oriented routines of problem-solving outside education on public spending on education/change in public expenditure minus expenditure on education as a percentage of GDP in 1975–2002	r = 0.59	s = 0.005	21
Degree of fiscal decentralisation/sub-national governments' share in total public expenditure, early 1990s	r = −0.60	s = 0.009	18
Fiscal competition between spending on education and spending on the social budget/size of social budget (% GDP) in 1975	r = −0.37	s = 0.10	21
Change in imports plus exports (% GDP) between 1975 and 2002 (percentage point difference)	r = 0.12	s = 0.60	21
Role of private spending/private spending on education (% public and private spending) 2002	r = −0.45	s = 0.04	21

Sources: Tables 7.1 and 7.2; Castles (1993); OECD (2005); OECD Economic Outlook (various issues); Schmidt (2005a, 2006).

7.3.2   Catch-up and Democratisation

The catch-up process in Spain, Portugal and Greece was particularly
strong. In these OECD countries, the forces of expenditure growth were
twofold. One was the catch-up imperative provided by relative economic
backwardness, the other was the pro-spending momentum given by the
transition from an authoritarian state to democracy (see Figure 7.1). The
economic catch-up effect is mirrored in the inverse association between
indicators of economic modernisation, such as the relative size of the
service sector in 1975 and education expenditure change from 1975 to 2002
(see Table 7.3). And the impact of the transition to democracy is at least
partly reflected in the inverse relationship between the age of democracy
and changing public education–expenditure ratios from 1975 to 2002 (see
Table 7.3).

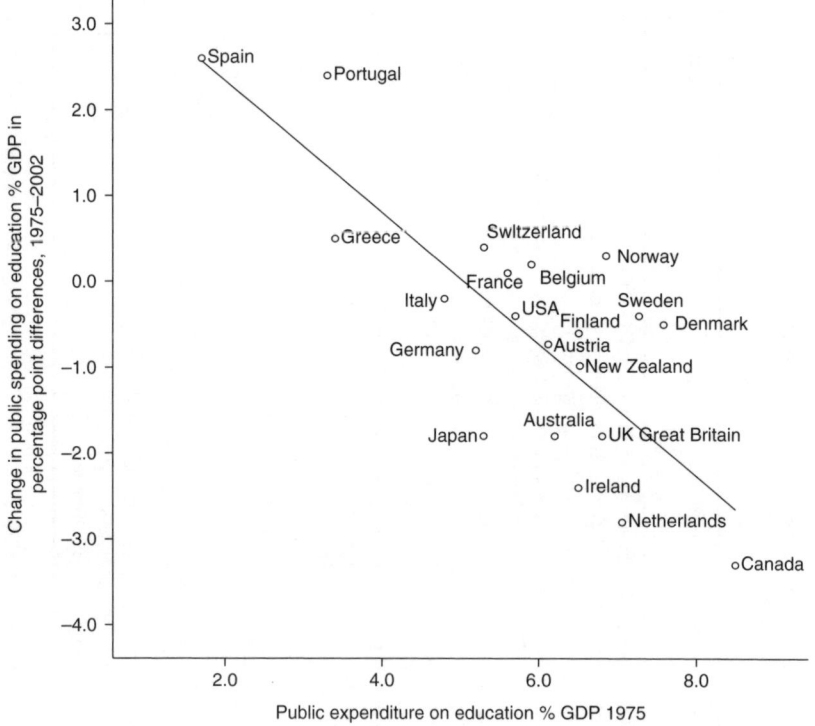

Sources: Table 7.1, column 5 (complemented by estimates for Denmark from OECD
(1985: 89) and Spain (1974) from Castles (1998: 177) and Table 7.2, column 6.

Figure 7.1   Catch-up in public spending on education, 1975–2002

7.3.3   Families of Nations

To what extent do 'families of nations' (Castles, 1993) play a role in shaping education budgets since the mid-1970s? The data analysis points to asymmetric relationships between expenditure trends and families of nations. The relationships are asymmetric, because only the expenditure profile in the member countries of the English-speaking family of nations changed in a consistent way: the proportion of GDP spent on public education budgets tended to decline in the 1975–2002 period in all English-speaking OECD countries. In contrast, no clear pattern emerged in the Nordic and German families of nations. That the members of the English-speaking family of nations chose the retrenchment path after 1974 may partly be attributable the prior existence of big spenders on education in this group of countries, but it also mirrors a culturally and politically deeply embedded stronger preference for constraining big government. But even that preference, it must be added, does not preclude noteworthy expenditure shifts after 1975. The increasing share of public education expenditure (as a percentage of GDP) in Great Britain after the Blair 'New Labour' government came to power in 1997 is an example, even if the magnitude of the policy shift involved no more than a 0.4 percentage point increase in the education budget (as a percentage of GDP) from 4.6 per cent in 1997 to 5.0 per cent in 2002 (see OECD, *Education at a Glance*, various issues).

7.3.4   Party Differences

In contradistinction to the view of the mainstream 'new politics' literature on social expenditure retrenchment (see Pierson, 2001), political parties do continue to matter in spending on education after 1975 and also in the most recent period. Partisan effects on education are, however, more complex than the classical exposition of the partisan theory of public policy in Hibbs (1977) and the 'new politics' literature suggest. It is not the difference between leftist and non-leftist governments that matters, rather it is the difference between Social Democratic parties in power and governments of a secular conservative complexion which counts. Examples of the latter include governments constituted by the British Conservative Party, the Australian Liberal Party, New Zealand's National Party, the Republican Party of the United States and Japan's Liberal Party.

Moreover, the distinction between short-term impacts and the long-term legacies of parties must be added to standard partisan theory. Partisan effects comprise not only contemporaneous short-term impacts (measured by a party A's cabinet seats share at a particular point in time or over a shorter period), but also the long-term legacy of party A on taken-for-granted policy positions in that society. The latter is measured by the long-term partisan complexion of government from a time-point early on in the post-war period to the date of the expenditure comparison in question.

The analysis of the data on spending on education in the democratic OECD countries after the turnaround in economic growth in the mid-1970s supports this view. First, the change in the relative size of the education budget between 1975 and 2002 covaries positively with Social Democratic parties in office in this period (measured by cabinet seats shares) and inversely with secular conservative parties in office. Moreover, the change in public spending on education is positively associated with the difference between Social Democratic and secular conservative cabinet seat shares. Furthermore, there is a significant correlation between the long-term legacies above all of governments of a secular conservative complexion in the period from 1950 to 1975 and the change in spending on education in the subsequent period (see Table 7.3 and Figure 7.2).

7.3.5   Institutional Configurations and Problem-solving Routines outside Education Policy

To a degree which varies from one country to another, the policy-making capabilities of governments are also contingent upon confining restrictions and enabling conditions. Among these, the strength or weakness of state-centred routines of problem solving and the degree of fiscal decentralisation matter a great deal. State-centred routines of problem solving of policy making outside education also make a state-centred approach to educational spending more likely. In contrast, a market-oriented distribution of labour between the government and the economy is liable to generate lower investment in public spending on education. Moreover, fiscal centralisation and decentralisation are also important determinants of change in education budgets. According to the data analysis, the governments of a country with a substantially decentralised fiscal policy will find it harder to raise public spending on education to high levels than a government in a country with higher levels of fiscal centralisation and, hence, greater manoeuvrability in fiscal policy, other things being equal.

Empirically, both hypotheses receive support from the data analysis. According to the correlation coefficients in Table 7.3 and the underlying data, levels and changes in state-centred routines of problem solving manifest themselves in further growth in public spending on education. In contrast, market-oriented problem solving makes the reduction or limitation of public budgets in education more likely. Table 7.3 demonstrates that fiscally decentralised countries perform in precisely the way in which

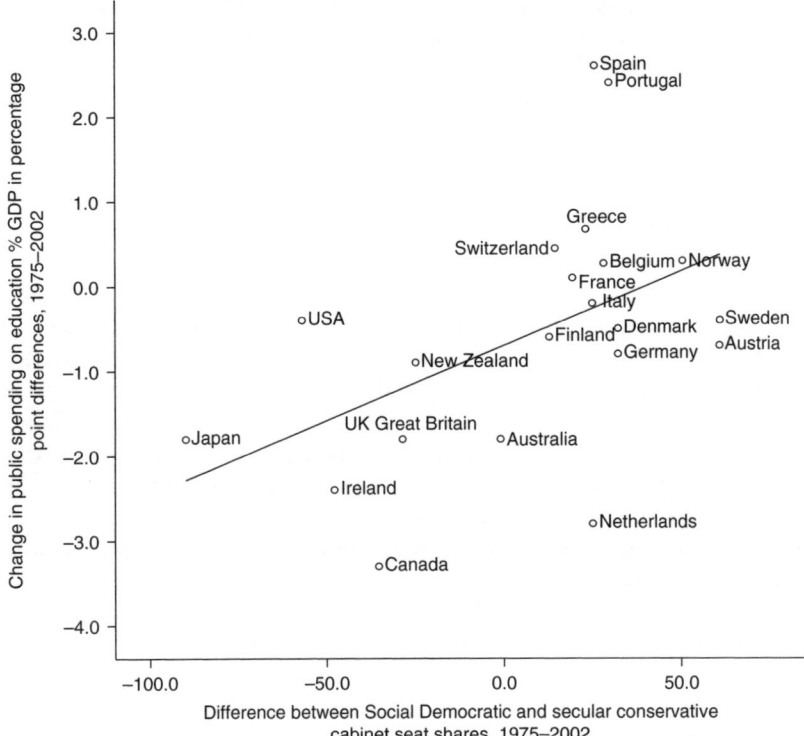

Sources: Table 1, Table 2, Schmidt (2006).

Figure 7.2   Change in education budgets and the difference between Social Democratic and secular conservative parties in office, 1975–2002

standard theories of federalism predicts. Under circumstances of tight constraint on public budgets, large spending items are subject to close scrutiny by governments seeking ways to reduce or limit the growth of public spending. Over the period 1975 to 2002, as Table 7.2 demonstrates, fiscal decentralisation has permitted governments in federal nations such as Canada and Australia to make particularly marked cuts in what were once very high levels of public spending on education.

7.3.6   Crowding Out

To what extent has education been exposed to crowding out? According to a standard crowding-out hypothesis, a high level of public debt and, above all, high net interest payments as a percentage of GDP constrain all other policy areas. According to Busemeyer (2006) and Nikolai (2006a, 2006b), public spending on education in OECD countries is subject to this mechanism. Just as dramatic may be the impact of spending on social policy, particularly in those countries in which the social budget consumes as much as two-thirds of the total outlays of government, such as Germany (Schmidt, 2004). Under such circumstances, the allocation of a large proportion of national resources to social policy objectives is likely to constrain all other fiscally costly policy areas.

The empirical relationship between social budgets and the education budgets is, however, rather more complex than is sometimes implied (see Busemeyer, 2006; Nikolai, 2006a, 2006b; Wolf, 2005, 2006). Social budgets constrain education budgets, but they do so in a degree which varies from country to country. The overall tendency has been that a large (small) share of social budgets as a percentage of GDP has gone hand in hand with large (small) education budgets. Moreover, large (small) percentage changes in social budgets have tended to covary with larger (smaller) percentage changes in education. However, there is also a noteworthy inverse relationship between change in education budgets after 1975 and the size of the social budget prior to or at the beginning of the retrenchment period. The big spenders on the welfare state at that time, such as Germany and the Netherlands, were particularly prone to cut public spending programmes on education, not least because of their efforts to maintain the structure of the welfare state. It is not by chance that these two countries now have education budgets that are exceptionally small in comparison to the size of their social spending (Schmidt, 2004).

7.3.7   Globalisation Effects?

Does globalisation matter in spending on education? According to a widely shared view, the threat of globalisation since the early 1980s has resulted in a 'race to the bottom' in the public provision of goods, services and market-correcting regulation. While retrenchment policies have been particularly ambitious in some of those countries most exposed to massive increases in the openness of the economy, the data analysis reported in Table 7.3 does not point to systematically significant relationships. This finding is not consistent with the standard globalisation-based account of public expenditure development in recent decades, or with the hypothesis, identified in Chapter 2 above, as a possible reformulation of that account, that, what globalisation effects there have been, have been restricted to core spending. Such effects have not been present in the arena of educational expenditure over the past quarter-century.

7.3.8 The Role of Private Spending

While the much-debated 'threat of globalisation' is not identifiable in the data on education expenditure, a significant impact can be attributed to a variable which has almost completely been neglected in the comparative analysis of public policy, namely private spending (the few exceptions include Schmidt, 2004; Busemeyer, 2006). That bias has been responsible for under-estimating the relative importance of total expenditure on education, including its public and private components. Moreover, the bias in the literature in favour of public activities has disregarded the extent to which the volume of national resources devoted to public spending on education has been dependent on private spending. Private spending on education and training, it must be added, plays a major role in a particular group of OECD countries. This group of countries includes Korea (where private spending accounts for 41 per cent of total expenditure on education in 2002) and, to cite examples from the sample of the established democracies studied in this chapter, the United States and Japan (26 per cent of total expenditure on education), Australia (25 per cent), Canada (19 per cent), New Zealand (18 per cent), Germany (17 per cent) and Great Britain (15 per cent) (calculated from OECD, 2005: 184; data for Canada are for 2000, source: OECD, 2003: 243).

Because comparable data on private spending data on education are not available for all the countries of our sample in the pre-2000 period, the relationship between public and private spending on education can be tested only with data from the early twenty-first century. However, existing data suggest that the role of private spending on education was not so different in earlier decades. Thus the data for 2002 may be regarded as proxy indicators of private spending profiles in the past. These indicators are part of a noteworthy inverse relationship: the larger the role of private spending, the stronger the inclination to opt for retrenchment of public expenditure, and the smaller the role played by private spending, the less likely were governments to cut back public financing of education budgets (see Table 7.3). This pattern is partly a function of a substitution processes. In countries in which retrenchment of spending on education budgets went comparatively far, such as Canada, the US, Australia, New Zealand, the United Kingdom and Germany, private spending was, at least, sufficient to compensate for a sizeable part of the cut-back in public spending. The education sectors that were privileged by the compensation of private spending differ from one country to the other. In the United States, for example, most private financing of education flows into tertiary education (Busemeyer, 2006) and, precisely for this reason, this sector was largely sheltered from fiscal retrenchment. In contrast, broadly one half of private spending on education in Germany is attributable to private companies' investment in the vocational training of employees (Klemm, 2003; Baethge, 2003). Thus, in the German case, the education and training of the industrial working class received much stronger support than tertiary education.

7.4 PATTERNS OF RELATIONSHIPS

The data presented in this chapter suggest that education budgets have contributed to the retrenchment of public expenditure over recent decades. However, retrenchment in education actually commenced in the mid-1970s, not in the 1980s. This tends to contradict both globalisation hypotheses and the argument of Chapter 2 of this volume that core spending cut-backs were initiated by the impact of a growing debt burden. There are, however, two caveats. In some countries, the intensity of welfare state retrenchment exceeded that of educational spending, for instance, in Germany after the change in power from the Social Democratic government to the Christian-Democratic-Liberal coalition in 1982 and until the late 1980s.[5] Nor is it the case that all OECD countries experienced retrenchment in education. Some maintained constant education budgets as a percentage of GDP or, indeed, as in the case of the countries of the New Southern Europe, experienced a marked increase in spending.

The findings of the present study shed more light on the social and political causes of retrenchment and expansion in education budgets. According to these findings, retrenchment opportunities have varied from one country to the other. Expenditure cuts were most likely in countries in which the following conditions were fulfilled (see Table 7.3):

- the country was a big spender on education (as a percentage of GDP) prior to the retrenchment period and, hence, in a sense, maintained a budget reserve rendering cut-backs in spending more tolerable than where prior spending was more frugal;
- it had a high level of economic development and, hence, smaller incentives and smaller opportunities for catching up;
- it was a well established democracy and, hence, lacked the specific momentum given by progressive regime change;
- it belonged to the English-speaking 'family of nations' and, hence, to a group of nations marked by a clear cultural preference for an alternative conception of social equality: equality of opportunity in preference to state intervention designed to procure equality of conditions;
- it was characterized by a party composition of central government dominated by market-friendly secular conservative parties rather than by leftist parties;

- it was fiscally decentralised;
- its state-centred traditions of problem solving were relatively weak, and, hence, it offered a potentially larger role for private solutions, including private spending on goods and services;
- it was characterized by a greater role of private spending on education as an alternative to public spending or as a compensation for cutbacks in public expenditure.

This constellation of variables may be regarded as the most advantageous environment for retrenchment efforts. In the sample of countries investigated in this study, Canada is the best example of such a constellation of forces. Among the countries of this study which approximate the retrenchment optimum, albeit less perfectly than Canada, are the US, Great Britain, New Zealand, Japan and Ireland. It therefore comes as no surprise that retrenchment in these countries went farther than in most other OECD member countries. The Irish case stands out, since a long period of massive economic growth – from 1987 and, above all, in the second half of the 1990s – offered especially favourable conditions for cutting the proportion of national resources going to education without undue opposition.

Under what conditions did the public authorities in the OECD democracies of the post-1974 period opt for the alternative trajectory – not in favour of retrenchment, but rather in favour of constant or increasing education budgets? The expansionary trajectory was most likely under the following conditions:

- where there was a relatively small education budget (as a percentage of GDP) prior to the retrenchment period and where, hence, there was no slack in the budget making cutbacks more easily tolerable;
- where there was a lower level of economic development and, hence, larger incentives and greater opportunities for catching up;
- in a new democracy and, hence, possessing the policy-making momentum given by the regime change process;
- in countries outside the English-speaking 'family of nations';
- where the party composition of government was dominated by state-centred leftist or centre–leftist parties, such as the West European Social Democratic parties;
- where there was fiscal centralization;
- where there was a strong tradition of a generalised state-centred mode of problem solving;
- where private educational spending played an insignificant role, and, hence, there was no alternative to, or obvious means of compensating for, cut-backs in public expenditure.

This constellation of forces provided an optimal environment for expanding public spending on education even in a period of reduced growth rates. In the sample of countries analysed in the present study, Spain and Portugal as well as Greece are the major examples of that configuration. It has been largely for these reasons that these countries opted for massively expanding education budgets in the period under investigation.

7.5   THE INDEX OF RETRENCHMENT PROMOTERS IN EXPENDITURE ON EDUCATION

The explanation of changes in public spending on education from 1975 to 2002 advanced so far has been anchored in what Mancur Olson called the social and political 'causes' of societal outcomes (Olson, 1982: 4). We are now in a position to summarise these explanations in an index of push-and-pull factors of retrenchment in education budgets. This index is constructed from variables which are significantly related to the change in public spending on education as displayed in Table 7.3. The index is an additive, unweighted summary of the total number of factors which, according to the data analysis in the preceding sections of this chapter, have been conducive to fiscal retrenchment in education.[6]

The procedure chosen here can be conceived of as a simple, elementary, albeit powerful and easily accessible substitute for a classical regression-based multivariate explanation. Owing to the small number of cases (21 countries), a classical regression-based multivariate analysis is not capable of integrating a larger number of predictor variables. It rather tends to select only an unsatisfactory low number of significant predictors. A pooled time-series design would offer in principle a way out of the dilemma that the small number of cases and the large number of potentially explanatory variable create (see Busemeyer, 2006; Nikolai, 2006a, 2006b). However, the large discrepancies between the estimates of education expenditure in the major data sources employed in this study, that is, OECD (1985), OECD (1992) and the most recent volumes of *Education at a Glance*, such as OECD (2005), render pooled time-series particularly risky. It is largely for this reason (but also in order to maximise the accessibility of the study), that the data analysis in this chapter rests mainly on the combination of a series of, mostly, rather strongly significant, bivariate correlations, careful inspection of the relationships between the explanatory variables and construction of an index summarizing the essential information of each of the predictor variables.

The scores of this index vary from 1 and 2 (that is, favourable conditions for expansion and unfavourable circumstances for retrenchment) in the

South European states and Switzerland, to 3 and 4 (in France, Austria and Finland), 5 (as in Germany), 6 (Ireland, Japan and Norway), 7 and 8 (in the UK, New Zealand and Australia), 9 (in the US) and 10 in Canada.

The explanatory power of the index is high: it is significantly correlated with the change in public spending on education budgets from 1975 to 2002. The association is positive and strong: the higher the retrenchment potential (measured by the total number of retrenchment promoters in a country), the greater the de facto retrenchment in public spending on education and training (r=−0.71). And the lower the total number of obstacles to retrenchment, the greater the expansionary stance in financing education (see Figure 7.3). The two alternative retrenchment indicators fully support this finding (see Table 7.2). They, too, are significantly related to the change in spending on education in 1975–2002 (r=0.64, s=0.002 in

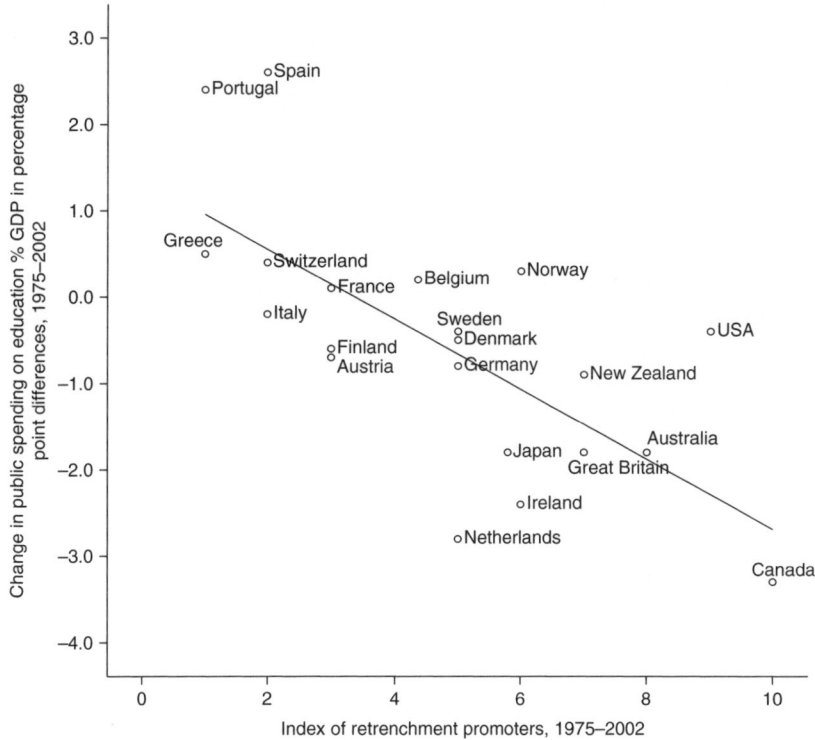

Sources: Tables 7.1, 7.2, 7.3.

Figure 7.3   Change in public spending on education and the index of retrenchment promoters, 1975–2002

the case of trichotomized indicator and $r=-0.65$, $s=0.001$ in the case of the dichotomized measure).[7]

That Canada's retrenchment profile has been more pronounced than that of all other countries in the sample, the index suggests, can be explained by the large number of powerful promoters of retrenchment policy. In Canada, all relevant predictors from Table 7.3 point to powerful promoters of retrenchment. Similar results, albeit not quite as clear-cut as in the Canadian case, can be obtained for the other retrenchment cases, including the US, Australia, Great Britain and New Zealand.

In sharp contrast, the promoters of retrenchment in the new democracies were, by any conceivable standard, weak, while the promoters of expansionary education budgets were numerous and powerful. The dominance of promoters for expanding public spending on education mirrors a route to economic modernity in which human capital-oriented public policy plays an important role.

7.6 CONCLUSIONS

There are several noteworthy conclusions to be derived from this study of the development of public spending on education since the mid-1970s. First, there is the issue of which policy sectors have been most exposed to contractionary forces conducive to public sector retrenchment, and the evidence presented here is unequivocal that education has been one such area, even though not all OECD countries experienced cutbacks.

Second, the difference between retrenching education expenditure or, alternatively, maintaining or increasing the relative size of the education budgets is attributable to a wide variety of factors. Most prominent amongst these have been catch-up and 'catch-down' processes, but institutions, problem-solving routines of state- or market-centred complexion and membership in the English-speaking family of nations have also been important determinants. Moreover, the partisan composition of governments continues to make a major difference, with respect both to party-related legacies and to short- or medium-term impacts of political parties on the substance of public policy.

Third, the data on public spending on education do not support a globalisation-based interpretation. Education is an arena has in which domestic politics (including democratisation, partisan legacies and institutional differences) has largely shaped the trajectory of recent expenditure development.

Fourth, and finally, the analysis of spending on education in the OECD world suggests that an approach focusing attention on the joint impact of public and private spending and on substitution processes between them promises to be a valuable tool for gaining a fuller understanding of why financing education varies between nations as much as it does.

NOTES

1. The difference between this estimate and the sum of the three estimates from the sub-periods results from the differences in the expenditure estimates in OECD (1985, 1992, 2005) and earlier versions of *Education at a Glance*. See for details Table 7.1 and Table 7.2.
2. See also OECD (2005: 180–82) on factors influencing changes in national expenditure on education between 1995 and 2002.
3. For example, GDP per capita in 1973 (measured by Maddison's estimates of International Geary–Khamis dollars per capita, see Maddison, 2003) is inversely related to the interval-scaled retrenchment indicator of Table 7.2 (Pearson correlation coefficient $r=-0.44$, number of cases (N)=19, significance level (s): 0.6).
4. The correlation between the level of deindustrialisation in 1980 (see Iversen, 2001: 54–5) and the interval-scaled retrenchment indicator (see Table 7.2) is $r=-0.45$, $s=0.04$, $N=21$. The change in deindustrialisation and the retrenchment indicator are significant at the 0.06-level ($r=0.39$, $N=21$).
5. The most comprehensive study of this period is Schmidt (2005b).
6. The cut-off point chosen for the classification of a variable as an obstacle or as a promoting factor for retrenchment is defined by the arithmetic mean of that variable. The variables list comprises (1) the relative size of the education budget (as a percentage of GDP) at the beginning of the retrenchment period, (2) the level of economic modernisation at the same time-point (measured by service sector employment as a percentage of total employment in 1975), (3) the age of democracy variable (measured by a new-democracy dummy), (4) membership in the English 'family of nations' (measured by a dummy-variable), (5a) the difference between the cabinet seat shares of social democratic parties and secular conservative parties from 1975 to 2002, (5b) the party legacy variable (measured by the Social Democratic cabinet seat share in the period from 1950 to the beginning of the retrenchment period (1974), (6) fiscal decentralization, (7) the degree of state-centred traditions of problem solving in public policy, (8) the size of the social budget at the beginning of the retrenchment period, and (9) the role of private spending on education (measured by private expenditure as a percentage of total expenditure on education in 2002).
7. A note on multicollinearity must be added. Some of the determinants of the change in education expenditure are significantly correlated, such as state-centred routines in problem solving, membership of the Nordic family of nations and indicators of left–centre parties in office. However, the degree of multicollinearity of the variables included in the index does not generally exceed the critical threshold of $>+0.8$ or <0.8. Borderline cases are the following two pairs of variables: public expenditure on education in 1975 (% GDP) and age of democracy ($r=0.80$), as well as public expenditure on education in 1975 (% GDP) and service sector employment 1975 ($r=0.80$).

REFERENCES

Baethge, M. (2003), 'Das berufliche Bildungswesen in Deutschland am Beginn des 21. Jahrhunderts', in K.S. Cortina, J. Baumert, A. Leschinsky, K.-U. Mayer and L. Trommer (eds), *Das Bildungswesen in der Bundesrepublik Deutschland*, Reinbek: Rowohlt, pp. 525–80.

Busemeyer, M.R. (2006), *Die Bildungsausgaben der USA im internationalen Vergleich*, Wiesbaden: Deutscher Universitäts-Verlag.

Castles, F.G. (ed.) (1982), *The Impact of Parties on Public Policy*, London: Sage.

Castles, F.G. (ed.) (1993), *Families of Nations. Patterns of Public Policy in Western Democracies*, Aldershot, UK and Brookfield, USA, Hong Kong, Singapore and Sydney: Dartmouth.

Castles, F.G. (1998), *Comparative Public Policy. Patterns of Post-war Transformation*, Cheltenham, UK and Northampton, MA, USA: Edward Elgar.

Esping-Andersen, G. (1990), *The Three Worlds of Welfare Capitalism*, Cambridge: Polity Press.

Hibbs, D.A. (1977), 'Political parties and macroeconomic policy', *American Political Science Review*, **71**(4), 1467–87.

Klemm, K. (2003), 'Bildungsausgaben: Woher sie kommen, wohin sie fließen', in K.S. Cortina, J. Baumert, A. Leschinsky, K.-U. Mayer and L. Trommer (eds), *Das Bildungswesen in der Bundesrepublik Deutschland*, Reinbek: Rowohlt, pp. 215–50.

Leibfried, S. (2005), 'Social policy. Left to the judges and the market?' in H. Wallace and M. Pollack (eds), *Policy-Making in the European Union*, 5th edn, Oxford: Oxford University Press, pp. 244–78.

Maddison, A. (2003), *The World Economy. Historical Statistics*, Paris: OECD.

Nikolai, R. (2006a), 'Determinanten der öffentlichen Bildungsausgaben in alten und neuen OECD-Staaten im Vergleich', in M.G. Schmidt, M.R. Busemeyer, R. Nikolai and F. Wolf (eds), *Bildungsausgaben im inter- und intranationalen Vergleich. Bestimmungsfaktoren öffentlicher Bildungsausgaben in OECD-Staaten* (unpublished manuscript), Institute of Political Science at the University of Heidelberg.

Nikolai, Rita (2006b), 'Intranationaler Vergleich: die Schweiz', in M.G. Schmidt, M.R. Busemeyer, R. Nikolai and F. Wolf (eds), *Bildungsausgaben im inter- und intranationalen Vergleich. Bestimmungsfaktoren öffentlicher Bildungsausgaben in OECD-Staaten* (unpublished manuscript), Institute of Political Science at the University of Heidelberg.

OECD (1985), *Social Expenditure 1960–1990. Problems of Growth and Control*, Paris: OECD.

OECD (1992), *Public Education Expenditure, Costs and Financing: An Analysis of Trends 1970–1988*, Paris: OECD.

OECD (2003), *Education at a Glance. OECD Indicators 2003*, Paris: OECD.

OECD (2005), *Education at a Glance. OECD Indicators 2005*, Paris: OECD.

Olson, M. (1982), *The Rise and Decline of Nations. Economic Growth, Stagflation, and Social Rigidities*, New Haven and London: Yale University Press.

Pierson, Paul (ed.) (2001), *The New Politics of the Welfare State*, Oxford: Oxford University Press, pp. 410–57.

Rose, R. and P.L. Davies (1994), *Inheritance in Public Policy: Change without Choice in Britain*, New Haven: Yale University Press.

Scharpf, F.W. (1987), *Sozialdemokratische Krisenpolitik in Westeuropa*, Frankfurt a.M. and New York: Campus.

Schmidt, M.G. (1996), 'When parties matter: a review of the possibilities and limits of partisan influence on public policy', *European Journal of Political Research*, **30**(2), 155–83.

Schmidt, M.G. (2004), 'Die öffentlichen und privaten Bildungsausgaben in Deutschland im internationalen Vergleich', *Zeitschrift für Europa- und Staatswissenschaften*, **2**(1), 7–31.

Schmidt, M.G. (2005a), *Sozialpolitik in Deutschland. Historische Entwicklung und internationaler Vergleich*, Wiesbaden: VS.

Schmidt, M.G. (ed.) (2005b), *Bundesrepublik Deutschland 1982–1989. Finanzielle Konsolidierung und institutionelle Reform* (Geschichte der Sozialpolitik in Deutschland seit 1945, ed. Bundesministerium für Gesundheit und Soziale Sicherung and Bundesarchiv, vol. 7), Baden-Baden: Nomos.

Schmidt, M.G. (2006), 'The party composition of governments in democratic OECD member countries (1945–2005)', Institute of Political Science at Heidelberg University (SPSS-File).

Schmidt, M.G., M.R. Busemeyer, R. Nikolai and F. Wolf (2006), *Bildungsausgaben im inter- und intranationalen Vergleich. Bestimmungsfaktoren öffentlicher Bildungsausgaben in OECD-Staaten* (unpublished manuscript), Institute of Political Science at the University of Heidelberg.

Wilensky, H.L. (1975), *The Welfare State and Equality*, Berkeley: University of California Press.

Wolf, F. (2005), 'Die Bildungsausgaben der Bundesländer im Vergleich', *Gesellschaft – Wirtschaft – Politik*, **4**, 411–23.

Wolf, F. (2006), *Die Bildungsausgaben der Bundesländer im Vergleich*, Münster: LIT Verlag.

8. The real race to the bottom: what happened to economic affairs expenditure after 1980?

Herbert Obinger and Reimut Zohlnhöfer

8.1 INTRODUCTION

Public interference in economic affairs was a commonplace of the post-war political economy of Western capitalism. Sparked by the past experience of economic depression and war, public intervention in economic and social affairs was increasingly seen as a means of guaranteeing economic stability, growth and full employment. In the aftermath of World War II, it was seen as proper for the state to play a leading role in the coordination of economic reconstruction and development, particularly in countries suffering from serious war-induced damage to the economic and public infrastructure. Framed by the growing influence of Keynesian ideas, a consensus emerged across the advanced democracies that public intrusion in economic affairs and generous welfare state programmes could help to smooth the business cycle and cope with the market failures to which decentralized co-ordinated market economies were inherently prone. The period between 1960 and 1980 was, therefore, one of unprecedented enthusiasm for activist expenditure policies coupled with a growing involvement of government in economic affairs (Tanzi and Schuknecht, 2000; Cusack and Fuchs, 2003; Castles, 2006).

An aspect of this development was that airlines, railways, postal services and telecommunications, the supply of electricity, gas and water, as well as a broad range of local services such as waste disposal, were directly provided by public enterprises in many countries. By means of cross-subsidisation between sectors, this 'public infrastructure state' also fulfilled social welfare functions by providing services equal in quality irrespective of the local resource base and, in areas such as energy and transport, frequently adjusted to the ability of consumers to pay. Hence public utilities became, in a sense, and to varying degrees in different countries, an 'outer skin' of the welfare state (Leibfried, 2005: 271), encasing and supporting the direct cash transfer programmes of the income maintenance state. In some countries, large parts of heavy industry (the steel industry, ship-building and mining) and even banks were nationalised. In many cases, state-owned enterprises were politically utilised as employment buffers, social laboratories or as instruments for promoting regional economic development. However, public interference in the commercial decisions of these industries often led to efficiency costs, which, in turn, fuelled demands for public subsidies to balance the losses accrued by these public corporations.

In the 1970s and early 1980s, this optimistic faith in the beneficial effects of big government came to a halt. Deteriorating economic performance in the wake of the oil shocks and the failure of many governments to cope with emergent stagflation led to scepticism concerning the involvement of government in economic affairs and finally to a realignment in economic policy. In the early 1980s, with the first moves occurring in the English-speaking countries, the state increasingly became seen as part of the problem rather than as a tool for overcoming macroeconomic imbalances. Soon, however, neo-liberal ideas spread across the globe. This process was accelerated and reinforced by international organisations and triggered a major rethinking of the role of the state in economic and social affairs. Rolling back the state to its core functions was more and more seen as offering a major comparative advantage in the international economy and as a prerequisite for unleashing the dynamic of market forces.

In this chapter, we examine whether, in comparative terms, this reorientation in economic policy was accompanied by a decline in public expenditure on economic affairs. Focusing on the period between 1980 and 2004, we show that the 'tyranny of past commitments' (Tanzi and Schuknecht, 2000: 20) characterising so many fields of public expenditure does not hold for the economic activities of the state. Using the COFOG data set, we show that public spending in this area manifested a remarkable decline right across the OECD world. Unfortunately, however, the COFOG data set does not have sufficient country coverage or cover sufficient years to allow anything like a comprehensive analysis. We thus pay special attention to a sub-category of governmental spending on economic affairs, namely industrial subsidies and state aid to economic activities, for which far more comprehensive data are available. Here, again, we discover substantial cross-national decline in governmental transfers paid to industry. Moreover, in this area of spending, retreat by the state is paralleled by strong convergence. Overall, our findings suggest a sort of 'race to the bottom' with respect to the involvement of government in economic affairs.

The remainder of the chapter is organised as follows. We begin our analysis by mapping recent developments in public spending on economic activities as measured according to the COFOG classification. In addition, we report recent spending trajectories of industrial subsidies and state aid in advanced democracies. Next, we derive hypotheses from various theoretical approaches of comparative public policy research potentially capable of accounting for cross-national differences in the extent of governmental intervention in economic affairs. We then provide an empirical analysis of the factors driving the extent and changes of industrial subsidies in the OECD world. The final section discusses the findings.

8.2   THE INVOLVEMENT OF GOVERNMENT IN ECONOMIC AFFAIRS

In this section, we utilise diverse data sources to map recent developments in public spending on economic activities in advanced OECD democracies. More specifically, we are interested in whether spending levels and changes in the cross-national dispersion of spending are indicative of expenditure convergence over recent years. However, before presenting the empirical findings, some words on the measurement of convergence are required. In general, convergence denotes increasing similarity of policies over time. However, convergence is a multifaceted concept and the literature distinguishes several variants of the phenomenon (Knill, 2005: 768–9). The most common way of gauging the extent of convergence is to compare the variation of policies at two points in time. A decline in statistical measures of dispersion such as the standard deviation and coefficient of variation (CV) is denoted as σ (sigma) convergence. Whereas σ-convergence focuses on the cross-sectional dispersion, β (beta) convergence denotes an inverse relationship between the initial value of a particular policy indicator (in our case the level of spending on economic activities) and its subsequent growth.[1] A simple test for β-convergence is to regress the initial value of a particular policy indicator on its subsequent growth rate for the period of interest. If the estimated coefficient for the initial value shows a negative sign and is statistically significant in this baseline model, there is evidence of absolute β-convergence. This concept of convergence is, thus, equivalent to a process of catch-up by policy laggards or – in the case of a decreasing mean over time – a 'catch-down' by the highest spending countries.

8.2.1   State Interference in Economic Affairs: COFOG

The Classification of Functions of Government (COFOG) breaks down total public expenditure on economic affairs into nine sub-categories. Table 8.1 shows total public spending on economic activities as a proportion of

Table 8.1   *Spending on economic activities in OECD countries, 1990–2002*

	1990	1996	2002	Change 1990–2002	Change 1996–2002
Australia	—	—	—	—	—
Austria	—	4.70	5.00	—	0.30
Belgium	6.00	4.70	4.60	−1.40	−0.10
Canada	—	—	—	—	—
Denmark	4.60	4.50	3.60	−1.00	−0.90
Finland	6.50	7.00	4.90	−1.60	−2.10
France	—	3.60	3.20	—	−0.40
Germany*	5.30	4.40	4.00	−1.30	−0.40
Greece	4.70	4.10	5.50	0.80	1.40
Iceland	8.60	6.70	6.20	−2.40	−0.50
Ireland	5.70	5.80	5.20	−0.50	−0.60
Italy	6.10	4.70	4.30	−1.80	−0.40
Japan	4.40	5.30	4.50	0.10	−0.70
Luxemburg	5.90	6.30	5.10	−0.80	−1.20
Netherlands	—	5.00	5.10	—	0.10
New Zealand	—	—	—	—	—
Norway	8.70	6.40	5.10	−3.60	−1.30
Portugal	5.80	5.80	4.80	−1.00	−1.00
Spain	—	—	4.50	—	—
Sweden	—	4.90	4.80	—	−0.10
UK	4.20	2.90	2.70	−1.50	−0.20
USA	3.70	3.50	3.70	0.00	0.20
N	14	18	19	14	18
Mean	5.73	5.02	4.57	−1.14	−0.44
SD	1.48	1.14	0.84		
Range	5.00	4.10	3.50		
CV	0.26	0.23	0.18		

Notes: * 1990 figure refers to 1991.

Source: data as given in Appendix 3B.

GDP in advanced OECD countries from 1990 onwards. The figures reported in the table reveal considerable cross-national differences in the involvement of government in economic affairs. In 1990, spending levels ranged from 3.7 per cent of GDP in the United States to 8.7 per cent in Norway. Even more interesting is the evidence of expenditure decline over these years. For the 14 countries for which data are available in both 1990 and 2002, mean levels of spending went down by around 20 per cent, from 5.73 per cent of GDP in 1990 to 4.57 per cent in 2002, with cutbacks experienced in no less than four-fifths of the countries. A similar picture emerges for the period between 1996 and 2002 for which data for 18 OECD democracies are available.

The retreat of the state from economic activities was paralleled by convergence. The summary statistics displayed in the last rows of Table 8.1 provide strong evidence of σ-convergence in public expenditure devoted to economic affairs with all the statistical measures of dispersion declining over time. As indicated by the negative slope of the regression lines in Figure 8.1, σ-convergence was accompanied by β-convergence. The coefficients for the initial spending level reported below the figure are statistically significant at the 1 per cent level. The negative sign of the estimated coefficients suggests that the rollback in public spending on economic activities was strongest in countries with initially high spending levels. This effect explains almost two-thirds of the change in public expenditure in this area over the period between 1990 and 2002. The decline in the mean and the presence of σ- and β-convergence together provide strong prima facie evidence of a race to the bottom with respect to the involvement of the state in economic affairs during these years.

Unfortunately, the available COFOG data only extend over a relatively short period of time. Moreover, nations such as Australia, Canada, New Zealand and Switzerland are not covered at all. Although we are able to identify important trends in cross-national spending on economic activities by means of descriptive statistics, the COFOG data set is neither suitable for conducting multivariate statistical analysis nor can it be used to examine long-term trends. In what follows we therefore focus on a particular segment of public expenditure related to economic affairs, namely industrial subsidies and state aid in OECD and EU countries.

8.2.2 Subsidy Levels in OECD Countries

Subsidies represent a major component of governmental activity in economic affairs as defined by COFOG. In the post-war period, virtually all governments have provided assistance to sectors such as agriculture, manufacturing, mining and transport. In addition, governments have not only financed employment programmes and general measures to reduce regional economic disparities, but have also provided subventions supporting R&D activities and foreign trade.

Based on the Systems of National Accounts (SNA), the OECD provides data on subsidy payments of governments to industry in its member states. Under the OECD classification, subsidies are referred to as direct payments that government units make to enterprises. Other types of assistance such as credit subsidies, tax concessions and subsidies to consumers are not taken into

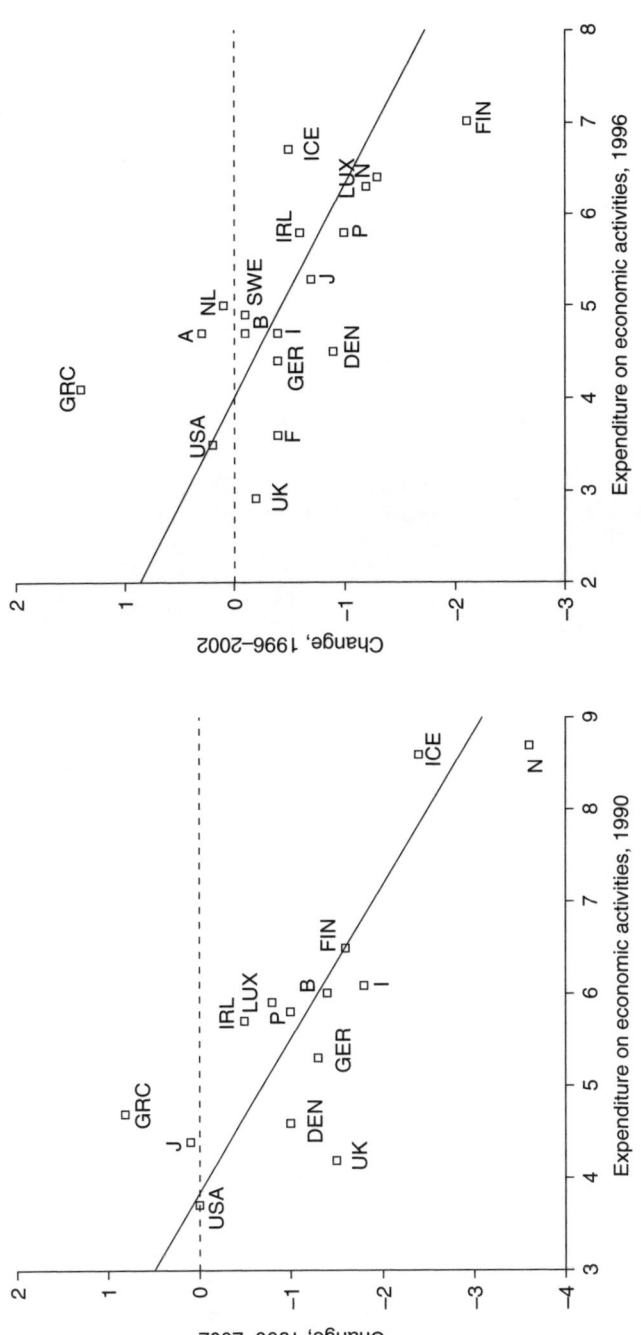

Notes: Change, 1990–2002 = 2.26 − 0.59 (4.69) expenditure, 1990;
R^2 = 0.65; n = 14; t-statistics in parentheses.

Notes: Change, 1996–2002 = 1.73 − 0.43 (3.49) expenditure, 1996;
R^2 = 0.43; n = 18; t-statistics in parentheses.

Figure 8.1   *The relationship between change in spending on economic activities between 1990 and 2002 (left-hand side) and 1996 and 2002 (right-hand side) and initial spending levels*

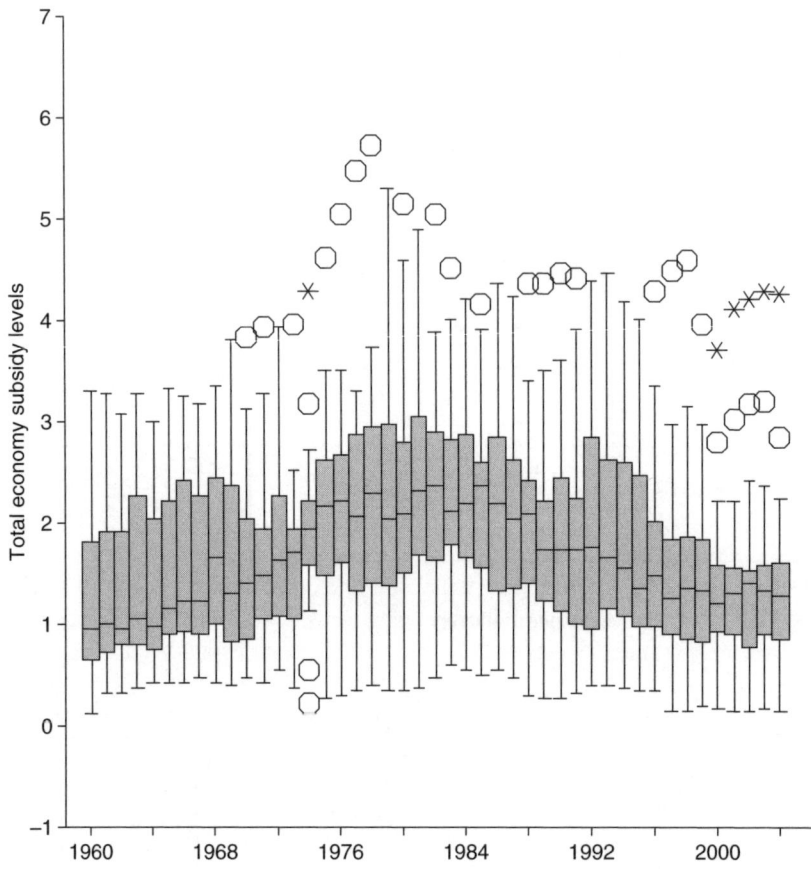

Figure 8.2   Total economy subsidy levels, 1960–2004

account (Lee 2002: 5). Subsidy levels, that is, subsidies as a percentage of
GDP, can be calculated from the OECD *Economic Outlook* database. The
latest version of this data set (OECD, 2005) provides information on subsidies granted by core OECD member states since 1960. Missing data for some
countries were supplemented using information provided in OECD *Economic
Outlook* no. 63 (June 1998).[2] Switzerland, however, is a problematic case,
because the latest OECD data only cover the period since 1990. Moreover, we
cannot use older versions of the database to construct a consistent time-series
dating back to the 1960s because of a marked rupture in the data.

The development of subsidy levels in the 20 OECD countries since 1960
reveals a pattern that can be described as an 'accordion effect'. Figure 8.2
shows boxplots mapping the cross-national dispersion of subsidies (as a per-

Table 8.2   Total economy subsidy levels as a percentage of GDP,
1960–2004

Year	Mean	SD	Range	N
1960	1.32	0.95	3.18	14
1965	1.51	0.87	2.92	18
1970	1.58	0.90	3.37	19
1975	2.23	1.01	4.35	20
1980	2.37	1.14	4.80	20
1985	2.28	0.96	3.65	20
1990	1.82	1.06	4.21	20
1995	1.58	1.02	3.37	20
2000	1.23	0.67	2.63	20
2004	1.24	0.69	2.70	20

Note: Switzerland not included.

centage of GDP) for the period between 1960 and 2004, while Table 8.2 reports the corresponding summary statistics. The boxplots as well as the descriptive statistics show an increase in governmental payments to business between 1960 and 1980. Moreover, the steady rise in expenditure levels over this period was paralleled by an increasing cross-national dispersion. Government support to industry peaked in 1980, when subsidy levels stood at an average of 2.4 per cent of GDP. This was also the time-point of maximum cross-national dispersion: in 1980, the United States only devoted 0.35 per cent of GDP to industrial support while governmental payments to industry in Norway were a massive 5.15 per cent of GDP. Since 1980, subsidy levels and cross-national differences have been declining and, by the new millennium, had reached levels, if anything, rather lower than those of the early 1960s.

Table 8.3 reports levels and changes of subsidies in 20 OECD countries between 1980 and 2004. The figures displayed in the last rows of this table provide strong evidence for the existence of families of nations (Castles, 1998). Throughout the period, industrial subsidies were lowest in the English-speaking countries and highest in Scandinavia. Subsidy levels in continental and southern Europe are located in-between these extremes. Even more striking is the dramatic decline in industrial subsidies throughout the OECD world. With one exception, all these nations have considerably reduced governmental assistance to industry over the past 25 years. This rollback of subsidies has been particularly strong in the Scandinavian countries and in the countries of Southern Europe. Since these were the families of nations with the highest levels of industrial support in 1980, it comes as no surprise that the measures of dispersion reported in Table 8.2

Table 8.3   *Level and change of total economy subsidies as percentages of*
                GDP, 1980–2004

	1980	1990	2004	Change 1980–1990	Change 1990–2004	Change 1980–2004
Australia	1.44	1.32	1.32	−0.12	0.00	−0.13
Austria	3.09	3.01	2.84	−0.07	−0.17	−0.24
Belgium	2.79	1.66	1.60	−1.13	−0.06	−1.19
Canada	2.74	1.48	1.17	−1.26	−0.31	−1.57
Denmark	1.65	2.45	2.20	0.80	−0.25	0.55
Finland	3.16	2.83	1.29	−0.33	−1.55	−1.87
France	2.13	1.81	1.29	−0.32	−0.52	−0.84
Germany	2.08	2.01	1.27	−0.07	−0.74	−0.81
Greece	1.99	1.22	0.14	−0.77	−1.08	−1.85
Ireland	2.44	1.13	0.59	−1.31	−0.54	−1.85
Italy	2.70	1.88	1.07	−0.82	−0.81	−1.63
Japan	1.50	1.09	0.86	−0.41	−0.24	−0.64
Netherlands	1.77	2.25	1.53	0.48	−0.72	−0.24
New Zealand	1.46	0.27	0.31	−1.19	0.04	−1.15
Norway	5.15	4.48	2.25	−0.67	−2.23	−2.90
Portugal	4.60	1.73	1.64	−2.88	−0.09	−2.96
Spain	1.06	1.06	1.05	0.00	−0.01	−0.01
Sweden	3.38	3.61	1.44	0.24	−2.18	−1.94
Switzerland	n.a.	3.57	4.26	n.a.	0.69	n.a.
UK	1.96	0.68	0.53	−1.28	−0.15	−1.43
USA	0.35	0.46	0.34	0.11	−0.12	−0.01
MEAN (OECD 20)*	2.37	1.82	1.24	−0.55	−0.52	−1.14
Mean English-speaking countries	*1.73*	*0.89*	*0.71*	*−0.84*	*−0.18*	*−1.02*
Mean Continental Europe	*2.37*	*2.15*	*1.71*	*−0.22*	*−0.44*	*−0.66*
Mean Scandinavia	*3.33*	*3.34*	*1.79*	*0.01*	*−1.55*	*−1.54*
Mean Southern Europe	*2.59*	*1.47*	*0.98*	*−1.12*	*−0.50*	*−1.61*

Notes: English-speaking nations: USA, UK, New Zealand, Australia, Canada and
Ireland. Continental Europe: Austria, Belgium, France, Germany and Netherlands.
Scandinavia: Denmark, Finland, Norway and Sweden. Southern Europe: Greece, Italy,
Portugal and Spain.* = without Switzerland.

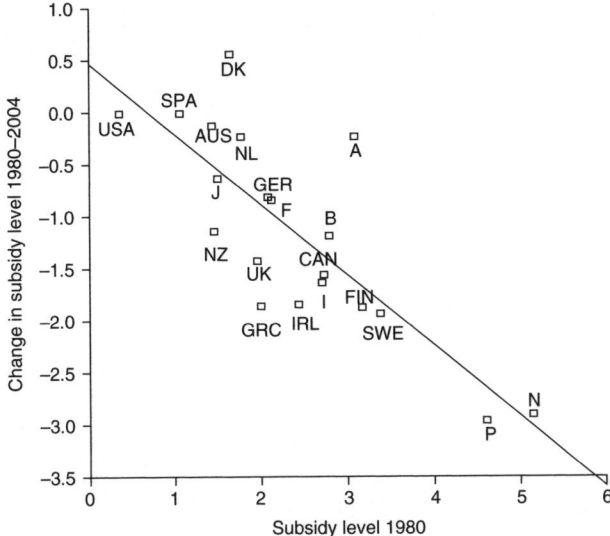

Note: Change 1980–2004=0.46−0.67 (5.68) subsidy level 1980; R^2=0.67; n=20; t-statistics in parentheses.

Figure 8.3 β*-convergence of subsidies as a percentage of GDP, 1980–2004*

as well as the scatterplot shown in Figure 8.3 are indicative of strong convergence. The bivariate regression reported at the right-hand side of Figure 8.3 confirms the presence of β-convergence: The estimated coefficient for initial subsidy levels is not only statistically significant at the 1 per cent level, but is also a powerful predictor of change in subsidies in the subsequent period. Once again, the evidence for a race to the bottom is overwhelming.

8.2.3   State Aid in Europe

In this section we focus on subsidies in EU member states. Since the European Community provides data for different sectors, we can draw a more nuanced picture of recent developments in this area. Subsidies for agriculture and fisheries play a prominent role in EU countries. Therefore the data set differentiates between total state aid and total state aid less agriculture, fisheries and transport. Note that grants to railways, a major component of total subsidies granted by government in many countries, are not included in these figures. In 2004, subsidies to railways amounted to €24.7 billion in the EU-15[3] (EC, 2005: 16).

Table 8.4 Total state aid as a percentage of GDP in the EU-15, 1992–2004

Country	Total aid 1992	Total aid 1992 less agriculture, fisheries and transport	Total aid 2004	Total aid 2004 less agriculture, fisheries and transport	Change in total aid (1992–2004)**	Change in total aid less agriculture, fisheries and transport (1992–2004)**
Austria	1.0*	0.30*	0.60	0.20	−0.40	−0.10
Belgium	1.0	0.70	0.30	0.20	−0.70	−0.50
Denmark	0.40	0.30	0.70	0.50	0.30	0.20
Finland	2.80*	0.50*	1.50	0.40	−1.30	−0.10
France	0.70	0.40	0.50	0.40	−0.20	0.00
Germany	1.6	1.40	0.80	0.70	−0.80	−0.70
Greece	2.2	1.60	0.30	0.20	−1.90	−1.40
Ireland	0.80	0.40	0.70	0.30	−0.10	−0.10
Italy	1.70	1.40	0.50	0.40	−1.20	−1.00
Luxemburg	0.80	0.60	0.30	0.20	−0.50	−0.40
Netherlands	0.40	0.20	0.40	0.20	0.00	0.00
Portugal	0.80	0.50	1.10	0.80	0.30	0.30
Spain	0.70	0.40	0.50	0.40	−0.20	0.00
Sweden	0.50*	0.30*	1.00	0.80	0.50	0.50
UK	0.30	0.20	0.30	0.20	0.00	0.00
Mean	1.04	0.61	0.63	0.39	−0.41	−0.22
SD	0.72	0.46	0.35	0.22	0.67	0.50
Range	2.50	1.40	1.20	0.60	—	—
CV	0.69	0.75	0.56	0.56	—	—

Notes: * = 1995; ** Austria, Finland and Sweden: 1995–2004.

Source: http://europa.eu.int/comm/competition/state_aid/scoreboard/indicators/k1.html#data (24.1.2006).

In the early 1990s, total state aid in member states on average amounted to 1.04 per cent of GDP (see Table 8.4). Total aid covers manufacturing, services, coal, fisheries, agriculture and transport with the exception of railways. Almost 60 per cent of this volume, equivalent to 0.61 per cent of GDP, was granted to manufacturing, services and coal. These averages, however, mask substantial cross-national differences in terms of the sectoral allocation and the extent of state aid in member states. In 1992, total state aid ranged from 0.3 in the UK to 2.8 per cent of GDP in Finland. In sectoral terms, 80 per cent of total state aid was granted to agriculture and fisheries in Finland, whereas the corresponding share was only 12 per cent in Germany. In line with the subsidy data compiled by the OECD, the data provided by the Commission show a substantial decline in state aid over time and across all sectors. Total state aid decreased from 1.04 per cent of GDP in 1992 to 0.63 per cent in 2004. Subsidies to manufacturing, services and coal fell from 0.61 in 1992 to 0.39 per cent of GDP in this period. Overall, the average volume of state aid in the EU-15 in 2004 was about 40 per cent lower than 13 years earlier.

Even though all sectors, with the exception of agriculture and fisheries, have been subject to cutbacks in the 1990s (EC, 2001: 24), it is interesting to highlight the rollback of state aid in particular sectors in more detail. The transport sector, for example, experienced major cutbacks in the wake of the liberalisation of the airlines. In the steel sector, the decline was even more dramatic. This radical rollback can be attributed to efforts of the EC, OECD and WTO to reduce distortions in the international steel market. Significant cutbacks, albeit less pronounced, can also be observed for the coal and the shipbuilding sectors (EC, 2005: 11–19; EC, 2001: 28ff).

Overall, the data point to a substantial decline in state aid within a relatively short period of time. Similarly to the developments in industry subsidies described above, this downward trend was accompanied by convergence. The summary statistics section of Table 8.4 shows a decline in all measures of dispersion over time. In addition to σ-convergence, there is also evidence of β-convergence (see Figure 8.4). Hence cutbacks were most pronounced in the nations with the highest levels of state aid in the early 1990s. This effect is extremely strong and explains about 80 per cent of the variation of change in state aid in Europe.

However, it must be emphasised that this remarkable decline in state support occurred largely during the 1990s (see Figure 8.5). More recently, expenditures have levelled off. Instead of further retrenchment, member states have redirected state aid from supporting individual sectors to so-called 'horizontal objectives' such as promoting energy saving, regional economic development, R&D, employment aid and small and medium-sized enterprises (SMEs). In the EU-15, 84 per cent of total state aid (less agriculture,

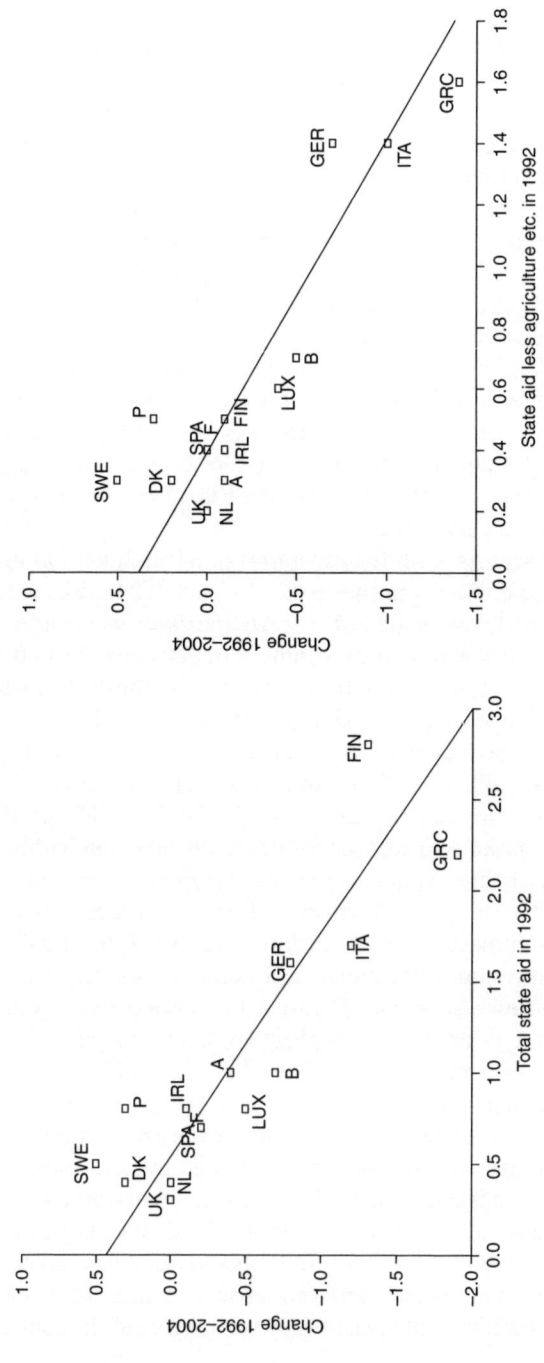

Notes: Change (1992–2004) = 0.379 − 0.976 (7.48) State aid 1992; R^2 = 0.81; n = 15; t-statistics in parentheses.

Notes: Change (1992–2004) = 0.437 − 0.813 (6.58) State aid 1992; R^2 = 0.77; n = 15; t-statistics in parentheses.

Figure 8.4 β-*convergence of state aid in the EU, 1992–2004*

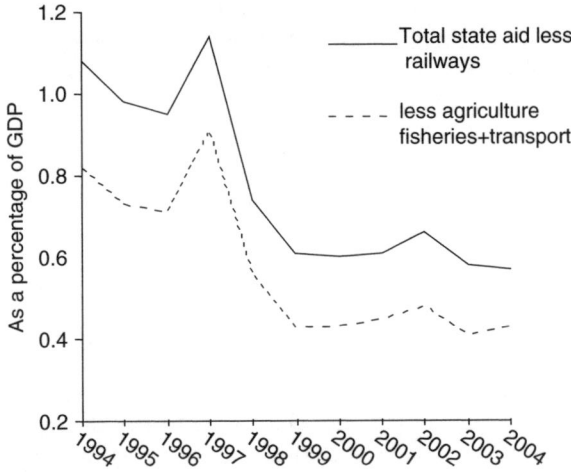

Source: EC (2005:12).

Figure 8.5   *State aid as a percentage of GDP in the EU-15, 1994–2004*

fisheries and transport) was utilized in this way in 2004, whereas the corresponding share was only about 50 per cent in the mid-1990s (EC, 2005: 21).

8.3   EXPLAINING RECENT DEVELOPMENTS IN INDUSTRIAL SUBSIDIES IN THE OECD

In this section we seek to identify the factors determining the level and dynamics of industrial subsidies over the past 25 years. Relying on the major schools of thought in comparative public policy research, we briefly develop some hypotheses, which may help to explain differences in levels and changes in subsidies among OECD countries. We then proceed to expose these hypotheses to an empirical test.

8.3.1   Hypotheses

Policy inheritance
As Rose and Karran (1987) have observed, policymakers are heirs at least as much as choosers and it is often rather difficult to alter the trajectory of policy once it is embarked upon. This is also true for subsidies. Subsidies are often granted on a medium-term basis and, thus, cannot be cut with immediate effect. Moreover, short-term changes in the level of subsidisation may have severe unintended effects, which may lead governments to abstain from

radical change in subsidy levels. Even the European Commission is reported to have 'recognised that, like drug withdrawal, it is dangerous to cut the dose overnight' (Wilks, 2005: 123). Therefore we expect the *level* of subsidy payments to be positively related to the extent of subsidies in the past.

On the other hand, it has already been demonstrated that there has been strong convergence in subsidy levels. Hence we assume that countries starting from comparatively high levels of subsidy increase their subsidies less (or cut subsidies more) than countries with a low starting level. In other words, we expect a negative relationship between the initial level of subsidisation and change in subsidies over time. The data for subsidy levels are taken from OECD *Economic Outlook*, numbers 77 and 63.

Socio-economic changes

It has often been argued that policy changes represent the reactions of governments to pressing economic challenges. This may also be the case for state support to industry. For example, one might expect that processes of deindustrialisation would be associated with a decline in subsidies just because most subsidies went to manufacturing industries which are now of decreasing importance. We use Iversen's and Cusack's (2000: 331–2) measure of deindustrialisation, which is defined as '100 minus the sum of manufacturing and agricultural employment as a percentage of the working-age population', using values for 1980, 1990 and 2001 and the differences over time as appropriate.[4]

Similarly, governments that are confronted with dismal economic growth, high unemployment and excessive public debt may well be more likely to resort to the recommendations of the supply-side economists who have dominated the economic policy discourse since the 1980s (Hall, 1993; Boix, 1998). According to this view, it is imperative to roll back the state's influence on the economy as far as possible in order to create incentives for economic activity, which, in turn, will result in stronger growth and increasing employment. Subsidies are particularly problematic from this perspective, because they reduce an economy's potential to adapt to new circumstances and may lead to an inefficient allocation of resources. Given these distorting effects of subsidies, many economists have suggested that subsidies should be drastically curtailed. The hypothesis we examine here is that governments are likely to be more inclined to follow this advice if they are confronted with unsatisfactory economic performance (Zohlnhöfer, 2003). This suggests that high rates of economic growth and low rates of unemployment will be associated with continuingly high levels of subsidisation, as low growth and high unemployment increase pressures on governments to launch growth-stimulating measures, including subsidy cuts.[5] We use average unemployment ratios between 1973 and 1980, 1980 and 1990, 1990 and 2003 and 1980 and 2003, as well as the changes between these points in time (source: OECD Labour Force Statistics, various issues). Data for economic growth are taken from OECD Historical Statistics and Penn World Table 6.1.

The state of public finances may also have direct effects on subsidisation policies. A government confronted with high levels of public debt or a high budget deficit will search for options to tackle this problem. Expenditure cuts may be particularly urgent when debt interest payments are high. Since subsidies are often criticised as inefficient economic policy instruments and because tax increases are unpopular, it seems reasonable to suppose that state aid will be an immediate target for retrenchment where spending cuts are perceived as being inevitable. Therefore both the change and the level of subsidy payments should be negatively related to public debt at the beginning of each period of observation (1970, 1980, 1990; source: OECD Economic Outlook, various issues). Theoretically, we would also expect public deficits to be negatively related to subsidy spending. However, because of the danger of reverse causality (high spending might cause deficits while deficits might cause spending cuts) we have refrained from using deficits as an independent variable. Instead we have used average net debt interest payments between 1980 and 1990 and between 1990 and 1999 (source: OECD Economic Outlook, various issues).[6] The expectation would be that governments that have to expend greater resources on debt repayment are likely to be under greater pressure to cut spending on subsidies (cf. the argument of Chapter 2 above).

Political parties
Partisan theory essentially argues that political parties' positions on the relationship between state and market are pivotal to the distinction between bourgeois and left parties (von Beyme, 2000: 89). While bourgeois parties favour market solutions in economic policy, left parties tend to emphasise the role of the state for a well functioning economy (Schmidt, 2002; Zohlnhöfer, 2003). Since subsidies are an interventionist economic policy instrument *par excellence*, we expect subsidy levels to be higher and subsidy cutbacks to be smaller under left governments. In contrast, right parties should prefer lower levels of state support and larger cuts in subsidies. The partisan complexion of government is measured by the share of cabinet seats held by each party family. Left parties are social democratic, socialist and (post)-communist parties, while liberal, conservative and centre parties are categorised as right parties. These latter parties, together with Christian democratic parties, are classified as bourgeois parties.[7]

Political institutions
Comparative public policy research has shown that political institutions, by configuring actor constellations, actor strategies and patterns of interaction,

can exert a major impact on policies in diverse policy fields. It is our assumption that spending on subsidies will be no exception to this rule. According to veto-player theory (Tsebelis, 2002), it can be argued that a change of the status quo will become more difficult as the number of veto players increases. The reason is that, with an increasing number of actors, it becomes more likely that at least one of the actors will veto a change of the status quo, either because of programmatic dissent or because important political allies, interest groups or decisive parts of the electorate oppose the reform, thereby making such a veto opportune for electoral reasons. The implication is that strong institutional pluralism produces a status quo bias and suggesting the hypothesis that *changes* in subsidy levels will be smaller in political systems with many powerful veto players. At the same time, we would expect the *level* of subsidies to be lower in veto-prone polities, where policy makers, *ceteris paribus*, face more difficulties in increasing subsidies than in Westminster-style polities. Institutional pluralism is measured by Manfred Schmidt's (2000: 352) index.

Interest groups
The political economy of subsidies is characterised by the fact that the benefits of financial state aids are particularly concentrated on the enterprises receiving the subsidies and their employees, while the costs are dispersed amongst the whole electorate (regarding the financial resources used) or are even disputed (concerning the effects of subsidies on economic efficiency). Therefore it is reasonable to assume that the way interest groups are incorporated in economic policy making will make a big difference to subsidy expenditure outcomes.

Encompassing organisations that internalise the external costs of their behaviour are likely to pursue economically more responsible policies than small groups that focus only on the advantages accruing to their own narrow constituency (Olson, 1982). Given today's mainstream economics' scepticism about the economic effects of subsidies, this argument might lead one to expect that subsidy levels would be lower in corporatist countries (characterised by more encompassing organisations) than in pluralist ones. However, the economic effects of subsidies continue to be a matter of debate (cf. Thöne, 2003: 16–24) and there is probably agreement that, under certain circumstances, in certain sectors and for a certain time, subsidies can be useful – with the controversy focused on the nature of the circumstances, sectors and duration. It is therefore possible that encompassing organisations may also argue for higher subsidies. Given their more direct access to policy makers in corporatist systems, this suggests that high levels of corporatist intermediation may actually lead to higher subsidy levels and make a rollback of subsidies more difficult. We have used Siaroff's (1999) index of 'economic integration' as a measure for corporatism.

External challenges

It is often argued that the economic policies of nation states are increasingly monitored or even punished by international financial markets under circumstances of high capital mobility (Siebert, 1998). As a consequence, credibility becomes a major goal of governments (Freitag, 2001), which may feel obliged to respond by adopting orthodox economic policies including cuts in subsidy levels. Moreover, a rollback of subsidies may improve a government's budgetary position, which is, in itself, of central importance for the actions of international capital markets (Mosley, 2000). Hence both levels of and change in subsidies should be negatively related to the level of a country's trade and capital market openness.[8] Trade openness is measured by the sum of exports and imports divided by two (averaged over different periods in time; data from Armingeon et al., 2005), while data for capital market openness in 1980, 1990 and 1993 are taken from Quinn (1997).

European integration is also likely to have an impact on policies of subsidisation. At least two channels of influence can be distinguished. First, the European Commission operates a formally rather strict regime of state aid control. Article 87.1 TEC stipulates that 'any aid granted by a Member State or through State resources in any form whatsoever which distorts or threatens to distort competition by favouring certain undertakings or the production of certain goods shall, in so far as it affects trade between Member States, be incompatible with the common market'. Though articles 87.2 and 87.3 TEC allow for a number of exceptions, the European Commission is given a rather strong position: state aids need to be explicitly permitted by the Commission and the Commission can decide that member states have to abolish subsidies that are found to be incompatible with the common market (article 88.2 and 88.3 TEC). While the prevailing policy approach up to and including the early 1980s could best be characterised as one of 'pragmatic neglect', the Commission 'began to take a much more rigorous line towards subsidies from the mid-1980s onwards' (McGowan, 2000: 129, 131). Stephen Wilks (2005: 123) even argues that 'the state aid regime has chalked up significant successes and has consolidated an historic move away from state subsidisation of industry'.

Second, the fiscal pressures on the EU member states stemming from the Treaty of Maastricht and its deficit criteria could well play an important role. European governments aspiring to join the Monetary Union (EMU) in 1999 were required to achieve public deficit levels of below 3 per cent of GDP by 1997. Therefore the deficit criterion (and its follow-up in the stability and growth pact) put these governments under intense fiscal strain, arguably giving them a greater incentive to reduce subsidy (and all other expenditure) levels than non-EMU countries. The effects of EU and EMU are measured by dummy variables for the respective member states in the different periods.

8.3.2 Empirical Analysis

We analyse the determinants of cross-national differences in subsidies in two ways: first by looking at levels of spending as percentages of GDP at three different points in time (1980, 1990, 2004) and second by analysing changes in spending as percentages of GDP between these time points, that is, for the periods 1980–1990, 1990–2004 and 1980–2004. We present best-fit models for each dependent variable plus models showing different specifications of particular theoretical relevance.

The evidence provided by the models featuring in Table 8.5 does, indeed, suggest that politics can help explain the variation in the subsidy levels in OECD countries. To begin with, we find significant partisan impacts on the level of industrial subsidies in 1980. Left governments show systematically higher expenditure on subsidies (equation 2) than right cabinets (1), irrespective of whether Christian Democrats are classified as right parties or not. Moreover, in the 1980 model, there is also evidence that institutional pluralism impedes spending. The higher the number of veto players in a country, the lower the extent of state support. This effect fails to reach statistical significance in some specifications, but generally by a small margin. Using other indicators of institutional pluralism than Schmidt's does not substantially alter the picture. Finally, while, as predicted, higher economic growth rates went along with high rates of subsidisation, there was a negative, although not quite significant, association between levels of economic affluence and spending on subsidies as a percentage of GDP.

The results for subsidy levels in 1990 are similar, albeit not identical to those for spending levels in 1980. We find a positive impact of the previous spending level and again significant partisan effects, even though the latter are somewhat weaker than previously. In particular, the negative effect of right parties only remains significant when Christian Democratic parties, the least liberal of the bourgeois parties in terms of economic policy, are excluded. The weakening of the partisan effect is not really all that surprising, however, as the subsidy level of 1980, which explains a large part of the subsidy level in 1990, is itself, to a substantial degree, shaped by the partisan complexion of government.[9] Contrary to the 1980 findings, institutional pluralism does not even come close to statistical significance in 1990. The same is true for economic growth. On the other hand, two other variables turn out to be positively and significantly related to the level of subsidy payments, namely the financial position of government and the system of interest group relations. Thus, the lower were a government's net

Table 8.5   Determinants of subsidy levels as percentages of GDP in OECD countries (1980, 1990, 2004)

| | Dependent variable: subsidies as a percentage of GDP | | | | | | |
| | 1980 | | 1990 | | | 2004 | |
	(1)	(2)	(3)	(4)	(5)	(6)	(7)
Intercept	3.025*** (6.106)	0.789 (1.555)	−1.054*** (3.162)	2.207*** (5.253)	0.692 (1.189)	−0.482 (1.492)	−0.554 (0.821)
Subsidy level 1980			0.445*** (4.448)	0.443*** (4.395)	0.403*** (4.964)		
Subsidy level 1990						0.663*** (6.078)	0.674*** (4.646)
Cabinet share of bourgeois parties (1950–1980)	−0.029*** (5.143)						
Cabinet share of left parties (1950–1980)		0.027*** (4.873)					
Cabinet share of right parties (excl. Christian Democrats) (1950–90)				−0.017*** (4.459)	−0.010** (2.640)		
Cabinet share of bourgeois parties (1950–2004)							0.001 (0.122)
Real economic growth (1973–79)	0.480*** (3.658)	0.476*** (3.853)					
Institutions (Schmidt, 1996)		−0.216* (2.013)				0.247*** (2.877)	0.240** (2.334)
Corporatism (1980s)			0.590*** (5.607)		0.345*** (3.187)		

Table 8.5 (continued)

	Dependent variable: subsidies as a percentage of GDP						
	1980			1990		2004	
	(1)	(2)	(3)	(4)	(5)	(6)	(7)
Average net debt interest payments (1980–90)				-0.189^{***} (4.621)	-0.127^{***} (3.354)		
Adj. R^2	0.647	0.686	0.812	0.821	0.886	0.675	0.657
N	18#	18#	20†	20†	20†	21	21

Notes: Unstandardized regression coefficients; t-statistics in parentheses. $* \ p \leq 0.10$; $** \ p \leq 0.05$; $*** \ p \leq 0.01$; # = Portugal, Spain and Switzerland are excluded because of missing information on subsidy levels in 1980 (Switzerland) or on partisan complexion of government due to authoritarian regimes until the 1970s (Portugal, Spain); † = Switzerland is excluded because of a lack of information on the subsidy levels in 1980.

Sources: See text.

debt interest payments between 1980 and 1990 and the more interest groups were integrated in economic policy making in the 1980s, the higher was subsidy spending by governments.

The pattern changes once more for subsidy levels in 2004. While the effect of policy inheritance remains strong, the impacts of the partisan complexion of government and corporatism collapse. When the policy inheritance variable is dropped from the regression, however, the expected effects resurface. The sign of the estimated coefficient for institutional pluralism has turned positive. Hence countries with high institutional pluralism manifested higher subsidy levels in 2004 than countries with fewer veto players.

We did not obtain significant results for the other variables hypothesised as being possibly linked to spending levels. This is true for variables measuring economic problems such as deindustrialisation, unemployment, economic growth and GDP per capita (except in 1980), public debt or net debt interest payments (except in 1990). Nor does integration in the world economy appear to exert an impact on subsidy levels. This holds for trade as well as financial market integration. Surprisingly perhaps, neither the EU – despite its rigid regime of state aid control – nor the EMU have an impact on the extent of subsidies, with coefficients well below the level of statistical significance.

Overall, the findings for levels of industrial subsidies suggest that significant change has taken place between 1980 and 2004. Whereas the level of subsidy expenditure in 1980 can be attributed to the partisan complexion of government and institutional pluralism, the effects of these variables either vanish (political parties) or change their direction of influence (veto points) over time. In order to locate the nature of this transformation, we now focus on the determinants of *changes* in subsidies since 1980. Our findings are summarised in Table 8.6.

The most important finding for all three periods analysed is that subsidy levels in OECD countries have converged dramatically. This is evident from the highly significant negative coefficient of the subsidy level at the beginning of each period. Thus the multivariate regressions presented here strongly corroborate the findings already presented in section 2.

Concerning the political determinants of changes in subsidy payments, the results are mixed. We find the expected negative impact of right (not necessarily bourgeois) parties on change in subsidy levels for the period between 1980 and 1990, implying that right parties increased subsidies less or cut more than their leftist counterparts. Partisan differences disappear, however, for the periods 1990–2004 and 1980–2004. For the former period, the signs of the estimated coefficients for both party families actually change compared to the 1980s. Thus, other things being equal, left parties imposed larger cuts than right parties between 1990 and 2004. This tilt in the impact

Table 8.6   Determinants of changes in subsidy expenditures as a percentage of GDP in OECD countries (1980–90, 1990–2004, 1980–2004)

	Dependent variable: change in subsidy levels						
	1980–90			1990–2004		1980–2004	
	(8)	(9)	(10)	(11)	(12)	(13)	(14)
Intercept	−1.05*** (3.162)	1.548*** (3.433)	0.327 (0.622)	−0.482 (1.492)	−0.706 (1.378)	−0.369 (1.105)	−0.725 (1.476)
Subsidy level 1980	−0.555*** (5.544)	−0.416*** (3.613)	−0.617*** (6.952)			−0.818*** (8.167)	−0.759*** (6.448)
Subsidy level 1990				−0.337*** (3.089)	−0.313** (2.623)		
Cabinet share of right parties (excl. Christian democrats) (1980–1990)		−0.011** (2.608)					
Cabinet share of bourgeois parties (1950–1990)			−0.01** (2.262)				
Cabinet share of bourgeois parties (1990–2004)					0.004 (0.570)		
Cabinet share of left parties (1980–2004)				0.247*** (2.877)			0.003 (0.468)
Institutions (Schmidt 1996)					0.220** (2.212)		0.116 (1.062)

Corporatism (1980s)	0.590***		0.468***			0.380***	0.331**
	(5.607)		(5.000)			(3.609)	(2.784)
Average Net Debt interest payments (1980–90)		−0.176***	−0.065*				
		(3.455)	(1.776)				
Adj. R²	0.691	0.536	0.795	0.456	0.434	0.773	0.761
N	20†	20†	20†	21	21	20†	20†

Notes: Unstandardised regression coefficients; t-statistics in parentheses. * $p \leq 0.10$; ** $p \leq 0.05$; *** $p \leq 0.01$; † = Switzerland is excluded because of a lack of information on the subsidy level in 1980.

Sources: See text.

of parties on industrial subsidies is graphically shown in Figure 8.6. These effects are not, however, strong enough to be statistically significant.

In contrast, we find a significant positive coefficient for the Schmidt index of institutional pluralism for the period between 1990 and 2004, suggesting that countries with many veto players have imposed smaller cuts in subsidies than countries with few veto players. The third significant political determinant of changes in subsidy levels is corporatism, which turns out to be positively related to changes in subsidy levels between 1980 and 1990 as well as between 1980 and 2004. Thus it would appear that countries with corporatist systems of interest mediation have reduced subsidy payments to industry more hesitantly compared to pluralist countries. Finally, economic problem pressures resulting from high net debt interest payments accelerated a rollback of subsidies in the 1980s. This result supports the argument of Chapter 2 of this volume that the skyrocketing interest payments faced by highly indebted countries in the 1980s due to massive interest rate rises did indeed put pressure on core expenditure, evidently not least spending on subsidies.

As in the case of subsidy levels, a number of variables failed to have an impact on changes in subsidy payments during any of the periods analysed. This is true for most socio-economic variables (with the exception of net debt interest payments in the 1980s) and also for all indicators of economic globalisation as well as of European integration.

8.4   CONCLUSION

Public spending on economic activities has declined dramatically in recent years. Unlike other areas of public expenditure development, where the diagnosis of a 'race to the bottom' has been falsified by the evidence of comparative research, in the area of economic affairs, this is a phenomenon that does genuinely appear to have taken place. Moreover, as expenditure has declined, it has also converged, leaving countries' spending profiles far more alike than was the case in the early 1980s.

It thus comes as no surprise that partisan differences in government spending on subsidies have decreased, if not disappeared altogether in the wake of this race to the bottom. While we do, indeed, find that right parties, which we expected to favour market solutions in economic policy, spent less on subsidies in the 1980s, this difference had disappeared by the 2000s. Thus subsidisation may be added to the economic policy instruments which do no longer distinguish parties of the left and the right.

The temporal parameter instability of the impact of political parties on changes in subsidy levels identified in this chapter seems to be mainly a

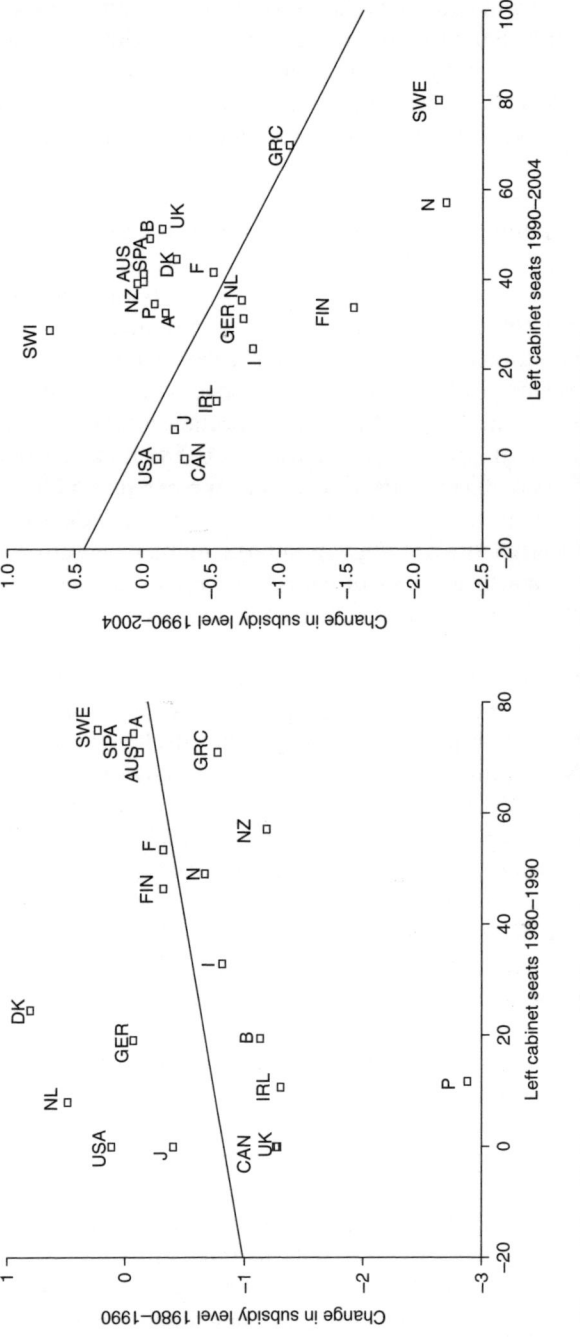

Figure 8.6   Cabinet seats of left parties and changes in subsidy levels, 1980–90/1990–2004

result of timing and catch-up. Cutbacks in subsidies were first (that is, in the 1980s) implemented by bourgeois cabinets. In the 1990s, when many governments were forced to rein in their budget deficits, left cabinets also started to scale down subsidy payments to industry. Given the historically inherited high levels of subsidies paid to industry in these latter countries, this rollback was massive in scale and explains the reversed partisan impacts over time.

Similar temporal parameter instability was also observed for the impact of political institutions. While institutional pluralism exerted a negative effect on levels of subsidisation in 1980, by 2004 the effect had turned around. The latter finding is supported by the analysis of changes in subsidy levels between 1990 and 2004 that appears in figure 8.7, which also reveals a positive institutional pluralism effect. The explanation for this effect is that both findings confirm the expectation that high institutional pluralism tends to preserve the status quo. Essentially, what changed between 1980 and 2004 was the direction of the pressure on the status quo. In 1980, many governments were still increasing spending on subsidies and those governments dealing with a large number of veto players were more severely constrained in pursuing this policy than governments in Westminster-style democracies. Thus the latter continued to maintain higher subsidy levels than the former. A decade later, the picture had changed, with most governments now seeking to reduce their spending on subsidies. Again, the governments facing many veto players were more limited in their freedom to move than those with lesser institutional constraints. This time, however, the countries with many veto players ended up with higher subsidy expenditures because they had a harder time cutting subsidies. This last point is illustrated by Figure 8.7.[10]

However, it is not altogether clear which factors have been most instrumental in triggering the downward and convergent trend in public expenditure devoted to economic affairs. At first glance, the usual suspects, particularly globalisation and the EU, appear to be unlikely candidates, given that these indicators do not feature significantly in our regression modelling. In the case of the EU, where variation between member and non-member states should have been readily observable, this result is probably decisive and indicative of the failure of the EU to exercise significant additional pressure on its members for a reduction of subsidies. Such a result is not one that scholars of European competition policy will find particularly surprising. Indeed, it is very much in line with Francis McGowan's (2000, 131ff.) conclusions on the European Commission's state aid policy that 'in practice its bark is worse than its bite. Although there are exceptions . . . in most major cases . . . the Commission has agreed weak compromises with the relevant member governments, approving the aid subject

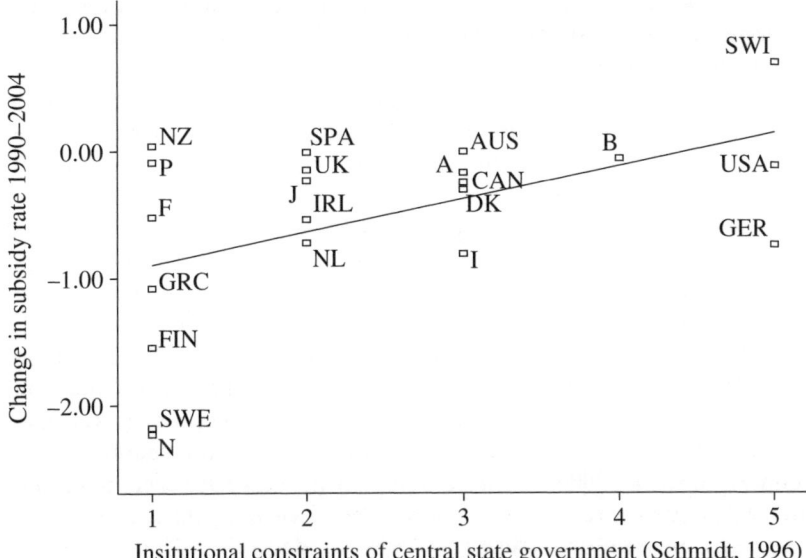

Figure 8.7   *The relationship between change in subsidy levels, 1990–2004 and institutional constraints on central state government*

to relatively modest conditions'. In addition, EU directives on state aid exclude general measures which are not selective; that is, measures which may benefit many firms in a country (Lee, 2002: 5; Thöne, 2003: 29), and also allow for exceptions.

The globalisation finding is less decisive. If increasing economic integration had been experienced in all these countries in much the same way, then globalisation might have constituted a triggering event without showing up as a significant predictor of differences in levels of expenditure. For the regressions explaining *changes* in subsidy levels, we also tested for the impact of a variable measuring changes in capital market integration. However, this also failed to achieve statistical significance.

Theoretically, it could still be argued that globalisation does not catalyse neo-liberal reforms per se, but only exerts effects on countries that are confronted with considerable economic problem loads resulting from a lack of adaptation. If this hypothesis were correct, we might expect that more far-reaching changes would occur when economic problems were greater (cf. Zohlnhöfer, 2005). With one exception, however, this is not what we find in the data either. Most indicators of economic problem loads remain statistically insignificant most of the time and none is statistically significant in the latter part of the period of observation (level 2004, change 1990–2004) which should be characterised as one of growing internationalisation of the economy. Moreover, the fact that high net debt interest payments are negatively related to the level of subsidies in 1990 and to change in subsidy payments in the 1980s, is convincingly explained by the interaction of high debt and extraordinarily high interest rates during the 1980s, which boosted interest payments and thus put pressure on other areas of public expenditure (see Chapter 2 above).

Therefore our findings do not support the interpretation that growing economic integration has caused a process of expenditure convergence. There is, however, one close contender to globalisation as a potential explanation of convergence, namely a diffusion of neo-liberal policy ideas since the 1980s that has made economic policy instruments increasingly more similar right across the OECD world. This spread of neo-liberal ideas and the resulting shift towards supply-side economic policies may well have been triggered by an increasingly globalised mode of transnational communication (Knill, 2005: 769–72). Governments may have been induced to emulate policies perceived to be successful elsewhere and they may also have found themselves under pressure to accede to the advice of and the policy models promoted by international organisations such as the IMF, the WTO, the OECD or the EU (cf. Simmons and Elkins, 2004; Armingeon and Beyeler, 2004; Henisz et al., 2005). However, this possibility of increasingly globalised policy diffusion is one which could only be taken beyond the speculative realm by means of further empirical research.

NOTES

1. Note that β-convergence does not necessarily lead to σ-convergence (see Barro and Sala-i-Martin, 1995: 31–2).
2. This mainly refers to the early 1960s and to Germany prior to reunification.
3. Note that total state aid in Europe amounted to €56.4 billion, or 0.63 per cent of GDP in 2004.
4. Data provided by Francis G. Castles.
5. However, the opposite effect is also conceivable. Economic turbulence may lead to increases in subsidy levels because of efforts to prop up declining industries.
6. Missing data provided by Uwe Wagschal.
7. Data provided by Manfred G. Schmidt.
8. Note that one could also argue that globalisation leads to higher spending on subsidies because governments may seek to attract foreign direct investment via state aid.
9. The effects reported for subsidy levels in 1990 and 2004 do not substantially change in most cases when the subsidy level of the previous period is dropped from the equations. The only noteworthy change is that the variable for corporatism in the 1990s turns out to be positively and significantly related to the level of subsidisation in 2004. Nevertheless, since our results strongly suggest that the trend of expenditure on subsidies changed around 1990, we hold that the inclusion of the subsidy level of the previous period is necessary.
10. The positive effect of institutions on subsidies is in part driven by the Swiss case, which is exceptional in that Switzerland as a veto player-prone polity was the only country

significantly to increase subsidy levels between 1990 and 2004. If Switzerland is dropped from the analysis, the effect loses statistical significance but still comes close to it, and the sign remains unchanged.

REFERENCES

Armingeon, K. and M. Beyeler (eds) (2004), *The OECD and European Welfare States*, Cheltenham, UK and Northampton, MA, USA: Edward Elgar.

Armingeon, K., P. Leimgruber, M. Beyeler and S. Menegale (2005), 'Comparative political data set 1960–2003', Institute of Political Science, University of Berne.

Barro, R.J. and X. Sala-i-Martin (1995), *Economic Growth*, New York: McGraw-Hill.

von Beyme, K. (2000), *Parteien im Wandel. Von den Volksparteien zu den professionalisierten Wählerparteien*, Wiesbaden: Westdeutscher Verlag.

Boix, C. (1998), *Political Parties, Growth and Equality*, Cambridge: Cambridge University Press.

Castles, F.G. (1998), *Comparative Public Policy*, Cheltenham, UK and Lyme, USA: Edward Elgar.

Castles, F.G. (2006), 'The Growth of the Post-war Expenditure State: Long-term Trajectories and Recent Trends', TranState Working Paper, no. 35, University of Bremen.

Cusack, T.R. and S. Fuchs (2003), 'Parteien, Institutionen und Staatsausgaben', in H. Obinger, U. Wagschal and B. Kittel (eds), *Politische Ökonomie*, Opladen: Leske+Budrich.

EC (European Commission) (2001), *Ninth Survey on State Aid in the European Union*, COMM (2001) 403, Brussels 18.7.2001.

EC (European Commission) (2005), *Report State Aid Scoreboard*, COMM (2005) 624, Brussels 9.12.2005.

Freitag, M. (2001), 'Politische Grundlagen glaubwürdiger Wirtschaftspolitik: Österreich und die Schweiz im internationalen Vergleich', *Österreichische Zeitschrift für Politikwissenschaft*, **30**(3), 275–90.

Hall, P.A. (1993), 'Policy paradigms, social learning, and the state. The case of economic policymaking in Britain', *Comparative Politics*, **25**(3), 275–96.

Henisz, W.J., B.A. Zelner and M.F. Guillén (2005), 'The worldwide diffusion of market-oriented infrastructure reform, 1977–1999', *American Sociological Review*, **70**(6), 871–97.

Iversen, T. and T.R. Cusack (2000), 'The causes of welfare state expansion. Deindustrialization or globalisation', *World Politics*, **52**(3), 313–49.

Knill, C. (2005), 'Introduction: cross-national public policy convergence: concepts, approaches and explanatory factors', *Journal of European Public Policy*, **12**(5), 764–74.

Lee, F. (2002), *OECD Work on Defining and Measuring Subsidies in Industry*, Paris: OECD.

Leibfried, S. (2005), 'Social policy. Left to the judges and the markets?', in H. Wallace, W. Wallace and M.A. Pollack (eds), *Policy-Making in the European Union*, Oxford: Oxford University Press.

McGowan, F. (2000), 'Competition policy. The limits of the European regulatory state', in W.H. Wallace (ed.), *Policy-Making in the European Union*, Oxford: Oxford University Press.

Mosley, L. (2000), 'Room to move: international financial markets and national welfare states', *International Organization*, **54**(4), 737–73.

OECD (2005), *Economic Outlook Dataset*, Paris: OECD.

Olson, M. (1982), *The Rise and Decline of Nations. Economic Growth, Stagflation, and Social Rigidities*, New Haven: Yale University Press.

Quinn, D. (1997), 'The correlates of change in international financial regulation', *American Political Science Review*, **91**(3), 531–51.

Rose, R. and T. Karran (1987), *Taxation by Political Inertia. Financing the Growth of Government in Britain*, London and Boston: Allen & Unwin.

Schmidt, M.G. (2000), *Demokratietheorien. Eine Einführung*, Opladen: Leske + Budrich.

Schmidt, M.G. (2002) 'The impact of political parties, constitutional structures and veto players on public policy', in H. Keman (ed.), *Comparative Democratic Politics*, London: Sage.

Siaroff, A. (1999), 'Corporatism in 24 industrial democracies: meaning and measurement', *European Journal of Political Research*, **36**(6), 175–205.

Siebert, H. (1998), 'Disziplinierung der nationalen Wirtschaftspolitik durch die internationale Kapitalmobilität', in D. Duwendag (ed.), *Finanzmärkte im Spannungsfeld von Globalisierung, Regulierung und Geldpolitik*, Berlin: Duncker & Humblot.

Simmons, B.A. and Z. Elkins (2004), 'The globalisation of liberalisation: policy diffusion in the international political economy', *American Political Science Review*, **98**(1), 171–89.

Tanzi, V. and L. Schuknecht (2000), *Public Spending in the 20th Century. A Global Perspective*, Cambridge: Cambridge University Press.

Thöne, M. (2003), *Subventionskontrolle. Ziele–Methoden–internationale Erfahrungen*, Berlin: edition sigma.

Tsebelis, G. (2002), *Veto Players: How Political Institutions Work*, Princeton and Oxford: Princeton University Press.

Wilks, S. (2005), 'Competition policy. Challenge and reform', in H. Wallace, W. Wallace and M.A. Pollack (eds), *Policy-Making in the European Union*, Oxford: Oxford University Press.

Zohlnhöfer, R. (2003), 'Der Einfluss von Parteien und Institutionen auf die Staatstätigkeit', in H. Obinger, U. Wagschal and B. Kittel (eds), *Politische Ökonomie. Demokratie und wirtschaftliche Leistungsfähigkeit*, Opladen: Leske + Budrich.

Zohlnhöfer, R. (2005), 'Globalisierung der Wirtschaft und nationalstaatliche Anpassungsreaktionen. Theoretische Überlegungen', *Zeitschrift für Internationale Beziehungen*, **12**(1), 41–75.

9. A mortgage on the future? Public debt expenditure and its determinants, 1980–2001

Uwe Wagschal

9.1 INTRODUCTION

An important aim of this book is to extend the reach of political economy research by focusing on public expenditure programmes largely untreated in the comparative literature. The huge body of work on social expenditures has – to a very considerable extent – crowded out research on other policy areas. This crowding out has been a function of the growing predominance of social programmes, which, in total, now amount to around 50 per cent of all government expenditures in the OECD world (see Chapter 2). Valuable insights for the analysis of the other half of public spending – what Castles earlier has called core spending – can be obtained from the COFOG classification (Classification of the Functions of Government), which is the most useful functional categorisation available to researchers (see Chapter 3). The present chapter draws attention to one of the largest core spending categories of all: interest payments on the public debt. Although, as we shall see, in some countries during some recent periods, interest payments have constituted the largest core spending programme of all, in the COFOG classification, interest payments are only a sub-category of General Public Services, which, as noted in Chapter 4, is essentially COFOG's residual expenditure category.

Since the mid-1970s, the subject of debt expenditure has gained in importance, with many Western industrialised countries (for the first time in history, under conditions of peace and democracy) facing increased public debt and deficits. The consequences for governments of a substantial debt interest burden can be extremely serious, adversely affecting their chances of retaining power in democratic elections. That is because high levels of public debt undermine political stability and reduce the capacity of governments to supply public goods. These consequences occur because interest payments arising from the accumulated public debt absorb an increasingly larger proportion of the total government outlays and tax revenues. The marked reduction of core public spending corrected for net interest payments that occurred in the 1980s and early 1990s (see Chapter 2 above) was a phenomenon of precisely this kind. In this period, increasing public debt expenditure served to disguise real cuts in core expenditure that were occurring across the OECD.

This situation was particularly acute in certain countries where extraordinarily large proportions of total outlays were devoted to debt service payments. In 1994, 27.9 per cent of Greek public expenditure was on debt interest. In Italy, in 1993, the figure was 22.6 per cent and, in Belgium, in 1990, 22.4 per cent. Looking at debt interest spending as a share of overall government revenues, the picture for the early 1990s was even grimmer, with seven OECD countries temporarily spending 20 per cent or more of revenues on debt interest payments (with an all-time high of 34.2 per cent in Greece in 1994).

Economists have long explored this issue, arguing that economic factors provide a sufficient account of the factors shaping the size of a government's debt expenditure. At first sight, it does, indeed, seem that the extent of the debt expenditure cannot easily be influenced by governments, since it is largely determined by the inheritance of debt accumulated over the long term and by prevailing interest rates. Section 9.2, however, does identify some additional determinants of debt interest expenditure and draws attention to differences in the normative frames through which debt is construed by both economists and governments. Section 9.3 gives a descriptive overview of cross-national data on the extent of debt interest payments in the years after 1980. Hypotheses identifying the factors shaping the debt interest burden are formulated in Section 9.4, while Section 9.5 presents the main empirical findings.

9.2   PUBLIC DEBT INTEREST PAYMENTS: A THEORETICAL OVERVIEW

In principle, the budget equation of the government is quite simple: expenditures have to equal all inflows, that is, tax revenues, social contributions, fees, seignorage, income from economic activities, revenues from privatisation, international budget contributions and the public deficit. This last residual category balances the budget equation. The accumulated public deficit (minus repayments) equals the public debt. The interest on the outstanding public debt has to be paid as a price for the sum borrowed. The cost of public debt service is substantially determined by three variables.

These variables are, in turn, determined by other socio-economic, international, political and institutional factors.

1. *The size of the public debt and deficit*: all things equal, as public debt increases, the greater the money outstanding and borrowed by the government.
2. *Interest rates*: higher interest rates lead to higher payments for interest on the public debt.
3. *Debt management*: full use of capital markets, various financial instruments and a high quality of managers and organisation may make it possible to reduce interest payments.

Empirical research on the determinants of the public debt and deficits is well established (Persson and Svensson, 1989; Roubini and Sachs, 1989; Alesina and Perotti, 1994; Wagschal, 1996; DeHaan and Sturm, 1997; Franzese, 2002). The most relevant hypotheses and findings are presented in sections 9.4 and 9.5.

What determines the interest rate? Economists offer various explanations, the Fisher parity being most prominent. Fisher argued that the nominal and the real interest rate are connected via the (expected) inflation rate. A 1 per cent increase in the inflation rate leads to a 1 per cent increase in the nominal interest rate. At the end of the nineteenth century, Knut Wicksell argued that there is a 'natural (interest) rate' and a market rate ('money rate of interest'). The latter is influenced by demand and supply in the capital market, whereas the natural rate is the real interest rate in the real market, equalizing the capital supply and investment demand. An economy is in equilibrium when market and natural rates are equal. The assumption is that, where there is a (long-run) constant natural rate and a lower market rate, this will stimulate investment until interest rate convergence takes place. Böhm-Bawerk, an Austrian economist, introduced 'time' as a factor relevant to the understanding of interest rates. He argued that interest is not the price for money borrowed, but for the period of time a creditor is willing to lend the money. Finally, John Maynard Keynes stressed the importance of liquidity preference. In his view, the interest rate is a price for the wish to hold money in cash rather than a price for investment demand.

Other economic factors like the rate of economic growth, the current account and exchange rates are also regarded as significant determinants of the interest rate. In particular, it is often postulated that the long-run growth rate should equal the long-term interest rate because it is a proxy for the return of the overall amount of capital within the economy.

In addition to these economic factors, political variables have increasingly come to be seen as important, with political stability (as a proxy for credibility and the capacity to effect debt repayment), central bank independence, constitutional expenditure limitations and governmental stability variously seen as vital in shaping interest rate expectations. Moreover, Alesina et al. (Alesina, Grilli and Milisi-Ferreti, 1993) argue that capital controls are more likely to be imposed by strong governments and this will keep interest rates at a significantly low level.[1] On the other hand, some political factors, such as elections or changes in the composition of governments, have proved of dubious value in explaining the development of interest rates (Johnson and Siklos, 1996). The impact of the budget deficit itself turns out to be significant for the interest rate in the OECD world (Gupta and Moazzami, 1996).

Debt management has to be differentiated in two respects. First, there is the question of the terms or conditions pertaining to debt instruments, that is, the maturity date, whether the debt is internal or external, the kind of issued bond (for example, zero bonds will have no direct interest payment), selling techniques or the share of marketable debt are all potentially parameters relevant to improved performance. In general, there is a trade-off between the time-horizon and interest payments. The longer the amortisation period, the smaller (all things being equal) are annual interest payments. However, over the long run, overall interest payments are higher than when the government decides to pay them off more quickly.[2] Second, most OECD countries have implemented institutional reforms of the state agencies responsible for the administration of the debt (OECD, 2005a).[3] The impacts of these reforms are difficult to assess, though it is plausible to suppose that there are positive effects. Nevertheless, debt management is not a factor as influential in shaping the extent of debt repayment as either the size of the public debt or prevailing interest rates.

Normative judgments of public debt, deficits and interest payments differ hugely. Keynesian doctrine is closely associated with the idea of running deficits at times of economic crisis, and the demand-side argument was one key concept in the 'Golden Era' of the welfare state. The most extreme variant of this view was put forward by Abba Lerner in the 1940s, when he argued, in his theory of functional finance (Lerner, 1979), that governments should, above all, be responsible for avoiding unemployment and inflation, with public spending, deficits and the interest rate all used as instruments to achieve these goals. From this perspective, balanced budgets have no special significance (Lerner, 1979: 88) and debt interest payments are not seen as having any negative effect. In a closed economy, interest payments by the government remain in the country and only have distributional effects within the country. When looking at the aggregate of the national product, the effect of increased interest payments is of a shift between sectors. Debt is not a problem because, as Lerner famously put it: 'We owe it to ourselves'.

However, negative judgments of public debt predominate in the political economy literature. According to David Ricardo, public debt was 'one of the most terrible scourges ever invented to afflict a nation' (Ricardo, 1951: 197, first published 1820). Most of the numerous public choice studies are also highly sceptical about public debt, since this school of thought usually imputes bad intentions to governments. Advocates of this school believe governments manipulate policy outcomes either to seek re-election or to try to influence the policy of their successor governments (Persson and Svensson, 1989; Alesina and Tabellini, 1990). During the economic crises of the 1970s and 1980s, the Keynesian logic was the subject of heated debate (Buchanan and Wagner, 1977). Buchanan, in particular, sought to propose new institutions and redesign old ones, such as tax and expenditure limitations, which would make governments less prone to spend too much or to accumulate deficits (Wagschal, 2002).

9.3   INTEREST PAYMENTS AND PUBLIC DEBT IN INTERNATIONAL COMPARISON

The choice of the dependent variable is crucial. Interest payments can be presented as a share of GDP, as the percentage of expenditures or revenues or even per capita. It also makes a difference whether the data are displayed for the general or central government. The most important distinction is between gross or net debt interest payments. The first includes all interest payments, whereas the latter subtracts government income from dividends, property income or other asset revenues from gross interest payments. Gross interest payment data are more suitable for analysis, but data on net interest payments are more readily available. There is no determinate relationship between revenues from dividends or interest and the service of the public debt, since a government has to pay the gross interest. However, Figure 9.1 shows a strong correlation ($r=0.84$; $n=23$) between gross and net debt interest payments for 23 OECD countries.

Given the reasonably close correspondence between these measures and the greater availability of net debt data for the period under investigation, much of our subsequent analysis, including the time-series presented in Figure 9.2, is for net debt interest payments as a percentage of GDP. A further problem is data quality: for some countries, figures for net debt interest payments as a percentage of GDP differ substantially in different adumbrations of the relevant OECD data set.[4] According to Figure 9.1, Norway and Luxembourg spend least on public debt, while Belgium and Italy head the list of big spenders amongst these 23 OECD countries. According to Figure 9.2, the OECD average peaked during the mid-1990s

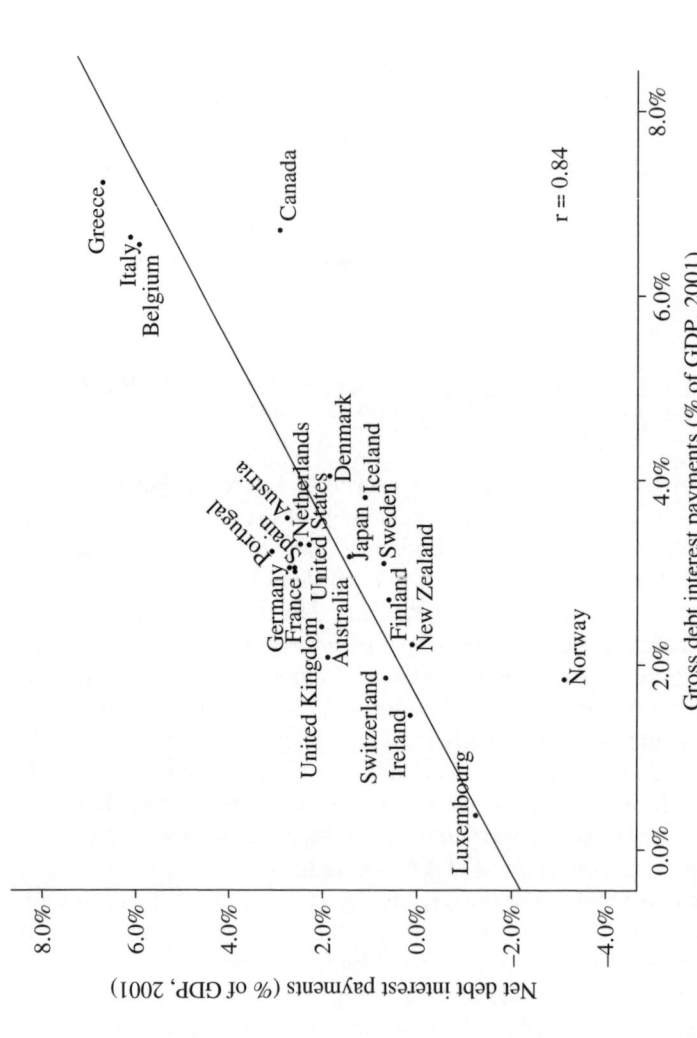

Source: Gross debt interest payments: OECD Main Economic Indicators (2005c) and net debt interest payments: OECD Economic Outlook Database (OECD 2005b); n = 23.

Figure 9.1   Gross and net debt interest payments in 23 OECD countries as a percentage of GDP, 2001

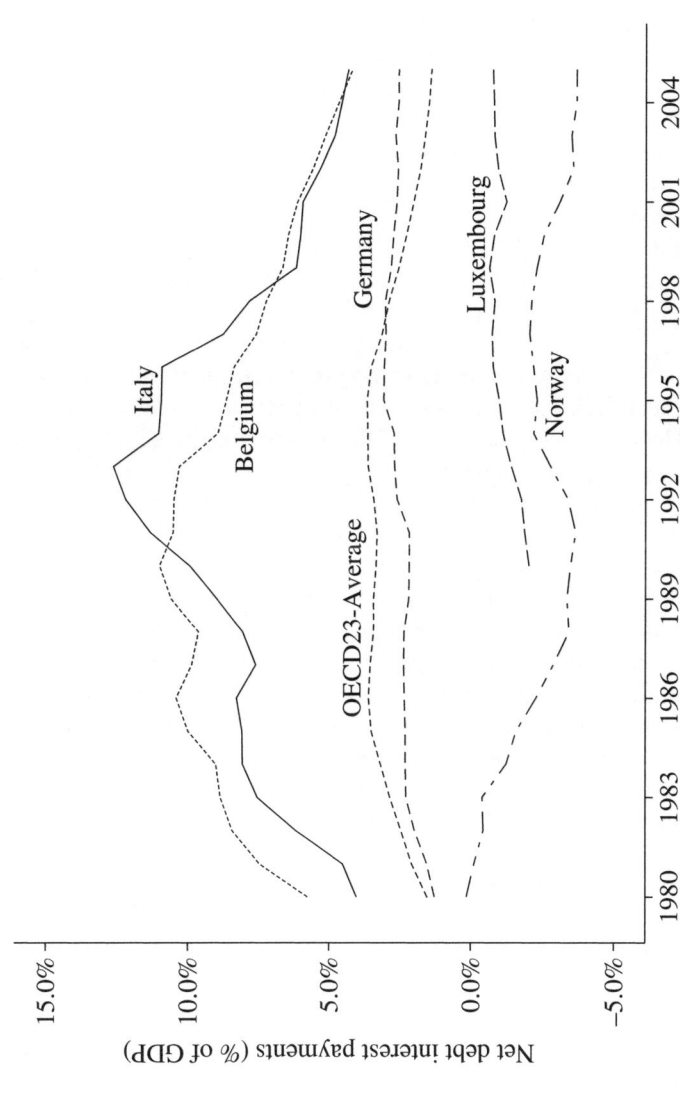

Source: OECD Economic Outlook Database (OECD, 2005b). The average relates to all 23 countries for which data are available. Note that data for New Zealand are only included from 1986 onwards and for Switzerland and Luxembourg from 1990 onwards.

Figure 9.2 Net debt interest payments (percentage of GDP) in the OECD, (1980–2005)

and has been decreasing ever since. This development is similar to the overall variation of the public debt in the OECD world. The public debt peak of the countries analysed was reached in 1995, with an average of 73 per cent of GDP. It slowly decreased to an overall average of 63 per cent in 2005 for the 23 countries shown in Figure 9.1.

The correlation between public debt and net debt interest payments is straightforward. Figure 9.3 shows a clear and strong correlation ($r=0.60$; note for 2001 $r=0.71$; $n=23$) between these variables. This rather technical relationship turns out to be one of the main causal explanations for the dependent variable.[5] However, the correlation between public debt and gross interest payments is even stronger ($r=0.77$, $n=23$). The outlier cases in Figure 9.3 shed some light on the problematic use of the dependent variable. Japan is the most indebted OECD country and would normally be expected to pay much more for its debt service. Norway, the second outlier, is a special case because of its huge revenues from natural resources. New Zealand is also a mysterious case: according to government finance statistics for New Zealand dating from 2005, interest payments exceed the property income. However, according to the OECD, the country actually has a negative debt burden, that is, a surplus.

Although there has been a long debate on the influence of deficits on interest rates, the long-term correlations for the period 1960 to 2000 are also straightforward enough. Analysing correlations over time, it becomes apparent that large deficits produce significantly higher short- and long-term interest rates (typical correlations are about $r=-0.4$, but, for some countries, like Belgium, the figure is closer to -0.9). However, cross-sectional correlations reveal that there is no substantial association between the level of the public debt and the size of the deficit. The determination of the interest rate depends on several factors. In addition to economic variables, institutional and political factors also seem to have an influence – political stability, central bank independence or political credibility; for example, membership of the EMU is a sign for market actors that governments are willing to stick to rules.

Figure 9.4 shows the development of long-term interest rates for the OECD average and several selected countries. Countries highly indebted in the 1980s, such as New Zealand, Greece, Ireland and Italy, have reduced their interest rates to a much greater extent than other countries. On average, interest rates declined from a peak in 1982 (15.2 per cent) to a minimum in 2005 (3.8 per cent). The current level of interest rates is roughly one-quarter of that in the early 1980s, resulting in much lower debt service payments. On the one hand, members of the EMU and the Eurozone, such as Greece (deviating from the general trend until the early 1990s), Italy and Belgium, have gained tremendously in credibility and stability. On the other, countries

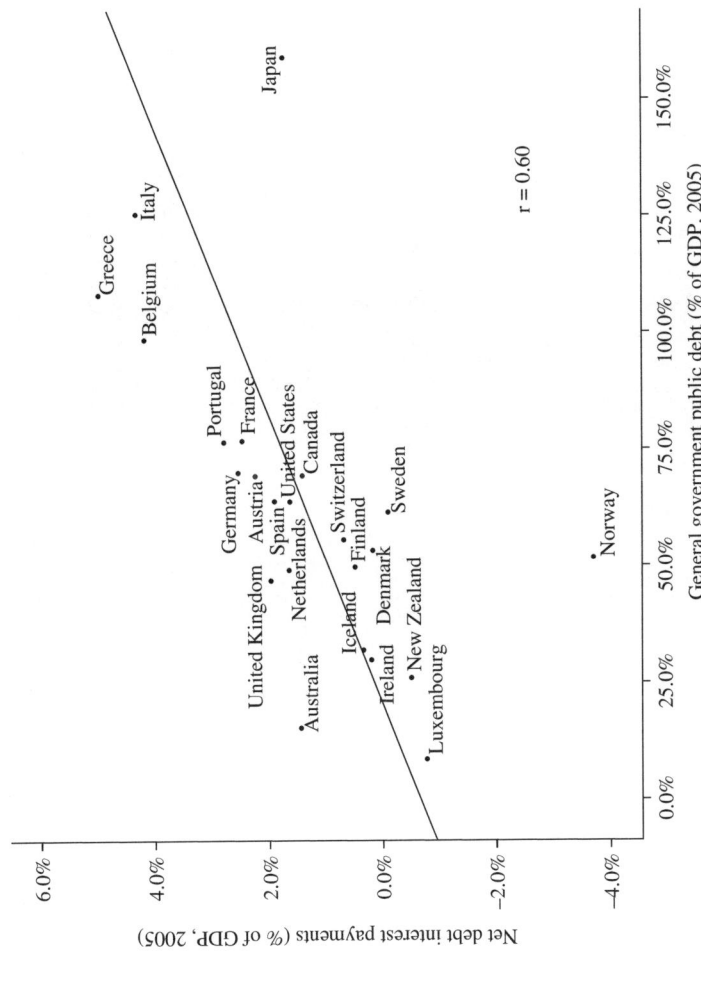

Source: OECD Economic Outlook Database (OECD, 2005b) and national data sources for Switzerland.

Figure 9.3   Public debt and net debt interest payments in 23 OECD countries, 2005

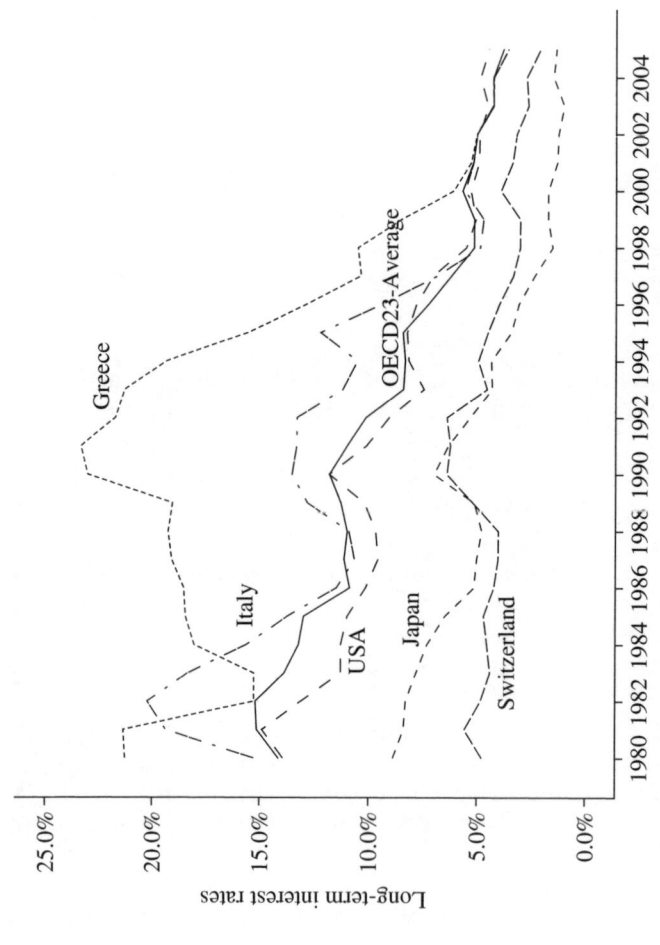

Source: OECD Economic Outlook Database (OECD, 2005b). Data for Greece are short-term interest rates. Data for Iceland are taken from the IMF. Part of the data for Luxembourg are from the EU. Data for Iceland, which has experienced the highest interest rates, are not separately displayed in this graph.

Figure 9.4 Long-term interest rates, 1980–2005 (ten-year benchmark government bond yields)

such as Switzerland, Austria and Germany, which formerly experienced a comparative advantage because of the lower interest rates over the long run, have lost out in comparison. This long-lasting decline in interest rates, also an effect of more flexible capital markets, has allowed policy makers greater freedom of manoeuvre for alternative spending decisions.

A descriptive overview of net debt interest payments and public debt is presented in Table 9.1. It also shows the 'family means' for the various families of nations or 'worlds of welfare' as described by Esping-Andersen (1990). In 1980, the overall average level of spending was about 1.5 per cent of GDP. It increased very rapidly and reached its maximum in 1995 (3.6 per cent of GDP), at the time when the average level of public debt also peaked. Thereafter, net debt interest payments declined very rapidly (2001: 2.0 per cent of GDP, 2005: 1.4 per cent of GDP), mainly owing to decreasing interest rates and debt reduction. However, cross-national variation in the debt levels of the different families of nations remains high and increased slightly between 1980 and 2001. In the early 1980s, the Scandinavian countries experienced the lowest public debt ratios, whereas in 2001 the Anglo-Saxon world performed best. Japan, the Latin cluster and the Continental welfare states increased levels of public debt very significantly. Convergence of debt interest payments only becomes evident after 1990. However, the variation is still very high.

Bringing both main explanatory factors together, we have a reasonable model to explain net and gross debt interest payments in the OECD world (see Table 9.2). Both variables, the public debt and the interest rates, have the correct sign and are highly significant. The explanatory power of the model is very high. The coefficient of determination also increases substantially when excluding the outliers, Norway, Japan and Canada, and the importance of interest rates decreases at the same time. Focusing on the dependent variable at different points in time, it becomes apparent that the interest rate has become less important over time. This can be explained by the overall convergence of this variable. It should be noted, however, that there is still a considerable degree of unexplained variation in this model. As noted earlier, the nature of a country's debt management strategy might account for some part of this unexplained variation. There are also country-specific factors which are not accounted for in the model. In the Norwegian case, oil revenues obviously make a big difference. For Switzerland, its role as the largest fund manager of assets worldwide, in conjunction with long-term political stability and the central bank's entrenched low interest rate policy, has led to long-term interest rates almost as low as in Japan, where the central bank has pursued a zero rate policy over many years. Additional possible relevant political and other economic factors are not included in the model.

Table 9.1   *Levels and changes in net debt interest payments and public debt in 23 OECD countries, 1980–2001*

Country	Net debt interest in % of GDP (1980)	Net debt interest in % of GDP (2001)	Change of net debt interest (1990–2001)	Public debt in % of GDP (2001)	Change of public debt (1980–2001)
Australia	2.4	1.9	−1.6	21.5	−3.6
Canada	−0.2	2.9	−2.2	82.9	39.6
Ireland	3.8	0.1	−6.0	35.3	−37.4
New Zealand	—	0.1	−4.1	35.7	−9.3
United Kingdom	3.4	2.0	−0.7	41.1	−12.9
United States	1.8	2.3	−1.1	58.0	21.1
Family mean	*2.3*	*1.6*	*−2.6*	*45.8*	*−0.4*
Austria	1.3	2.8	0.1	70.2	33.6
Belgium	5.8	6.1	−4.9	111.6	34.1
France	0.7	2.6	0.4	63.8	32.9
Germany	1.3	2.6	0.4	59.3	28.2
Luxembourg	—	−1.2	0.8	6.7	1.0
Netherlands	2.2	2.5	−1.6	59.5	12.5
Family mean	*2.3*	*2.6*	*−0.8*	*61.8*	*23.7*
Denmark	0.9	1.9	−1.8	53.3	9.6
Finland	−1.0	0.6	2.4	50.9	39.1
Iceland	−0.5	1.1	−0.2	47.3	24.6
Norway	0.2	−3.1	0.4	33.2	−14.3
Sweden	−0.9	0.7	1.4	63.4	20.6
Family mean	*−0.3*	*0.2*	*0.4*	*49.6*	*15.9*
Greece	1.9	6.7	−3.1	114.4	91.5
Italy	4.0	5.9	−4.0	124.5	66.4
Portugal	2.5	3.1	−5.2	62.5	29.7
Spain	0.1	2.7	−0.3	61.6	43.3
Family mean	*2.1*	*4.6*	*−3.1*	*90.8*	*57.7*
Japan	1.2	1.4	0.2	142.3	92.7
Switzerland	—	0.7	0.3	54.0	9.7
Family mean	*1.2*	*1.0*	*0.2*	*98.1*	*51.2*
Summary statistics					
Overall mean	1.5	2.0	−1.3	63.2	24.0
CV / Catch-up	115.6	110.4	−0.77	52.2	−0.19

Sources and notes: Data were taken from OECD Economic Outlook Database (OECD, 2005b), national sources for Switzerland and its public debt. CV designates the coefficient of variation, which is reported for measures of levels. Catch-up is the correlation between the level of spending at the beginning of each period and change in spending during that period (columns 4 and 6).

Table 9.2　Base model for the explanation of general government net and gross debt interest payments (percentage of GDP) in 2001 (OECD)

	(1) Net debt interest payments	(2) Gross debt interest payments	(3) Net debt interest payments	(4) Gross debt interest payments
Constant	−4.79	−2.91	−2.35	−1.70
	(−2.96)**	(−2.91)**	(−2.08)	(−2.64)*
General govern-ment public debt ratio (2001)	0.05	0.04	0.06	0.05
	(5.36)***	(7.54)***	(8.41)***	(12.11)***
Long-term interest rate (average 1991–2001)	0.52	0.51	0.12	0.27
	(2.56)*	(4.07)**	(0.76)	(2.99)**
N	23	23	20	20
F-statistic	16.58***	34.28***	41.17***	97.07***
Adj. R^2	0.59	0.75	0.81	0.91

Note:　This table shows the coefficients of the OLS-regressions. *t*-values in brackets. * = 0.05 significance level, ** = 0.01 significance level, *** = 0.001 significance level. All models were checked for multicollinearity, i.e. only variables with a VIF value of less then 2 are included. In equations 3 and 4, Norway, Japan and Canada are excluded.

The overall picture shows that net interest payments have become more important over the years: as public debt rose, debt service payments also increased substantially. Nevertheless, the situation has improved slightly during the past decade after the peak in the mid-1990s. Three reasons can be identified: (1) interest rates dropped substantially and, at present, variation is very small. This is due to several factors, the European integration process, huge capital supply and low growth rates being the most important; (2) restrictions imposed on public debt and deficits, mainly the Maastricht criteria, also had a significant positive effect. This holds true even though several Euro countries have failed to meet the Maastricht criteria in past years; (3) governments have made policy shifts in the consolidation process of the budget. The focus is now on sustainable public finances, with policy shaped by increasingly severe budgetary constraints, by the pressures exerted by international capital markets, which give lower rating scores for poor performance increasing capital costs, and by new institutional arrangements such as the European Stability and Growth Pact (SGP), adopted in 1997 and designed to improve budgetary discipline within the EMU.

9.4   HYPOTHESES ACCOUNTING FOR PUBLIC DEBT AND INTEREST RATES

As pointed out in sections 2 and 3, interest payments will be directly affected by the size of the public debt, interest rates and the quality of debt management. However, these variables themselves can be explained by other factors. Hypotheses identifying factors accounting for the size of the public debt may be derived from various theories and different schools of thought (Schmidt, 2000): (1) the theory of socio-economic determinants, (2) partisan theory, (3) power resources theory, (4) political–institutional theory, (5) theories focusing on the effect of international factors (globalisation hypotheses), and (6) path dependency theory.

Empirical studies focusing on the political determinants of interest payments are rare. Studies focusing on economic factors dominate the literature. Caselli, Giovannini and Lane (1999), for example, use a model with five independent variables: the interest rate on government bonds; the size of the primary surplus; the debt to GDP ratio; the inflation rate and the rate of growth of real GDP. Recent work by Sanz and Velásquez (2002) also focus on GDP per capita and demographic factors.

Within the 'theory of socio-economic determination', economic factors like economic growth, unemployment, inflation or the misery index are the dominant variables in explaining public debt and deficits. Demographic variables (Boix, 1998), such as the size of the aged population or urban density, are also seen as factors stimulating the growth of public finances. The state in this context is regarded as an object, the actions of which are determined by outside forces, and the socio-economic approach assumes little direct influence by governments. Public policy is largely seen as a reaction to developments in society and the economy, and actors, parties, institutions and power distributions are regarded as being of minor importance.

According to the partisan theory, the constituencies of the parties have different public policy preferences (Hibbs, 1977; Schmidt, 1996) and parties adopt the preferences of their social constituencies. In an older public choice tradition, starting with Downs, the assumption is that parties elaborate policy positions with the aim of maximising offices and votes. Partisan theory further postulates that, once elected, incumbent parties implement policies in accordance with the preferences of their constituency. This also implies that governments have the capacity to act upon and to implement these policies.

A number of public choice studies suggest that governments use the public debt to influence the policy of their successors (Persson and Svensson, 1989; Alesina and Tabellini, 1990). Both theories focus on the behaviour of governments when they are in danger of not being re-elected.

Persson and Svensson analyse the behaviour of conservative governments in office. They argue that a conservative and 'stubborn' government will generate a high debt and high deficits to influence the politics of its probable 'left' successor. A high level of debt is likely to mean that the successor government will not be able to initiate all its ideologically preferred programmes. So the 'low spender' influences the 'big spender'. Alesina and Tabellini (1990) also focus on the strategic role of public debt. They consider two parties with different objectives in public policy: for example, one prefers more 'defence expenditures' and the other favours more 'social welfare expenditures'. The authors identify three conditions under which the public debt might be higher than its social optimum (Alesina and Tabellini, 1990: 404): (a) The larger the degree of polarisation between alternating governments; (b) the higher the probability that the current government will not be reappointed; and (c) the more downwardly rigid is public consumption. The empirical tests of these theories are not convincing, with the only variable proving significant in the Alesina and Tabellini model being the downward rigidness of public spending (Wagschal, 1996: 121).

The standard view with respect to partisan politics is that left governments will produce higher debt, which is justified by their 'Keynesian' preferences and their tendency to spend more. This view has been challenged by the 'partisan tax smoothing model' (Wagschal, 1996), suggesting that conservative governments produce higher deficits than labour governments. The reasoning behind this hypothesis stems from the constituencies of the parties. The driving force for higher deficits is once again voter preferences, but in this model those of the bourgeois side of politics. Because of their ideology, right-wing governments always want to cut tax rates and deficits, largely to reduce the tax burden for their clientèle. The theory assumes that the government has the capacity – at least, to some extent – of choosing between taxes and deficits as sources of revenue. Since the core constituency of bourgeois parties benefits more from tax cuts than low-income groups, governments achieve their re-election by using this policy instrument, which increases the real income of their electorate. It is therefore quite obvious that a bourgeois government will cut tax rates even at the cost of increasing deficits. Until the mid-1990s, the empirical results supported this 'partisan tax smoothing hypothesis'. However, as a consequence of the adoption of the Maastricht criteria, globalisation and tax competition, this empirical regularity is no longer apparent. However, with respect to the determination of interest rates, it seems plausible to hypothesise that left-wing governments will have lower credibility on financial and capital markets, producing a mark-up for interest rates.

The theory of power resources of competing interest groups is closely related to partisan theory. This line of theorising has two main variants: the class-struggle approach (Korpi, 1991) and the rent-seeking approach suggested by Mancur Olson (1992). Power resources theory has contributed significantly to explaining public debt and deficits. Union density, corporatism and strike activity are clearly factors pushing public spending and taxation (Steinmo and Tolbert, 1998; Garrett, 1998). In terms of interest rates, a clear negative correlation between strike activity and levels of interest rates can be expected, since capital markets react very sensitively to threats to political stability. Institutional analysis has become very prominent in discussing public finances. Since the causality is sometimes extremely complex, the following short summary can only give a brief overview. Very prominent factors in explaining public debt and interest rates are political stability (Alesina, 1989; Alesina and Tabellini, 1988) and the credibility of policy makers. Political stability includes at least two aspects: first, a broader 'political system' focus and, second, a focus on specific aspects of the institutional setting. Typical political system variables are the age of a democracy, the distinction between consensus or competitive democracies (Lijphart, 1999), the level of political conflict and violence in a society or specific factors measuring the level of stability (Alesina, 1989; Wagschal, 1996). Governmental instability, that is, the number of changes in office, the average duration of governments or the frequency of elections, involves variables capturing aspects of the institutional setting. A theory developed by Roubini and Sachs (Roubini and Sachs, 1988, 1989) suggests that 'strong government' is an institution preventing increases in deficits. The hypothesis postulates that the more parties are involved in government the weaker that government will be. 'Multiparty governments' will run larger deficits, because instability will be greater and because more actors claiming financial resources are in power. Empirical results for tests of this hypothesis are not very convincing. Strong government has no direct impact on debt and deficits when measured using a variety of different operationalisations (Wagschal, 1996; Borelli and Royed, 1995). However, it is useful to look at these factors again when analysing debt interest payments.

The credibility argument is particularly important for explaining variations in interest rates. Specific institutions, such as an independent central bank (Alesina, 1989; Grilli et al., 1991; Cukierman et al., 1992), are directly linked to this argument. Other institutions, such as federalism or the constraints on governments pursuing expansionist policies, for example measured by the degree of what Scharpf (1987) describes as 'fiscal difficulty', may also have an impact. Constitutional regulations or limitations on governments' freedom of manoeuvre in the budgetary process (Buchanan, 1980; Wagschal, 2002) may also lead to higher credibility. International rating companies like Moody's, Standard and Poors or Fitch assess countries for their credibility and it turns out that countries with tax and expenditure limitations (TEL) have lower deficits and also better ratings, that is, credibility on the capital markets, than countries which do not.

The influence of veto players (Tsebelis, 2002) is a further factor which has been hypothesised as influencing budget and reform processes. Empirical findings concerning the size of the budget show no clear tendency, whether larger or smaller. However, in respect of budget reform, the number of veto players has been demonstrated to have a significant negative influence on the extent of change (Bawn, 1999). That being so, the number of veto players may be hypothesised as being likely to have a limiting effect on deficits and the interest rate.

The international linkages of the economy also have to be considered. From national income accounting, it is possible to derive an influence of the trade balance on the budget. This is known as the 'twin-deficit' hypothesis (Abell, 1990; Kearney and Monadjemi, 1990). This proposition claims that a trade deficit coincides with a deficit in the government budget. Along these lines, findings from public policy research stress the importance of the 'degree of openness of the economy' and involvement in international trade in shaping the size of the public budget and, hence, potentially the size of the deficit and accumulated public debt (Cameron, 1978; Katzenstein, 1985; Saunders and Klau, 1985).

Finally, the path dependency argument stipulates that present policies (and, hence, to a greater or lesser degree, their outcomes) are a function of their own past and history. This autocorrelation is obvious in many social science phenomena and can be explained by transaction costs, institutional rigidities and experiences. In public finance, the path dependency argument is also prominent, for example, in explaining taxation levels (Rose and Karran, 1987). Although the cost and knowledge arguments are evident, sticking to past solutions also poses risks in a changing environment. In the end, a system is 'locked into' its specific historical context and model. Moreover, path dependency is a clear recipe for perpetuating mistakes in policy strategy.

Table 9.3 summarises the possible causal effects of most of the hypothesised relationships discussed in the text above. These variables are used in the empirical analysis that follows to assess their impact on public debt, interest rates and net debt interest payments.

9.5 EMPIRICAL FINDINGS

The cross-sectional regression models featuring in Table 9.4 are designed to test the hypotheses outlined above in respect of the level of public debt in

Table 9.3   Hypotheses on possible determinants of public debt, deficits and interest rates

Variable (high values lead to . . .)	Hypothesised effects on public debt[1]	Hypothesised effect on real interest rates	Effect on net debt interest payments as a share of GDP and comment
GDP per capita	⇔	⇓	⇓
Inflation	⇓	⇔, ?	⇓
Unemployment	⇑	⇔, ?	⇑
Economic growth	⇓	⇑	⇓
Old age dependency ratio	⇑	⇔, ?	⇑
Current balance	⇓	⇑	?; 'Twin deficit' argument
Trade dependency/ globalisation	⇑, ⇓	⇓, ?	
Exchange rate	⇔, ?	⇑	?;
Left party strength	⇑, ⇓	⇑	? Different hypotheses
Strength of Christian Democrats	⇑, ⇓	?	? Different hypotheses
Liberal and Conservative Parties	⇑, ⇓	⇓	? Different hypotheses
Corporatism	⇑	⇔, ?	⇑ Via increasing spending
Strike activity	⇑	⇑	⇑ Less credibility/stability
Consensus democracy	⇔, ?	⇓	⇓ Increases stability
Veto player structure	⇓	⇓	⇓
Central bank independence	⇓	⇓	⇓
Political stability	⇓	⇓	⇓
Credibility rating	⇓	⇓	⇓
Strong government	⇓	⇓	⇓
Federalism	⇓	⇓	⇓
Membership of EMU mechanism	⇓	⇓	⇓

Notes: The direction of the hypothesised influence is not yet proven. Furthermore, interaction effects and non-linear effects are not considered.
[1] Note that, where the financial balance is the dependent variable, the hypothesised effect should be reversed due to the coding of the variable (see equations 4 and 5 in Table 9.4).

2001 and changes in the size of the deficit between 1990 and 2001. A first point to note is the presence in equation 1 of some degree of path dependency, with the level of debt in 2001 moderately dependent on the inherited debt level of 1980. However, the actual correlation between 2001 and 1980 debt levels is not that high ($r=0.35$), indicative of substantial change in

Table 9.4 *Determinants of public debt as a percentage of GDP in 2001 and average of financial balances as percentage of GDP, 1990 to 2001*

	(1) Public debt (2001)	(2) Public debt (2001)	(3) Public debt (2001)	(4) Financial balances (ø 1990–2001)	(5) Financial balances (ø 1990–2001)
Constant	20.59 (0.77)	−154.77 (3.61)**	8.11 (0.14)	−2.40 (0.90)	7.86 (3.71)**
Public debt ratio (1980)	0.64 (2.43)*				
Real GDP growth (ø 1980–2001)	−13.65 (2.56)*		−6.36 (0.91)		
Old age adj. dependency ratio (2000)	1.25 (2.32)*		5.45 (2.59)*		−0.12 (3.31)**
Credibility (Moody's rating, ø 1980–2001)	7.12 (1.85)	17.47 (4.48)***			
Unemployment rate (ø 1991–2001)				−0.14 (1.12)	
GDP per capita (1000 US$, cur. prices, 2001)				0.14 (2.22)*	
Change social sec. exp. (1990–2001)				−0.23 (2.30)*	
Gross interest expenditures (2001)				−0.72 (3.67)**	
Current balance (ø 1990–2001)					0.25 (2.55)*
Strike activity (ø 1980–2001)					−0.003 (1.56)

Table 9.4 (continued)

	(1) Public debt (2001)	(2) Public debt (2001)	(3) Public debt (2001)	(4) Financial balances (ø 1990–2001)	(5) Financial balances (ø 1990–2001)
Veto player (Tsebelis, ø 1980–2001)		9.55 (2.26)*			−0.62 (2.03)
Siaroff's corporatism index		8.60 (1.58)			
Population (Log. 2000)		13.99 (4.68)***			−0.47 (2.05)
% of Social Democratic cabinet seats (ø 1980–2001)			−0.64 (2.57)*		
Government duration (ø days, 1980–2001)			−0.34 (1.99)		
N	23	23	23	23	23
F-statistic	8.41**	10.39***	6.80**	14.68***	13.12***
Adj. R²	0.574	0.631	0.513	0.713	0.734

Notes: This table shows the coefficients of the OLS-regressions. t-values in brackets; * = 0.05 significance level; ** = 0.01 significance level; *** = 0.001 significance level.

some countries, with Japan an exemplar of rising debt levels and Ireland of falling ones.

The most important factors in explaining public debt and deficits are socio-economic determinants, including the old-age dependency ratio, the average real growth rate and the current balance. However, some other economic factors unreported in Table 9.4 are also influential, including inflation and, to a lesser extent, unemployment.[6] Aggregating both inflation and unemployment as components of the so-called 'misery index' (an indicator of the overall extent of a country's economic difficulties) does produce a strong correlation with the financial balance ($r = -0.62$) and a weak correlation with the public debt ($r = +0.34$). Compared to prior research in this field, it appears that these core factors have become less prominent in explaining debt and deficit performance (Wagschal, 1996). One factor, however, has gained in importance: a country's population size. High population countries, it would appear, especially the USA, can, to some extent, externalize the cost of public debt (see equation 2 in Table 9.4). Within the European Union, a clear tendency for higher deficits can also be observed for the countries with large populations, which have better opportunities for evading the full strictures of the Maastricht criteria.

Partisan complexion has also become less important in the determination of public debt and deficits. Until the early 1990s, despite the Keynesian logic, there was a rather strong and clear relation between the strength of leftist parties in government and comparatively low indebtedness. This relationship has been affected by globalisation, economic difficulties, the Maastricht criteria and tax competition and, today, the association, while still present, is more muted (see equation 3 in Table 9.4). Corporatist variables and strike indicators are also no longer of any real importance. Focusing more closely on the bourgeois parties, there are also no significant variations for different party families (for example, Liberals, Christian Democrats and Conservatives).

Institutional determinants can be clearly observed, although not necessarily those expected. The implication of veto player theory is that deficits and debt levels will be lower where veto players are most numerous, and some empirical studies (such as Bawn, 1999) support this argument. However, the relationships between public debt level in 2001 (see equation 2 in Table 9.4) and financial balances in the same year (see equation 5 in Table 9.5) and the veto player data supplied by George Tsebelis are wrongly signed and around the 0.05 significance level.

The findings in Table 9.4 reveal that political stability, measured by strike activity rates and by government duration, is only moderately related to the outcomes. Also Alberto Alesina's (1989) ordinal indicator for the OECD countries (high values equal low stability) shows only weak explanatory power. Bivariate correlations for this additional indicator (not shown in Table 9.4) show the expected tendency, but with rather low magnitudes. The correlations with the level of public debt (2001: r=0.26), the change of public debt between 1980 and 2001 (r_s=0.27) and average financial balances (1990–2001: r_s = −0.44) are modest.

Despite this poor finding, it is also possible to approximate political stability via country risk ratings. Data from rating companies like Moody's, whose indicator I have used for country stability ratings, vary over time.[7] The rating scale consists of 21 different items, differing from triple A (Aaa) to D. Usually these ratings are used by financial markets for calculating a risk premium for interest. This credibility indicator is highly correlated with the long-term interest rate and also with the political stability of a country. Thanks to better data coverage, this indicator was used in the multivariate regressions (see equations 1 and 2 in Table 9.4), where it manifests moderately strong explanatory power.

Other institutional factors such as federalism, EU membership, central bank independence and the 'strong government' variables postulated by Roubini and Sachs (1989) and Lijphart (1999) manifest no significant impact. At first sight, this seems contradictory when compared to the impact of political stability. However, both indicators use the number of parties in government or the extent of the majority status of governments as defining elements, but it is obvious that these aspects cover only a fraction of what is conveyed by the notion of political stability. Another indicator proves more relevant in this context. As suggested by the hypothesis that politicians maximise the size of their budgets, it turns out that the greater the number of ministers in a government, the higher the public debt and deficits (correlation around 0.5).

Two 'technical' factors directly linked to the budget, the extent of gross interest payments for public debt and change in the level of social security spending (equation 4 in Table 9.4), turn out to be significant. Financial leeway is clearly absorbed by higher interest spending which also supports the 'inheritance hypothesis'. The level of social security spending does not play any role in explaining the dependent variables, although change in social spending between 1990 and 2001 has an influence on the financial balance. An increase in social security spending leads to a larger budget deficit.

We now turn to the analysis of the determinants of the nominal long-term interest rates. We focus on two dependent variables: average nominal long-term interest rates for the period 1991 to 2001 and for 1980 to 2001. This distinction is made because the main focus is on the long-run causal explanation of structural effects. The first point to note is that our results suggest that economic growth rates do not play an important role in explaining (nominal) long-term interest rates. In cross-sectional

Table 9.5 Political and institutional determinants of long-term interest rates

	(1) Long-term interest rates (ø 1991–2001)	(2) Long-term interest rates (ø 1980–2001)	(3) Long-term interest rates (ø 1991–2001)	(4) Long-term interest rates (ø 1980–2001)	(5) Long-term interest rates (ø 1980–2001)
Constant	6.58	8.48	8.84	16.07	13.98
	(6.19)***	(4.44)***	(7.01)***	(5.77)***	(5.01)***
Political stability	0.54	1.26	0.86	1.83	1.33
(Alesina)	(2.04)	(2.68)*	(4.13)***	(3.78)***	(2.65)*
Strike activity (period corresponds to the dependent variable)	0.002	0.003			
	(1.82)	(2.06)			
Index of central bank independence (Alesina)	−0.57	−1.21			
	(−2.32)*	(−2.67)*			
Current balance (period corresponds to the dependent variable)			−0.18	−0.54	−0.41
			(−3.69)**	(−4.50)***	(−3.26)**
Population (Log. 2000)			−0.41	−1.12	−0.95
			(−3.71)***	(−4.48)***	(−3.92)**
Credibility (Moody's rating, ø 1980–2001)					0.84
					(2.11)*
N	21	21	23	23	23
F-statistic	15.65***	21.05***	19.48***	23.65***	22.06***
Adj. R²	0.653	0.750	0.716	0.755	0.793

Notes: This table shows the coefficients of the OLS-regressions, *t*-values in brackets; * = 0.05 significance level; ** = 0.01 significance level; *** = 0.001 significance level.

regressions, in correlation analysis and in pooled time-series designs, this factor is close to irrelevance. Correcting the nominal interest rate with the annual inflation rate does not improve the picture: real interest rates also are not significantly affected by economic growth. A variety of institutional and political factors turn out to be much more relevant.

As predicted by economic theory, inflation is one of the strongest explanatory determinants of interest rates. This holds true for correlation and multivariate regressions, for example for the period 1980 to 2001, average inflation correlates $+0.61$ with long-term interest rates and, for the period 1990 to 2001, the relationship is even stronger ($r = +0.70$). There is also a medium-strong positive correlation between the effective average exchange rate[8] and the interest rate. The development of a currency is linked to inflation as well as to interest rates. A high interest rate will promote capital inflows and this tends to appreciate the currency. On the other hand, this appreciation will shift a country's trade profile: it is likely that exports will shrink with a tendency towards lower interest rates. Finally, the current balance has a strong and significant impact. Countries with a positive trade balance, that is (mainly) an excess of exports over imports, are also likely to experience a substantial inflow of capital which will tend to reduce interest rates.

In addition to economic factors which are reported here in tabular form, Table 9.5 shows the impact of political and institutional factors on long-term interest rates. Indicators of political stability, such as the credibility ratings, the Alesina indicator (1989) and average strike activity, all feature as significant and influential predictors of outcomes. Central bank independence is also relevant. Delegating the competence to set interest rates to independent institutions has clear economic advantages, since interest and inflation rates are significantly lower where this is the case.

Surprisingly, the size of population has a significant and strong (negative) impact on interest rates. It is usually argued that interest rates will decline when population declines. However, there is no empirical connection between the level of interest rates and the growth rate of the population. A second demographic relationship is established between an ageing society and interest rates. Most studies suggest that increasing life expectancy will lead to lower interest rates. One possible explanation of the finding reported in Table 9.5 might be that large countries have larger markets and therefore fewer problems with capital supply.

It is often argued that high levels of public debt tend to produce an increase in interest rates (England, 2002). This may hold true from a theoretical point of view, but empirical data show just the opposite sign in regression analysis or no significant impact over the past two decades. Although the crowding out argument appears compelling in theory, other institutional factors, such as flexible capital markets, independent central banks, exchange rates and increasing political stability, appear to have worked in the opposite direction.

Putting the results together, the story told by our analysis is as follows: Table 9.2 indicates that public debt and interest rates largely explain the size of debt interest payments. Tables 9.4 and 9.5 are designed to identify the relevant causal determinants of these two variables, with a special focus on socio-economic, political and institutional variables. The combinations of these explanatory factors are displayed in Table 9.6.

Obviously, socio-economic factors are the most important determinants of the three different dependent variables. Especially high economic growth since 1980 has reduced debt interest payments substantially (see equations 1, 3 and 4 in Table 9.6). The old-age dependency ratio is also very important, except in regard to the explanation of gross debt interest. The current balance also matters, but to a lesser extent. As expected, political factors such as political stability are also relevant. However, the salience of the credibility indicator declines in strength, because of the overall increase in credibility in the OECD world (see equations 1, 3 and 4 in Table 9.6). The partisan complexion of government, measured by the cabinet strength of Social Democracy, has a dampening effect on interest payments, originally due to the lower indebtedness of countries with left governments, especially in Scandinavia.

9.6   CONCLUSION AND OUTLOOK

The development of net debt interest payments after 1980 was first marked by an upward trend until the mid-1990s and has since fallen substantially. Empirically, two major driving forces account for variation in debt interest payments (both gross and net): the extent of borrowing (that is, public debt and deficits) and debt service (that is, interest rates). Roughly 70 per cent of variation can be explained by the two factors together. After the mid-1990s, the downward trend of interest rates gave governments more leeway for other spending priorities: average long-term interest rates in the OECD countries analysed here are only around a third of what they were in the early 1980s. A third factor, which cannot be measured in an appropriate way, is the quality of public debt management. Since the early 1990s, more than half of the OECD countries have substantially reformed the institutions and processes responsible for public debt. Almost certainly, this helps to explain why debt repayment levels have been declining.

Public debt and interest rates themselves depend on other factors. The theoretical literature points to economic as well as political and institutional variables. Empirical findings show the importance of some economic explanatory indicators, especially economic growth and inflation. Economic

Table 9.6   *Socio-economic and political determinants of general government net and gross debt interest payments as percentages of GDP*

	(1) Net debt interest payments (2001)	(2) Net debt interest payments (2001)	(3) Gross debt interest payments (2001)	(4) Net debt interest payments (ø 1990–2001)	(5) Net debt interest payments (ø 1990–2001)
Constant	0.91	–3.12	5.00	–0.25	–3.80
	(0.63)	(3.49)	(2.97)**	(0.11)	(2.58)
Real GDP growth (ø 1980–2001)	–1.11		–1.12	–1.02	
	(3.95)**		(3.55)**	(2.35)*	
Old age adj. dependency ratio (2000)	0.09	0.18	–0.00	0.10	0.21
	(2.81)*	(5.65)***	(0.10)	(1.95)	(4.31)***
Credibility (Moody's rating, ø 1980–2001)		–0.15			0.29
		(0.54)			(0.74)
Political stability (Alesina)	0.91		0.91	1.81	
	(2.89)*		(2.48)*	(3.72)**	
Cabinet share of social democrats (ø 1945–2001)	–0.03		–0.03	–0.05	
	(2.61)*		(–1.95)	(2.47)*	
Current balance (ø 1980–2001)		–0.22			–0.19
		(2.39)*			(1.63)
N	23	23	23	23	23
F-statistic	19.632***	14.96***	6.75*	14.78***	11.48***
Adj. R^2	0.772	0.656	0.511	0.715	0.590

Notes: This table shows the coefficients of the OLS-regressions, *t*-values in brackets; * = 0.05 significance level; ** = 0.01 significance level; *** = 0.001% significance level.

growth reduces public debt as well as the inflation rate (the latter, at least, theoretically). Inflation and nominal interest rates are positively connected. The overall effect on net debt interest payments was positive, indicative of a stronger covariation with interest rates.

Two political and institutional factors turn out to be highly relevant: political stability and (economic) credibility. Safe conditions are appreciated by capital markets. However, other political institutions and social conditions are also important for both factors.

These findings fit the general thrust of the findings elsewhere in this volume. Convergence is visible for many of the expenditure categories analysed in this book. Since the early 1990s, cross-national interest rate variation within the OECD area has been reduced to a large extent (see Figure 9.4). Variation in cross-national public debt levels has also declined, although to a smaller extent. All in all, strong convergence in net debt interest payments can be observed, especially over the past decade and this, in turn, has contributed significantly to the overall convergence of aggregate spending patterns reported in Chapter 2.

The future development of interest payments depend on a variety of factors. For an understanding of the debt arithmetic and its dynamics, one way forward is to simulate the development of public debt and public debt service over time. The groundbreaking research in this field was by Domar (1944). The Domar model is rather simple and uses constant parameters over time for simulation. In principle, there are two models: one excluding and the other including inflation (Gandenberger, 1981: 45f.; Blaas and Matzner, 1981: 118ff.). The simple model excluding inflation starts by calculating the gross national product, which is dependent on a start value and a fixed constant real growth term. A simulation based on actual data for the OECD averages shows a future increase in public debt and also in interest payments. However, the Domar model is especially sensitive to growth rates, interest rates and inflation for the limits of the debt to GDP ratio. The empirical results have shown that governments can only influence these factors indirectly. For example, they can create a political and institutional environment favourable to political stability and credibility. Such policies, which governments have been seeking to refine and entrench over recent decades, have some promise of containing interest rates and, in the long-term, reducing the burden of public debt.

NOTES

1. On the other hand, a well functioning capital market should (theoretically) produce a larger supply of capital and lead to lower interest rates in the long run.

2. Moreover, the amount of interest varies depending on the choice of repayment method: (a) a fixed sum for each period of interest and repayment leads to high interest payments and small repayments at the beginning, but high repayment in the end; (b) the repayment of an equal sum over the period leads to decreasing interest payments and decreasing overall payments; (c) repayment of the credit in one sum at the end of the repayment period will result in constant interest payments over time.

3. In many countries, debt management has been improved by the adoption of more flexible and professional organisation, including new instruments, financial market tools and benchmarks to drive the portfolio risks of government debt. In Britain, the responsibility for debt management was transferred from the Bank of England to the Debt Management Office in 1998. A similar shift took place in Germany in 2000, with responsibilities handed over to a new institution, the 'Finanzagentur'.

4. Three of many examples may highlight the problem: OECD *Outlooks*, nos 58, 63 and 78, report the following values for Belgium (1989): 9.7 per cent, 9.3 per cent and 10.6 per cent; for Australia (1989): 1.9 per cent, 1.8 per cent and 3.7 per cent; and for Norway (1994): -0.1 per cent, -0.8 per cent and -2.2 per cent. In what follows, I use the latest OECD figures from OECD *Outlook* no. 78 (OECD, 2005b).

5. The magnitude of the correlation coefficient decreases over time; for example, in 1992, the correlation was close to 0.8.

6. For example, the average inflation rate (1991 to 2001) is moderately correlated with the average financial balance for the same period ($r=-0.53$). On the other hand, unemployment (ø 1991–2001) is rather weakly correlated with the average financial balance ($r=-0.40$) and very weakly with the level of public debt ($+0.16$).

7. I want to thank Alexander Kockerbeck, Vice President Senior Analyst of Moody's Frankfurt, for supplying me with the data.

8. The effective exchange rate is the exchange rate of the domestic currency vis-à-vis other currencies (for example, US dollars) weighted by their share in either the country's international trade or payments. The variable is measured in relation to the year 2000 ($= 100$). Higher values reflect the appreciation of the currency.

REFERENCES

Abell, J.D. (1990), 'Twin deficits during the 1980s: an empirical investigation', *Journal of Macroeconomics*, **12**, 81–96.

Alesina, A. (1989), 'Politics and business cycles in industrial democracies', *Economic Policy*, **8**, 57–98.

Alesina, A. and R. Perotti (1994), 'The Political Economy of Budget Deficits', NBER Working Paper no. 4637, Cambridge, Mass.

Alesina, A. and G. Tabellini (1988), 'Credibility and politics', *European Economic Review*, **32**, 542–50.

Alesina, A. and G. Tabellini (1990), 'A positive theory of fiscal deficits and government debt', *Review of Economic Studies*, **57**, 403–14.

Alesina, A., V. Grilli and G. Milisi-Ferreti (1993), 'The Political Economy of Capital Controls Independent', NBER Working Paper no. W4353, Washington.

Bawn, K. (1999), 'Money and majorities in the Federal Republic of Germany: evidence for a veto players model of government spending', *American Journal of Political Science*, **43**, 707–36.

Blaas, W. and E. Matzner (1981), 'Nachlassendes wirtschaftliches Wachstum und Staatsverschuldung', in D. Simmert and K.D. Wagner (eds), *Staatsverschuldung kontrovers*, Cologne: Verlag Wissenschaft und Politik.

Boix, C. (1998), *Political Parties, Growth and Equality. Conservative and Social Democratic Strategies in the World Economy*, Cambridge: Cambridge University Press.

Borelli, S. and T. Royed (1995), 'Government strength and budget deficits in advanced democracies', *European Journal of Political Research*, **28**(2), 225–60.

Buchanan, J. (1980), 'Procedural and quantitative constitutional constraints on fiscal authority', in W. Moore and R. Penner (eds), *The Constitution and the Budget*, Washington, DC: American Enterprise Institute.

Buchanan, J. and R. Wagner (1977), *Democracy in Deficit. The Political Legacy of Lord Keynes*, New York: Academic Press.

Cameron, D. (1978), 'The Expansion of the public economy: a comparative analysis', *The American Political Science Review*, **72**, 1243–61.

Caselli, F., A. Giovannini and T. Lane (1999), 'Fiscal discipline and the Cost of public debt service: some estimates for OECD countries', IMF working paper no. 55.

Cukierman, A., S. Webb and B. Neyapti (1992), 'Measuring the independence of central banks and its effect on policy outcomes', *The World Bank Economic Review*, **6**, 353–98.

DeHaan, J. and J.-E. Sturm (1997), 'Political and economic determinants of OECD budget deficits and government expenditures: a reinvestigation', *European Journal of Political Economy*, **13**, 739–50.

Domar, E. (1944), 'The "burden of the debt" and the national income', *American Economic Review*, **34**, 798–825.

England, R. (2002), *Global Aging and Financial Markets: Hard Landings Ahead?*, Washington, DC: CSIS Press.

Esping-Andersen, G. (1990), *The Three Worlds of Welfare Capitalism*, Cambridge: Polity Press.

Franzese, R. (2002), *Macroeconomic Policies of Developed Democracies*, Cambridge: Cambridge University Press.

Gandenberger, O. (1981), 'Theorie der öffentlichen Verschuldung', in W. Gerloff (ed.), *Handbuch der Finanzwissenschaft, Band III*, Tübingen: Mohr Siebeck.

Garrett, G. (1998), *Partisan Politics in the Global Economy*, Cambridge: Cambridge University Press.

Grilli, V., D. Masciandaro and G. Tabellini (1991), 'Political and monetary institutions and public financial policies in the industrial countries', *Economic Policy*, **13**, 341–92.

Gupta, K. and B. Moazzami (1996), *Interest Rates and Budget Deficits: A Study of the Advanced Economies*, London: Routledge.

Hibbs, D. (1977), 'Political parties and macroeconomic policy', *American Political Science Review*, **71**, 1467–87.

Johnson, D. and P. Siklos (1996), 'Political and economic determinants of interest rate behavior: are central banks different?', *Economic Inquiry*, **34**, 708–29.

Katzenstein, P. (1985), *Small States in World Markets*, Ithaca: Cornell University Press.

Kearney, C. and M. Monadjemi (1990), 'Fiscal policy and current account performance: international evidence on the twin deficits', *Journal of Macroeconomics*, **12**, 197–219.

Korpi, W. (1991), 'Political and economic explanations for unemployment: a cross-national and long-term analysis', *British Journal of Political Science*, **21**, 315–48.

Lerner, A. (1979), 'Funktionale Finanzpolitik und Staatsschuld', in E. Nowotny (ed.), *Öffentliche Verschuldung*, Stuttgart: Fischer.

Lijphart, A. (1999), *Patterns of Democracy. Government Forms and Performance in Thirty-Six Countries*, New Haven: Yale University Press.

OECD (2005a), *Central Government Debt: Statistical Yearbook 1994–2003*, Paris.

OECD (2005b), *OECD-Economic Outlook Database*, Paris.

OECD (2005c), *Main Economic Indicators*, Paris.

Olson, M. (1992), *Die Logik des kollektiven Handelns: Kollektivgüter und die Theorie der Gruppen*, Tübingen: Mohr Siebeck.

Persson, T. and L. Svensson (1989), 'Why a stubborn conservative would run a deficit: policy with time-inconsistent preferences', *Quarterly Journal of Economics*, **104**, 325–45.

Ricardo, D. (1951), *The Works and Correspondence of David Ricardo, Vol. IV Pamphlets and Papers 1815–1823*, ed. P. Sraffa, Cambridge: Cambridge University Press.

Rose, R. and T. Karran (1987), *Taxation by Political Inertia. Financing the Growth of Government in Britain*, London: Allen & Unwin.

Roubini, N. and J. Sachs (1988), 'Political and economic determinants of budget deficits in the industrial democracies', NBER Working Paper No. 2682, Cambridge, MA.

Roubini, N. and J. Sachs (1989), 'Political and economic determinants of budget deficits in the industrial democracies', *European Economic Review*, **33**, 903–33.

Sanz, I. and F. Velázquez (2002), 'Determinants of the Composition of Government Expenditure by Functions', European Economy Group Working Paper no. 13/2002.

Saunders, P. and F. Klau (1985), 'The role of the public sector, causes and consequences of the growth of government', *OECD – Economic Studies*, No. 4, 4–239.

Scharpf, F.W. (1987), Sozialdemokratische Krisenpottik in Europa, Frankfurt, Campus.

Schmidt, M.G. (1996), 'When parties matter: a review of the possibilities and limits of partisan influence on public policy', *European Journal of Political Research*, **30**, 155–83.

Schmidt, M. (2000), 'Die sozialpolitischen Nachzüglerstaaten und die Theorien der vergleichenden Staatstätigkeitsforschung', in H. Obinger and U. Wagschal (eds), *Der gezügelte Wohlfahrtsstaat. Sozialpolitik in reichen Industrienationen*, Frankfurt a. M.: Campus.

Steinmo, S. and C. Tolbert (1998), 'Do institutions really matter? Taxation in industrialized democracies', *Comparative Political Studies*, **31**, 165–87.

Tsebelis, G. (2002), *Veto Players. How Political Institutions Work*, New York: Sage.

Wagschal, U. (1996), *Staatsverschuldung. Ursachen im internationalen Vergleich*, Opladen: Leske+Budrich.

Wagschal, U. (2002), 'Verfassungsbarrieren als Grenzen der Staatstätigkeit', *Schweizer Zeitschrift für Politische Wissenschaft*, **2**, 51–87.

10. Moving beyond expenditure accounts: the changing contours of the regulatory state, 1980–2003

Nico A. Siegel

10.1 FROM MARKET RESTRICTING REGULATION TO COMPETITION ENABLING RE-REGULATION[1]

In most chapters of this book, historical accounts of public expenditure are used to explore whether systematic retrenchment has occurred in OECD countries by examining expenditure trends and their determinants in the post-1980s. This chapter has a similar intellectual concern, but differs insofar as it focuses on the extent of product and labour market regulation as two key dimensions of the size of government. In contrast to expenditure-based accounts of public policy patterns, comparative inquiries analysing the scope and density of formal rule setting and legal regulatory policy provisions (best summarised as 'government regulation' studies[2]) have predominantly relied on 'small n' comparisons or case studies. There are manifold reasons for this striking division of labour between quantitative expenditure analysis and qualitative studies investigating regulatory policies. Owing to a lack of standardised indicators of the scope of government regulation, quantitative studies have mainly relied on expenditure data.[3] With the exception of the OECD, none of the major international organisations providing data on government expenditure has published cross-national time-series on the various aspects of government regulation.

The lack of systematic quantitative comparisons of the extent of government regulation in different OECD countries marks an important gap in the literature. Although expenditure-based accounts of public policy offer many crucial insights, the relatively weak correlations between expenditures and the extent of product market regulation shown in Table 10.1 demonstrate that they do not provide an exhaustive, or even perhaps a representative, picture of the changing role and size of the state in advanced capitalist societies. Because that is so, we are left with the question of whether the

Table 10.1   Product market regulation and public expenditure, 1980–2003

		General government total expenditure, % GDP		Spending on economic affairs
Mean value	1980	0.42 (N = 21)		—
regulatory	1990	0.53 (N = 21)		0.33 (N = 13)
provisions	2003	0.35 (N = 21)		0.47 (N = 17)
	1980–2003	0.45 (N = 21)	1990–2003	0.46 (N = 13)
		(0.62)* (N = 20)		

Notes: Shown are values for Pearson's r, N = number of countries; * excluding Ireland.

Sources: Total general government outlays from OECD *Economic Outlook*, various volumes; *Spending on Economic Affairs* from Obinger and Zohlnhöfer, this volume, chapter 8; data on regulatory provisions, Conway et al. (2005), OECD International Regulation database; see also explanatory notes in text and for Table 10.2.

descriptive and analytical findings of expenditure-based accounts of government policies give us anything like a full picture of contemporary patterns of public policy transformation.

On the basis of a priori reasoning, we might expect that, in countries with high levels of public expenditure, that is, big tax and welfare states, there would also be likely to be more extensive government regulation limiting the role of market mechanisms.

In fact, as Table 10.1 and Figure 10.1 both show, the statistical association between various changes in total government outlays and the economy-wide role of product market regulation is indeed positive. However, the statistical association is of only moderate magnitude, with only the 1990 correlation reaching the 0.05 significance threshold. As can be seen from Figure 10.1, Ireland is an obvious outlier, as a radical decline in total government spending as a percentage of GDP in the post-1980 period was not matched by a radical downscaling of economic regulation according to the OECD estimates of regulatory change. Excluding the exceptional case of Ireland, the coefficient *r* increases by almost 40 per cent, from 0.45 to 0.62.

However, although the relationship is significant, there remains a large share of statistical variation unaccounted for. Thus there are reasons for supposing that, through examination of the changing contours of government regulation, there is a real potential for adding something important to the picture revealed by comparative analyses of government expenditure trends. This is likely to be particularly true in the realm of economic affairs, where, in contrast to welfare spending, government expenditure was

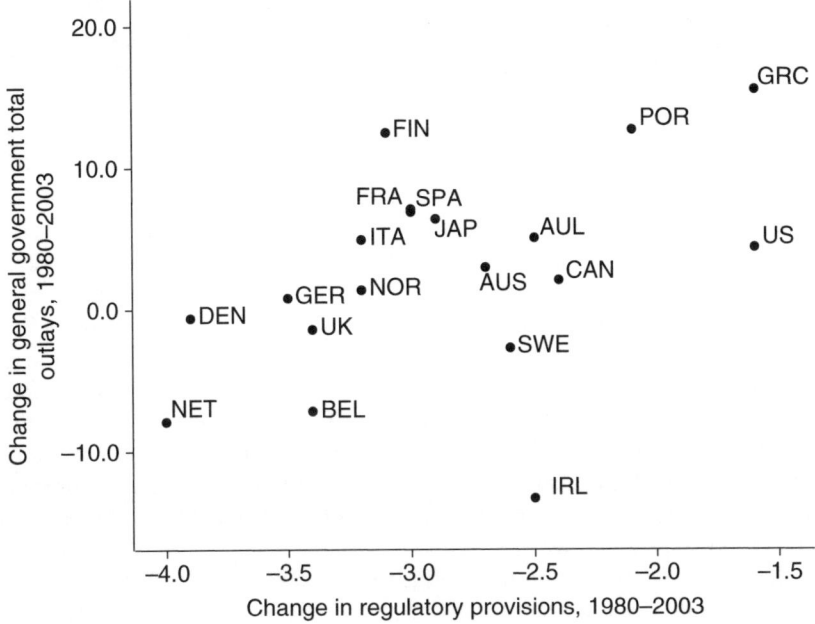

Figure 10.1 *Changes in levels of regulatory provisions and public*
expenditure, 1980–2003

remarkably reduced during the 1990s (see, in particular Chapter 8 of this volume).

The shortage of macro-quantitative analysis of government regulation is a particular problem, given that, during the past two decades, a rapidly growing body of literature has investigated what is commonly referred to as the end of the positive or Keynesian welfare state and the 'rise of the regulatory state' (Majone, 1994, 1997; for a critical review, cf. Moran, 2002). The increasing importance of regulatory reforms and regulatory management on governments' agendas across the Western world has led some authors to the conclusion that we are witnessing a 'global diffusion of regulatory capitalism' (Levi-Faur, 2005). Indeed, it is the general view of recent research undertaken in this area that the reform of regulatory provisions became a key economic policy issue in all OECD countries during the 1990s.

In the overwhelming majority of studies that have investigated patterns of regulatory change from a cross-national perspective, authors have emphasised the importance of in-depth 'process investigations' of regulatory changes. A number of these studies have identified and tried to account for what might be summarised as the seemingly paradoxical relationship between privatisation, liberalisation and (preliminary) deregulation on the one hand, and the mounting pressure on policy regulators for competition enabling reregulation on the other hand. In this literature, it is almost a given that the simple notion of state retreat is misleading (Wright and Müller, 1994). As Richardson has summarised the UK experience, politically induced initiatives to 'bring markets [back] in' had triggered an unexpected dynamic of 'Doing Less by Doing More' (Richardson, 1994). The increasing relevance of regulatory reforms that aim at putting in place market-enabling policy regimes has resulted in what may be described as 'regulation *for* competition' (Levi-Faur, 2005). Privatisation and market-enforcing liberalisation have not wiped out government regulation per se, but have led to less regulation *against* markets and fostered the growth of market-*enabling* or *enforcing* regulatory policy frameworks. As Vogel succinctly summarises this transformation, 'freer markets' mean 'more rules' (Vogel, 1996), with the decline of administrative and economic anti-market regulations preceding the rise of competition enabling reregulation and 'regulatory governance' (OECD, 2002).

By and large, the lesson to be learnt from qualitative studies of regulatory reform – namely, that more market-oriented policies have not resulted in a radically downsized state – seems to confirm the broad picture drawn by most comparative analyses of government expenditure trends for the post-1980 period (for example, Castles, 1998). However, as we demonstrate below, quantitative measures of *competition-restricting regulation* in key economic sectors do indicate a decline in *market-restricting* regulation in the 1990s. Thus the rise of the regulatory state may imply a greater emphasis on regulatory policies, for the most part aimed at reducing the salience of regulations against markets.

10.2   QUANTITATIVE MEASURES OF REGULATION

In what follows, we shall focus on two major dimensions of government regulation: (a) economic and administrative regulations affecting the regulation of product markets, and (b) an important social dimension, labour market regulation; that is, legal provisions affecting employment contracts.

In a first step we will introduce and explore a range of quantitative data measuring the extent of market-restricting regulations in product markets. The indicators we use measure the extent of regulatory provisions (hereinafter *REGPRO*) in six non-manufacturing sectors in which the state has played a major role as the provider of public utilities for much of the twentieth century: the supply of gas, electricity, railways, air transport, telecommunication and post services. The OECD has produced a time-series of sector-specific regulatory provisions for each of these non-manufacturing sectors, plus the regulation of road freight for the period 1975–2003.

The OECD has also developed a more complex measure for *economy-wide* product market regulation (in the following *PMR*). However, to date, the OECD has published estimates of these more complex measures for only two years, 1998 and 2003. The OECD figures reflect a sophisticated and hierarchical indicator system, comprising 16 sub-indicators (Conway et al., 2005: 8f; Jochem and Siegel, 2004). Although the set of indicators the OECD has used in its measures of regulatory provisions might be criticised for not offering an exhaustive list of administrative and economic regulation, it provides a reasonable proxy for internationally variable patterns of market-restricting regulation in those economic sectors in which one might expect important dynamics of change due to a paradigmatic shift in economic policy making away from Keynesianism and towards supply-side economics (Hall, 1989).

The PMR indicator system also allows us to focus on important sub-dimensions of regulatory reform patterns in OECD countries as it measures different aspects of economic and administrative regulation, summarised under such headings as 'state control', 'barriers to entrepreneurship' and 'barriers to external trade and investment'. However, in what follows, owing to restrictions of space, we will analyse only the aggregate summary measures of product market regulation and regulatory provisions. Thus this chapter provides a macroscopic exploration of regulation patterns and not a more detailed, microscopic investigation of regulatory changes.

In section 10.5, we investigate one area of social regulation that is closely related to key issues in comparative welfare state research: namely, employment protection legislation (hereinafter *EPL*), which mirrors important features of the protection of workers and employees against managerial prerogatives concerning hiring and firing practices (OECD, 1999). The OECD has calculated country-specific EPL values for both permanent (or standard) and temporary employment contracts for the period 1985–2003. The EPL indicators comprise sub-indicators for collective and individual dismissals, such as severance payments, notice periods and a range of other aspects of employment contracts (Nicoletti et al., 2000: 43). Employment protection legislation is an important regulatory feature of broader patterns of national 'labour regimes', largely neglected in the analysis of 'politics against markets'. Only recently have comparative accounts of the welfare state paid more attention to EPL and emphasised the decisive contribution of labour market regulation to welfare regimes (Esping-Andersen, 1999; Samek Lodovici, 2000).

There are, of course, many other important aspects of government regulation that we are unable to cover within the brief ambit of this chapter. By using aggregate indicator scores, we necessarily neglect the 'hows' of regulation – for example, differences in the institutional functioning of regulatory agencies – which have been the subject of considerable scholarly investigation (for example, command-and-control vs. incentive-based regulation: see Baldwin et al., 1998). Nor do we consider issues concerning differences between implementation practices and formal regulatory provisions. Our focus here is that of the rest of this volume: exploring the determinants of hitherto largely unused measures of the reach of the state and seeking to ascertain whether that reach has diminished in recent decades.

PMR and EPL represent two crucial dimensions of government regulation, which are not only highly correlated with each other,[4] but which have also started to attract enormous attention among economists interested in assessing the effects of regulatory provision as specific institutional features of national economic systems. A rapidly growing body of literature has started to explore the systematic links between the various measures of product market regulation and economic growth and between employment protection legislation and unemployment and employment growth (Layard et al., 2005; Nicoletti and Scarpetta, 2003). These studies have used various measures of PMR and EPL as *independent variables* inserted on the right-hand side of econometric models.

The purpose of this chapter and the perspective reflected in its research design is radically different. We are not interested here in finding answers to undoubtedly fascinating questions such as whether, how and to what extent product market and labour market regulations affect important aspects of welfare production. Our aim is to use available data on product and employment protection legislation to locate trends in the development of regulatory controls and, wherever possible, to locate the factors shaping such trends. Thus, in this chapter, both PMR and EPL figure as *dependent variables*.

10.3   HYPOTHESES

The theoretical approaches that guide our variable-oriented analysis are firmly rooted in the tradition of comparative public policy studies. They are, however, less representative of the impressive body of literature we find in the regulation literature. The main reason for this is that we do not engage with the major economic theories of regulation, which have been predominant for a long time in the economic literature on regulation (Stigler, 1971; Ogus, 1994). These theories are often of a more prescriptive than analytical character, and, where analytical, rarely offer much of explanatory value when used for cross-national comparisons over time. As our aim is to establish some systematic links with expenditure-focused accounts of public policy of the kind featuring elsewhere in this volume, we draw on a standard set of theories that have figured prominently in comparative analysis of public expenditure trends in OECD countries.

A major aim of this exploratory study is to establish whether these variables, so prominent in public expenditure analysis, can also account for variation in the trajectory of regulatory provision. The standard theories of comparative public policy analysis, from which we derive our hypotheses, offer plausible predictions concerning the likely relationships between socio-economic and political variables on the one hand and cross-national similarities and difference in policy patterns on the other. We would, however, expect those relationships to be less direct than in the realm of government expenditure. Where expenditure change is quite frequently immediately shaped by socio-economic forces, regulatory change is framed by legislative and/or bureaucratic processes and decision making often only indirectly sensitive to such forces. In what follows, we list the hypotheses featuring in our subsequent analysis and locate the theoretical expectations guiding their formulation.

10.3.1   Socio-economic Factors and 'Problem Pressure'

Although the relationship between key variables of socio-economic development and regulatory policies is less obvious than in the case of spending trends, we will control for two types of important socio-economic background factors, which may affect the timing and the extent of regulatory change. We assume an inverse relationship between economic performance (measured by annual real GDP growth for specified periods) and the extent of regulatory reforms. The assumption is that, in countries with notoriously low economic growth in the post-OPEC I era (1974–82), the political pressure to liberalise regulatory provisions should have been stronger during the 1980s than in countries that managed to steer their economies rather more smoothly through the period 1974–82. Whereas we would expect a clear negative relationship between economic performance in the post-OPEC I period and regulatory reforms during the 1980s, we do not expect such a strong link between economic performance and regulatory reforms in the 1990s. Why so? Our assumption is based on the literature on the changing role of political ideas, which suggests that one of the most striking changes in the political economy of most advanced democracies was the diffusion of a supply-side economic policy paradigm after the recession of the early 1980s (Hall, 1989). Thus we would expect that changes in regulatory reforms during the 1990s already reflected a diffusion of a transnationally shared economic policy paradigm, and would therefore assume that reform patterns would be marked by a convergent dynamic towards less market-restricting regulatory regimes.

The second problem factor we take into account is the level of public debt at the beginning of our two periods of investigation. Obviously, debt reflects both economic and political factors (on which, see Chapter 9 above). Although the relationship between increasing debt and mounting pressure for restrictive policy measures is less clear-cut in the area of economic regulation than in the case of budget processes, it is reasonable to suppose that the pressure for liberalisation would be greater, the higher the GDP share of government liabilities.

10.3.2 Politics

We take into account theories that stress the importance of the political power of collective actors, in particular the 'parties do matter' theory suggesting that the partisan composition of (central) governments is an important factor shaping national policy profiles (at least, over the long run). Hence we deploy measures of cabinet seat shares for various families of parties. Our expectation is that Left parties will have tried to utilise their power resources in favour of more market-restricting regulatory policies, particularly in the area of employment protection legislation, and within a context of high interest group pluralism, that is, low levels of corporatism and coordinated policy making, reflecting a political economy unfavourable to a coordinated Social Democratic supply-side economic policy approach. In contrast, our expectation is that bourgeois parties would favour less market-restricting patterns of government regulation and would have been in the vanguard of regulatory reform during the 1980s. Again, we would expect partisan factors to be less relevant during the 1990s due to the transnational diffusion of a regulatory paradigm resulting in less market-restricting government regulation.

10.3.3 Institutions

We utilise the crucial insights of institutional theories focusing on the impact of constitutional structures on public policy outcomes (Schmidt, 1993). Here, we mainly focus on the question of whether countries with constitutional structures manifesting a high degree of institutional pluralism – that is, a low extent of power concentration in the hands of central governments – tend to have less densely regulated product and labour markets than those concentrating political steering power in the hands of central governments.

Analysis of change in regulatory policy might, however, yield a different picture from that resulting from the investigation of levels. In countries with a high degree of institutional fragmentation, central governments may face more and more powerful veto players blocking regulatory reform initiatives than governments in countries with only a few institutionally anchored veto players.

10.3.4　Legal Origins Theory

The literature analysing country profiles of product market and employment protection legislation has emphasised the role of different legal traditions shaping regulatory policy patterns (Nicoletti and Scarpetti, 2003; Botero et al., 2004). The major line of distinction runs between countries in which the 'common law' tradition prevails (mainly the English-speaking countries and former British colonies), and the 'civil law countries' of the European continent (and some Asian nations like Japan). Common Law countries tend to rely less on legal rule setting, which emphasises standardised procedures, but place more emphasis on juries and independent agencies. In contrast, the Civil Law tradition puts more weight on a stringent codification of the legal system and statutory rights (for example for employees), resulting in comprehensive and clearly defined legal rule-sets to be applied and interpreted by less independent judges.

Studies analysing the impact of legal traditions on market institutions are particularly prominent in the 'law and economics' literature. There we find important cross-national investigations; for example, of corporate ownership and corporate governance systems (La Porta et al., 1998). More recent studies have also analysed cross-national variations in labour law (Botero et al., 2004). In a manner similar to studies analysing product market regulation, these comparative inquiries have reported convincing evidence that the most densely regulated labour markets are to be found in Civil Law countries.

Within the group of Civil Law countries three subgroups are distinguishable:

- a French-speaking group, comprising the BENELUX countries, but also the Southern European economies of Italy, Spain and Portugal;
- a German legal tradition reflected in the legal system of Germany, Austria, Switzerland, Greece and Japan;
- a somewhat independent Nordic legal tradition that is typical of the Scandinavian countries included in our analysis.

In general, we would expect the most striking differences in regulatory patterns to be between Common Law countries and the rest of the OECD world. We would also expect a rank order within the group of Civil Law countries, with the most restrictive regulatory patterns in the state-prone French tradition, followed by the German and, finally, coming closest to the Common Law system of the English-speaking world, the countries adhering to the Nordic legal tradition.

10.3.5   Catch-up and Catch-down

Just as in other chapters of this book, in the area of market-restricting regulation we expect to observe a convergent trajectory of development. However, this is a convergence better described as 'catch-down' than catch-up. The catch-up tendencies observed in previous chapters are generally an effect of the maturation of spending programmes. We expect to encounter a 'catch-down' dynamic, because the thrust of regulatory reform has been towards cutting back on market restrictions across the board. Thus it is a plausible assumption that those countries with the most restrictive regulation profiles will have been those facing the strongest pressures to liberalise their regulatory regimes. 'Catch-down' occurs where, as well as a general trend towards decline, the countries manifesting the greatest decline are those with the initially highest values.

10.3.6   Globalisation

Finally, we include in our analysis variables derived from theoretical approaches focusing on the effects of globalisation on public policy patterns. Just as in the case of expenditure trends, the link between policy outcomes and external economic vulnerability can be viewed positively or negatively. Analogously to Cameron's classic compensation hypothesis that trade exposure is associated with greater welfare spending (Cameron, 1978), one might expect higher levels of domestic market regulation, particularly labour market regulation, in countries whose economies are highly dependent on international trade, offering workers in exposed sectors a more finely meshed safety net against the potentially adverse effects of international trade. However, a quite different relationship, of the kind implied by contemporary theories of a 'race-to-the-bottom' in social spending, might well hold in the sphere of product market regulation, with countries heavily involved in international trade taking a less restrictive regulatory stance to maximise their flexibility in the face of international competition. It is possible, too, that the logic of compensation simply does not apply in the regulatory sphere, suggesting the possibility of the null hypothesis: that changes in regulation are not directly linked to a country's exposure to international trade and capital markets.

10.4   EMPIRICAL RESULTS: PRODUCT MARKET REGULATION

The OECD has collected and published summary measures of regulatory provisions (the plural form is an OECD usage employed throughout this chapter) in seven non-manufacturing sectors and information on various sub-dimensions of product market regulation. The indicators cover a wide range of aspects of economic and administrative features of product market regulations. The weighted figures for PMR are normalised on a 0–6 scale. The higher the index scores, the more salient competition-inhibiting government regulation. The 'raw materials' for this aggregate indicator are 800 data entries the OECD has collected for each of the countries which are included in its International Regulatory Data Base.[5]

Whereas product market regulation indices, as presented in Table 10.2, are based on economy-wide estimates of the role and scope of government regulation, the summary indicators of the extent of regulatory provisions are based on average regulation scores for the six non-manufacturing sectors plus the regulation of road freight. The reason why we do not rely exclusively on the more representative economy-wide regulation scores is a purely pragmatic one, as it would only allow us to analyse changes over a very short time period. As we are interested in patterns of change for the whole post-1980 period, we use the somewhat more narrow summary scores for regulatory provisions.

Table 10.2   Regulatory provisions and product market regulation, 1980–2003

	Regulatory provisions, non-manufacturing sectors					Economy wide product market regulation		
	1980	1990	1980– 1990	2003	1990– 2003	1998	2003	1998– 2003
Australia	4.0	3.9	−0.1	1.5	−2.4	1.3	0.9	−0.4
Austria	5.1	4.5	−0.6	2.4	−2.1	1.8	1.4	−0.4
Belgium	5.5	5.3	−0.2	2.1	−3.2	2.1	1.4	−0.7
Canada	4.3	2.7	−1.6	1.9	−0.8	1.4	1.2	−0.2
Denmark	5.5	4.7	−0.8	1.6	−3.1	1.5	1.1	−0.4
Finland	5.5	4.6	−0.9	2.4	−2.2	2.1	1.3	−0.8
France	6.0	5.2	−0.8	3.0	−2.2	2.5	1.7	−0.8
Germany	5.2	4.6	−0.6	1.7	−2.9	1.9	1.4	−0.5
Greece	5.7	5.7	0.0	4.1	−1.6	2.8	1.8	−1.0
Ireland	5.7	5.0	−0.7	3.2	−1.8	1.5	1.1	−0.4

Table 10.2   (continued)

	Regulatory provisions, non-manufacturing sectors					Economy wide product market regulation		
	1980	1990	1980–1990	2003	1990–2003	1998	2003	1998–2003
Italy	5.8	5.8	0.0	2.6	−3.2	2.8	1.9	−0.9
Japan	5.1	3.5	−1.6	2.2	−1.3	1.9	1.3	−0.6
Netherlands	5.6	5.6	0.0	1.6	−4.0	1.8	1.4	−0.4
New Zealand	5.2	3.7	−1.5	2.1	−1.6	1.4	1.1	−0.3
Norway	5.5	4.5	−1.0	2.3	−2.2	1.8	1.5	−0.3
Portugal	4.7	5.3	0.6	2.6	−2.7	2.1	1.6	−0.5
Spain	5.0	4.7	−0.3	2.0	−2.7	2.3	1.6	−0.7
Sweden	4.5	4.4	−0.1	1.9	−2.5	1.8	1.2	−0.6
Switzerland	4.5	4.2	−0.3	2.8	−1.4	2.2	1.7	−0.5
UK	4.4	3.0	−1.4	1.0	−2.0	1.1	0.9	−0.2
US	3.0	2.3	−0.7	1.4	−0.9	1.3	1.0	−0.3
OECD mean (21)	5.0	4.4	−0.6	2.2	−2.2	1.9	1.4	−0.5
Coefficient of Variation	0.14	0.22		0.31		0.26	0.21	
Catch–up coefficient			0.14		−0.69			−0.90
Families of legal origins (group-specific mean values)								
Common Law	4.4	3.4	−1.0	1.9	−1.5	1.3	1.0	−0.3
Civic Law	5.3	4.8	−0.5	2.4	−2.4	2.1	1.5	−0.6
Scandinavian	5.3	4.6	−0.7	2.1	−2.5	1.8	1.3	−0.5
German	5.1	4.5	−0.6	2.6	−1.9	2.1	1.5	−0.6
French	5.4	5.3	−0.1	2.3	−3.0	2.3	1.6	−0.7

Notes:
Catch-up: Shown is the correlation coefficient r measuring the strength of the statistical association between the levels of regulatory provision/product market regulation at the beginning of a period and the change of regulatory provisions for product market regulation for the periods 1980–1990, 1990–2003, 1998–2003.
Common Law countries: Australia, Canada, Ireland, New Zealand, UK, US; *Civic Law* countries: a. *Scandinavian group*: Denmark, Finland, Norway, Sweden; b. *German group*: Austria, Germany, Greece, Japan, Switzerland; c. *French group*: Belgium, France, Italy, Portugal, Spain.

Source: OECD International Regulation Data Base and Conway et al. (2005), various tables.

Table 10.2 summarises information on the two types of OECD indicators of regulatory provisions we use in this chapter. Regardless of whether we use the narrower indicator REGPRO or the more inclusive PMR estimates, the clear pattern of change that is indicated by Table 10.2 is of a decline of 'regulation against markets'. The mean index score for the 21 OECD democracies we have included for the REGPRO measure decreased between 1980 and 2003 from an average of 5.0 in 1980 to 4.4 in 1990 and to an all-time low of 2.2 in 2003. This finding stands in stark contrast to the kind of pattern we obtain for most OECD countries in respect of post-1980s total outlays and social spending. However, it provides a nice match with the changes in government expenditure on state subsidies and economic affairs identified in Chapter 8 of this volume.

The English-speaking Common Law countries pioneered in terms of regulatory reforms during the 1980s. In contrast, the 1990s witnessed a strong convergent dynamic. As we can see from the summary statistics at the bottom of Table 10.2, although all countries moved in the same direction, coefficients of variation actually increased between both 1980 and 1990 and 1990 and 2003. However, looking at the relationship between the initial level and change over time, the catch-up coefficient measuring β-*convergence* over time gives an entirely different picture. An inspection of the catch-up coefficient mirrors important changes in the cross-country patterns we observe for the 1980s and 1990s. Whereas, for the 1980s, the statistical correlation between initial levels of regulatory provisions and their change over the decade is weak and positive ($r=0.14$), indicating a modestly divergent policy reform trend, we find a strong negative association between the initial level of regulatory provisions in 1990 and the subsequent changes between 1990 and 2003 ($r=-0.69$). Moreover, for the short five year interval 1998–2003, the statistical association between the level of economy-wide product market regulation in 1998 and the subsequent change between 1998 and 2003 is a stunning $r=-0.91$.

This picture of convergence over time fits well with the results of multiple regression analyses discussed below. During the 1980s, policy reforms aimed at reducing the scope and intensity of market-restricting government regulation were not driven by a common logic or shared liberalisation paradigm. Rather, changes in regulatory provisions for the 1980s reflected country-specific political 'lead' and 'laggard' constellations. The picture we get of aggregate regulation measures largely confirms the findings of qualitative studies. In the two biggest English-speaking countries, the downward trend in regulation was substantially a consequence of the profound shift in power towards programmatically reformist Conservative parties, which embarked on radical pro-market policies and pioneered the adoption of privatisation and liberalisation measures during the 1980s.[6] In contrast to the 1980s, the 1990s witnessed the rise of a more general policy pattern resulting in more market-enforcing regulatory reform steps throughout the OECD area. This decline in regulation 'against' markets occurs in parallel with the rise of the regulatory state (Majone, 1997).

Given the remarkable decline in anti-market regulation of product markets in the post-1980 period, what are the factors that have driven regulatory reform in OECD countries and what are the political constellations that have reduced the speed and intensity of reform? Tables 10.3A and Table 10.3B report the results of multivariate regressions. We find strikingly different determinants of change for the 1980s and the post-1990 period and the results prove to be robust, controlling for other socio-economic and political variables omitted for reasons of space. For the 1980s, we find the expected negative relationship between the share of cabinet seats for Conservative parties and changes in regulatory provisions (1980–90). Table 10.3A also reveals an interesting finding concerning the link between the partisan composition of governments and regulatory reforms in the 1980s. Our measure of cabinet seat shares of bourgeois parties does not comprise only secular Conservative parties, but all centre and centre–right parties. Hence our indicator for bourgeois party incumbency includes not only secular centrist parties like the Democrats in the US or the Liberals in Canada, but also the Christian Democratic parties of Western Europe. This more inclusive indicator for bourgeois party incumbency included in model specification A3 scores slightly stronger (in terms of statistical significance levels for partial regression coefficients) than our measure of Conservative cabinet seats in model A2, suggesting that, during the 1980s, the shift towards pro-market policies became a more widely-spread policy ambition of all 'major parties of the right'.

The level of regulatory provisions in 1980 shows the expected (negative) sign, but is significant only at the 10 per cent level as long as we do not control for bourgeois partisan incumbency (model A1 vs. A3), again supporting the finding that the dynamics of regulatory reform were driven mainly by political factors during the 1980s. The term controlling for the legal origins explanation is not significant if we control for bourgeois party incumbency (model A5).

Neither the indicator of institutional pluralism nor that of trade openness is statistically significant even at the 10 per cent level. Moreover, it may also be noted that neither our economic performance indicator (model A8) nor the public debt term (A9) features as a significant predictor of change in regulatory reforms. Thus we reject the notions that regulatory reform in the 1980s was mainly a consequence of economic underperformance in the post-OPEC I period or that it was a government response to fiscal crisis. Rather it is clear that it was a political enterprise of rightist parties, which

Table 10.3A   Regression results: determinants of changes in regulatory provisions, 1980–1990

	Model A1	Model A2	Model A3	Model A4	Model A5	Model A6	Model A7	Model A8	Model A9
Constant term	-0.789	0.976	1.65**	1.855**	1.477**	1.659**	2.004**	1.849***	1.64**
	(-1.16)	(1.36)	(2.54)	(2.76)	(2.17)	(2.45)	(2.69)	(3.17)	(2.46)
Level of REGPRO (1980)	0.553	-0.228	-0.335*	-0.401***	-0.377**	-0.330**	-0.399***	-0.425***	-0.335**
	(0.39)	(-1.71)	(-2.85)	(-3.25)	(-2.62)	(-2.64)	(-2.95)	(-3.52)	(-2.68)
Cabinet seat shares Conservative parties (1979–1989)		-0.015***							
		(-5.99)							
Cabinet seat shares Bourgeois parties (1979–89)			-0.017***	-0.015***	-0.013***	-0.016***	-0.016***	-0.017***	-0.016***
			(-6.47)	(-5.83)	(-5.28)	(-5.64)	(-6.80)	(-6.41)	(-6.42)
Interaction cabinet seat shares left parties *interest group pluralism				0.002**					
				(2.07)					
Legal origin (4 scale)					0.121				
					(1.29)				
Trade openness (1979–89)						-0.001			
						(-0.12)			
Institutional pluralism							-0.074		
							(-0.80)		
GDP growth (1979–89)								0.132	
								(1.51)	
Government Debt (level 1980)									0.001
									(0.03)
R^2	0.01	0.54	0.66	0.72	0.69	0.66	0.67	0.70	0.66
F	0.15	19.10	22.97	15.79	15.77	16.25	16.68	15.64	15.55

Notes: The figures reported here are unstandardised regression coefficients and t-values based on robust standard errors as calculated by STATA 9.0 in parentheses; * $p \leq 0.1$; ** $p \leq 0.05$; *** $p \leq 0.01$.

Table 10.3B   Regression results: determinants of changes in regulatory provisions, 1990–2003

	Model B1	Model B2	Model B3	Model B4	Model B5	Model B6	Model B7	Model B8	Model B9
Constant term	0.390	−0.344	−0.478	1.101	0.252	0.400	0.418	0.377	0.383
	(0.66)	(−0.43)	(−0.40)	(1.64)	(0.37)	(0.65)	(0.69)	(0.48)	(0.61)
Level of REGPRO (1990)	−0.599***	−0.475**	−0.483**	−0.811***	−0.505**	−0.607***	−0.596***	−0.589***	−0.593***
	(−4.07)	(−2.77)	(−2.35)	(−4.30)	(−2.26)	(−3.59)	(−4.02)	(−3.97)	(−4.20)
Cabinet seat shares Conservative parties (1979–89)		0.008							
		(1.97)							
Cabinet seat shares Bourgeois parties (1989–2002)			0.007						
			(0.87)						
Interaction cabinet seat shares left Parties*interest group pluralism				0.005					
				(1.54)					
Legal origin					−0.094				
					(−0.60)				
Trade openness (1989–2002)						0.003			
						(0.29)			
Institutional pluralism							−0.026		
							(−0.20)		
GDP growth (1989–2002)								0.004	
								(0.02)	
Government debt (level 1990)									0.001
									(0.09)
R²	0.50	0.55	0.52	0.59	0.50	0.50	0.50	0.50	0.50
F	16.58	13.11	8.92	15.00	9.31	7.73	8.11	7.95	8.94

Notes: The figures reported here are unstandardised regression coefficients and t-values based on robust standard errors as calculated by STATA 9.0 in parentheses. * $p \leq 0.1$; ** $p \leq 0.05$; *** $p \leq 0.01$.

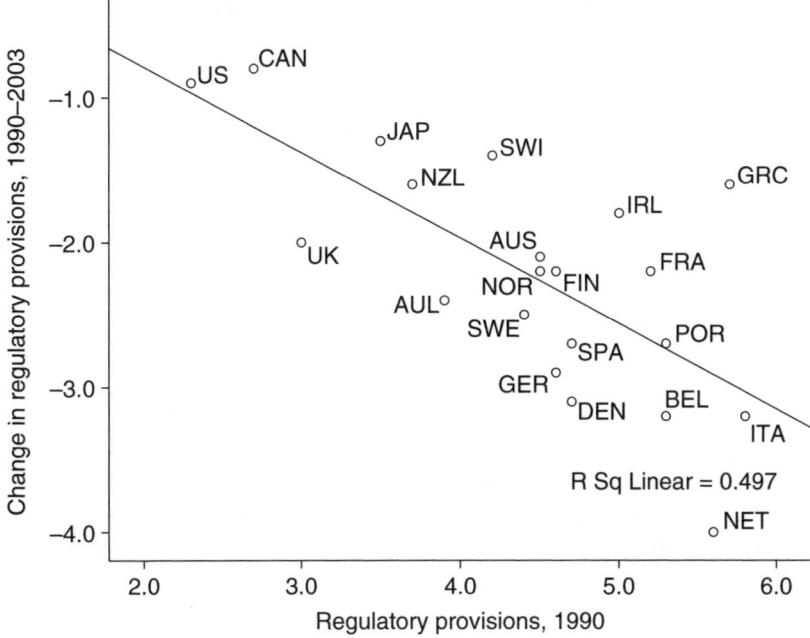

*Figure 10.2   Level of regulatory provisions in 1990 and changes,
1990–2003*

used the undoubted facts of low economic growth, high unemployment and growing public deficits to legitimate their privatisation and liberalisation initiatives.[7]

As can be seen from Tables 10.3A and 10.3B, the factors that have shaped regulatory reforms in the 1980s and 1990s are quite different. As all the model specifications for the post-1990 period show, the initial level of regulation in 1990 is the strongest predictor for the regulatory reform taking place between 1990 and 2002. This is also reflected in Figure 10.2, in which we have plotted changes in regulatory provisions between 1990 and 2003 against the level of our REGPRO indicator for the year 1990.

The interaction term between left party incumbency and interest group pluralism is significant in the model specifications for changes between 1980 and 1990 (model A4, Table 10.3A). However, this is only the case where ordinary OLS standard errors are calculated, and significance levels fall below even the 0.1 threshold in models based on robust standard errors for the post-1990 period (see model B4, Table 10.3B). Nevertheless, our analysis yields (at least, for the 1980s) some evidence of a protective regulation pattern characteristic of political economies characterised by strong left parties, but simultaneously exhibiting a lack of policy coordination due to a high degree of interest group pluralism.

Puzzling at least at first sight are the positive signs for the partial coefficient for the cabinet shares of Conservative and/or bourgeois parties for the post-1990 period (models B2 and B3 in Table 10.3B). However, the results are less puzzling if we bear in mind the consequences of changes in regulatory provisions in countries with high shares of right-of-centre parties in the 1990s: in these countries, the level of regulatory provisions was already comparatively low in 1990.[8] In other words, in many countries in which bourgeois parties were in office between 1990 and 2002, much less was left for the Right to do in terms of further privatisation and liberalisation initiatives. In contrast, the strong catch-up dynamic we find for the post-1990s period is partly a result of the fact that, in many countries in which left-of-centre parties were strong, levels of regulatory provisions were higher at the beginning of the decade. Indeed, the correlation between Social Democratic cabinet seats (1990–2002) and levels of regulatory provisions in 1990 was strong and positive (r=0.63). This does not necessarily suggest that the laggards of regulatory reforms in the 1980s became the leaders during the 1990s. Rather, in many OECD countries in the 1990s, there was much more left for the Left to do, in terms of pushing back market restrictive regulations, than there was left to the Right.

Two further results of our multivariate analyses are worth reporting, since they raise important questions about the role of two sets of variables, which have often been very important in quantitative accounts of public policy patterns relying on expenditure data. Neither trade openness nor our indicator of institutional pluralism came out as significant from our model specifications. Although we find the expected sign for our measure of institutional pluralism and the level of regulatory provisions in 1980 (r=−0.43, N=21), indicating that countries with a high degree of institutional pluralism also tended to have somewhat lower regulation scores than countries with highly centralised political systems, subsequent changes did not reflect a further braking effect on change generated by fragmented constitutional structures. In general, we found surprisingly weak empirical evidence for the impact of macro-institutional indicators on the reform of regulatory patterns in OECD member countries in the post-1980 era (cf. Bartle, 2002).

The other remarkable finding suggested by our bivariate and multivariate explorations of regulatory changes is the weak link between levels and changes in trade openness and levels and changes of regulation. There is one exception, which is not really all that surprising: for the relationship between trade openness and the OECD regulation measure of 'outward oriented policies' (or rather: regulations), we found the expected negative bivariate association of r=−0.51. For the broader indicators measuring levels and changes of sector-specific regulatory provisions and PMR, further analyses did not yield any evidence of a significant association between increasing trade openness and a decline in market-restricting regulatory provisions. What is worth noting, however, is that the relationship between levels of trade openness and regulatory provision in 1980 was positive, whereas the relationship with change was negative if not statistically significant. Heroic conclusions about the first signs of 'a race to the bottom tendency' on the basis of such a negative coefficient would be hazardous. Taken at face value, what we may possibly be seeing here are some signs of the correction of a formerly positive linkage, somewhat in the manner of the same reversal in core spending trends in the 1980s identified in Chapter 2's earlier overview of expenditure aggregates.

As already noted in the analysis of the changes of regulatory provision in the 1990s, a strong pattern of convergence, indicated by a statistically highly significant catch-up coefficient is the most remarkable finding. However, the international and transnational diffusion of ideas and paradigms in economic policy making, favouring market-enabling regulatory policy reforms and the increasing role of economic and political internationalisation, should not be prematurely ruled out as potentially important contextual factors conditioning the overall decline in regulatory provisions.

10.5   EMPIRICAL RESULTS: EMPLOYMENT PROTECTION LEGISLATION

The liberalisation and flexibilisation of employment rights has been a key issue on the reform agenda of most OECD countries during the 1990s (Nickell, 2003). In particular, the regulation of temporary employment contracts has become a major target of reform. The analysis of EPL deserves particular attention as it points to a welfare-related policy dimension, which only emerged as a central topic of comparative welfare state analysis in the late 1990s. However, the existence of socially protective labour law, defining the legal restrictions on the hiring and firing prerogatives of companies, might well be considered a central component of welfare state 'decommodification'. According to Esping-Andersen, who does not consider the regulation of employment law in the original version of his regime typology, but includes it in his subsequent work, employment protection legislation might even 'be regarded as the labour market equivalent to social citizenship rights' (Esping-Andersen, 1999: 122).

The analysis of EPL is important as employment protection contributes in various ways to the stratification of labour market outcomes. In countries with very rigid legislative systems, there are theoretical reasons for expecting insider–outsider problems and some empirical evidence to suggest their presence (OECD, 1999). Insider–outsider conflicts appear to be particularly strong if the scope and magnitude of employment protection differs between regular and other forms of employment contracts. The main dividing line runs between employment protection legislation for permanently employed 'core staff' and the weakness of such protection for employees in casual, part-time, fixed-term or other forms of precarious employment. However, as earlier in the case of PMR, we are not seeking to contribute to research on the effects of regulation, but rather to examine EPL as an important dimension of the regulatory pattern of modern economies and as a dependent variable in our study of the changing contours of government regulation.

In what follows, we will analyse data on employment protection legislation for which the OECD has provided a time-series dating back to 1985. From a public policy perspective that considers the dynamics of employment protection legislation mainly as an important dimension of changing regulation patterns, one finding is especially striking. As Table 10.4 reveals, during the 1990s, several OECD countries embarked on an asymmetric strategy of reducing the restrictiveness of EPL regimes, more or less exclusively liberalising temporary employment contracts. Between 1985 and 2003, the flexibilisation and deregulation of employment law for temporary employment contracts was particularly pronounced in Belgium, Denmark, Germany, Italy, the Netherlands and Sweden. For none of these countries do the OECD data provide evidence of a significant reduction of employment protection for regular employment. Advocates of this reform pattern tend to refer to such developments as 'targeted flexibilisation'. Opponents of the reforms interpret the outcome of this strategy of labour market segmentation as evidence of a process of asymmetric deregulation of employment rights.

As Table 10.4 presents data for a rather limited time period, it does not allow us to draw any conclusions about substantial dynamics of change before 1985. It is crucial to bear this in mind, as countries scoring low on employment protection levels in 1985, such as all Common Law countries, may well have undergone substantial liberalisations of their labour market regulations prior to that year.

For the two sub-measures as well as for the aggregate EPL measure, both indicators of convergence indicate a significant decline of variation over time. However, regardless of reduced variation, group-specific EPL profiles are still quite pronounced. In contrast to regulatory provisions affecting product markets, the dividing line runs more clearly between the English-speaking (Common Law) countries and the rest of the OECD world. Having said this, the decline of EPL in respect of temporary employment

Table 10.4   Employment protection legislation, 1985–2003

	Overall measure			Regular employment			Temporary employment		
	1985	2003	1985–2003	1985	2003	1985–2003	1985	2003	1985–2003
Australia	0.90	1.20	0.30	1.00	1.50	0.50	0.88	0.88	0.00
Austria	2.20	1.90	−0.30	2.92	2.37	−0.55	1.50	1.50	0.00
Belgium	3.20	2.20	−1.00	1.68	1.73	0.05	4.63	2.63	−2.00
Canada	0.80	0.80	0.00	1.32	1.32	0.00	0.25	0.25	0.00
Denmark	2.30	1.40	−0.90	1.52	1.47	−0.05	3.13	1.38	−1.75
Finland	2.30	2.00	−0.30	2.79	2.17	−0.62	1.88	1.88	0.00
France	2.79	3.00	0.21	2.51	2.47	−0.04	3.06	3.63	0.57
Germany	3.20	2.35	−0.85	2.58	2.68	0.10	3.75	2.03	−1.72
Greece	3.60	2.80	−0.80	2.46	2.41	−0.05	4.75	3.25	−1.50
Ireland	0.90	1.10	0.20	1.60	1.60	0.00	0.25	0.63	0.38
Italy	3.60	1.90	−1.70	1.77	1.77	0.00	5.38	2.13	−3.25
Japan	2.12	1.80	−0.32	2.44	2.44	0.00	1.80	1.25	−0.55
Netherlands	2.70	2.10	−0.60	3.08	3.05	−0.03	2.38	1.19	−1.19
New Zealand	0.90	1.50	0.60	1.35	1.70	0.35	0.38	1.25	0.87
Norway	2.90	2.60	−0.30	2.25	2.25	0.00	3.54	2.88	−0.66
Portugal	4.19	3.70	−0.49	5.00	4.33	−0.67	3.38	3.00	−0.38
Spain	3.80	3.10	−0.70	3.88	2.61	−1.27	3.75	3.50	−0.25
Sweden	3.50	2.20	−1.30	2.90	2.90	0.00	4.08	1.60	−2.48
Switzerland	1.10	2.20	1.10	1.16	2.86	1.70	1.13	1.63	0.50
UK	0.60	0.70	0.10	0.95	1.12	0.17	0.25	0.38	0.13
US	0.20	0.20	0.00	0.17	0.17	0.00	0.25	0.25	0.00
OECD mean (21)	2.28	1.94		2.16	2.14		2.40	1.77	
Coeff. Variation	0.54	0.44		0.51	0.40		0.70	0.59	
Catch–up coeff.			−0.74			−0.64			−0.80
Legal Families									
Common Law	0.72	0.92	0.20	1.07	1.24	0.17	0.38	0.61	0.23
Civic Law	2.90	2.35	−0.55	2.60	2.50	−0.10	3.21	2.23	−0.98
Scandinavian	2.75	2.05	−0.70	2.37	2.20	−0.17	3.16	1.94	−1.22
German	2.44	2.21	−0.23	2.31	2.55	0.24	2.59	1.93	−0.65
French	3.38	2.67	−0.71	2.99	2.66	−0.33	3.76	2.68	−1.08

Notes:
Indicator value range: 0–6, with *high* scores indicating restrictive employment protection legislation. All values shown are based on a set of disaggregated indicators measuring various components and dimensions of employment protection legislation, such as procedures for individual and collective dismissals, for severance payments and various other rules concerning hiring and firing. Data for New Zealand shown in 1985 column are values for 1990.
Catch-up: Shown is the correlation coefficient *r* measuring the strength of the statistical association between the levels of employment protection in 1985 and the change in EPL between 1985 and 2003.

Source and further information: Nicoletti et al. (2000: table A3.11 p. 84 and pp. 40–42), OECD: Employment Protection Time Series, Paris.

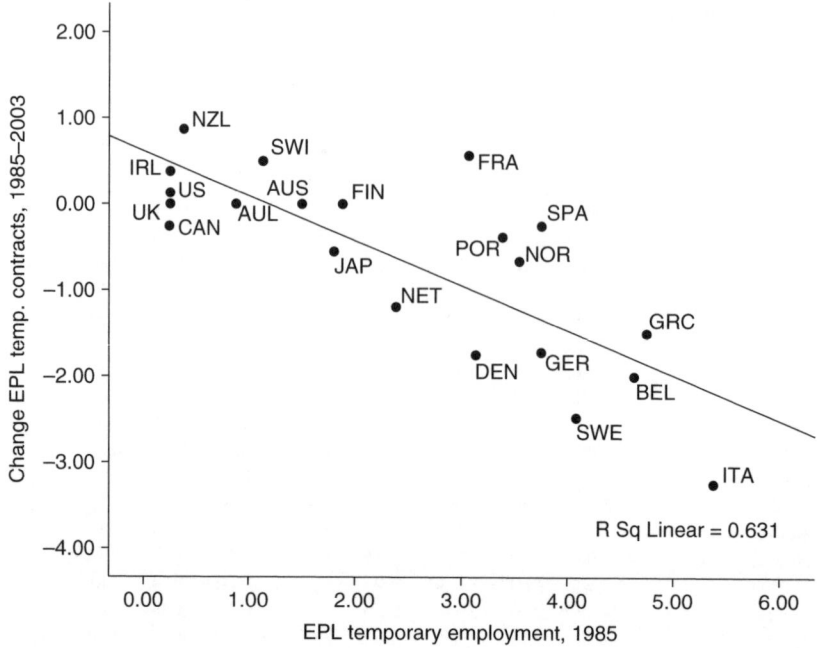

*Figure 10.3   Level of employment protection for temporary contracts in
1985 and changes, 1985–2003*

contracts between 1985 and 2003 is remarkable across all country groups,
including the EU countries,[9] although, because of the lack of change in
respect of permanent contracts, not as pronounced as in the area of
product market regulation.

When analysing the changes of EPL for the last two decades, one faces
the problem that changes in overall measures of employment protection
legislation are relatively small. Once again, this reflects the very limited
changes of the EPL indicators for regular employment for most countries.
Hence, in what follows, we will focus exclusively on changes in the indicator for *temporary work contracts*, as it is in this area that we find significant
changes (and variation) in our dependent variable.

As can be seen in Figure 10.3 and in Table 10.5, the findings for temporary employment contracts are broadly similar to the findings for regulatory provisions of product markets in the post-1990 period, with
convergence, by a long way, the most dominant trend. Apart from the
catch-up term, the interaction term between Left incumbency (1984–2002)
and interest group pluralism is the strongest factor. Model 6, in which both

Table 10.5 *Regression results, determinants of changes in EPL for temporary contracts*

	Change in EPL for temporary employment 1985–2003							
	Model 1	Model 2	Model 3	Model 4	Model 5	Model 6	Model 7	Model 8
Constant term	0.616***	0.726***	0.932***	0.591**	0.570***	1.695**	0.686***	0.636***
	(3.46)	(2.15)	(2.91)	(3.79)	(3.81)	(4.05)	(3.10)	(3.52)
Level of EPL temp. 1985	−0.520***	−0.542***	−0.570***	−0.672***	−0.733***	−0.730***	−0.528***	−0.527***
	(−5.94)	(−4.82)	(−5.72)	(−6.49)	(−7.67)	(−7.77)	(−5.71)	(−6.05)
Cabinet seat shares, Conservative parties (1984–2002)		−0.002						
		(−0.44)						
Cabinet seat shares, bourgeois parties (1984–2002)			−0.004					
			(−1.05)					
Cabinet seat shares, Social Democratic parties (1984–2002)				0.013				
				(1.32)				
Cabinet seat shares, left parties (1984–2002)					0.018*			
					(1.87)			
Interaction cabinet seat shares left parties*interest group pluralism (1984–2002)						0.007		
						(3.35)***		
Trade openness (1984–2002)							−0.004	
							(−0.98)	
Institutional pluralism								−0.073
								(−0.57)
R^2	0.63	0.63	0.64	0.68	0.72	0.80	0.64	0.64
F	35.26	17.27	18.03	36.80	50.01	31.86	17.33	18.34

Notes: Shown are unstandardised regression coefficients and t-values based on robust standard errors as calculated by STATA 9.0 in parentheses; * $p \leq 0.1$; ** $p \leq 0.05$; *** $p \leq 0.01$.

are included, explains exactly 80 per cent of the variation in the change of EPL for temporary contract between 1985 and 2003.

The coefficient for Left cabinet seats (1984–2002) is significant (at the 0.1 threshold) even if we do not take into consideration the interest group system indicator. The share of Conservative governments and bourgeois parties show the expected signs, but do not pass conventional significance tests. As in the case of product market regulation, this lack of a statistically significant relationship is not that surprising if we take into consideration that the level of EPL in 1985 was negatively correlated with cabinet seats of the major parties of the Right in the post-1985 period (r = −0.68).

Measures of trade openness and institutional pluralism are insignificant, suggesting that neither state structures nor dependence on international trade have decisively shaped the scope of change in temporary employment regulations. The same holds for socio-economic variables like the level of the unemployment rate, suggesting that, from a purely cross-national perspective, variable patterns of change in EPL were not a response to different levels of reform pressure. However, we are aware that genuine times-series analysis might arrive at different results, as it is the country-specific experience of increasing unemployment (regardless of unemployment levels in other countries) which should be regarded as the major push factor in the liberalisation of fixed work contracts.

10.6   DISCUSSION AND CONCLUSION

Compared to earlier findings in this volume, our quantitative analysis of regulatory provisions of product markets and employment protection legislation reveals both similarities and differences:

1. Similarly to the findings regarding changes in 'core expenditure' and those relating to expenditure for subsidies and economic affairs, we have found striking evidence of convergent patterns of product market regulation, most remarkably for the post-1990 period.
2. This descriptive finding is closely related to an analytical one. According to our multivariate analyses of multidimensional quantitative OECD regulation indices, political factors have become much less important in determining changes in the scope of government regulation than they were in the 1980s. Changes in the scope of government regulation in the 1990s were mainly driven by a dynamic of convergence amounting to what may be described as a 'catch-down' process. However, a question we have not addressed systematically is how statistically significant coefficients for convergence can be supplied with a

theoretically substantive explanation or causal mechanism. One plausible explanatory framework emphasises the increasing relevance of the transnational diffusion of a supply-side economic policy paradigm which, although filtered through national political institutions and processes, has resulted in somewhat convergent regulatory reform patterns. Establishing whether this was so was beyond the scope of the exploratory and quantitative exercise we have undertaken in this chapter. It is a matter that could probably only be properly addressed by qualitative studies capable of analysing changes in policy discourses.

3. According to the OECD measures we have used throughout this chapter, the trend towards less market-restrictive regulation is weaker in the domain of employment protection legislation than in that of product market regulation. Although a convergent dynamic was also identified for the EPL measure for temporary work contracts, our findings suggest that political factors remain somewhat more salient in this welfare state-related area of social regulation. What are particularly striking are the asymmetric policy reform paths characterising EPL reforms in most OECD countries. While EPL for temporary work contracts has been liberalised in most OECD countries, in the majority of countries, EPL for regular employment contracts has not been dismantled. As a consequence of this selective reform trend, the insider–outsider segmentation of OECD labour markets has been further increased. However, the advocates of this reform dynamic suggest that this asymmetric development should not be criticised as a further segmentation of labour law, but rather argue that it reflects a selective flexibilisation of regulatory provisions, improving the employment opportunities of the long-term unemployed and other disadvantaged jobseekers, at least in the long run.

Overall, our findings suggest similarly distinct patterns of change when comparing different domains of regulation, as does the comparison of changes in social expenditure with non-social expenditure dynamics. The increasing role of market-enabling 'reregulation' and the decline of market-restricting regulatory patterns has been much stronger in the area of product market regulation than in the case of employment protection legislation. Again, we may conclude that welfare-related policies have been more resilient to changes than policies affected by an epochal paradigm shift in economic policy. As we have focused on a rather narrow set of quantitative indicators measuring the extent of market-restricting regulation in only one area of social regulation, our findings are preliminary and it is quite possible that they are not representative of more general patterns of change in social regulation concerning, for example, health and safety regulation.

Because of our relatively narrow focus on quantitative indicators, we have ignored questions which are related to the qualitative dimension of regulatory reforms. Thus it is important to note that, although our findings suggest convergent dynamics towards less market-restricting and more competition-enabling regulation of product markets, this does not necessarily mean that the outcome of regulatory reform processes is less state regulation per se or that national styles of regulation no longer matter at all. Moderately distinctive country patterns of economic regulation still persist despite the strong dynamic of convergence-dominating trends in regulatory reform since about 1990. Even in an area like the telecommunications sector, where the convergent dynamic from monopoly to competition has been particularly striking, the institutional set-up of national regulatory agencies still differs considerably across countries (Tenbücken and Schneider, 2004). Thus our results should not be misinterpreted as evidence for the proposition that national regulation profiles have been completely eroded. However, what our quantitative exploration of product market regulation clearly does suggest is that the 1990s have witnessed a profound turn towards more market-complementary government regulation. The future will prove whether and when we may witness a more profound spillover effect towards one of the last bastions of market-restricting regulatory policy regimes: national welfare states.

NOTES

1. The author would like to express his gratitude to Francis G. Castles for his editorial input and helpful comments on successive drafts.
2. As Hood et al. (1999: 3) have rightly pointed out, regulation is 'a much used word rarely defined with precision, but broadly denoting the use of public authority (often in the hands of specialized agencies) to set and apply rules and standards'. For a discussion of alternative definitions of regulation, see Baldwin et al. (1998).
3. Once more, exceptions prove the rule: see, for instance, the data collected in a research project chaired by Volker Schneider at the University of Konstanz, measuring different dimensions of privatisation in various economic sectors for 26 OECD countries and the period 1970–2000/01 (Schneider and Tenbücken, 2004). Botero et al. (2004) have collected and analysed data on labour law in 85 countries.
4. For 21 OECD countries, the correlation between the level of product market regulation and employment protection legislation in 2003 is $r=0.76$ (i.e. it is significant at the 0.01 threshold). One economic theorem proposes that companies in highly regulated product markets can afford higher levels of employment protection legislation and still break even. A second, related, explanation focuses on preferences of workers and suggests that in highly regulated product markets employees tend to prefer high levels of employment protection, one reason being their difficulties in finding new jobs in the case of unemployment (Königer and Vindigni, 2003).

5. On the details of the OECD product market regulation indicator system, see Nicoletti et al. (2000) and Conway et al. (2005). I am grateful to Mr Paul Conway, OECD, for further clarifications based on a personal interview in March 2005 and written correspondence.
6. In the Antipodean countries it was the Labour parties which initiated major regulatory reform steps.
7. This might partly be a consequence of the decision to regress on changes over quite long time periods of ten and 13 years. We did not use pooled times-series in our analysis for this chapter, basically because of the data structure of the dependent variable. Quite similarly to the analysis of changes in annual government expenditure, a time-series analysis might report more evidence for a statistically significant economic performance or debt indicator.
8. This is reflected in the negative relationship between the level of regulatory provisions in 1990 and the cabinet shares of Conservative parties for the period 1990–2002, r=−0.51.
9. As in the case of product market regulation, it would be highly plausible to consider EU membership as a major explanatory factor. However, because we analyse cross-sections across rather extended time periods rather than short times-series units, the impact of the EU cannot be a major concern of our analysis.

REFERENCES

Baldwin, R., C. Scott and C. Hood (eds) (1998), 'Introduction', in R. Baldwin, C. Scott and C. Hood (eds), *A Reader on Regulation*, Oxford: Oxford University Press, pp. 1–55.

Bartle, I. (2002), 'When institutions no longer matter: reform of telecommunications and electricity in Germany, France and Britain', *Journal of Public Policy*, **22**(1), 1–27.

Botero, J.C., S. Djankov, R. La Porta, F. Lopez-de-Silanes and A. Shleifer (2004), 'The Regulation of Labour', *Quarterly Journal of Economics*, **119**(4), 1339–82.

Cameron, D. (1978), 'The expansion of the public economy: a comparative analysis', *American Political Science Review*, **72**(4), 1243–61.

Castles, F.G. (1998), *Comparative Public Policy: Patterns of Post-war Transformation*, Cheltenham, UK and Lyme, USA: Edward Elgar.

Conway, P., V. Janod and G. Nicoletti (2005), 'Product Market Regulation in OECD Countries, 1998 to 2003', OECD Economics Department, Working Paper no. 419, OECD, Paris.

Esping-Andersen, G. (1999), *Social Foundations of Postindustrial Societies*, Oxford: Oxford University Press.

Hall, P. (1989), *The Political Power of Economic Ideas: Keynesianism across Nations*, Princeton: Princeton University Press.

Hood, C., O. James, G. Jones, C. Scott and T. Travers (eds) (1999), *Regulation Inside Government. Waste-Watchers, Quality Police, and Sleazebusters*, Oxford: Oxford University Press.

Jochem, S. and N.A. Siegel (2004), 'Staat und Markt in internationalen Vergleich. Empirische Mosaicksteine eines facettenreichen Arbeitsbeziehung', in R. Czada and R. Zintl, *Politik und Markt, Politische Vierteljahresschritt*, Sonderheft 34, Wiesbaden: Verlag für Sozialwissenschaften, pp. 351–88.

Königer, W. and A. Vindigni (2003), 'Employment Protection and Product Market Regulation', Institute for the Study of Labour, Discussion Paper 800, Bonn.

La Porta, R., F. Lopez-de-Silanes and A. Shleifer (1998), 'Corporate ownership around the world', *Journal of Finance*, **54**(2), 471–517.

Layard, R., S. Nickell and R. Jackman (2005), *Unemployment: Macroeconomic Performance and the Labour Market*, 2nd edn, Oxford: Oxford University Press.

Levi-Faur, D. (2005), 'The global diffusion of regulatory capitalism', *The Annals of the American Academy of Political and Social Science*, **598**, 12–32.

Majone, G. (1994), 'The rise of the regulatory state in Europe', *West European Politics*, **17**, 77–101.

Majone, G. (1997), 'From the positive to the regulatory state: causes and consequences in the change of governance', *Journal of Public Policy*, **17**(2), 139–67.

Moran, M. (2002), 'Understanding the regulatory state', *British Journal of Political Science*, **32**, 391–413.

Nickell, Stephen (2003), 'Labour market institutions and unemployment in OECD countries', CESifo DICE report 2/2003, London.

Nicoletti, G. and S. Scarpetta (2003), 'Regulation, productivity and growth. OECD evidence', *Economic Policy*, **April**, 9–72.

Nicoletti, G., S. Scarpetta and O. Boylaud (2000), 'Summary Indicators of Product Market Regulation with an Extension to Employment Protection Legislation', Economics Department Working Papers, no. 226, OECD, Paris.

OECD (1999), *Employment Outlook*, Paris: OECD

OECD (2002), *Regulatory Reforms in OECD Countries*, Paris: OECD.

OECD *International Regulation Data Base*, Paris: OECD.

Ogus, A. (1994), *Regulation: Legal Form and Economic Theory*, Oxford: Clarendon Press.

Richardson, J. (1994), 'Doing less by doing more: British government 1979–1993', *West European Politics*, **17**(3), 176–97.

Samek Lodovici, M. (2000), 'The dynamics of labour market reform in European countries', in G. Esping-Andersen and M. Regini (eds), *Why Deregulate Labour Markets?*, Oxford: Oxford University Press, pp. 30–65.

Schmidt, M.G. (1993), 'Theorien in der vergleichenden Staatstätigkeitsforschung', in A. Héritier (ed.), *Policy-Analyse* (PVS Sonderheft 24), Opladen: Westdeutscher Verlag, pp. 371–94.

Schneider, V. and M. Tenbücken (eds) (2004), *Der Staat auf dem Rückzug. Die Privatisierung öffentlicher Infrastrukturen*, Frankfurt a.M.: Campus.

Stigler, G.J. (1971), 'The theory of economic regulation', *Bell Journal of Economics and Management Science*, **2**, 3–21.

Tenbücken, M. and V. Schneider (2004), 'Divergent convergence: structures and functions of national regulatory authorities in the telecommunications sector', in J. Jordana and D. Levi-Faur (eds), *The Politics of Regulation. Institutions and Regulatory Reforms in the Age of Governance*, Cheltenham, UK and Northampton, MA, USA: Edward Elgar, pp. 245–67.

Vogel, S.K. (1996), *Freer Markets, More Rules. Regulatory Reform in Advanced Industrial Countries*, Ithaca: Cornell University Press.

Wright, V. and W. Müller (eds) (1994), 'The State in Western Europe: Retreat or Redefinition?', Special Issue of *West European Politics*, **17**(3).

Index

administrative complexity, *see* institutional pluralism

ageing population, *see* demographic factors

aggregate core spending, residual estimates 5–8

aircraft, *see* fixed-wing combat aircraft

aircraft carriers, costs 119, 121

Alesina indicator, *see* political stability

armed forces, *see* military personnel

arms race
  and military spending 109, 112, 113
  see also Cold War

Augustine, N.R. 119, 121

Australia
  core spending 23, 25, 56, 57, 68
  economic regulation 247, 255, 261, 265, 266
  economic services spending 56, 68
  educational spending 56, 68, 160, 164, 170, 173, 175, 179, 180
  general public services spending 56, 68
  industrial subsidies 192, 193, 209, 211
  military spending 56, 68, 108, 120
  public debt 56, 68, 220, 223, 226
  public order and safety spending 137, 138, 139
  social spending 22, 55, 56, 68
  state overhead spending 90, 92, 95–7

Austria
  conscription in 115
  core spending 23, 25, 55, 56, 57, 64, 68, 70
  economic affairs/services spending 56, 68, 70, 187, 189, 192, 193, 194, 196, 209, 211
  economic regulation 247, 255, 261, 265, 266
  educational spending 56, 68, 70, 160, 164, 170, 173, 179

general public services spending 56, 68, 70

military spending 56, 68, 70, 108, 111

public debt 56, 62, 68, 81, 220, 223, 225, 226

public order and safety spending 70, 135, 137, 138, 139, 155

social spending 22, 55, 56, 68, 70

state overhead spending 81, 82, 86, 89, 90, 92, 93, 98

battle tanks, statistics 117–18, 120

Baumol's disease 121, 124

Belgium
  conscription in 115
  core spending 23, 25, 61, 64, 70
  economic affairs/services spending 61, 70, 187, 189, 192, 193, 194, 196, 209, 211
  economic regulation 247, 255, 261, 264, 265, 266
  educational spending 61, 70, 160, 164, 170, 173, 179
  general public services spending 61, 70
  military spending 61, 70, 108, 111, 120, 126
  public debt 61, 62, 81, 216, 219, 220, 221, 222, 223, 226
  public order and safety spending 61, 70, 135, 137, 155
  public spending 55
  social spending 22, 61, 70
  state overhead spending 81, 82, 86, 89, 90, 91, 92, 93, 98

bomber aircraft, *see* fixed-wing combat aircraft

borrowing, *see* public debt

bourgeois parties, *see* Right partisanship

budgetary trade-offs, *see* trade-offs

Canada
  core spending 23, 25
  economic regulation 247, 255, 261,
    265, 266
  educational spending 160, 164, 170,
    173, 175, 177, 179, 180
  industrial subsidies 192, 193, 209,
    211
  military spending 108, 111, 120, 126
  public debt 220, 223, 225, 226
  social spending 22
  state overhead spending 90, 95–6
capital equipment (military) 116–19,
  119, 120, 121–6, 129
capital markets, and industrial
  subsidies 201, 205
catch-up/catch-down, *see* convergence
central bank independence, and public
  debt 232, 237, 238
civil law countries, and regulation 253,
  256, 265
COFOG (Classification of the
  Functions of Government)
  background 8–10, 44, 48–50
  categories 50–51, 52–4, 59, 60
  data
    1980s 54–7
    1990s+ 58–64
    validity of 52–3, 57, 58–61, 63, 65
  economic affairs category 186–8
  general public services category 75–6
  new classification 50–52, 59
  public order and safety category
    134–6, 156
Cold War
  military effects 60, 104, 107, 109, 114
  see also arms race; Soviet Union/
    Russia; Warsaw Pact
common law countries, and regulation
  253–4, 256, 257, 264, 265
conscription 114–16
consensual government 146, 147, 230,
  232; *see also* institutional
  pluralism
Conservative Party (UK), and public
  order and safety spending 146
Continental Europe, *see* Western
  Europe (continental)
contract employment, *see* temporary
  employment

convergence
  of debt interest payments 225, 241
  of economic affairs/services
    spending 187, 188, 191–3, 194,
    195, 205
  of educational spending 168–9, 170
  measurement of 186
  of military spending 112, 113
  of public spending 14–15, 21, 26–7,
    32, 41
  of regulation 254, 256, 257–8, 261,
    262, 263, 264–6
  of social spending 21
  of state overhead spending 82, 83
core spending
  data validity 57
  definition 55, 63
  and Left cabinet seats 34, 35, 38
  minus debt interest payments 24, 25,
    37–9, 55, 57, 64
  and policy inheritance 34, 38
  and public debt 34, 36–7, 38–9, 40
  residual estimates 5–8
  socio-economic factors 32, 34, 36
  statistics, sources 4–11
  trade factors 16, 30–31, 34, 35, 37–8,
    40
  trends 20–26, 55–7, 61, 64, 68–74
  see also economic affairs; economic
    services; educational spending;
    general government services;
    military spending; public debt
    interest payments; social
    spending
corporatism 200, 203, 205, 208, 232, 234
credibility, and public debt 229,
  230–31, 232, 233, 236, 237, 238,
  239, 240
criminal justice, *see* public order and
  safety spending; recorded crime;
  violent crime
crowding out 169, 173–4, 238–9; *see
  also* trade-offs

debt, *see* public debt
decentralisation, *see* fiscal
  decentralisation; institutional
  pluralism
defence spending, *see* military
  spending

deindustrialisation 33, 35, 36, 39, 167, 198, 205
democratisation, and educational spending 169, 170, 176, 177
demographic factors
  and core spending 34, 36
  and educational spending 167
  and military spending 128
  and public debt 232, 234, 235, 237, 238, 239, 240
Denmark
  conscription in 115
  core spending 23, 25, 55, 56, 57, 61, 64, 68, 70
  economic affairs/services spending 56, 61, 70, 187, 189, 192, 193, 194, 196, 209, 211
  economic regulation 247, 255, 261, 264, 265, 266
  educational spending 56, 60, 61, 68, 70, 160, 164, 170, 173, 179
  general public services spending 56, 61, 68, 70
  military spending 56, 61, 68, 70, 108, 111, 120, 126
  public debt 56, 61, 62, 68, 81, 220, 223, 226
  public order and safety spending 61, 70, 135, 137, 138, 139, 155
  social spending 22, 55, 56, 61, 68, 70
  state overhead spending 81, 82, 89, 90, 91, 92, 93, 98
development aid, *see* overseas aid
disposal of military equipment 121
Domar model of debt interest payments 241

Eastern Europe, *see* Soviet Union/ Russia
economic affairs spending
  background 184–5
  convergence 187, 188, 191–3, 194, 195, 205
  and product market regulation 246–7
  statistics, sources 186, 190
  trends 60, 61, 70–74, 186–8, 189
  see also industrial subsidies
economic growth
  and core spending 34

  and educational spending 169, 170, 176, 177
  and industrial subsidies 198–9, 202, 203, 205
  and public debt 232, 233, 235, 236, 238, 239, 240
  and regulation 259, 260
  and social spending 33
economic regulation, *see* regulation
economic services spending 55, 56, 68–9
economic slowdown 27–8, 258
Education at a Glance (OECD) 51–2, 162
education levels, and public order and safety spending 142, 143–4, 149, 150, 151, 152, 153–4
educational spending
  expansion patterns 164–5, 177–8, 179–80
  factors in
    convergence 168–9, 170
    crowding out 169, 173–4
    democratisation 169, 170, 176, 177
    families of nations 171, 176
    federalism 173
    fiscal decentralisation 169, 172–3, 177
    policy inheritance 167, 169
    political partisanship 167, 169, 171–2, 173, 176, 177
    private spending 169, 175–6, 177
    problem-solving routines 169, 172, 177
    public debt 173–4
    public spending 169
    social spending 169, 174
    socio-economic 166, 167, 169, 170, 176, 177
    trade-related 167, 169, 174
  and military spending 128
  retrenchment patterns 164–5, 166, 171, 175, 176–7, 178–80
  statistics
    data validity 45, 51–2
    methodology 178–9
    sources 162
  trends 159–62, 163–6, 170, 173
    1980s 55, 56, 60, 68–9, 160–61, 164–5

1990s+ 60, 61, 70–74, 159, 160–61,
164–5
employment
labour costs 124
and public spending 46
and state overhead spending 89–91,
92, 94–5, 98
see also military personnel;
unemployment; wages
employment protection regulation
convergence in 264–6
and insider–outsider conflicts 263–4,
269
measures 249
trends 264, 265–6, 269
see also temporary employment
English-speaking countries
core spending 23, 24–5
economic affairs/services spending
191, 192
educational spending 162, 171, 176
public debt 40, 225, 226
public order and safety spending 138
social spending 22, 24–5
state overhead spending 83, 97, 101
trade dependency 40
see also Australia; Canada; common
law countries; Ireland; New
Zealand; United Kingdom;
United States
ethno-linguistic fragmentation; *see*
minority ethnic groups
European Monetary Union 201–2,
205, 222, 227, 232; *see also*
Maastricht criteria
*European Sourcebook on Crime and
Criminal Justice* 134
European Stability and Growth Pact
227
European Union/Commission, and
state aid 193–7, 201, 205, 210–211
exchange rate, and public debt 232, 238
exports, *see* trade dependency

families of nations, *see* English-
speaking countries; Scandinavia;
Southern Europe; Western Europe
federalism 85, 86–7, 96, 97, 173, 232;
see also institutional pluralism
female labour force, effects 33, 36

fighter aircraft, *see* fixed-wing combat
aircraft
Finland
conscription in 115
core spending 23, 25, 55, 56, 57, 61,
64, 68, 70
economic affairs/services spending
56, 61, 68, 70, 187, 189, 192,
193, 194, 195, 196, 209, 211
economic regulation 247, 255, 261,
265, 266
economic services spending 56, 68
educational spending 61, 70, 160,
162, 164, 170, 173, 179
general public services spending 56,
61, 68, 70
military spending 56, 61, 68, 70, 108,
111
public debt 56, 61, 62, 68, 81, 220,
223, 226
public order and safety spending 61,
70, 135, 137, 138, 139, 155
social spending 22, 55, 56, 61, 68, 70
state overhead spending 81, 82, 89,
90, 91, 93, 98
fiscal decentralisation 169, 172–3, 177
Fisher parity, and interest rates 217
fixed-wing combat aircraft 118, 119,
120, 122–4, 125
foreign aid, *see* overseas aid
fragmented government, *see*
federalism; institutional pluralism
France
conscription in 115
core spending 23, 25, 64, 71
economic affairs/services spending
71, 187, 189, 192, 193, 194, 196,
209, 211
economic regulation 247, 255, 261,
265, 266
educational spending 71, 160, 164,
170, 173, 179
general public services spending 71
military spending 71, 108, 111, 118,
120
public debt, 1990s+ 62, 81, 220, 223,
226
public order and safety spending 71,
135, 155
social spending 22, 71

state overhead spending 81, 82, 89, 90, 91–2, 93, 98, 99

GDP
and public debt 232, 233, 240
and public order and safety spending 142–3, 145
general public services spending
data validity 53
definition 75–6, 79–80
trends 55, 56, 61, 62, 68–9, 70–74, 81, 81–2
see also public debt; state overhead spending
Germany
conscription in 115
core spending 23, 25, 56, 57, 61, 64, 68, 71
economic affairs/services spending 56, 61, 68, 71, 187, 189, 192, 193, 194, 196, 209, 211
economic regulation 247, 255, 261, 264, 265, 266
educational spending 45, 56, 60, 61, 68, 71, 160, 162, 164, 170, 173, 174, 175–6, 179
general public services spending 56, 61, 68, 71
military spending 56, 61, 68, 71, 108, 111, 118, 120, 126
public debt 56, 61, 62, 68, 81, 220, 221, 223, 225, 226
public order and safety spending 61, 71, 135, 137, 138, 139, 155
public spending 55, 56, 61, 68, 71
social spending 22, 26, 55, 56, 61, 68, 71
state overhead spending 81, 82, 89, 90, 91, 98
Global Terrorism Index 155
globalisation
and core spending 16, 30–31, 35
and educational spending 167, 174
and industrial subsidies 201, 205, 210, 211–12
and public debt 231, 232
and public spending 32
and regulation 254, 258, 259, 260, 262–3, 267, 268
and social spending 35

and state overhead spending 84, 86, 87–8, 99
see also trade dependency
Government Finance Statistics Yearbooks (IMF) 49
Great Britain, *see* United Kingdom
Greece
conscription in 115
core spending 23, 25, 61, 64, 71
economic affairs/services spending 61, 71, 187, 189, 192, 193, 194, 196, 209, 211
economic regulation 247, 255, 261, 265, 266
educational spending 61, 71, 160, 164, 170, 173, 178, 179
general public services spending 61, 71
military spending 61, 71, 108, 111, 120, 126
public debt 61, 62, 81, 216, 220, 222, 223, 224, 226
public order and safety spending 71, 135, 155
social spending 22, 61, 71
state overhead spending 81, 82, 89, 90, 91, 92, 98
gross domestic product, *see* GDP
gross public debt interest payments 219, 222, 225, 227, 236, 240

health spending
COFOG categories 60
and military spending 128
trends 55, 56, 60, 61, 68–9, 70–74
homicide levels, and public order and safety spending 140, 141
household income, and public order and safety spending 142, 143, 145, 151
housing spending 56, 60, 61, 68–9, 70–74

Iceland
core spending 61, 71
economic affairs/services spending 61, 71, 187, 189
educational spending 61, 71
general public services spending 71
military spending 71

public debt, 1990s+ 62, 63, 220, 223,
    226
public order and safety spending 61,
    71, 135, 137, 138, 139
social spending 61, 71
IMF, *Government Finance Statistics
    Yearbooks* 49
imports, *see* trade dependency
imprisonment, *see* prisons
income, *see* GDP; household income
income per capita, and military
    spending 112, 113, 128
income transfers, trends 55, 56, 60,
    68–9
industrial subsidies
    convergence 191–3, 194, 195, 205
    factors in
        capital markets 201, 205
        EU/EMU regulations 201–2, 205,
            210–211
        globalisation 201, 205, 210,
            211–12
        institutional pluralism 199–200,
            202, 203, 205, 206, 208, 210,
            211
        interest groups 200, 202, 203, 205,
            208
        policy inheritance 197–8, 203, 205,
            206
        political partisanship 199, 202,
            203, 205–6, 208–210
        public debt 199, 201–2, 204–5,
            207, 208, 212
        socio-economic 198–9, 202, 203,
            205
    refocusing 195, 197
    trends
        EU 193–7
        OECD 188–93
inequality 143–4, 147–8, 150, 152, 153;
    see also threat index
inflation, *see* price inflation
insider–outsider conflicts 263–4, 269;
    see also temporary employment
institutional factors, in public debt 230,
    231, 232, 235, 236, 240
institutional pluralism
    and industrial subsidies 199–200,
        202, 203, 205, 206, 208, 210, 211
    and public debt 230, 231

and regulation 252–3, 258, 259, 260,
    262, 267, 268
and state overhead spending 84, 85,
    86–7, 91–2, 96, 97, 99
see also consensual government;
    federalism
interest, *see* public debt interest
interest groups
    and industrial subsidies 200, 202,
        203, 205, 208
    and public debt 229–30, 232, 234
    and regulation 259, 260, 261–2, 266,
        267
International Crime Victim Survey 140
International Monetary Fund, *see*
    IMF
international trade, *see* globalisation;
    trade dependency
Ireland
    core spending 23, 25, 61, 64, 72
    economic affairs/services spending
        61, 72, 187, 189, 192, 193, 194,
        196, 209, 211
    economic regulation 246, 247, 255,
        261, 265, 266
    educational spending 61, 72, 160,
        164, 170, 173, 177, 179
    female labour force participation
        36
    general public services spending 61,
        72
    military spending 61, 72, 108, 111
    public debt, 1990s+ 61, 62, 81, 220,
        222, 223, 226
    public order and safety spending 61,
        72, 135, 137, 138, 139, 155
    public spending 55
    social spending 22, 36, 61, 72
    state overhead spending 81, 82, 89,
        90, 91, 93, 98
Italy
    conscription in 115
    core spending 23, 25, 61, 64, 72
    economic affairs/services spending
        61, 72, 187, 189, 192, 193, 194,
        196, 209, 211
    economic regulation 247, 256, 261,
        264, 265, 266
    educational spending 61, 72, 160,
        164, 170, 173, 179

general public services spending 61, 72

military spending 61, 72, 108, 111, 120, 126

public debt 61, 62, 81, 216, 219, 220, 221, 222, 223, 224, 226

public order and safety spending 61, 72, 135, 137, 155

social spending 22, 61, 72

state overhead spending 81, 82, 89, 90, 91, 93, 98

Japan 222, 225
  core spending 23, 25, 55, 56, 57, 61, 64, 68, 72
  economic affairs/services spending 56, 61, 68, 72, 187, 189, 192, 193, 209
  economic regulation 247, 256, 261, 265, 266
  educational spending
    private spending 175
    trends 61, 160, 162, 164, 170, 173, 177, 179
    trends (1980s) 60, 68, 160, 164
    trends (1990s+) 60, 61, 72, 160, 164
  general public services spending 56, 61, 68, 72
  military spending 56, 61, 68, 72, 108, 110, 111, 120
  public debt 56, 61, 62, 63, 68, 220, 222, 223, 224, 225, 226
  public order and safety spending 61, 72, 135, 137, 138, 139, 155
  social spending 22, 55, 56, 61, 68, 72

Keynes, J.M., on public debt 217, 218

labour market, *see* employment; employment protection regulation; female labour force; wages

Left cabinet seats
  and core spending 34, 35, 38
  and educational spending 167
  and industrial subsidies 199, 202, 203, 205–6, 208–210
  and public order and safety spending 146, 149, 150, 152, 153

and regulation 252, 259, 260, 261–2, 266, 267, 268

and social spending 33, 35

Left partisanship
  and public debt 229, 232, 235
  and public order and safety spending 145–7
  and public spending 29–30, 32
  and state overhead spending 85

legal traditions, and regulation 253–4, 256, 257, 259, 260, 264, 265

Lerner, A., on public debt 218

Luxembourg
  core spending 61, 64, 72
  economic affairs/services spending 61, 72, 187, 189, 194, 196
  educational spending 61, 72
  general public services spending 61, 72
  military spending 61, 72
  public debt 61, 62, 81, 219, 220, 221, 223, 226
  public order and safety spending 61, 72, 135, 155
  social spending 61, 72
  state overhead spending 81, 82, 89, 90, 92, 98

Maastricht criteria 227, 229; *see also* European Monetary Union

major surface combat vessels, statistics 116–17, 120

market-enabling regulation 248

military personnel
  conscription 114–16
  costs 90–91, 124, 126
  recruitment problems 129
  trends 113–16

military spending
  budgetary trade-offs 127–8
  capital equipment 116–19, 119, 120, 121–6, 129
  and conscription 116
  convergence 112, 113
  downward pressures 109–110
  and educational spending 128
  factors in
    arms race 109, 112, 113
    Cold War 60, 104, 107, 109
    demographic 128

income per capita 112, 113, 128
political partisanship 128
public debt 110, 112
trade-related 110, 112, 113
and social spending 105, 127, 128
statistics
   data validity 51–2
   sources 103–4, 116
   World War II 104
trends 104–9
   1980s 55, 56, 68–9, 105, 106–9,
      110–112
   1990s+ 60, 61, 70–74, 105, 106,
      107–8, 109, 110–112
minority ethnic groups, and public
   order and safety spending 142,
   144, 149, 150, 151–2, 153
misery index, and public debt 235
modernisation, of military equipment,
   costs 121
multi-party governments, *see*
   consensual government
multiple administrative units, *see*
   federalism; institutional pluralism

NATO, military personnel, costs 91
naval forces
   statistics 116–17, 120
   see also aircraft carriers
Netherlands
   conscription in 115
   core spending 23, 25, 55, 56, 57, 64,
      69, 73
   economic affairs/services spending
      56, 69, 73, 187, 189, 192, 193,
      194, 196, 209, 211
   economic regulation 247, 256, 261,
      264, 265, 266
   educational spending 56, 69, 73, 160,
      162, 164, 170, 173, 174, 179
   female labour force participation 36
   general public services spending 56,
      69, 73
   military spending 56, 69, 73, 108,
      111, 120, 126
   public debt 56, 62, 69, 81, 220, 223,
      226
   public order and safety spending 73,
      135, 137, 138, 139, 155
   public spending 56, 69, 73

social spending 22, 36, 55, 56, 69, 73
state overhead spending 81, 82, 86,
   89, 90, 91, 92, 93, 98
new politics
   and public spending 35, 36, 39
   and retrenchment 28–30
new social risks, and social spending
   28–9, 36
New Zealand
   economic regulation 256, 261, 265,
      266
   educational spending 160, 164, 170,
      173, 175, 177, 179, 180
   industrial subsidies 192, 193, 209, 211
   public debt 220, 222, 223, 226
   public order and safety spending
      137, 138, 139
   state overhead spending 90
non-social spending, *see* core spending
Nordic countries, *see* Scandinavia
Norway
   conscription in 115
   core spending 55, 56, 57, 61, 64, 69,
      73
   economic affairs/services spending
      56, 61, 69, 73, 187, 189, 191,
      192, 193, 209, 211
   economic regulation 247, 256, 261,
      265, 266
   educational spending 56, 60, 61, 69,
      73, 160, 162, 164, 170, 173, 179
   general public services spending 56,
      61, 69, 73
   military spending 56, 61, 69, 73, 108,
      111, 120, 126
   public debt 222, 225
      1980s 56, 69, 221
      1990s+ 61, 62, 81, 219, 220, 221,
         223, 226
   public order and safety spending 61,
      73, 135, 137, 138, 139, 155
   social spending 55, 56, 61, 69, 73
   state overhead spending 81, 82, 89,
      90, 91, 92, 98
nuclear weapons, US primacy in 116

OECD
   Education at a Glance 51–2, 162
   Social Spending Database 6, 48
   state aid, trends 188–93

OECD countries
military personnel trends 114
military spending 106–7
see also Australia; Austria; Belgium;
Canada; Denmark; Finland;
France; Germany; Greece;
Ireland; Italy; Japan;
Netherlands; Norway; Portugal;
Spain; Sweden; Switzerland;
United Kingdom; United States
overseas aid 80, 81, 94, 107, 108, 127–8

partisan tax smoothing model 229
path dependency, *see* policy
inheritance
peace dividend 60
police spending
factors in 140, 141, 142–3, 144, 145,
146, 150–52, 153–4
statistics 138, 139
availability of data 134–6
policy inheritance
and core spending 34, 38
and educational spending 167, 169
and industrial subsidies 197–8, 203,
205, 206
and public debt 228–9, 231, 232
and public spending 32
and social spending 33
political institutions, *see* federalism;
institutional pluralism
political partisanship
and educational spending 167, 169,
171–2, 173, 176, 177
and industrial subsidies 199, 202,
203, 205–6, 208–10
and military spending 128
and public debt 228–9, 232, 234,
235, 239, 240
and public order and safety
spending 145–7, 149, 150, 152,
153, 154
and public spending 15–16, 29–30,
32
and regulation 252, 257, 258, 259,
260, 261–2, 266, 267, 268
and state overhead spending 84, 85
see also Left cabinet seats; Right
cabinet seats
political stability, and public debt 230,

232, 234, 235–6, 237, 238, 239,
240
politics, *see* new politics
population size, *see* demographic
factors
Portugal
conscription in 115
core spending 23, 25, 61, 64, 73
economic affairs/services spending
61, 73, 187, 189, 192, 193, 194,
196, 209, 211
economic regulation 247, 256, 261,
265, 266
educational spending 61, 73, 160,
164, 170, 173, 178, 179
general public services spending 61,
73
military spending 61, 73, 108, 111,
126
public debt, 1990s+ 61, 62, 81, 220,
223, 226
public order and safety spending 61,
73, 135, 137, 138, 139, 155
social spending 22, 61, 73
state overhead spending 81, 82, 90,
91, 92, 93, 98
poverty, *see* inequality
power resource theory, and public debt
229–30
price inflation
and interest rates 217
and military spending 119, 121–6
and public debt 232, 235, 238, 241
prisons spending
factors in 140, 141, 142–3, 144, 145,
146, 147–8, 152–3
statistics 139
availability of data 134–6
private education, and public
educational spending 169, 175–6,
177
private finance initiative (UK) 46
private security industry, potential for
research 156–7
privatisation, and regulation 248
problem-solving routines, and
educational spending 169, 172,
177
product market regulation
convergence of 257–8, 263

and economic affairs spending 246–7
and globalisation 258, 259, 260,
　262–3
and institutional pluralism 258, 259,
　260, 262
and interest groups 259, 260, 261–2
and legal traditions 259, 260
measures 248–9
and political partisanship 257, 258,
　259, 260, 261–2
and public debt 259, 260
and public spending 245–6
socio-economic factors 258, 259, 260
trends 246, 255–6, 257–8, 261
proportional representation systems
　147
public administration, *see* general
　government services spending;
　state overhead spending
public debt
　advisability of 218–19
　COFOG classifications 50–51, 59
　and core spending 34, 36–7, 38–9, 40
　and educational spending 173–4
　factors in 233–4
　　credibility 232, 233
　　institutional 231, 232, 235, 236
　　interest groups 229–30, 232
　　policy inheritance 228–9, 231, 232
　　political partisanship 228–9, 234,
　　　235
　　political stability 232, 234, 235–6
　　social spending 233, 236
　　socio-economic 228, 232, 233,
　　　234, 235
　　trade-related 231, 232, 233, 235
　and industrial subsidies 199, 201
　and interest payments 222, 223,
　　225–7, 233, 236
　management of 218, 225
　and military spending 110, 112
　and regulation 259, 260
　trends 226
public debt interest payments
　COFOG classifications 48
　convergence 225, 241
　economic theory 216–19
　and educational spending 173–4
　effects 28, 37, 39, 215–16, 233, 236
　factors in 222, 225, 227

credibility 229, 232, 239, 240
institutional 232, 240
interest groups 232, 234
policy inheritance 232
political partisanship 232, 239, 240
public debt 222, 223, 225–7, 233,
　236
repayment methods 218, 242
socio-economic 232, 239, 240
trade-related 232, 240
future development 241
and industrial subsidies 202, 204–5,
　207, 208, 212
net and gross 219, 225, 227
and public debt 222, 223, 225–7,
　233, 236
and public order and safety 61
statistics 81, 216, 219–20, 223
data validity 219
trends
　1980s 21–4, 55, 56, 68–9, 221, 225,
　　226
　1990s+ 23, 61, 62–3, 221–2, 225,
　　226
see also core spending, minus debt
　interest payments
public debt interest rates 217–18, 222,
　224–5, 230–31, 232, 236–9
public employment, *see* employment
public order and safety spending
　criminal justice factors 139–42, 144,
　　149–50, 152, 153
　political factors 145–8, 149, 150,
　　151, 152, 153, 154
　socio-economic factors 142–5, 149,
　　150, 151–2, 153–4
　statistics 137, 138–9
　　data availability 134–6
　　data validity 137–8, 139, 148
　and terrorism 154–6
　trends 60–62, 70–74, 135, 136
public–private partnerships 45–6
public spending
　analysis, methodology 31–2
　convergence in 14–15, 21, 26–7, 32,
　　41
　and debt interest 28
　definition 45, 46–7
　and economic slowdown 27–8
　and employment 46

functional breakdown, *see* COFOG
and new politics 35, 36, 39
and policy inheritance 32
and political partisanship 15–16,
    29–30, 32
and regulation 45, 245–6, 247
separation of finance and provision
    45–6
and state overhead spending 84,
    85–6, 98–9
statistics
    data validity 45, 46
    sources 4–11, 47–52, 58
trade factors 32
trends 55, 56, 61, 68–74
see also core spending; social
    spending

recorded crime, and public order and
    safety spending 140–41
recruitment
    of military personnel 129
    see also conscription
regulation
    convergence in 254, 256, 257–8, 261,
        262, 263, 264–6
    definition 270
    and globalisation 254, 258, 259, 260,
        262–3, 267, 268
    and institutional pluralism 252–3,
        258, 259, 260, 262, 267, 268
    and interest groups 259, 260, 261–2,
        266, 267
    and legal traditions 253–4, 256, 259,
        260, 264, 265
    market-enabling 248
    and political partisanship 252, 257,
        258, 259, 260, 261–2, 266, 267,
        268
    and public debt 259, 260
    and public spending 45, 245–6, 247
    socio-economic factors 251–2, 258,
        259, 260
    trends in 246–7, 255–6, 257–8, 261,
        265–6
    see also employment protection
        regulation; product market
        regulation
repayment methods, for public debt
    interest payments 218, 242

residual estimates, of aggregate core
    spending 5–8
retrenchment, *see* individual topics and
    countries
Right cabinet seats
    and educational spending 167
    and industrial subsidies 199, 202,
        203, 205–6, 208
    and public order and safety
        spending 146, 149, 150, 152,
        154
    and regulation 252, 257, 258, 259,
        260, 262, 267, 268
Right partisanship
    and public debt 229, 232, 235
    and public order and safety
        spending 145–7
    see also secular conservative
        partisanship
Russia, *see* Soviet Union/Russia;
    Warsaw Pact

Scandinavia
    core spending 23, 24, 25
    economic affairs/services spending
        191, 192
    economic regulation 256, 265
    public debt 40, 225, 226
    public order and safety spending
        138
    social spending 22, 24
    state overhead spending 83, 88, 91,
        100
    see also civil law countries;
        Denmark; Finland; Iceland;
        Norway; Sweden
Schmidt index 146, 147, 148, 149, 150
Second World War, *see* World War II
secular conservative partisanship 169,
    171–2, 173, 176
security, *see* military spending; private
    security industry; public order and
    safety
SIPRI (Stockholm International Peace
    Research Institute) 5
    correlation with COFOG 51–2
SIPRI Yearbook 103–4
Social Democratic parties, and
    educational spending 169, 171–2,
    173, 176, 177

social protection spending, trends,
  1990s+ 61, 70–74
social spending
  convergence 21
  and educational spending 169, 174
  and Left cabinet seats 33, 35
  and military spending 105, 127, 128
  and policy inheritance 33
  and public debt 233, 236
  and public order and safety
    spending 147–8
  socio-economic factors 28–9, 32, 33,
    35–6, 39
  statistics, sources 4, 6, 47–8
  trade factors 33, 35
  trends 2–3, 20–21, 22, 24–5, 26, 55,
    56, 68–74
  see also health; income transfers;
    social protection
Social Spending Database, OECD 6,
  48
socio-economic factors
  in core spending 32, 34, 36
  in educational spending 166, 167,
    169, 170, 176, 177
  in industrial subsidies 198–9, 202,
    203, 205
  and public debt 228, 232, 233, 234,
    235, 237, 238, 239, 240
  and public order and safety
    spending 142–5, 149, 150,
    151–2, 153–4
  in regulation 251–2, 258, 259, 260
  in social spending 28–9, 32, 33, 35–6,
    39
  see also economic growth; GDP;
    trade dependency
SOCX, *see Social Spending Database*
Southern Europe
  core spending 23, 25
  economic affairs/services spending
    191, 192
  educational spending 176
  public debt 40, 225, 226
  public order and safety spending 138
  public spending 24
  social spending 21, 22
  state overhead spending 83, 101
  see also civil law countries; Greece;
    Italy; Portugal; Spain

Soviet Union/Russia
  military spending 106, 107, 120
  and the arms race 109, 112, 113
  see also Warsaw Pact
Spain
  conscription in 115
  core spending 23, 25, 64, 73
  economic affairs/services spending
    73, 187, 192, 193, 194, 196, 209,
    211
  economic regulation 247, 256, 261,
    265, 266
  educational spending 73, 160, 164,
    170, 173, 178, 179
  general public services spending 73
  military spending 73, 108, 111, 120,
    126
  public debt, 1990s+ 62, 81, 220, 223,
    226
  public order and safety spending 73,
    135, 137–8, 139, 148, 155
  social spending 22, 73
  state overhead spending 81, 82, 89,
    90, 91, 92, 93, 98
state aid, *see* industrial subsidies;
    overseas aid
state overhead spending
  calculation of 80–81
  case studies 94–7
  convergence 82, 83
  country rankings 98
  and employment 88–91, 92, 94–5,
    98
  and institutional pluralism 84, 85,
    86–7, 91–2, 96, 97, 99
  and political partisanship 84, 85
  and public spending 84, 85–6, 98–9
  research questions 76–8
  statistics 81–3
    data validity 82–3, 99
  and tax collection 92–3, 95
  trade factors 84, 85, 86, 87–8, 99
  trends 97, 100–101
strike activity, and public debt 230,
    232, 233, 235, 237, 238
strong government, and public debt
    230, 232, 236
subsidies, *see* industrial subsidies
Sweden
  conscription in 115

core spending 23, 25, 55, 56, 57, 64, 69, 74
economic affairs/services spending 56, 69, 74, 187, 189, 192, 193, 194, 196, 209, 211
economic regulation 247, 256, 261, 264, 265, 266
educational spending 56, 69, 74, 160, 164, 170, 173, 179
general public services spending 56, 69, 74
military spending 56, 69, 74, 108, 111, 120
public debt 56, 62, 69, 81, 220, 223, 226
public order and safety spending 74, 135, 137, 138, 139, 155
public spending 56, 69, 74
social spending 22, 55, 56, 69, 74
state overhead spending 81, 82, 89, 90, 91, 93, 98
Switzerland
conscription in 115
economic regulation 256, 261, 265, 266
educational spending 160, 164, 170, 173, 179
industrial subsidies 192, 209, 211
military spending 108, 111, 120
public debt 220, 223, 224, 225, 226
public order and safety spending 137, 138, 139

tanks, statistics 117–18, 120
tax collection, and state overhead spending 92–3, 95
tax cuts, and public debt 229
temporary employment, and regulation 263–4, 266–8, 269
terrorism 154–6
threat index 144–5, 149, 150, 151, 152, 153; *see also* inequality; violent crime
time-series analysis 31–2
trade balance, and public debt 231, 232, 233, 235, 237, 238, 240
trade dependency
and core spending 34, 35, 37–8, 40
and educational spending 169
and military spending 110, 112, 113
and social spending 33
and state overhead spending 85, 86
see also globalisation
trade-offs
and military spending 127–8
see also crowding out
trade openness, *see* globalisation; trade dependency

UN, *see* United Nations
unemployment
and employment protection 268
and industrial subsidies 198–9, 205
and public debt 232, 233, 235
and public order and safety spending 142, 143, 154
see also employment
United Kingdom
core spending 23, 25, 55, 56, 57, 61, 64, 69, 74
economic affairs/services spending 56, 61, 69, 74, 187, 189, 193, 194, 195, 196, 209, 211
economic regulation 247, 248, 256, 261, 265, 266
educational spending 56, 60, 61, 69, 74, 161, 164, 170, 171, 173, 175, 177, 179, 180
general public services spending 56, 61, 69, 74
military personnel, costs 126
military spending 56, 61, 69, 74, 108, 111, 118, 120, 126
eighteenth century 105–6
and price inflation 119
private finance initiative 46
public debt 56, 61, 62, 69, 81, 220, 223, 226
public order and safety spending 61, 74, 135, 137, 138, 139, 146, 155
public spending 56, 61, 69, 74
social spending 22, 56, 61, 69, 74
state overhead spending 81, 82, 88, 89, 94–5, 98
and institutional pluralism 91
and public employment 90–91, 92, 94–5, 98
and tax collection 92, 95
United Nations National Accounts 48, 49

United Nations Survey of Crime and Justice 134
United States
  core spending 23, 25, 55, 56, 57, 61, 64, 69, 74
  economic affairs/services spending 56, 61, 69, 74, 187, 189, 191, 193, 209, 211
  economic regulation 247, 256, 261, 265, 266
  educational spending 56, 60, 61, 69, 74, 161, 164, 170, 173, 175, 177, 179, 180
  general public services spending 56, 61, 69, 74
  military equipment 119, 120, 121–5
  military personnel, costs 124, 126
  military spending 6, 56, 61, 74, 106–7, 108, 111, 118, 126
  nuclear primacy 116
  public debt 56, 61, 62, 69, 81, 220, 223, 224, 226
  public order and safety spending 61, 74, 135, 137, 138, 139, 150, 155
  social spending 22, 55, 56, 61, 69, 74
  state overhead spending 81, 82, 92, 93
USSR, *see* Soviet Union

veto players 200, 202, 208, 210, 231, 232, 234, 235

violent crime
  and public order and safety spending 140–42, 144, 145, 149, 150, 152, 153
  see also threat index

wages
  and state overhead spending 88–9, 94–5
  see also employment
Warsaw Pact/Russia
  and military personnel trends 114
  military spending, capital equipment 116–19
welfare spending, *see* social spending
Western Europe (continental)
  core spending 23, 24–6, 40
  economic affairs/services spending 191, 192
  public debt 40, 225, 226
  social spending 22, 24–5
  state overhead spending 83, 88–9, 92, 100
  trade dependency 40
  see also Austria; Belgium; civil law countries; France; Germany; Luxembourg; Netherlands
World War II, military spending 104